SHOOTING ZODIAC

ROBERT GRAYSMITH

MONKEY'S PAW PUBLISHING, INC. - LOS ANGELES

Books by Robert Graysmith

Zodiac
The Sleeping Lady
Auto Focus
Unabomber
The Bell Tower
Zodiac Unmasked
Amerithrax
The Laughing Gorilla
The Girl in Alfred Hitchcock's Shower
Black Fire
Shooting Zodiac

Audio Books

Zodiac
Zodiac Unmasked
Black Fire

Film Adaptations

Zodiac
Auto Focus

SHOOTING ZODIAC

Published by Monkey's Paw Publishing, Inc.

This book is based on face to face, tape-recorded interviews conducted on scene by the author between 2003 and 2007.

Photos by the author unless otherwise noted.

Book & Cover design by Aaron Smith

ISBN: 978-1-7365800-5-9

Monkey's Paw Publishing, Inc.
Los Angeles, CA

www.monkeyspawpublishing.com

The "Monkey Paw" design is a trademark of Monkey's Paw Publishing, Inc.

In Memory of Inspector David Toschi, Detective Sergeant George Bawart, and Captain Ken Narlow, Heroes All

"SOMETHING DRAWS THE GIRL'S attention," David Fincher said. The maverick director paused at the spot along the shore Captain Ken Narlow had indicated. Something was not right. Fincher looked down at the rocky ground and the steep slope of the rotting tree as if he had not seen them before. Without a word he wheeled and walked some distance around to the adjacent peninsula. The retired detectives watched the celebrated filmmaker follow the curve of land and circle to a little inlet on the other bank. His head was down as he took long, athletic strides. Suddenly, he knelt and studied the ground. He picked up a fistful of earth, let it drift between his fingers, and watched as the wind carried the reddish particles away. He looked up at the road high above where the victims' car had been found, then looked back at the tree. Next, he tossed a few rocks in the air and gazed to the center of the lake where it was a couple hundred feet deep. Fincher wondered what other mysteries might be buried there. Further up, underneath the dam at Devil's Gate, was the narrow point of Putah Creek.

Fincher returned from his scouting trip and made an announcement. His voice was confident and clear, ringing out over the lake. "The other side of the little island out there is much more vertical than this side," he said. "I think that is the actual murder site."

"Let's go over and take a look," Narlow said and started north with Jamie Vanderbilt. "I'm not one hundred percent convinced this is the place." When Narlow reached the other side of the inlet, he clapped a hand to his forehead and then hailed Fincher and the rest of the men across the water. "My God!" he hollered, "I took you to the wrong spot!"

In that arcane way he had of penetrating to the heart of a riddle, Fincher had discerned the truth. He became quiet as he began working the puzzle of the open taxi door, the blood that should have been elsewhere, a bloody print that belonged to no one, and the shot nobody heard.

CONTENTS

PREFACE

EVERY SATURDAY consisted of sitting in the dark watching a triple feature, broken only by my race home to hear the radio adventures of *The Shadow*. Childhood was spent chasing about the country and across the world with my Air Force family. It was curious that no matter where we landed, the South, or New Mexico, or Japan, I never seemed to be able to catch the first or the last chapter of the fifteen weekly cliffhangers that were shown in those days. Whatever U.S. Air Base where we happened to be living at the time, my first priority was always to find the local theatre. I'd return each week to catch most of the storyline, but once again, before I could see the completion of one story or the beginning of the next, we'd have already moved once more. Incomplete beginnings and missing endings left my mind wondering what had happened in the prior weeks, and the possibilities of how the other cliffhanger chapters may have ended. It was a search for resolution. These cold openings, and missing endings, likely paved my way to appreciate the unresolved qualities of the legendary Zodiac case—the true story of a costumed, hooded killer, cloaked in ciphers and trailing untraceable letters.

The two young men at my book signing were more animated than most. There was an intentness and dedication about them that was unique. As one homicide investigator later said, "You had to like them." My meetings with producer Brad Fischer, and screenwriter Jamie Vanderbilt became *this book*—a "Making of" book that ends before the first scene is shot—the making of a story with no ending. From boardroom to fog-shrouded lake to posh San Francisco mansions and mayor's offices, I followed Brad and Jamie and director David Fincher as they climbed through the mountains and along desolate roads. Looming over us was always that moment of doubt if Fincher was going to be there at the end of the road. He was going to make the film his way, and at his price, and his satisfaction, that they had the facts, or not make it at all.

Part Hollywood boardroom drama and part true crime thriller, I was there as they battled a huge script that refused to be beaten, a case that refused to be solved, and a running time and a budget that were a stumbling block to their movie being greenlit. As Brad said no one has ever had such behind the scenes access as I had. I was there as Brad and Jamie and Fincher learned new facts and challenged old, and brought the period to life. The original investigators were lured out of their retirement holes by one of the most unorthodox, ethical, and exacting movie directors of our time. No mystery could stand up against this reluctant director. Or could it? I wondered what more was there to say about one of the most puzzling murder mysteries in history—*I was about to find out.*

Working with top experts in linguistics, forensics, psychology, and with new witnesses, Fincher makes speedy progress until he comes up against political intrigue and a police department that on the face of it seemingly wants to bury the case, that the fight to make his movie really begins.

I visualized a bleak landscape that might be a movie: fireworks in the sky, and marching readers carrying torches for truth. Brad, Jamie, and Fincher's mantra would be sung by the throng: For Toschi. For Darlene. For Paul and all the rest. For all those who fought to never forget and put what they learned on the screen for all to see—forever. These filmmakers, like many of you, picked up that torch and ran with it, in turn inspiring another generation of detectives. They approached it with integrity, exactitude, and obsession as so many before them had done.

In an episode of *The Simpsons*, a movie company comes to fictional Springfield to make a movie. The townsfolk cheat and rob them at every opportunity. Finally, the director says, "I can't wait until we get back to Hollywood where everyone treats you right and everyone keeps their word." That was exactly my experience. For four years, I watched and listened and questioned, all on tape and film, wondering if the three filmmakers would achieve any of their goals or none at all. Suspense lasted till the very end but no matter the outcome, I realized I was watching greatness in progress.

Here it is, a peek behind the curtain, you know, the one where the Wizard is named David Fincher.

—Robert Graysmith, San Francisco, July 30, 2021

SHOOTING ZODIAC

CHAPTER ONE

WATCHING FOR RATTLESNAKES

BRAD FISCHER'S TALKING CAR, still a rarity in 2003, guided him higher into the mountains. As he drove, he listened to the hiss of rain on tires, the sluggish sweep of wipers, and the NeverLost GPS prompting: "Head east on Airport Boulevard towards Highway 29 . . . turn left onto 29 North . . . *pok—pok—pok—beep—beep* . . ." Tucking in his chin for a wider view of the landscape, Brad swung the SUV north. The rain was slanting edgewise now and the windshield was misting. Traffic lights were reflected onto the black pavement. "Get in the right lane and take the downtown Napa/Lake Berryessa exit," the female voice further advised. "Merge onto Soscol Avenue. Turn right at the Silverado Trail . . ." A herd of colorful trucks from Calistoga, Oakville, and St. Helena thundered past along 29 South bound for the gourmet restaurants of Main Street. Their blinding headlights shone directly into the car, but Brad was still able to make out signage as they rumbled by: "Coppola Estate Winery, Rutherford," and "Beringer, St. Helena." He was in Wine Country. He was in the Napa Valley.

"My brother is a heart surgeon, a cardio-thoracic surgeon," Brad said. "My mother is a pediatric neurologist, my dad is a pediatric radiologist. My cousin, Michael Kaplitt, is a neurosurgeon who was profiled recently on *The New York Times* front page for performing the first-ever procedure of gene therapy in the brain for Parkinson's disease. As a Hollywood producer, I'm the black sheep of the family." New York-born, New-Jersey raised, Brad had majored in Film, History,

Theory, and Criticism at Columbia. "It was comparative literature," he explained as the rain began to fall harder, "but with movies instead of books." In 1998, the same year he graduated with a BA in Film Studies and Psychology, Brad became a protégé of legendary producer Mike Medavoy, co-founder and chairman of Phoenix Pictures. A year later, Medavoy promoted him to Director of Development, and last year had named him Vice-president of Production. Brad's job was to find, acquire, and develop motion picture projects for the LA-based production company. Brad consulted the heavy silver watch on his wrist. The time was 5:30 PM. Clear-headed, imaginative, analytical, and a chronic worrier, he seemed to carry the entire weight of the potential *Zodiac* movie project on his shoulders and probably did.

From the backseat, Jamie Vanderbilt, attired in black and almost invisible in the shadows, lifted his head to point out Joe's Auto Shop as they sped by. He got no answer. He returned to anguishing over his script. He had recently pitched his screen adaptation of *Zodiac*, his favorite book in high school, to Brad and Mike Medavoy who messengered it to director David Fincher to read. When Jamie was a sophomore at the USC film school, he saw *Se7en* at the three dollar theatre. "David is like a god to film students," Jamie explained, "one of the top guys. He did such groundbreaking things in his films that he inspired a new generation of filmmakers and creative people. So, I was very nervous about meeting him. When we did meet, I was very taken with him." Jamie compared the opportunity of working with Fincher to asking the prettiest girl to the prom—the worst she could say was, "No." To Jamie's delight, Fincher said, "Yeah."

Jamie is a member of a storied American family, the Vanderbilts, who insist on only one thing: he must sign his scripts "*James Vanderbilt.*" "I grew up in Connecticut," he said, "but my old family hut is in Newport, Rhode Island. The big old Vanderbilt place [an Italian Renaissance extravaganza] is called 'The Breakers,' a fairly common name when it's on the water and near the breaking waves. I joked to my parents that when I got my house in California I was going to call it 'Breakers *West.*' They weren't charmed."

As the two young filmmakers headed upward, they felt the change in altitude and temperature. Early Novembers in most other parts of Northern California tend to be chilly, wet, and prone to flooding, but Lake Berryessa was the exception. Higher up, it was sultry and uncomfortable. As they descended into a valley in a series of hairpin curves, they left the driving rain behind. They had intended to arrive at the lake during daylight, but the storm had delayed them. Jamie put his script to one side, but kept his hand on a manilla envelope containing black and white landscape photos. Their research trip into the mountains would be a failure without them. Then, what would David Fincher think? The director's advice echoed in the dark as if Fincher was sitting with them—"Verify everything in the script—Tell the real story of the real people whose lives this movie is about—Visit the real sites where their life-changing and life-ending events took place—This is no vacation. This is work, the hardest there is and it takes heart."

"Go for approximately two point seven miles," the feminine voice prompted. They were close now. There was no turning back. "Turn right at Capell Valley Road 128. Go approximately five miles." They sped by the Central Store, an orange rectangle in the twilight, spun right at Berryessa Knoxville Road—Spanish Flats, then crawled north along Knoxville Road to the entrance to Oak Shores. Except for a light-colored, older model car trailing a hundred or so yards behind them during their descent to the lake, they hadn't seen another vehicle. Jamie watched as the older car sped by and vanished around the bend onto Knoxville Road. Brad wheeled right past the empty guard gate (it was off season), completed a hard left around the circle, and traced the road around to Twin Oaks Ridge.

"Park in the second lot," the feminine voice suggested, electronically sexy in such a desolate location. Turning east, they cruised down to the lot. Brad nosed his SUV into a space and the filmmakers eased out onto the pavement. At the edge of the lot, they found a path, slid down the steep slope of the western shore, and started across an open area. The uneven ground was red, rocky, and pockmarked with hundreds of rattlesnake holes. They felt their way in the dimness, dislodging shale, looking out for rattlers, and tripping over exposed roots so twisted they might have been snakes. Brad and Jamie studied every rocky crevice, jagged outcropping, and fallen tree for triangular-shaped heads and black banded tails. Jamie listened for warning rattles. The rule was: "Leave the snakes alone and they will leave you alone." That was hard to do. There were a lot of snakes to leave alone. There were ten species at Lake Berryessa from King-snakes to Yellow-bellied Racers, but only the rattlesnakes were venomous.

The sweep of the wide basin and narrowness of its ever-changing peninsulas presented a grim landscape. It was the right time of year, the right time of day, and under the same conditions as the stabbings. How deserted Lake Berryessa had been that long ago late September afternoon in 1969, how remarkably spare, somber, and silent—as now.

"This place has never really changed," Brad said to Jamie. "It still feels haunted." He looked around as if expecting ghosts, but the only spirits abroad were those of the Patwin Native Americans and Mexican settlers of the valley, restless ghosts far below the surface where there had been a cemetery before it was relocated—water ghosts. To the north lay an underwater vineyard. Far to the southeast, lost in the mist and out of sight, was 304 foot Monticello Dam.

When the dam was completed in the mid-fifties, workers set the grasslands ablaze and diligently leveled oaks so huge that old Spanish maps showed them as landmarks. Then, the workmen chased the indigenous people into the hills and flooded the valley with a million acre feet of water, enough to keep any ghost anchored to the bottom and any secrets that the lake held. Close by the dam is the Devil's Gate, a 72 foot wide concrete funnel which is the largest spillway in the world. Nearby, flowed Putah Creek, the mouth of the lake, where fishing was allowed upstream from the speed restriction buoy, but not from the bridge. Along the eastern shoreline, Eticuera Creek to Monticello Dam, fishing and picnicking were prohibited. On the western bank, where Brad and Jamie were, angling and picnicking were encouraged and that was what had attracted the young couple to the lake that long ago, sunny, tragic day.

Just as dusk fell, the two filmmakers reached the grassy-muddy shore. Ahead, stood decaying oaks, skeletal picnic tables, and bleak fence posts, ethereal in the dimness. The leather and blue oaks had been drained of color. Dressed in black, Jamie was as dull and drab as the oaks. Lakeside, the iron water was sluggish, warm as soup, the faded light gritty. You could feel it under your eyelids.

"Such a beautiful place," Jamie lamented with a shake of his long hair, "and yet when you know what really happened here the beauty becomes sinister."

As the faintest twinkle of the first star appeared in the sky, they reached a slender ridge that is sometimes underwater and sometimes not and sometimes only an islet. Above and behind them and beyond tall trees, curved Knoxville Road. This was where the male stabbing victim's white Karmann Ghia had been parked by a makeshift fence and where the costumed killer had left no doubt he had been there. He had signed the car door in felt-tip pen with the dates of his earlier murders and autographed it with his symbol—a crossed circle, even noted the time of that day's attack: 6:30 PM. Afterward, he had sped down the mountain some fifty odd miles to Napa to call the police from a phone booth near their headquarters to tell them where to find his victims. In this way he could watch the technicians dust the phone box and the receiver he had just used for prints. Jamie wondered if this constituted new behavior for the killer or if it was something he had done in all of his attacks. It was a lead worth following up.

Brad and Jamie studied the silhouette of a dark oak across the spit and easily imagined the killer lumbering across the sand toward them, a dry wind tugging at the yoke of his square, black hood. At his belt hung a footlong knife, precut lengths of rope, a holster, and a blue-steel .45 semiautomatic which he had used only to threaten and get the victims down on the ground. That day, his military Wing Walker boots had left deep tracks in the sand, the same size, 10 1/2, that Jamie left behind now. Zodiac's footprints, though, had cut more deeply into the sand. He was heavier. Ominous, lethal, unknowable, Zodiac remained the great mystery and now these two amateurs had the audacity to attempt to solve it as they double-checked the facts, got the feel of the site, and set about creating a classic movie.

Jamie sniffed the air which smelled as if it were charged with the sulfurous vapors of lava flows. With his HDV camcorder, just made available to the general public, he panned the lake, aware every second that he was losing what little light remained. His camera, with its 1.33 megapixel, could see more than he could. At first, only whirling static showed in the viewfinder, but gradually the wide lake came into focus as a pointillist landscape—little dots that when you view them from a distance coalesce to form a complete picture. Atop a distant bluff, a streak of white caught Jamie's eye, and suggested a watching man, a white dog at his side. Jamie turned away to point out the images to

Brad, but when he looked back, the man and his pet were gone. At least, Jamie had trapped their images inside his camcorder where he visualized them struggling to be released.

He and Brad paused at a grassy spot at the head of a spit that is sometimes submerged and sometimes not, depending on the season and amount of rain. Brad dragged out a manilla envelope, opened the clasp, and retrieved aerial photos of the homicide scene that Captain Ken Narlow had taken. Brad felt a sense of urgency as he held each photo in the beam of their flashlight, and compared its image to the landscape before them. They had their work cut out for them. Earlier landmarks either were gone or had been altered by time, reconstruction of the shore, and heavy rains. All they had to work with was a lightning-shattered California oak and a picnic table or two. They listened carefully as if the voice of the lake would reassure them they were at the right spot. There was no answer. The water was still as death, the sky grayer, and the viscous basin blacker. Then, the lake came alive.

A "Cats paw" showed as a slight ripple on the rubber-cement water. Fish nipped at the surface, and sounded tiny splashes as they twisted among the weed beds, brush heaps, and sunken stumps of the shallows. Now, an odd trilling arose in the electrified air—rising wind playing music in the surrounding trees. Frogs began croaking incessantly, accented by the hoot of an owl. Jamie shot footage of what they prayed was the correct spot, put his camcorder back into its bag, and then turned away. Both men rapidly climbed to the lot, glancing behind as if something was gaining on them. The atmosphere around was bluer than the rain had been, but hot. The sharp edges of the landscape were distorted and defused. They heard rustling in the weeds that had gained purchase on the side of the ravine. The red earth was redder than ever in the beam of the flashlight. Moving was hard in the shifting sand, and uphill was worse. At last, they scaled the incline, skidding, and lurching through patches of mud. They reached the paved lot where they scraped the mud off their shoes and climbed into the SUV. Jamie paused only once and that was to study the empty bluff in the distance where a disquieting sense of a watcher and his dog remained. They drove upward from the lot and rushed left onto Knoxville Road. Teeming gray specks in the charged atmosphere seemed to pursue them. The lights of another vehicle momentarily blazed in Brad's rearview mirror as they barreled down the mountainside. He accelerated and left the lights far behind on the serpentine road. Inside Jamie's camcorder electrical bits teemed, undefined as a swarm of fleas. Inside the car, the air was prickly and uncomfortable. Jamie's ears were hot. His clothes were damp. His shoes were wet. Brad was bent intently over the wheel. The guiding voice was silent. They knew the way now. They knew some of the truth.

Returning to San Francisco, they stowed their equipment in their Clift Hotel suite and immediately descended to the downstairs bar to decompress. "Because we were so freaked out by the emotional hit of Lake Berryessa," Jamie recalled, "we made a conscious decision to drink until we dropped."

Over several hours in the newly renovated Redwood Room, they admired Philippe Starck's "sexy, redwood walls" and "whimsically luxurious" interiors, slumped at the bar, and drank. Jamie drank Captain Morgan and Coke. Brad drank Vodka tonic.

"We got drunker than we've ever been in our lives," Jamie said. "We drank ourselves into oblivion."

"It was a drunk to forget," Brad recalled. "It had been so chilling just to be at the lake that we were suffering from emotional exhaustion and began to speak to random people at the bar. It was Jamie who filled the strangers in, telling them we were 'two young guys from Hollywood.' They replied—'Oh, really—you work in the movie industry'—'Brad's a producer and you're a screenwriter?'—'You're planning a film? Is that so? That's really cool—.' Jamie told them that he didn't know yet if anything was going to come of our visit to the lake."

"Just as the listeners were gearing up for a really interesting conversation," Jamie recalled, "Brad depressed them by telling them what we had been through that afternoon.

"You know the Zodiac?" Brad said. "That's why we are getting so drunk."

Everyone knew the elusive killer who wrote the *San Francisco Chronicle*, *San Francisco Examiner*, and *Vallejo Times-Herald*. After hearing Brad and Jamie's story, the people could only gasp, "Oh, my God!"

"We were professional buzz-killers that night," Jamie remembered, "but invited our new friends up to our suite, squeezed into the room, and raided the mini-bar of liquor. We ordered more tonic and cranberry juice from room service—anything to just keep talking and not have to be alone. We didn't want to go to sleep. We didn't want our new friends to leave. We just wanted to drink."

When Jamie played his camcorder footage for their guests, the earlier darkness returned. Electronic flecks on the screen turned slowly upon themselves. The vague shapes of the surreal landscape, the shattered oaks, phantom picnic tables, and the blurred suggestion of a watching man and his dog, frightened everyone who saw them that night. It would have the same effect on others who later saw the video back in Hollywood. Earlier in their sleuthing process, Brad and Jamie had quoted as their forensic texts similar scenes in movies which is what they knew best. "Remember in *The Godfather* where they did this and did that," they would say, or "Remember in the knifing in *The Untouchables*, didn't they do this?" Their visit to Lake Berryessa was the first time Zodiac ceased to be a really interesting story to them and became something real. As their knowledge of the case deepened, they became more sensitive to the tragedy, the seriousness of it sunk in, and they dropped the movie analogies for good and asked others to do the same.

"Real people died there," Jamie said. His broad smile had faded. He didn't look boyish anymore. "This is not Hollywood fun and games. I don't want to go back alone. Next time, I want a whole film crew with me."

CHAPTER TWO
CORRALLING RATTLESNAKES

DAVID FINCHER WAS AFTER the truth.

It showed in the long, lean line of his mouth and determined thrust of his chin. He ran one hand over his face in exasperation. By 10:00 AM, the acclaimed director was trying to shoot Brad Fischer. Seated behind the wheel of a make-believe Yellow Cab, Brad was uncomfortable and showed it. Fincher's elaborate pantomime with a pretend 9-mm semiautomatic was only a part of his quest for the absolute facts in the unsolved Zodiac case. Inside his San Francisco Clift Hotel suite, Private Apartment 1417, a special three-bedroom, Fincher was hypothetically shooting the young producer. It is his custom to physically reenact scenes to see if they work, just as he constantly reframes his questions aloud as if trying them on for size. He is building a house and the foundation has to be solid. Today is the groundbreaking ceremony. Brad Fischer is the shovel.

"Brad's taking one for the team," Jamie Vanderbilt chortled from across the room. Brad glared at him. Jamie, as always, was dressed in black jeans and a gray, black-sleeved pullover. He is a friendly, open-faced twenty-eight year old of constantly changing appearances, all of them disheveled. His dark hair is as long and untamed as Johnny Wiesmuller's, the thirties movie "Tarzan" that he so uncannily resembles. "I'm a wide guy," Jamie admits, "—one hundred and eighty pounds and five feet, eleven and one half inches tall." Brad was also dressed in black, though it was not as if the young producer had any other choice. The airline had flown his luggage on to Hawaii and now Fincher was trying to tear his only remaining shirt. The director leaned over him, grasped his shirttail on the left-hand side and with all his might attempted to rip away a piece of cloth as the killer had. It was an awkward stretch requiring both hands. Fincher, a powerful man, should have been able to succeed, yet failed. He persisted. Finally, he took a step back and shook his head. He was going to get it right. That was his nature.

"David's one of those guys who'll do thirty-seven takes of a guy walking by just to get it right," Jamie said. Though the director possesses considerable visual skills as an artist, sculptor, photographer, and cartoonist (like his father Jack), he expresses himself best in film.

The notorious director of *Fight Club* and *Se7en* is dressed this morning in Levi's, a gray cardigan over a white tee shirt, and a black cap with a deep crown emblazoned with the numerals "64." His goatee is short, rounded, slightly graying, his sandy hair is close-cropped. His hazel eyes are brimming with sly humor. He is tall, six foot one, and at forty-one years old, weighs a trim one hundred eighty pounds. Today he is eager to combine the philosophical and sociological elements of the Zodiac case with compassion for the human beings involved and a search for truth, his truth.

Brilliant sunlight slanted through the high, north window. Except for a strong westerly wind the morning was springlike. Today, January 14, 2004, sun drenched all of downtown San Francisco. The strong light bleached Brad paler than usual. No matter the illumination, he always photographs overexposed. His neatly trimmed black hair, black brows, and dark-brown eyes stand out boldly in a fine-featured face. He is sleepy-eyed with an aquiline nose and determined chin. Of indeterminate age, he is certainly well under thirty, and of indeterminate height, though one would guess five foot, eight or nine—movie star height.

Today's *Chronicle* Headlines read: "Supreme Court OKs roadblocks to solve crimes," "The State will face a $6 billion budget shortfall, double what Governor Arnold Schwarzenegger predicts," "Unleashed Mars Rover, Spirit, set to explore crater bed," and "Doctor who killed 215 hangs self in prison." Inside, the wide, paneled room the mood is grim: white furniture set hard against black carpet; deep shadows enveloping the three black-garbed men gathered around a single straight-backed white chair. Fincher began to experiment with the position of the "cabbie" behind the wheel. "Where did the blood pool?" he asked, speaking deliberately as he circled the chair like a stalking lion. Brad, in the part of cabbie victim Paul Lee Stine, squirmed in the seat and made a face. Finally, he settled back on the gold cushion, fixed his eyes on the white ceiling (the floor of the penthouse above) and waited for the ordeal to be over. Fincher ceased pulling, leaned back, consulted his black binder, and scratched his goatee. He circled the chair again, then halted as an idea struck him. "Why had the blood from the cabbie's contact wound pooled on the passenger side and not at his feet?" It made no sense. Nothing in the case did. "O.K.," Fincher continued, "so Stine is shot here and goes forward and to the right. He's bent over the dashboard where the radio would be and gouting blood into the floor well. Then, the killer sits in the front-seat, and brings Stine's head into his lap." He experimented from a sitting position the difficulty of extracting the victim's wallet from his rear pocket and the keys from the ignition. He found this procedure equally hard. "And where did the Zodiac exit and where did he reenter the taxi and why did he wipe down the cab, if he did at all?"

If Zodiac had cradled his victim's head in his lap that night as three young eyewitnesses had reported, why were his trousers not drenched with blood? Two police officers who observed the killer from their patrol car minutes afterward should have been able to differentiate between the dark blue of his jacket and the deep brown of his pleated pants. Yet, they saw nothing. "The crotch of his pants is not soaked with arterial blood?" Fincher said. He shrugged. "They don't see what would be in the night a black stain?" The streets in San Francisco's posh Presidio Heights District were brightly lit at night. Its wealthy residents made certain of that. Fincher paused, folded his arms, and stared into space imagining the children's second floor vantage point on the other side of Washington Street. He lifted his head and calculated the angle of their view from that middle window. It was steep. Just how good a look would they have gotten? The three youngsters had witnessed the cabbie's murder thirty-four years earlier; thirty-four years later they were still traumatized, still fiercely clinging to their anonymity and privacy. Who could blame them? But, if Fincher was going to make a film, he had to know exactly what they had seen in the night and how well they had seen it. To do that, he would have to ask them in person.

"Again, here I reach across his body," Fincher said. He stood behind Brad, to his right, and leaned across his chest. "I'm going to grab his shirt and it's probably polyester. Tougher thing to rip than cotton. I'm gonna tear this end." Fincher, who bestows bone-crusher handshakes, has very strong hands, yet found it impossible from this angle to exert enough pressure with both hands to accomplish his task. "If the killer tore the shirt he was an extraordinarily powerful man. But, it might be done with a cut started in the seam." He had to answer all of these questions before he could find the truth. He would not shoot *Zodiac* without the truth. Finally, Brad was released from his prison.

The three filmmakers moved to a long mahogany table at the south end of the room and sat down in a slab of cold light. Their intent expressions were reflected in the high gloss of the polished table. Before Brad and Jamie had arrived, Fincher had spent the early morning at this table going over police reports in that reserved, compressed way he had, his mind filing each fact, mentally checking and rechecking it as if it were one of the boundless retakes in one of his films, then speaking his thoughts aloud to hear how they sounded to other ears and to his own. Now, here they were, fourteen stories above a busy San Francisco thoroughfare—fatigued, battered, obsessed—their eyes already glittering with purpose and something not quite sane. By now, too soon, the infection was running deep. By now, the sharpest scalpel could not have cut it out before it spread. There could be no turning back even if they had wanted to. They were after the truth and they were after a great movie. Silently, they studied the picture window across the room and thought of Dashiell Hammett, falling beams, Fate, and the sidewalk below.

"I grew up in San Anselmo in Marin County," Fincher explained. He gestured toward the north window, recalling "a very sunny and happy and safe environment," with forests, open spaces, welcoming nooks, and the ever-present fragrances of eucalyptus and evergreens. This small suburb, scarcely twenty miles away from Fincher's Clift Hotel suite, sits between the towns of Fairfax and Ross. In 1969, a shadow, coldblooded and venomous, fell over this Eden. Truncated little Park Way, where the Fincher family lived, is hemmed in by Ancho

Vista to the west and Hillsdale Drive to the east, and is eclipsed by cozy streets like Cottage and Bungalow. To the southeast, Park Way enters San Rafael to become 4th, and then 2nd Street where some of Fincher's favorite films were shot. A mile away from their three bedroom home, Frank Lloyd Wright's Marin County Civic Center hugs the freeway. Seen at night from the 101, the 858 foot long Administration Building is a pink and blue ocean liner at sea. Diffused yellow light streams through its portholes in the fog.

Fincher's abiding personal connection to the Zodiac dates back to his childhood. "I was about seven years old when all this was going on," he remarked as he rearranged the reference material on the long table for the umpteenth time. He wondered aloud if Zodiac had something to do with the bleak, unrelenting, and saturnine perception of mankind that runs through his films. He recalled peering from his school bus on its way to Isabel Cook Elementary on Sir Francis Drake Boulevard. Fixed-wing aircraft were circling above. Worried parents were driving behind. Black and white units, aerials whipping in the wind, were speeding alongside. "We had to follow school buses to school for weeks, if not months," Captain Tony Pearsall later recalled. "We got constant updates on sketches of what the shooter looked like and had the sketches taped up in our patrol cars."

"I remember riding the bus home from school," Fincher continued, "and asking my dad [*Life's* San Francisco Bureau Chief], 'Why is the Highway Patrol following us?' My dad, never one to soft-pedal things, took a long, deep breath, then turned slowly in his chair, and said, 'Oh yeah. There's a killer who has killed four or five people and calls himself Zodiac and has threatened to take a high-powered rifle, shoot out the tires of a school bus, and nail the kiddies as they come bouncing out.' I thought to myself, you work at home, you could, like, drive us to school.' What if Zodiac showed up in our neighborhood? What if it was our bus? You create even more drama about it when you're a kid because that is what kids do." Fincher vowed that if he shot *Zodiac* (and he was still very doubtful that he would) he would have a scene where a worried parent pulls his kid off the yellow bus and drives him to school.

"My next door neighbor's mother worked with the Marin County Sheriff's Department," Fincher continued, "and I heard some things that way. I remember that people were killed in the Marin Headlands and then later on when I was at Berryessa having lunch at that picnic table somebody said this is where the Zodiac stabbing took place. I was probably eleven." The period was etched in his memory. He recalled the morning Zodiac rang up defense attorney Mel Belli on live TV during *The Jim Dunbar Show*. His dad had taken the day off work to listen. Fincher wasn't sure that his dad ever found out it was a hoax call, a guy calling from a mental hospital. At dawn that morning, SFPD Homicide Inspectors Dave Toschi and Bill Armstrong picked up Belli at his eight million dollar mansion on Broadway to take him to the television studio. As they drove, the defense attorney hid on the backseat floor, "scared shitless," as Toschi put it, but with enough presence of mind to complain about the candy bar wrappers strewn about the floor of the Toschi family car.

"There's been very little written about the real David Fincher," Jamie explained, "there's tons of fan sites and speculation about what an amazing director he is. There's one book written based on one lunch with the guy. The great thing about David, and there are obviously a lot of great things about David, is that he is also known as being a perfectionist. His simple, single rule is, 'Do your best work on any given day and try to live it down.' The other nice thing about David is that he's pretty hard to offend. I'm always curious to hear what people think of *Fight Club*, the one film of David's that divides a lot of people. People either think *Fight Club's* a masterpiece or absolutely hate it. I loved it. It's about anarchy and it's very dark, very black and violent." One critic deemed Fincher's adaptation of Chuck Palahniuk's novel "simultaneously anti-Capitalist, anti-society, and anti-God." Jamie was glad Fincher had made a type of serial killer movie before, *Se7en*. "The danger for us," he said, "would have been to get a director who wanted to focus on all the purulent details. He's got that part of it out of his system. He is more interested in the people now."

"It's not our intention to do the recreations and the reenactments and do this kind of salacious thing," Fincher was saying. "I've seen enough serial killer movies to know that depravity is not what makes this interesting. I want to do something that is pretty unheard of in Hollywood in that I want it to be as factual as it can possibly be. I want it to be a document that people can look at and go, 'That's done.

You never have to do that story.' It will be a newspaper movie like

All The President's Men—which is certainly much more high-minded journalism. *Zodiac* is the story of a reporter determined to get the story at any cost and one who was new to being an investigative reporter. It is all about his obsession to know the truth. *All The President's Men* is the best model for this movie cause you're going to make a movie where you will know what the ending of the movie is. You're going to make a movie for the people who read the book. We're going to go to an enormous amount of trouble to make this as factually accurate as possible for people who really know the facts. Anybody who knows that, knows there is no real ending, there's no electric chair. For these people they're just going to get to the point where they say this is the character, these are the people he knew, these are the people who helped him, these are the things that he found out. Part of this movie is to make a document. If there is some new break in the case people will be able to look at it and say, 'If they had known this, this would have gone on in here and this is how this would have been skewed.' That's what it should be."

Brad consulted his silver watch, rose and walked to the double-hung window. Shading the glass against the glare with his hand, he peered down at the bustling throng on Geary Boulevard. It was a street buzzing with creativity. Impresario Ian Schrager's venerable Clift Hotel on the corner takes a huge bite out of the 400 block which includes the American Conservatory and Geary and Curren Theaters. Where the hell was Inspector Dave Toschi? Brad wondered, and not for the first time. By now, he should have completed his afternoon shift at North Star Security Services where he was a Vice President and Operations Manager. Maybe, the retired SFPD homicide detective could explain to Fincher whether the cabbie's shirt had been torn or cut, why the blood ended up where it did, why it pooled on the passenger side and not at the driver's feet, and why blood landed in absurd places and at nonsensical angles. Fincher had to know whether Zodiac left a bloody print, planted a false clue, or if someone in the crowd had touched the bloody cab and left their print. The director had to know or he wasn't shooting *Zodiac*. Everything was riding on Toschi. And so they waited and listened for the hum of the elevator or the sound of a knock. The room grew eerily silent.

Two blocks away, cable cars climbed Powell Street. The rattling cars caused quakes in the ground as they rumbled past the elegant St. Francis where victim Paul Stine's Yellow Cab had idled in a cloud of exhaust one warmish October night in 1969. At 9:00 PM, Geary Boulevard had been slick, busy, and lit with jig-jags of neon. Zodiac had probably lain in wait under the purple striped awning shrouding Harold's Newsstand and the Pinecrest Restaurant, the former 401 Smoke Shop, the later scene of the infamous "Poached Egg" murder. The restaurant's temperamental short order cook had made it known to his staff that he had an aversion to serving poached eggs because they reminded him of a painful past event. "You are never to take such an order off the menu," he roared. When a waitress broke his rule, he shot her to death, strolled outside, lit a cigarette, and calmly waited for the cops under the same striped awning where Zodiac had probably waited for Stine's cab.

Jamie checked his watch, though not as anxiously as Brad, the self-appointed executive in charge of worrying. Jamie doesn't worry. He never doubts good things will happen. Brad always worries. He knows bad things will happen. It's just a matter of waiting for them. As they awaited Toschi's arrival, they shared their hopes for a brilliant movie that seemed very far away at that moment. They still had to get their film bankrolled by a studio, a process known as green lighting, and lick a mammoth script that spans years. Brad picked out a comfortable chair in the spacious living room area and leaned back against white pillows piled like snow drifts, listened to the monotonous hum of traffic, lowered his eyes, and worried.

"I feel like the end of this movie is a guy goes to Ace Hardware," Fincher was saying, "waiting in line, the big guy is there in the fucking orange smock that says 'Lee' on it, his little pocket protector, bagging stuff and he says, 'Can I help you?' and the fucking end of the movie is the cartoonist going, 'He did it. That's all I need to know. I'm done with it.' I think Truman Capote wrote a really interesting thing in *In Cold Blood*—that there is no truth. You can't get the people back, you can't undo this really bestial behavior. Yeah, these are bad seeds. It's a cumulative effect of a lot of bad decisions crossing over at one point and horrible things happen. They lynch the guy and everybody goes, 'O.K.' [He claps his hands loudly to emphasize his point. The impact shakes the room. Brad jumps]. They don't sleep any better at night knowing they hung the guy."

"Take Two: I feel this is a movie about a cartoonist who is privy to this stuff who gets in and around and between all these things and sort of brings this stuff to a head and the end of the movie is a guy going into a hardware store and going, 'If I look at this guy and I know. I know he walks with a fucking limp and I know he's got diabetes and I know he can't see very well. If I know that's him, I know.'" Fincher upturned his palms. Like many people, he has a fear of spiders and snakes. "I have a therapist who tells me, 'The trick is to learn you can't corral all the rattlesnakes. You just got to know where they are.'"

Fincher was interrupted by a sharp knock at the door. It was just 5:00 PM.

David Fincher attempting to rip a swatch from Brad Fischer's shirt.

CHAPTER THREE

THE MEN IN BLACK

"MY GOD, I FEEL like I'm back in Homicide," Dave Toschi said as he surveyed the three filmmakers dressed in black. He shrugged off his trench coat, well-worn from innumerable chases and shootouts, and draped it over the same straight-backed chair where Brad had endured Fincher's reenactment of Paul Stine's murder. Underneath his trench coat, the retired detective was dressed in a tan sport jacket, charcoal gray pants, a lilac shirt, and a plum paisley-print tie. As Toschi bent forward, Fincher could see, strapped to his left side about three inches below his armpit, a special rig of Toschi's own design. It held an upside down leather holster containing a diamond-backed Cobra .38 Special, a vertical refill row of cartridges, and a pair of handcuffs. Steve McQueen had worn Toschi's rig in Peter Yates's 1968 Oscar-winner *Bullitt*. A 1975 photo depicts the broad-shouldered detective in black shirt, wide belt, and flared, window box design pants standing between the stars of *The Streets of San Francisco*. Back then Toschi's wide smile was a few watts brighter than Michael Douglas's and his face more expressive than Karl Malden's. The City's "Super Cop," "Trench Coat Dave," doesn't smile so much these days. The case has taken its toll. He favors his ankle, injured when he slipped on an oil slick in the police garage. His black, curly hair is snowy now, but still as full and springy as in his prime. Toschi has lost none of his keenness as an investigator, and is tough and fit. He still doesn't need glasses to read the finest print, has given up smoking plastic-tipped Tiparillo cigars, and in spite of a full day's work and overtime appears fresh. As the inspiration for Clint Eastwood's *"Dirty" Harry*, his many friends now jokingly call him "Dusty" Harry. The North Beach Italian native is charismatic, stylish, charming, relaxed—always. He speaks softly in low measured tones that hint at his fine singing voice. He is guarded in what he says. Even when asking caustic questions, he is kind, but there is about him a hint of wariness and a mind that recalls and analyzes a suspect's most minute body language. Like Fincher, he is a watcher and a listener.

Fincher's passion for the latest high tech equipment, especially digital, was evident this evening. Standing dead center on the long, polished table scattered with coffee cups and half-eaten Club sandwiches was the smallest tape recorder Toschi had ever seen. It was a machine so advanced that it came with a man to set it up. This morning that man had come to Fincher's suite and done just that. The author's CTR-111 battery-operated cassette tape recorder, slightly smaller than a shoe box, whirred next to it. While Fincher waited for Toschi, he had taken the time to sift the Zodiac correspondence into three neat stacks—verified letters, doubtful letters, and outright fakes. To one side, the director had made a pile of three books: *Zodiac* and *Zodiac Unmasked* (the basis of the proposed movie) and Jamie's screen adaptation. The latter would grow to alarming size as Brad, Jamie, and Fincher uncover new physical evidence, question every "fact," and find eyewitnesses who saw Zodiac without his hood. Fincher put down his yellow highlighter and extended a hand to Toschi.

"I don't want to disturb all your work," Toschi said politely, pushing aside a high box of papers so he could look directly into Fincher's eyes. Brad lit the white shaded lamp over the table. At 5:15 PM, the sun was already lowering as the two Davids began talking, feeling each other out. Toschi leaned forward while Fincher sat flatfooted, elbow resting on the table, chin cupped, and thumb folded into his palm.

"What makes this interesting to me is that the case is unsolved," the director said.

"We think it is solved," Toschi said.

Fincher nodded. A faint smile. An understanding smile. "We wouldn't be interested in making the movie if we were not this close. So when this cartoonist comes to you and says, 'I'm interested in Zodiac,' he hasn't said to you, 'I'm gonna go to Vallejo and I'm gonna talk to those guys.' He hasn't laid that out for you."

"He was totally different from other people who had asked about the case," Toschi replied, "you had to talk to him. And the case had been going on since October of 1969."

"By the time 1977 rolls around and you hear that he wants to write a book," Fincher said, "is it somewhere in your mind that you kind of go, 'This has lost so much steam?' Are you sitting there and thinking it needs somebody to come in and shake things up?"

"I was kind of spinning my wheels at that point," Toschi said. "Nothing was forthcoming. Nothing good."

"So you're not able to disclose information to him initially. You're not able to say, 'I've got these files here.'"

"I showed him the *closed* file cabinets full of the original letters and swatches of the shirt," he said. Finances were so tight at the department that Toschi and his partner shared the same desk, the same phone, even a single wooden nameplate an inspector had carved with Toschi's name on one side and Bill Armstrong's on the other. The only thing that belonged to Toschi was a rubber chicken hanging by its neck over his desk and Walter Matthau had swiped that while filming *The Laughing Detective* in their Homicide room. In 1969, Toschi was drowning in ink, working days and nights, sleeping on his desk top and leaving face prints on the blotter with just enough time to run home, grab a bite, and then rush back to be deafened by constantly ringing phones. "All the calls were killing us: 'What about that phone call I gave you yesterday on John Doe? What have you got on him?'" Toschi could not put citizens off too much without insulting them so he listened to everybody. "My partner was *B.S.*-ing me," Toschi said with a smile. "'Dave,' he says, 'You're better with people than I am so you talk to them.' So I did it. Eventually, our busy secretary wouldn't even go to him, but come to me first. Some odd people were coming into the office and Bill just kind of shied away from it. That's the way he was. Which was fine with me with so many other cases. I met some of the strangest, funniest characters, but you had to sit down and listen to them." Sometimes Toschi wanted to break up in laughter, but filled his notepad with his illegible scrawl in pencil.

"And they won't give you a switchboard to take stuff in?" Fincher asked, amazed.

"No. Contrary to what Chief of Inspectors Marty Lee was telling the media, the whole squad wasn't working on the Zodiac case. There were just the two of us." He and Armstrong had gotten calls from Australia, New Zealand, Scotland Yard, and the FBI who badly wanted to make the arrest of Zodiac and without letting Toschi and Armstrong in on it. "Two agents were assigned to work the case as a phony kidnapping out of Vallejo," he said, "so they could justify working on it. I never liked them. Never—at any time," Toschi said: a flicker of anger in an otherwise placid, polite demeanor.

"So two federal guys move to Vallejo," said Fincher, "and are kinda sniffing around . . ."

"They worked out of the SF Federal Building," Toschi said. "In reality they never went anywhere—just out to lunch."

"When the first two shootings happen in Vallejo, it's a little teenie thing," Fincher continued. "What are you hearing about it?" Fincher opens both hands, palms down when he asks questions, then turns them up as if to receive the answer like catching a football.

"We didn't call them serial killers then—for lack of a better word it was just some nut who was killing."

"Vallejo is still Vallejo," Fincher said. "That's happening across the Bay and SFPD doesn't have anything to say about it. Somebody calls and says, 'Remember the cipher guy Zodiac and the whole thing? Well, he's now shooting in San Francisco. *The Chronicle* just got this odd letter. You better come down right away and you see the thing.'"

Stine the cabdriver was shot on a Saturday night, Zodiac's letter with a bloodied swatch of shirt enclosed arrived on a Tuesday. Toschi and Armstrong got to the newspaper at Fifth and Mission about eleven that morning. Toschi recalled his excitement when they showed Coroner Boyd Stevens and Dr. Henry Turkel the swatch. "Oh, my God," Stevens said, grabbing Stine's shirt out of evidence and smoothing it flat on a body gurney. Carefully, he matched the swatch with a torn section. It fitted perfectly.

"The guy sits in the backseat of the [taxi]," said Fincher thoughtfully, "and he gets to a certain place. He's going to shoot the guy in the back of the head—behind his right ear. So he does that and he's going to get out of the back of the passenger side door and he's going to sit in front. He's going to have the guy's head in his lap. Now, in your mind, the teenagers are not mistaken? The guy definitely has the cabbie's head cradled. Is there an ass print of this guy? If you're holding someone and they're gouting blood [Stine has just been shot seconds earlier], obviously, he's not going to pick the guy up and sit under him, so probably Stine has slipped over to his left."

"He slipped over on his right side."

"He did?" Fincher was surprised. "O.K., Stine was shot and slipped to his right. Then the guy gets out of the backseat of the car, sets the guy up. There's got to be blood on the seat."

"There was very little blood on the seat," Toschi said. The stains had been confined to Stine's clothing, person and the well of the front compartment of the cab where it had pooled. Why was Fincher so interested in the way Stine was sitting? Toschi wondered. Was it just because he wants to get it on film properly?

"Just psychologically Fincher's very interested in behavior," Brad explained, "and in certain choices that the killer made as mundane as what part of the car he decided to get into and what part of the car he decided to leave from. Those choices are reflective of what Zodiac was thinking. David's very meticulous about all those details. When you look at the big picture, those details become fairly significant."

"Is the shirt torn?," Fincher asked Toschi. "It has to be cut to be torn." He looked expectantly at Toschi.

"Torn," Toschi said.

Fincher was not so sure, but continued. "So he brings the head wound, open head wound, into his crotch, which seems like a particularly strange thing to do, and then reaches and tears off the front left flap of the guy's shirt. Now all the pictures that I've seen, it looks like a very even tear."

"It had jagged ends."

"It did?" Fincher's eyes widened again. "What kind of shirt is it? Is this like a broadcloth?"

"Polyester-cotton—short sleeve green and white striped sport shirt with buttons."

"Polyester—does it tear? Especially at the edges where it's seamed? Cause this is the most difficult part of the shirt to tear. So if this was the front part where you would tuck the shirt in—." Fincher got up and experimented again on poor Brad's only shirt, pulling with all his strength, but only stretching the material further.

"His shirt could have been out of his trousers," Brad suggested as he tucked his own shirt back in.

"But, still, it takes some doing. I mean this is thick tensile strength. It takes a big, strong man to just pull and tear it. When he tears it away the fabric doesn't just rip."

"But it was not a very good fabric sport shirt," Toschi explained. "If he tore it where it's been sewn already, it's going to be easier."

"So he tears it along the seam and it's a foot by a foot?" Fincher asked. Toschi nodded. "So he's going to take that and it's going to tear across and then here's where it's buttoned." He pantomimed the movement. "He's going to tear down since the buttons and buttonholes don't come with it." Fincher's expression hardened. "Let's go back to that night again." His eyes were faraway. Abruptly, he assumed the persona of Zodiac, something he would do throughout his investigation. Fincher was breaking the 180 Degree Rule, a very important aspect of being a director. Crossing an invisible line drawn through the center of the camera view plate in a filmed sequence results in a certain particular jump where it appears that two people have suddenly switched places and become each other. In this case, the result was uncanny.

"I come to San Francisco on Saturday night and I go, 'I'm going to get me a cabbie cause I can take this guy wherever the fuck I want.' I know a couple of things, even with my limited 120 IQ. I'm bringing two pairs of gloves, whether or not I'm going to be seen hailing a cab, I'm going to have gloves, I'm going to have my gun with me, and then when I pull to a place where I'm comfortable where its dark enough, secluded enough, I'll off this guy. And I want my trophy and maybe I'm disorganized enough not to know what my trophy is going to be, whether I'm going to get the guy's keys and send keys to the *Chronicle* or I'm going to get his shirt. But, the notion, if I've got to walk away—I've got my car parked a couple of blocks away or I'm going to go and get on a bus—the thing I'm staying away from is this gouting head wound. A 9-mill! [Fincher claps his hands together as if a gun is firing—*BLAM!*] That occluded making a seal and the amount of blood described at the scene. The notion that I'm going to cradle his head, and we saw what happened to Jackie Kennedy—she was covered in blood, doesn't make any sense. Do you think there's a chance the guy gets out of the backseat, opens the door, the cabbie's head is in the footwell, sits on the edge of the seat and reaches across as opposed to cradling his head?" Toschi, stunned by Fincher's uncanny performance, doesn't know if the cabbie's head was on Zodiac's lap or at an angle when the killer went through Stine's pockets. "But there's no spatter or drip on the front-seat," he said. "It's all in the footwell." Fincher took a sip from a white cup perfectly centered on a small black tray. "We had no witnesses except for the kids across the street who called . . . there is no 911 then. They have to call the operator. Nine-fifty this guy is shot. Ten-fifteen you're on the scene." Fincher has raised more questions than Toschi can answer in the time left. He had arrived late and it was nearly time for him to get home to his wife. Lights were springing on outside. Fincher looked Toschi straight in the eye as if to hold him.

"I want to take you back to the night that Stine was killed," he said. From the look on Toschi's face, he knew that terrible night was the last place the ace detective wanted to go. He wanted to go home. He wanted to see his bride. Fincher could see his toes were pointed toward the door.

"The Saturday night Stine died, I was wiped out," Toschi began. "The stabbing death of a fireman Friday night in the Haight-Ashbury, was the fourth homicide I'd caught that week. It was also my partner Bill Armstrong's birthday." That night Toschi had laid out his clothes like a fireman—slacks, trench coat, hushpuppies—inhaled his dinner, showered, and gotten to bed by eight o'clock. His wife was watching TV when the phone rang twice, three times. "Dave, Dave," she called. "It's probably for you."

"Oh, my God," Toschi had moaned, rolled out of bed, lifted the receiver, grabbed for his notepad, and listened to the police operator.

"It's a bad one, Dave, a Yellow Cab driver."

"Any suspects?"

"Nothing."

"You got the Crime Lab rolling?"

"Yes."

"Have you called my partner yet?"

"I haven't called your partner yet."

"I'll call him," Toschi said, and hung up.

"You get in a car and you go down there and it's probably less than twenty minutes after the shooting?" Fincher said. Toschi nodded.

Outside Fincher's suite, fog was rolling down Geary Boulevard just as it had been that long ago October night in 1969. "That's pretty amazing. You got nothing. You just got a cab. It seems fairly innocuous because cab drivers get robbed a lot."

"But they don't always get killed," Toschi said.

David Fincher, Brad Fischer, and Jamie Vanderbilt
with Inspector David Toschi.

CHAPTER FOUR

THE CANARY-YELLOW CAB

"SO YOU GO, 'AW, fuck!'" Fincher continued. "So you get out and you look at the scene. He tented his eyes as if framing a shot for his next movie whatever that might be. He was playing Toschi now, taking on some of his mannerisms. "You go, 'Lot of blood.' The first people you want to talk to are the two uniformed officers. 'Talk to me. What have you got? Has anybody stopped anybody, any suspects?' Two other cops are making a report and units from the Park Police and another precinct station from the other side of Golden Gate Park are circling the area. You've got this single gunshot wound, and it seems like business as usual. Two policemen reported a lumbering white male. The two officers, Don Fouke and Eric Zelms, are out of Richmond District. Are these the two guys on the scene when you get there?"

"No," Toschi said. "There was a mistake in communication." Obviously, it was something he didn't want to talk about.

"I understand that." Fincher cupped both hands and rested his chin as if his head was too heavy. He was not interested in who was culpable, but why Stine's body ended up where it did: upper torso slumped in a semi-supine position (on his right side) on the front-seat passenger side, head facing north and resting on the floorboard. Fincher now became the cabbie, acting the pose out, leaning this way and that. "You're shot here." He pointed to a spot. "You're going to fall this way. You're going to bleed profusely this way. That makes sense. So you've got a pretty good entry wound." But no exit wound. Why? When

Zodiac discharged his 9-mm into the cabbie's skull at the superior and anterior attachment of his right ear, he created a classic contact wound: ragged, torn skin with blackened edges. The molten slug traced a right to left downward path through the central surface of the right temporal lobe. It struck a bone and, spinning end over end, penetrated the mid-portion of his left cheekbone where it shattered into four pieces that embedded in the cheek muscle.

"So his brains basically are scrambled by expanding gases [and the sudden increase of intracranial pressure produced by the entrance of a high velocity projectile]," Fincher said. "He going to go this way first." He leaned as far left in his seat as he could. "Probably away from the blast, or he's gonna go twist. If he falls to the right, then the killer gets in. The killer sits on the front-seat, pulls the body close to him, but the body can bleed into the footwell. He's got blood on his shoes, but he's not covered in blood. So he's going to reach across and tear this shirt. He dips the cloth in the blood to make sure police can tie this [swatch] to the cabbie. He puts the swatch in his pocket."

With no exit wound and no blood pressure, the shooter could remain unbloodied merely by keeping Stine's head inclined to the left since only gravity exerts any action on blood flow after death. After Stine was pulled onto the right front-seat, the blood pooled in the well through the entry wound. Fincher changed the subject. He had something else to ask. "Something got the young witnesses' attention," he said to Toschi. "Was it the lights? The struggle inside the cab? Another noise? A shot?" Sound, an important part of Fincher's films, always intrigued him.

"Nobody heard a gunshot," Toschi said.

"If not a shot, then what? Even a 9 mill at close range is going to make a *pop*. From shooting blanks in movies, I know 9-mm are loud handguns. Is it possible in your estimation that the gun was silenced? Did Zodiac take credit for having a silencer? So, this is the first 9 mill kill, right? It's always been .22s until now. We don't know the make of the gun."

"It could have been one of three types," Toschi began.

"One would have been the Luger," Fincher interjected. "Its short recoil system is most effective for use with a 9-mm parabellum." Its inertia factor dictates a minimum basic weight. "On a Luger, the back moves, but the barrel stays. On all the rest the entire top assembly slides." Fincher pointed his right hand like a gun. "So the tops going to fly—there's probably more noise with a gun with the slide and ejector than with the German Luger because everything kind of breaks back here. It's probably the quietest of all the guns. Or it could have been the Beretta [The Beretta Modello 51 features a slide stop which retains the slide to the rear when the magazine is empty]. Or it could have been the Browning."

A Browning 9-mm semiautomatic model 1935 High Power has a fixed sight, a blade in front, a U notch in rear and a thirteen round detachable double-staggered line box magazine in the butt. The HP works on a locked breech system appropriate to the heavy round it fires. After the first manually loaded round is fired, the barrel and slide recoil together until a wedge-shaped cam unlocks the slide which flies to the rear automatically stripping a round and chambering it for the next shot. The Browning has a right hand twist, a six and six, and ejects the casing to the right which is consistent with the casing found in the cab. Fincher was sure the weapon had been one of those guns.

At 11:15 PM, the night of Stine's murder, Toschi had gotten an uninterrupted look from the middle window where the children had watched. Then, he had seen their view was sharply angled from two floors up down onto Washington Street. The kids had not heard the shot, only noticed a dome light inside the Yellow Cab and the open right front passenger door. One called the other, "Hey, look." They watched grabbing, pulling, and deliberate movements inside the cab until they realized a fight was going on and called the police. Toschi had heard them out, but wasn't getting what he wanted. The children were sobbing. Conditions in the room were horrible. The body was still on the street below. Red lights were flashing from a couple of radio cars. A dozen people had crowded around the cab. The coroner's wagon was there. Officers were still trying to talk to people. As Fincher listened to Toschi, he had an idea for a shot in his film: he could shoot the crime scene from that middle window and replicate what the children had seen. Then, Fincher asked himself, What had Toschi seen? Perhaps, more than he knew. Was there a clue lodged in his memory and, if so, could he extract it?

Toschi recalled that for three and a half hours "all the souls that were available," twenty-five to thirty people, were in action below. The coroner took the body away at 1:00 AM. When he left the scene, heavy fog was crawling down Washington Street and swallowing up the few hardy onlookers still lingering. The director asked himself a troubling question—had Zodiac been among that crowd of spectators that had gathered? Had he been captured on film in the crime scene photos taken that night? Did those seventeen photos still exist? And if they did, could he find them?

"What's your gut feeling, Inspector, about the chance that the famous bloody fingerprint taken from the Stine cab could possibly be from somebody other than the killer? Highly likely? Highly unlikely?" Silence. "So the suspect reaches in and he's going to hold Stine's head to the muzzle of the gun. The guy is going to start to bleed instantly. There could be blood on his hand when he steadies himself."

"He didn't lean into the cab," Toschi said. As always, he was careful in what he revealed to civilians. "The children would have seen him. And all the windows were closed."

"The thing that I question and seems strange to me," Fincher said, "is that there's always been this fingerprint. And yet the only thing we know about Zodiac for sure is that he takes the time and works in a meticulous way to wipe down the taxi cab. These teenage witnesses don't say whether or not he was wearing gloves. I don't buy a guy wiping his fingerprints down from the scene. He could be wearing gloves. It's not as though there's anything suspicious about a guy wearing gloves and he's hailing a cab. I think you have to say someone other than the suspect touched that cab. The most important thing is that you can't exclude anyone because of print. You ordered an officer at the scene not to let anybody touch the cab. Obviously everybody knows you're not supposed to touch the fucking cab."

"Cops are as human as anybody else," Toschi said. He shook his head sadly. "They're curious about seeing a dead body—where's my crime scene then? I'm concerned because I'm never going to get it back again."

"We know from [Zodiac's] letters that he's revising history as he goes," Fincher said. "'I'm putting airplane glue on my fingers. *Ha. Ha. Ha.*' We know he's been killing in Vallejo. He's making a trip to San Francisco to shoot a cabdriver which is a perfect random killing.

How come that fingerprint? What is there to lead us to believe there is a legitimate chance that someone of such intellect is going to make such a mistake? But you've got gloves on. Why are you going to take them off? If he doesn't have gloves, then he doesn't have a 160 IQ. So the kids see him wipe down the dash?"

"He's seen wiping or touching, but we don't know exactly why," Toschi said. He made a swirling clockwise motion with his left hand. "One of the kids said he put the rag back into his pocket. The shirt swatches didn't have that much blood on them, but they did have blood."

"Now, I'm going to amend my earlier criticism of the IQ issue," Fincher said, taking the role of the killer again. The role was always chilling. Take Two: "You've got your hands in your pockets. You hail a cab. You leave a handprint on the door. You fold it shut. You get in. Hands in the pockets. You can or cannot have airplane glue on your fingertips. You're taking your gun with you so you're not worried about that. *Boom!* You kill the guy. He falls back. You can't take fingerprints off of cloth. So then you tear the shirt, then dip the thing in blood or perhaps—was there any blood on the dashboard?"

"Minimal," Toschi said. "I could see it in my flashlight."

"Atomized spatter." Fincher said. Take Three: "Then you take the shirt, you put it in your pocket, you walk around, then you take your jacket and wipe the cab, making sure you get the whole panel, in case you touched the door and don't remember, and you're out of there. Pretty simple. Again, there's so much lore about this now. There are people saying he dipped the cloth in blood and smeared the side of the cab. Nonsense. The next day you get a call from someone you genuinely respect and they say, 'We've got two partials.' Where?"

"Left, left rear of the door on the door jamb on the outside," Toschi said. "Partials on the post. In blood. Inspector Bill Hamlet thought it was part of the left hand. They were good enough to rule somebody out, not good enough to get a warrant and say those are your prints."

"Do you believe that given the printing that was done on Arthur Allen that you could have gotten a match to the partial?" Fincher asked. Toschi nodded. "So when those came back negative, then that must exonerate him."

"We speculated that someone that we didn't eliminate at the scene had to have touched the cab and walked away."

"It's never seemed to me that Arthur Leigh Allen could be dismissed as a suspect because of these prints and you concur with me on that?" Toschi did. "If you've come to San Francisco to shoot somebody, the preeminent thing in your mind is to escape detection and the gold standard for evidence in 1969 is fingerprints. Is Zodiac's needling in his letter exaggerated in any way to make his point?"

"Extremely exaggerated. Like, 'You dummies. I was there the whole time laughing at you.' I don't think he was there at all. I think he wanted to get out of there as quickly as he could. He had done what he set out to do and thinking, 'I almost got caught.' Might have wet his pants over that one."

"So," Fincher conjectured, again assuming the persona of Zodiac, "you scout the area before you take the cab to see where you will park your car. And you get there, 'Eww. I feel better a block further. Drive on.' The irony is that by killing a cabbie you're giving yourself a twelve to fourteen hour head start. There's no way you're going to associate this with the Vallejo murders."

"But it's not a lovers' lane killing like Vallejo," Toschi said. "This is a poor cab driver who doesn't have more than fifteen bucks on him and he blew him away."

"Now explain to me how this works," Fincher said. "I'm the Zodiac and I'm on Mason and Geary and it's difficult for me to get a cab driver to take me out to the Presidio, so I'm going to call the dispatcher and say I want a cab. And then I'm going to hope to flag him down." At 9:45 PM, a call had come in to Yellow for a cab to 500 9th Avenue, Apartment # 1. "Did he flag Stine down or . . ."

"He flagged him down."

"Explain to me how it is that I, as the Zodiac, have any degree of certainty that Dispatch will send to the Presidio a cab I'm going to be able to flag down at Geary and Mason. If you want to kill someone you look through the people who are easy for you to get access to. Cabdrivers are high on that list, next to prostitutes. Its like Serial Killer 101. So it makes sense to me this is happenstance. Someone calls Stine. Stine is on his way there and he's at the wrong place at the wrong time, pick up a guy and figure, 'I'm on the way to the Presidio anyway.'"

But what if Zodiac also made that first call?

"What Paul Stine initially wrote down on his way bill was Washington and Maple [the east-north corner, one block east of Washington and Cherry]," Toschi said, "and that's where specifically the killer intended to go." But, Zodiac didn't. Instead, he went a block further. "Why? Who or what did Zodiac see at that intersection that scared him off? Was there another witness? If so, could Fincher and his neophyte detectives find him? Toschi studied the director. One expert people-reader judging another. His take on Fincher: "Such a perfectionist." Now, Toschi's mind again was on the cozy home he shares with his wife. This is where he yearns to be. This is where he has to be. He wants to be anywhere but that fog-shrouded corner in 1969. "My bride knows I'm here, talking to some high-powered people, that I was here to tell you the truth." He rose and pushed back his chair. "I didn't know what to expect when I walked into this room. You made me feel relaxed within thirty-seconds. I was here to tell you the truth."

"What's more important than the truth is that it is your subjective view of the events," Fincher said. "That's more important than an objective view. We're beyond being a reconstruction. So I trust implicitly and that's the difference, that's the thing we need to do now. He believed in intuition; Toschi has plenty of that. "We want to learn all we can from you."

"And I from you," Toschi said. "You get intuitive and if you're not intuitive and you want to be a cop, especially a detective, you're not going to be a good detective. You've got to listen and you have to look and then hope the truth will register and your brain will start clicking."

"Do you believe that instinct is the most important thing," Fincher asked. "Let me qualify this. The first time you ever saw Arthur Leigh Allen was when you went to talk to him at his work [at the Pinole Oil Refinery on August 4, 1971]. What's your first impression when you see him coming down the hallway? At this point you don't know anything about him. He's just a bunch of 'somebody said this about him' and 'somebody said that about him.'"

Toschi paused at the door, hand on the knob, trench coat draped over his arm. Fincher had nailed him to the spot with his question. "My first impression was that he was very uncomfortable. Arthur Leigh Allen's flatfooted, but I sense he could move if he had to. There is a power and cunning about the man. You think to yourself, 'This guy looks good.' You could tell that he was very concerned he's going to get fired and thinking he's being embarrassed."

"Did you get a reaction from Allen that this is a hit?" Fincher asked. "Let's talk about that for a second. He's a smart guy. He's nervous in the situation. He's not yet a convicted child molester." It chills Fincher that there are "a hell of lot more molested children by Leigh out there" than suspected. "Leigh's already tearfully lost a job at a school. This situation is very similar to him—'The principal would like to see you. Is it true you touched a child?' 'Yes, I did.' 'You're fuckin' out of here!' This is a reiteration of that for him as he's coming up the hallway. This has happened to him before and it resulted in the loss of his livelihood. Now he's not meeting with the principal. He's meeting with the SFPD. He comes into this room and sits down and you guys go, 'We want to talk to you about Zodiac.' Is he sweating?"

"Yes, but trying not to show it," Toschi said. The more the suspect held himself in check the more the detectives struggled to remain calm. He looked much bigger in the flesh than they had anticipated. Because of his thin hair and broad, high forehead, he appeared to be in his early forties. "He's touching up his hair."

"A pedophile from Vallejo colors his hair?" Fincher said in amazement.

"That's in the official Zodiac description—the reddish tint and crewcut were always consistent."

"Obviously if you color your hair you have gray roots." The two cops had said Zodiac's hair was gray in the back. "You saw him again after the search of his trailer." Toschi nodded. He recalled a good-sized camper parked off wheels next to a white and blue sailboat, a shed, a white Oldsmobile and a Honda 350 motorcycle. Inside the trailer, it was very dirty and in disarray—old books and newspapers strewn all over. "You close the door behind you," Fincher continued, "then Allen drives up [in a Karmann Ghia]. He's my height, six-one, about thirty pounds heavier. He comes up and leads with his forehead or leads with his gut?" Toschi indicated that it was mostly his gut. "That's why he's flatfooted, because he locks his knees."

"He's big all the way around. He's got a big tire and a fairly substantial rear."

"Is he more gorilla-like in that his shoulders sort of slope down?"

"Yeah, like an avocado . . . as excited as I was at seeing Allen again one foot away from me I could see the anger in his face at us being on his home grounds [his trailer]. You could feel the latent strength in him even though he was getting older; his mind was working. You could almost hear the brain cells clicking and I could feel the evil in him. I was just thankful that I was armed."

"You can see that he's angry because his chin's down when he's looking at you."

"I'm getting his evil eye."

"And what is his evil eye?" Fincher asked. "Is it Gloria Swanson [in 1950's *Sunset Boulevard*] looking over the cheekbones?" Fincher often used movie analogies in his sleuthing, something Brad and Jamie had ceased since their visit to Lake Berryessa in November, and Fincher soon would.

"No, its full face. He played very, very dumb and I said, 'We've met before,' and he kept staring and staring. You could feel the anger building. The Sonoma County plainclothes deputy was so excited I thought he was going to handcuff him. I was trying to be low key, but knowing we're staring at someone who is very likely a serial killer." Toschi had the door open now with one foot in the hall.

"It's really nice to have these little bits and pieces," Fincher concluded, closing his thick binder and rising, hand extended. "Thank you, Inspector, for coming down. If we come back, may we impose upon you again?"

Toschi nodded, slipped on his rumpled old Burberry, and patted the pockets for his car keys. "I never leave without my trench coat," he said with a forced smile, obviously still troubled by the case after all these decades, still saddened by the death of Paul Stine and his inability to bring him Justice. Brad and Jamie rose to say goodbye. The door closed behind him and the room suddenly felt empty.

Like a jigsaw puzzle these little bits and pieces were coming together. Eventually, these contradictory and disordered fragments would form a complete picture which Fincher would then film "and see the money guys at the premiere." He knew *Zodiac* was a tough sell: "There are no car chases in it—people talk a lot in it. It's about a cartoonist and a murderer who never got caught. So yeah, the studio is nervous. Sitting back in his chair, Fincher could already visualize the murder scene on the screen: from Washington and Cherry Streets, downtown San Francisco is glowing, lit with a new kind of light that the director is only just now refining. If *Zodiac* is green lighted, it will look like no movie before and will change the ways people see movies forever. It involved another kind of snake than a rattler, a Viper, which would soon be in his hands. As he pondered the long, difficult cinematic journey ahead with its many dead ends, he laid down an unbreakable ground rule to his two partners who had retaken adjoining seats on the opposite side of the table.

"It is anathema to rely on any secondary or tertiary source," Fincher said. "Police reports are the rule. That and the people who were there. Let's find everyone we can who was materially involved in the investigation, and let's sit down across from them, look them in the eye, ask them direct and sometimes difficult questions, and then hear what they have to say. The only thing we have going for us is that the movie is about these guys who get sucked down the rabbit hole of the Zodiac case."

"There is something in these characters [the cartoonist, the inspector, the reporter] that exists in all of us," Brad said, "the capacity for becoming consumed by something so fully, that day after day, night after night, you can't ever truly put it away. It has the potential to be an incredibly destructive force."

While their investigation was in full force, what they haven't counted on is that they too might be sucked down the same rabbit hole as those who had lost themselves in the process of chasing the murder story and become part of it. Even now, they were skirting its edges and that rabbit hole is bottomless and deadly. All things are possible in Hollywood, but in the Land of Fantasy, the Truth is hard to find. Fincher had grown quiet and was staring out the big window toward San Anselmo where for him it had all begun. He was once more working out the riddle of the open taxi door, the blood that should have been elsewhere, a bloody print that belonged to no one, and the shot nobody heard.

Those questions might never be answered to his satisfaction. He was, as Brad and Jamie knew, a perfectionist and as such never satisfied. Famously, Fincher has said, "Movies are never completed, they are abandoned."

CHAPTER FIVE
VERACITY

BY TUESDAY, FEBRUARY 3, 2004, all three filmmakers had returned to Los Angeles and retreated to their respective caves. David Fincher was ensconced inside his Hollywood Boulevard office, an 11,000 square foot former bank with a tower. All the miniature castle lacked were battlements and a moat.

Jamie Vanderbilt had returned to the home he shared with his lovely fiancée, Amber Freeman, a professional interior decorator. At the top of a wide, curving staircase, Jamie's disorganized study stood in sharp contrast to Amber's sophisticated designs. His desktop was crowded with scripts, a glass ashtray, coffee cups, a Stephen King thriller, and a gold lamp with a white shade. Against the rear wall stood a narrow, three-shelf bookcase containing Jamie's research volumes. Right of the bookcase, the tan blinds were up and the window was halfway open. Jamie took a deep breath, relaxing after his stressful trip. The wind seemed fresher here, the sun sparkling on the backyard pool brighter than he had remembered.

Brad Fischer had returned to his second floor office at Phoenix Pictures in Culver City and was worrying over a long list of impossible interviews spread out on his desktop. Without these interviews, David Fincher would *not* shoot *Zodiac*. At the top of the list was the name of Sandy Panzarella, a former acquaintance of the prime suspect. Brad wasted no time arranging a meeting with him for Friday in Manhattan Beach.

"We had breakfast at a restaurant at 9:30 AM," Brad reported, and quickly added. "And, no, it wasn't the International House of Pancakes [where victim Darlene Ferrin had worked], and, no, it wasn't Terry's [where the chief suspect, who lived nearby, had stalked Darlene], but a place called The Kettle." Brad had no difficulty in spotting Panzarella from across the room. He was wearing a sweatshirt from the Bel Air Country Club where he and his buddy, *Unsolved Mysteries* host Robert Stack, used to meet to hash over the Zodiac case for hours. Brad hailed him and they began to talk. It was Panzarella who had contacted Brad, and it was through him that Brad hoped to entice his former college roommate, Don Cheney, to speak with them. Both had important information on Zodiac. Sandy was eager to help, but Cheney would still require some persuading to meet with them. The plan was to fly Panzarella to Washington State and reunite him with Don Cheney and go from there.

"Sandy's a really sweet guy," Brad told Jamie afterward, "open to talking to us and genuinely interested in helping. He's really looking forward to our trip." That is, if they could make it happen. Cheney was a tough nut to crack.

Next, Brad initiated delicate negotiations to speak with the brother and sister-in-law of the prime Zodiac suspect. The young producer knew he had to be sensitive. One false step might lose them the interview. He considered calling cold, but after several late night discussions with Jamie decided to send the couple a single letter on company stationery to give them confidence that they were dealing with reputable people like Mike Medavoy, Chairman and CEO of Phoenix Pictures, creator of over three hundred films, including eight Best Oscar Winners. Only Toschi and Armstrong and Vallejo Detective Jack Mulanax had ever spoken with the beleaguered couple in any depth. By Wednesday, Brad was still slaving over the letter.

"Brad bugged me to death about that letter," Jamie said. "He went through innumerable drafts. He would call me at eleven o'clock at night and go, 'What do you think of this?' and give me a paragraph he had read to me three hours ago. And you know what he had changed? Three words!"

"By the twentieth version that's a lot of changes," Brad said defensively.

"And you ask me to hurry up writing the script," Jamie said.

Brad read his latest draft aloud, identifying himself as a producer and executive at Phoenix Pictures: "For the past year and a half, we've been developing a movie based on Robert Graysmith's books, *Zodiac* and *Zodiac Unmasked,* both of which detail controversial suspicions about your brother's involvement in the case. Our ability to even approach the starting gate with the film depends in full on the willingness of the people who were involved to sit face to face and speak openly with us." He explained that Fincher's template for their film is *All the President's Men,* "which is also based on a real story that happened to real people." To avoid second or thirdhand accounts, Brad underscored that it was essential they speak with them. "Most of those threads lead back to you and your wife and we would greatly value your perspective." Brad assured them they had no interest in publishing any part of their forthcoming conversation and hoped that the brother and sister-in-law would allow Fincher and himself "the opportunity to meet in person so that you can judge for yourself."

"Well, what do you think of this version?" Brad asked.

"You've changed two words," Jamie said. "Just send it already." Jamie was impressed. Brad's letter contained words rarely found in a Hollywood dictionary—"veracity," "integrity," "evenhandedness," "journalistic integrity," and "the greatest degree of authenticity."

Brad slept on his decision and Friday afternoon sent the all-important letter to the couple by FedEx, then went back to nailing down the meeting with Cheney. So far, he was having no luck. In the evening he returned home to read new scripts, a job that Amy Carr, the Phoenix Pictures research/story director, had handled the last four years. Brad lived in a 1920s garden-courtyard-style apartment complex of twenty-five individual addresses. "There's a little coy pond when you first walk up," he said, "and there are steps. It's got three-stories. It's got hardwood floors. It's got character." Tonight, though, the young executive's room seemed empty. Brad's job consumed him to the exclusion of almost everything else. He was logging in one hundred and fifty calls in a single day, and the women in his life didn't like it. When it came down to choosing between his job and his love life, his career always won hands down.   "It's hard in the business because it's so demanding," Brad explained, "and often times I think a lot of people, even though they understand rationally it's your job and it's something you're passionate about, don't always understand what your priorities are. Emotionally, I've always gotten to a point where girlfriends have said, 'You're choosing your job over me. And I'm second.' And what can I say to that? It's the truth."

His apartment was tastefully furnished with one exception—a discolored white hat from Columbia sitting in a place of honor on top of his television set. It was the filthiest object he owned. "If this hat could talk . . ." he often said. "Some scientists believe it can," Jamie would add.

As for the murderous negotiations over the *Zodiac* deal and budget, Brad could say little except it involved multiple studios and a few volatile personalities. "The talks are fascinating though backbreaking, but so far, so good," he said with a forced smile. The strain told in his voice. There is a slight tremor to his hand, congenital, not from the multiple trials he was enduring. Another sleepless night and the next evening, still on tender hooks, he waited for the brother and sister-in-law to respond to his letter which had been delivered to them that morning. The next morning, Brad rang up Inspector Toschi, hoping he was coming around to letting them use his name in the film. Using everyone's real name and securing life rights were another Fincher requirement that could determine whether he shot *Zodiac* or not.

"I just hope that in the end I come out of it looking O.K.," Toschi said.

"Dave," Brad said, "let me tell you something. There are only two heroes in this story and that's Graysmith and you."

On Monday morning, February 9, Brad called Cheney in Washington State. As feared, Cheney was uninterested. "Pretty much everything I have to say about this I've already said," he said tentatively. By the end of the conversation, Brad had reassured him and Cheney was O.K. with seeing Fincher and excited by the idea of his former roommate, Sandy Panzarella, coming up to Washington. That was the true selling point.

"I haven't seen Sandy in a long time," Cheney said.

"I think we're going to head up there in about two weeks," Brad said. "I've been talking to Sandy. He's really a hoot and eagerly looking forward to our trip."

Meanwhile, there was still no word from the brother and sister-in-law. Finally, on Tuesday, February 17, Brad could wait no longer and followed up his letter by phone. To his surprise, the suspect's brother picked up immediately. "We're thinking about it," he said. "We'll have an answer by Monday." As Brad went over his calendar afterward, he saw there was a scheduling conflict. That was the same day as their scheduled trip to see Cheney. At 5:00 AM, Wednesday, he and Lou Phillips, Senior Vice President of Phoenix Pictures Production, Post-Production, and Music, flew to San Francisco to meet with the mayors of two Bay Area cities. Brad, who had had no sleep the night before, dozed off on the plane ride there (and on the way back). They arrived at 8:15 AM, for their 10:00 AM meeting with the Mayor of Vallejo. A light rain was falling.

Just as Brad put one foot into the Mayor's office, the sister-in-law called. He quickly stepped back into the hallway. "I can't really talk right now," she said. "I wanted to let you know that I'm very protective of my husband. When's a good time to talk? I have some very direct questions."

"I'll have some very direct answers," Brad said.

"Good," she said, and suggested a time when she would let Brad know what she and her husband had decided. Brad strode into his meeting, a great weight lifted from his shoulders. The Vallejo Mayor was aloof at first, sizing them up a little bit, but heard them out along with a few local officials he had brought in to listen. Phillips opened up first, speaking briefly about who the filmmakers were and that this was an introductory visit. "We're working on this movie about the Zodiac," Phillips said, "and we hope to shoot the whole movie in San Francisco and Vallejo. It's a really big film, anywhere between eighty and one hundred million dollars."

"Also, one of the things that's very important to us," Brad said, "is making a film that is truly authentic. They'll be filming on the exact spots where the story took place. David Fincher wants to be scrupulous with the details. We would love to have access to official files on the case itself."

The Vallejo chief of police, wasn't available, so they conferred instead with Captain Dave Jackson, an athletic, silver-haired cop who had studied at the knee of Vallejo Detective Sergeant George Bawart, former Zodiac lead detective and a lead investigator for seventeen of his twenty-eight years with VPD. Jackson had joined Bawart, who was retired now, for the searches of the prime suspect's house and basement in 1991 and 1992. Fischer and Phillips were saying their goodbyes in the hallway outside the mayor's office when the mayor sidled up.

"Who knows?" he said, "Maybe you'll solve the case."

"We'll settle for making a great movie," Brad replied.

"We would obviously love their cooperation," he told Lou outside, "and their help in offering us any incentives financially for the production."

Oakland, Vallejo's neighboring city, already offered sales tax credits to film companies plus an employment tax credit of $5.30 an hour to any production company employing city residents. San Francisco did not—a problem.

Brad called George Bawart, though he didn't expect to reach him. Wednesdays, George was usually out sailing his "Bye George" along the Sacramento Delta waterways with Jan, his wife of twenty-three years. Jan, a Sacramento gal, funny, bright, and goodnatured, was a district manager who traveled a few days a week. Surprisingly, she was home today and answered the phone. The rain had kept Bawart home at his workshop building a remote-controlled plane.

"I would love to touch base with you," Brad told Bawart when he came to the phone. Sadly, the detective recalled how little SFPD had kept him in the loop: "But nobody calls me on this Zodiac stuff these days, except Graysmith. Tell you what, I'll go through the eighties' stuff in my attic to see what I had. It's just a lot of old copies of everything. You've probably got everything I've got." Not quite, Brad thought. Who knew what material had been sitting in Bawart's attic all these years in the heat and dust. "I'll pull some down for you," he promised.

"Bawart is very open," Brad told Phillips afterward, "and is considering meeting with us at some point." All through the conversation with Bawart, Brad had been trying to visualize the retired detective. His voice was husky, powerful and filled with energy and good humor. Captain Jackson had described a muscular, overweight man, but hinted to Brad that Bawart had gone through some drastic changes so he should be prepared. Brad did not know what to expect when they finally met. Bawart's reputation was that he was "tougher than a junkyard dog."

At 1:30 PM, the filmmakers drove over the Bay Bridge to confer with San Francisco's new mayor, Gavin Newsom. "The mayor's thirty-six-years old," Brad said. "He's a slick guy, really smart, and progressive, really impressive." He combs his dark hair in a high pompadour, has a penchant for green Hermes ties and is one of the best dressed men in America. A Catholic Democrat, he was married to courtroom-commentator Kimberly Guilfoyle Newsom. At this moment, the Mayor was riding a seventy percent approval wave. The city was struggling under a $300 million deficit when he slashed his nearly $170,000 salary by fifteen percent and urged other city government high earners to do the same. He hoped to raise ten million. He got less than $300,000. Mayor Newsom had filled top city posts with women such as Joanne Hayes-White, whom he had appointed the city's first female fire chief on Day 3 of his administration. He replaced Police Chief Alex Fagan with Heather Fong as Acting Chief.

"I'll tell you something," Brad told Phillips, "seeing the difference between the Vallejo Police Department and City Hall in San Francisco, you really get a sense of the small town versus the big city. San Francisco City Hall is huge. It's like the Vatican." They looked up at the Beaux-Arts dome glistening in the mist. At 2:15 PM, they mounted a wide marble staircase to Mayor Newsom's office and stepped into a whirlwind of television cameras, news crews, and reporters. Lights and cables snaked everywhere. The roar of many voices stunned them. Today was a historic civil rights moment.

Four days earlier, Newsom had authorized the city clerk to begin issuing marriage licenses to same-sex couples. Today, Day 24 of his administration, four thousand people had lined up in the rain outside City Hall to start what was called the "Winter of Love." Partners for over fifty years, Del Martin and Phyllis Lyon were the first couple to marry; teacher Michael Eaton and banker Sean Higgins were among the first dozen. Two thousand people crowded into the grand ballroom at the Hyatt Regency for a giant wedding reception. "We're right there in the midst of all these same-sex marriages taking place," Brad said. They were hanging around in the waiting room when Brad found himself on camera. Then, they went up and sat with Newsom.

"Did we come on a bad day?" Brad asked the Mayor, taking in

the whirlwind around them. Newsom laughed. Brad and Phillips settled into comfortable leather chairs and told him what he had told the Vallejo Mayor. The nearly $100 million movie would be filmed on location in San Francisco and the North Bay at the exact locations of the *Zodiac* story.

"San Francisco in the 1970s is so much a part of our story, it is important to capture as much as we can of the city," Brad said.

While a shooting schedule is usually about three and a half to four months, Fincher's schedule, if he shot Zodiac, would be much longer because of the logistics involved. There was one thing in their favor. The Mayor was eager to attract more movies to the Bay Area. He dreamed of building up San Francisco as a "Digital Hollywood," a high-speed network enabling digital media companies to flash films to satellite offices and clients worldwide. Film industry spending in the city had sunk from $461 million in 1996 to $138 million in 2002—a deficit just under the $350 million George Lucas was spending constructing a new digital arts center in the Presidio. It was set to open next year. San Francisco once averaged eight studio films a year, but over the last five years not one major motion picture had been shot on location there. The city's television and film industry languished with a loss of over $700 million of indirect spending benefits.

"The Mayor is very open to giving us the incentives we need," Brad said as he and Lou descended the marble steps out onto the Plaza. "He was very, very willing and eager to cooperate, absolutely, any help he could provide as far as the police files or police help would be beneficial. The movie business in Hollywood opens doors. It seems very presumptuous for Hollywood to be coming in and asking for files and reports—it's not our domain. I expected to have a lot more resistance than we've had from the police and city officials." That would come later, when doors started being slammed in their faces. Brad hoped Mayor Newsom would introduce them to former San Francisco Mayor and now US Senator Dianne Feinstein who lived in Presidio Heights where the cabbie was killed. The case had shaken her. Afterward, she got a number of crank calls and letters.

"Mike Medavoy knows her really well," Brad said. "Dianne could be helpful to us."

When they reached the Hall of Justice, Chief Fong was busy

streamlining the top police brass, so they sat down instead with Lt. Nicole Greeley. As acting liaison between the Police Department and filmmakers, the tall, willowy officer gave them the name of the person officially on the cold case, former Homicide Inspector, Kelly Carroll and they arranged a date to see the investigator.

In his office at Phoenix Pictures, Mike Medavoy was listening to Governor Arnold Schwarzenegger comment on the chaotic scene that was San Francisco's City Hall and thinking of his guys in the midst of it all. "San Francisco's actions are directly contrary to state law and present an imminent risk to civil order," Schwarzenegger was saying as he ordered Attorney General Bill Lockyer to prevent the city from granting marriage licenses to same-sex couples. Medavoy knew the new governor well. He had worked with him on *The 6th Day*, at the time Phoenix Pictures' biggest picture and the first which Medavoy had given himself a producer's credit. "I did it for two reasons," he explained, "Arnold asked me to produce the film, thereby sharing the creative risk with him, and I wanted to be more actively involved in this particular film because the subject matter [human cloning] interested me." At home, Jamie paused over his mammoth script, still apprehensive that the brother and sister-in-law weren't going to respond to Brad's entreaties, and listened to the Governor's speech. "Since Mike Medavoy is good friends with Arnold," he said half-seriously, "is there anyway to have him call the couple and say, 'This is the Governor of the State of California. Please talk to these guys.'"

THE NEXT DAY, THURSDAY, February 19, Brad and Lou Phillips returned to Los Angeles. By 10:00 AM, they were entering a third floor office in the Frankovich Building on W. Washington Boulevard. Their mission was to update producer Arnold W. Messer, President and Chief Operating Officer of Phoenix Pictures, on their progress. Ten years earlier, after two decades in the industry, Messer and Medavoy had launched Phoenix Pictures together. Messer, a Nebraska native, graduate of Harvard Law School, and former Senior Counsel of Columbia Pictures Television, was lean, silver-haired, and well-dressed.

"Our Washington trip is set for Monday to go up with Panzarella," Brad told him, "and David and Jamie and myself to see Cheney."

Brad left the office to discover that the sister-in-law had called during the meeting and he had missed her. His heart skipped a beat. He wondered if he had lost his chance. But, his worry was all for nothing. When he called her back, she seemed pretty positive about the interview. Afterward, he ran over their brief conversation with Jamie, trying not to read things into it, but underscoring the meeting's importance. "She asked me if we were going to use real names," he said. "I told her, 'Yes.' That kind of hit her a little hard. She said, 'You have no idea the number of people who have called us and ended up on our doorstep.' 'I can only imagine,' I told her. I might hear from her again today. Keep your fingers crossed." Brad called her again, but got the machine and left a recorded message. While he could see no reason why she wouldn't call back, he considered all the dire possibilities. Finally, he consoled himself that she had been reluctantly leaning toward meeting with them in their last conversation though she was understandably hesitant.

That afternoon, Brad realized he had a problem. "The schedules," he sighed, tossing them back onto his desk, "are really getting difficult—with David, Jamie, and myself." Fincher's motion control shoot for :30 and :15 television commercials for HP Technologies was to begin the same day as their scheduled flight to visit Cheney. Fincher made a good living without making movies. Brad called Cheney, who didn't really travel, and asked the former civil engineer if he could come to them instead.

"The only problem I have with traveling," he said, "is that it's a small seat."

"Don, we'll fly you first class the whole way," Brad promised. "We'll put you up in a suite in a hotel in Beverly Hills."

There was a pause, then Cheney said, "Well, that doesn't sound so bad."

Now that Cheney had agreed to come to Los Angeles, Brad called to update Sandy Panzarella who replied, "Did you tell Don that he's going to have to use all his miles?"

At least, the meeting with Cheney and Panzarella was set in concrete—if nothing else happened. "The King of Worriers" was putting in overtime.

By Friday, February 27, Brad, Jamie, and Fincher were prepared to meet with them to authenticate their statements. Brad and Jamie could see why Fincher had placed this meeting at the top of his list. With such a wildly dramatic case—unbreakable ciphers, taunting letters to the police, a hooded costume, science fiction-like weapons such as an electronic gunsight (which Fincher doubted and Brad did not), and a brilliant, physically strong madman, there was always the temptation to embellish a case that had entered into myth. Their two-day conference was to begin at Phoenix Pictures at 10:30 AM, but Cheney, whom they had put up at the St. Regis, wanted to delay the meeting until afternoon.

"Sandy and Don are going to get here by 1:00 PM," Brad told Jamie. "While we're waiting for Cheney, we can speak with Fincher alone. He's bound to be in a good mood. He's thrilled that we've got the meeting."

Sandy Panzarella arrived on the dot and Cheney walked in ten minutes later. The two friends had not seen each other since they resided with Leigh Allen's brother back in their college days. Both looked healthy and vigorous, but Cheney didn't recognize Sandy.

Sandy stood up and said, "Hey, Don," and extended his hand.

Cheney took his hand, shook it, then said, "Who am I talking to?"

Panzarella did a double-take.

"It's Sandy!" he said.

Cheney looked at him.

"You've changed a hell of a lot more than I have," he said.

Fincher smiled. "For the first time since they were interviewed by the police in the 1970s," he said, "we have put Don Cheney and Sandy Panzarella in a room together to ask them to tell us every detail of their story."

"It was New Year's Day 1969," Cheney began, "when I had this conversation with Leigh and I never saw him again after that. The first thing we talked about was the watch his mother had given him for his 35th birthday [December 18, 1968, two days before the kids were killed out on Lake Herman Road]. It was in the box with the card and he asked me what I thought of it. He had the attitude that maybe his mother had stiffed him and given him a cheap watch, but the watch was a Zodiac watch—very expensive for the time, $110, and made for skin divers like Leigh. He had wanted this watch for over a year. Cheney remembered the first time Leigh had mentioned the watch. They had been in his basement home and Leigh had been leafing through the December 1967 *Playboy* which had a striking orange, green, and purple psychedelic cover. On Page 65 of the Gala Christmas issue, Leigh saw that the bottom third of that page had been given over to a black and white ad for the Zodiac Sea Wolf, the "world's most popular skin diver's watch." As its symbol, the Zodiac watch had a striking crossed-circle logo.

Zodiac might have been born at that moment.

Cheney then recounted his August 26, 1967, conversation with Leigh Allen. That day they had been hunting and Leigh had been complaining about his flat feet. When they returned to his room, they discussed hunting, "The Most Dangerous Game," and the feasibility of attaching a penlight to a gun barrel to hunt people through the woods at night. "He had just been fired from Valley Springs," Cheney recalled, "and it looked like he wasn't going to teach anymore. I was concerned about what he was going to do and I tried to kind of pep him up and talk to him about career choices." Leigh was reading the August issue of *Amazing Stories*. Jack Vance's "The Man from Zodiac," was featured on the cover. The story was about a man who offers his services as the field representative of Zodiac Control. Zodiac will maintain order and fight enemies of those who sign a contract with Zodiac. In one of Zodiac's letters to the *Chronicle* he had written he was about to lose control.

"Well, you've been fired from this job," Cheney ventured, "and you've been knocking around for a couple of months." On March 10, 1967, he had been fired from Valley Springs for touching girls inappropriately. "What're you going to do?"

"I'm going to do contracts," Leigh had replied immediately, claiming a local crime boss wanted him to provide a demonstration before he hired him as a hitman.

"Leigh wanted to be Mike Hammer," Cheney told Brad, Jamie, and Fincher. He started talking about how he was going to be a professional criminal. He said he would give himself an identity and write letters to the editor and he'd have a name and it would be Zodiac. I told him I thought he could have a better name than that. He wasn't having any of that. 'That's the name I want and that the name I'm going to use,' he said, and then talked about setting up a random killing site."

Cheney was used to Leigh's joking and, at first, passed his boast off as another of his jests. Sometimes he cloaked his ideas in the guise of writing a novel. "Leigh liked toying with people and laughing at them,"

Cheney continued. "He then asked me how to disguise his handwriting and told me how he would wear makeup to change his appearance if he killed people. He again mentioned how much fun it would be hunting people and how he would send letters to the police to confuse them. They would be taunting letters. He liked that. He intentionally misspelled words to be funny.

"He told me that he would attach a flashlight to a gun for sighting in the dark. That same day, he used that phrase about 'picking the little kiddies off as they come bouncing off the bus.' He was into a rant into his feelings about the establishment about the school system so that was part of blowing off steam. I said to Leigh, 'You really better think about this stuff before you commit yourself to do anything and he said, 'It's too late for that.'"

Leigh took Cheney to an IHOP mere yards away on the next block where he wanted to show him this attractive waitress who worked at the pancake house. "What do you think of her," he asked. "I'm interested in her." She was Darlene Ferrin. They got in Leigh's car. "We went back around to Lake Herman Road," Cheney said. "We stopped there and Leigh lingered there to look at the place. And he described what he would like to do. As we sat at that spot he kept slipping from future tense to past tense, I began to think this was already history. I cautioned Leigh not to think like that. It was going to get him in trouble. He said it was already too late."

Brad and Jamie made notes on each of his statements. Most were in the published book and in police reports that George Bawart had compiled when it looked like they were about to arrest Allen. Brad patted his binder. Safely inside was a copy of Bawart's report with which he could authenticate the dates. Cheney tended to jump around in his speech, one day to the other, as if it was happening on the same day. Nothing new, yet Fincher was satisfied. He was looking for something more than a rerun of known facts. He found his answers in Cheney's eyes and in his body language and in the cadence of his speech. Cheney floated a number of unusual theories. One was that the Betty Lou Jensen murder on Lake Herman Road was a warning from Zodiac to his next victim, Darlene Ferrin. "Darlene said she knew Betty Lou," Cheney suggested. "She told her friend Bobbi Ramos, 'I knew those kids who were killed out on Lake Herman Road. I knew the girl.'

The fact that they look so much alike there is a good possibility it was a demonstration. 'This girl looks like you—here you go,' Zodiac might have thought."

Before the meeting, all three filmmakers had been a little iffy on Cheney. He seemed too perfect, Jamie thought, and decided to reference this in his script: "So let me get this straight. He unveils his entire evil master plan on New Year's Day?" For an hour, Fincher, Brad, and Jamie sat across from Cheney, listened to him, looked him in the eye, and decided, "This is not a guy who is trying to dine out on the story. He really believes this is the guy and this is what happened to him, though over the years all the events may have been cobbled into happening on the same day."

"Cheney's a very credible guy," Brad agreed. "He really is trying to tell the truth about this." Panzarella as always was forthright and backed Cheney up. There was one last question. "When did Cheney come to believe that what Allen had told him was the truth?"

"It was in late 1969," Cheney answered. "I had relocated to Pomona. A composite drawing in profile caused me to connect Zodiac to his former friend, Leigh Allen. Three or four months after I began working at the Fluor Company, an engineering and chemical company in Southern California, I was having breakfast in the new Task Force Center when my brother-in-law pointed out a wanted composite in a newspaper."

"That looks like your buddy, Leigh," he said.

"I took the paper, studied the profile drawing, and agreed it was of Leigh Allen except for the hair and absence of glasses."

Fincher thought it odd that Cheney had apparently had known nothing of Zodiac's murder spree back in the Bay Area. Eventually, he had put the facts together, and reported his suspicions to Lieutenant Bud Savage of the Concord PD, but nothing came of it. On January 10, 1970, still concerned, Cheney contacted Lieutenant Slade of Pomona PD about Leigh Allen with the same result.

"That Cheney did that in January 1970," Jamie said, "falls perfectly in line with the explosion of Zodiac panic and automatically makes Cheney more credible."

Fincher consulted the time line. After Fluor had finished a huge contract, they had major layoffs which included Cheney. For about a year he worked at a big paper mill in Laverne a few miles up from his house and continued to sit on his suspicions. On July 15, 1971, Cheney spoke with Panzarella who contacted the Manhattan Beach PD who took down Cheney's statement and relayed it to Toschi and Armstrong at SFPD.

As everyone chatted and sipped their coffee, Fincher casually leafed through a copy of Armstrong's impeccable handwritten notes of his last meeting with Cheney. On July 23, 1971, he confirmed Cheney's reliability with Panzarella. On August 5, he called Cheney. Twenty-one days later, he flew down and saw him in person at Manhattan Beach. Cheney had been back in the Bay Area for several months when Armstrong interviewed him on September 8, 1972. They met in the lobby of the Bechtel Corporation at 50 Beal Street in San Francisco where Cheney repeated his suspicions about Leigh Allen. On October 4, Toschi left Armstrong a typed message:

"Cheney is leaving for Minnesota next Wednesday and will be there for the next two years."

Fincher closed the binder and rubbed his eyes. He still could not account for the lapse of time between Cheney seeing the composite and acting on his suspicions. "The one thing he seems particularly squirrelly on," he said after some thought, "is the date of his conversation with Leigh Allen in relation to the date he became curious about coming forward to Pomona PD. Cheney originally said that the conversation was eleven months and twenty days before the first killing. It's not till late '71 or '72, which is, of course, after a lot of this information has been printed. It's certainly not feasible that Cheney is unaware of Zodiac's activities in Northern California and unaware of the 'shooting little kids as they come off the bus' remark which was widely publicized. So he comes to Pomona police nearly a year after the real shit storm of Zodiac, which is really the school bus stuff, to say, 'I know who this guy is because I had this conversation with him.' Granted, there's three months in there that we're foggy on because Pomona police blew him off."

"When Brad and I came out of the first day's meeting with Cheney and Panzarella," Jamie added, "Fincher turns and says to me, 'I believe him.'" Such a statement from such an analytical mind as Fincher's carried tremendous weight. Their trips to the Bay Area had borne fruit, as evidenced by the files and reports from various sources that Brad had collected in his three-ring binder.

Yet, in an earlier recorded interview, Cheney had been positive of the dates. "It was on November 16, 1970," he said, "while I was at Fluor and a few months after seeing the composite drawing, that I saw Zodiac's threat in the *Los Angeles Times* about shooting out the tires on a school bus and read Zodiac's unique 'kiddies' quote for the first time." He said this was a phrase Allen had said to him when he came down to Cal Poly in his Austin Healy to see his brother and Panzarella. "Until then," Cheney added, "I had forgotten the crucial details of my conversations with him, that he was going to call himself Zodiac. Leigh had been fired from his teaching job and said he was so angry he wanted to 'kill the little kiddies as they came bouncing off the bus.' It was too specific a remark to be chance. That stuck with me all my life. And that's the phrase that was later used by the Zodiac killer."

Like a bloodhound, Fincher still needed to track down any documentation to verify Cheney's memories. He had to find that now-yellowed square of newsprint that recalled to Don Cheney's mind Allen's remarks about shooting "the kiddies as they came bouncing out of the school bus." With it came the date of a long ago moment, of words spoken in a dismal basement by a dismal man. To verify Cheney's statements further, Brad needed to track down the profile drawing of Zodiac without glasses that he claimed to have seen. A police composite drawn in profile alone is unusual. Expert composite artists such as Jeannie Boylan, and Tom Macris of San Jose PD, rarely draw profiles. With a profile the difficulty of centering a full face does not exist. This suggested a nonprofessional artist may have drawn the unidentified composite. Further, Cheney recalled the drawing was in pencil, not conte crayon, a compressed powdered graphite stick which easily converts to line art that reproduces well. There were seven known Zodiac composite. First was police artist Robert Mackenzie's three Identikit sketches of a man observed by a trio of college women at Lake Berryessa on September 27, 1969, the day of the stabbings. Because of marked differences between the three Berryessa portraits, one, the "official" composite drawing, was released over three days later to various newspapers *outside* Napa. The second Berryessa composite was never circulated. The third was published locally on October 1. The

SFPD's wanted poster showed not one, but two drawings of Zodiac.

Of these five, none were in profile. On February 23, 1971, *Denver Post* staff artist Joe Barros circulated a sixth and seventh Zodiac composite with glasses and without glasses. "While looking at the description drawing done by the San Francisco police artist," Barros said, "I became sure the look of the guy can't be right. I made this sketch from their composite, only changing the features to lifelike detail." The UPI wire service transmitted Barros' composites to most metropolitan and smaller circulation papers in Southern California. None were in profile.

There was an eighth possibility which was unknown to Toschi and Armstrong because of the lack of cooperation between jurisdictions. Vallejo PD Sergeant John Lynch had ordered a composite of a menacing man in a suit who hung out at Darlene Ferrin's painting party shortly before her murder at Blue Rock Springs. Darlene's sister, Linda, had described "a middle-aged man named 'Lee,' heavyset with a very round face and a peculiar stare, a cold stare." Lynch had insisted his artist work with Linda and draw a composite of the man in profile. When this new composite was done, Lynch produced a *ninth* Zodiac composite from his binder and compared them. Except for the chin the two were identical. "Surviving Blue Rock Springs victim Mike Mageau only saw the subject's face from the profile, side view, and did not recall seeing a front view, Lynch said. "There was nothing unusual about his face, other than it appeared to be large, but Mike Mageau said he could possibly recognize the man responsible if he had a profile view." It now made sense why Lynch had insisted on a profile composite to compare with Mageau's composite. Vallejo Officer Steve Baldino had also agreed the profile was "probably the same individual" who had frequented Terry's Restaurant where Darlene last worked and where he followed her to continue his harassment of her.

Like a bloodhound, Fincher still needed to track down any documentation to verify Cheney's memories. He had to find that now-yellowed square of newsprint that recalled to Don Cheney's mind Allen's remarks about shooting "the kiddies as they came bouncing out of the school bus." With it came the date of a long ago moment, of words spoken in a dismal basement by a dismal man.

Brad could not get the two Zodiac profile composites out of his mind. How had those two drawings gotten into a Southern California newspaper for Cheney to see? He was surfing websites one day when he spied a picture of SFPD Inspector Jim Deasy taken by Gary Fong on May 3, 1981. Brad looked closely. There was a wanted poster on Deasy's desk. He enlarged the photo, but it was still not clear. He enlarged it again and once more until he was able to see that the poster was a *profile* composite of Zodiac. Brad called Cheney for verification.

"I'd be happy to see if I recognize this as being the right one," Cheney said. Brad hung up to await his reply once he received the composite by overnight mail. If he had found the missing Zodiac composite it would prove Cheney was telling the truth and entice Fincher to continue his private investigation and they their verification of the facts in the mystery. Brad waited to hear back. Just after 3:00 PM, his phone rang. It was Cheney.

"Thanks for getting back to me," Brad said.

Cheney got right to the point. "The composite in the photo enlargement you sent," he said, "was *not* the one I saw."

"It would have been easy for Cheney to say it was the one," Brad recalled, "but again he had been truthful."

Vallejo Detective Bawart had also believed Cheney when he underwent three lie detector tests in Washington State to validate his remarks. On April 9, 1991, examiner R. W. Yunck had conducted the first polygraph test at the General Investigation Section on Martin Way in Olympia. The test came up inconclusive. "That's not uncommon," Bawart had reported. "They ran Cheney again on April 24 inside the Polygraph Unit." He was again advised of his Constitutional Rights which he waived a second time on the same form he had earlier signed. Once more, Yunck administered the test and asked the relevant question:

"Did you hear Lee Allen in late 1967 or early 1968 talk about 'shooting the little darlings as they came bouncing off the bus?'"

"Yes."

On May 2, Yunck administered a *third* test. In Polygraph Report, # PIO-91-0-0254, the expert wrote that, "Based on the physiological responses produced by the subject on three (3) polygraph charts, in the opinion of this examiner, he was not attempting deception when he answered 'yes' to the relevant question." To be certain, examiners

Detective W. D. Tufts and Detective W. S. Warner carefully reviewed the examination and agreed with Yunck's numerical evaluation and conclusion that Cheney was telling the truth.

"Yes, Cheney was telling the truth," Bawart had acknowledged, "but to be one hundred percent certain he was not involved in the thing in any way, we determined that he was out of the area when the killings were going on."

As one policeman remarked at the time, "If Cheney's story is true, then Arthur Leigh Allen *has* to be Zodiac."

On Wednesday, March 3, at 6:30 PM, Brad's assistant, Diego, placed a call to Jamie at his home (Jamie was a bit of homebody). "It has been insane this week," Brad told him excitedly when he got on the phone. "I spoke to the sister-in-law—I left a message yesterday and she called me back today. And she said they were familiarizing themselves with Cheney's assertions which they already knew about." When Cheney stayed with them, he told them what he had told Armstrong. "I think that one of the big reasons why they are doing this is to set the record straight and make sure everything is accurate. She said, 'We will meet with you in San Francisco.'"

Even with the best movies there's always a part where their existence becomes tenuous. Mike Medavoy, Arnie Messer, and Brad had been negotiating with six competing studios, among them Sony, to release and bankroll *Zodiac*. "Arnie Messer's the business side and Mike Medavoy's the creative side," Jamie explained, "and they teamed up to put Phoenix together. They're very old friends." And Brad? "Brad's the responsible one: 'We gotta worry about the page count. We gotta worry about the studio. We gotta worry about the budget.' I tell him, 'That's great, Brad, but I gotta worry about the story.'"

The next day, things became complicated fast. "The way it worked out was this," Brad said, "Phoenix was talking to Sony because they wanted to make the picture at Sony and they were the studio across the street. David Fincher had been meeting with a couple of other people. Phoenix knew about this [Brad and Arnie Messer are in one way the combatants in the negotiations, an impossible situation for the young producer]." Fincher was over at Warner Brothers the day they made the deal with Sony in a meeting with Jeff Robinov, President of Production at Warner Brothers. He was telling him about *Zodiac* and Robinov was really, really excited.

At the same moment, Arnie Messer went across the street and without informing Fincher made a deal with Sony for the movie. "I said to Arnie, 'Arnie you can't do this. David is at Warner Brothers having a meeting with them. We can't make a deal with Sony under those circumstances. We have to wait until he is out and have a conversation with them.'"

"And David, when he heard,—not to put too fine a point on it—" Brad said, "David lost his shit."

"I'm sitting there getting more money for our movie and you guys go and do this," Fincher told him.

"He's my boss," Brad said. "What was I supposed to do?"

"Tackle him!" Fincher said. "Don't let him get across the street to make that deal!"

CHAPTER SIX

FINCHER'S VISION

ON MARCH 4, BRAD received more bad news. "There is a disagreement between Fincher and Sony on what the cost of the movie should be," he explained. "As you know, we went ahead and made a deal for *Zodiac* with Sony and Sony now controls the project. Our home is pretty much at Sony. We have a special relationship, and we've got to try to make it work. Amy Pascal made *Panic Room* with David, so we had every confidence that it would be done at Sony. It might still be done there. Amy's holding on to this thing and doesn't want to let it go. They really want *Zodiac*. What happened was that she arrived at a number that was below what David wanted."

"The movie is greenlit at this price," Amy had told Fincher. "You can put any actor in it you want. We're not going to hold you up in terms of a list of actors."

"It's not acceptable," Fincher had replied. "I need more."

She's at seventy. He's at eighty. She wants less. He wants more.

"The negotiation originally taking place with Sony," Brad elaborated, "was about how much David would get to make the movie, how much the movie would cost. David said he needed eighty-million dollars with certain actors. The price fluctuates with a particular actor. Its one of those bizarre, but common processes in Hollywood where the studio says, 'We'll finance it for this amount of money if you deliver an actor from the pre-approved list.' And of course the list of actors is some ridiculous one—from Tom Cruise, Tom Hanks, Brad Pitt,

Leonardo DiCaprio—to all the stars of the moment, most of whom are not right for the part. If you deliver a budget for that price and one of these actors, then you are greenlit and everybody's pay or play, everybody gets their fee. The rights to the book are bought, Jamie gets his script, we get our fee for producing the film, and David gets his fee for directing the film. But David will resist any outside pressure to go for a star not suited for the part. He wants to make *Zodiac* with Jake Gyllenhaal, not Tom Cruise." Fincher had earlier reached a similar budget impasse on *Fight Club*. "It was about what would get lost with that cut," he told author Sharon Waxman for her *Rebels on the Backlot*. "That five million dollars is not going to come from Eastman Kodak, it's not going to come from Teamsters, it's going to come from visual effects, it's going to come from sets, from costumes, it's going to come right off the screen." Fincher and Amy Pascal also disagreed on the running time. Fincher wanted two hours and forty minutes. Sony wanted a running time of two hours and fifteen minutes.

"Every movie Fincher's done had something that he needed to get to move forward," Jamie explained, "and for every movie that didn't get made was because one of those things didn't happen." He passed on *Catch Me If You Can* to do *Panic Room*. He rejected *Batman Begins* and *8 MM* to direct *Fight Club*. He's walked away from projects such as *The Black Dahlia* which he was going to direct as a five hour, eighty-million dollar miniseries. Studio backing did not agree, so Fincher moved on to *Zodiac*. For the same reason, he walked away from a skateboarding movie about the Venice, California youth subculture of extreme skateboarders. "You know why it fell apart? There was a pier that David needed, one of the set pieces in the film. David said right from the beginning, 'I need this pier. If I can have this pier I'm gonna make the movie. If I can't get this pier, I'm not making the movie.' He felt he needed to either find one that was appropriate or have one built. They couldn't find the kind of pier that he needed and it would have been too expensive to build so he didn't do the movie."

When David's journalist father, "Jack" Fincher, died in April, he left behind the eighth draft of a wonderful script—*Mank*, a biopic of screenwriter Herman Mankiewicz. *Mank* had a similar, unyielding Fincher "must have"—the movie had to be shot in black and white as befitting the late 1930s, early 1940s period. Fincher vowed it would be made—without compromise, without surrender, and in black and white. Fincher, a rare mix of fine and commercial artist, was hard for Hollywood to figure. Somehow, he had managed to combine the fine and the profane. He simultaneously has control of his art, creating on his own terms, and is paid for it—"Enterprise in the service of Art."

"He will never compromise his vision," Brad said, "even if it means walking away. It wasn't like the goal posts changed at the end, that first he needed three things, then a fourth thing, and then a fifth. It was the same with *Zodiac*. He had told the studio what he had to have. So the negotiations are just sitting there. Amy Pascal won't go up and David won't come down." It was going to take eighty-million dollars to make the movie Fincher's way. Brad knew there were other studios. Paramount and Warner Brothers in particular would give Fincher what he needs. Brad believed that Amy needed to make the movie on David's terms or release the project and let *Zodiac* go elsewhere. He remained assured the movie would be made with or without Fincher. Still, he had confidence it would remain on David's desk.

"In my heart of hearts I hope so. Fincher is such a perfect guy for *Zodiac*," he said. "The other day Mike Medavoy was speaking to Sherry Lansing [Sherry runs Paramount] and she was asking Mike what was happening with *Zodiac*. Paramount wants very much to do it." Besides Sony, Phoenix had been negotiating with six competing companies, among them Paramount, to release and bankroll *Zodiac*.

"Mike has worked with her and I was developing something with her," Brad said. "I had our Morgan Freeman movie, *Resurrecting the Champ*, that Rod Lurie was going to direct. It's not going to happen there. It's going to happen somewhere else. It's tricky developing stuff with studios cause you never know who you're dealing with." When Phoenix first had the Freeman movie it was before Donald DeLine replaced John Goldwyn who was there under Sherry Lansing.

"Sherry and Donald really love *Zodiac* very much," Brad said, "so what I think will probably happen is that it will move from Sony over to Paramount and Paramount and Warners may become partners."

Brad and Jamie's search for the facts in the Zodiac case continued. Brad called Vallejo Police Sergeant Don DiStefino, who had taken over the Zodiac case from George Bawart, to arrange for them to see the Zodiac files.

"You can come up to Vallejo," he said, "and see pretty much of everything we still have—Darlene Ferrin's clothes . . . the blouse and patterned slacks."

"Honestly, I can't believe it," Brad said joyfully. He was surprised that DiStefino didn't think Zodiac was Leigh Allen. "Really?" Brad asked, "Why?" But the sergeant didn't really have a good answer. In San Francisco constant work was taking a toll on Toschi who had been virtually president of North Star Security since his boss's sudden illness.

"Apparently, I've picked up some bronchitis in my chest," he said. "I was working security at the Temple until about 1:00 PM, then I was feeling a little weak, a little strange, and coughing a lot. I got the shakes, so I went to the doctor. He said the bronchitis was taking over my body and gave me an antibiotic shot. I went to bed for about an hour, slept, and when I awoke my hands were freezing and my bride got a little concerned about me. But I'm a little bit better and I'll go back to work Monday." Allegedly, a staffer who had quit to form his own company had been luring away their clients. But this was only rumor. No matter the cause, they had lost forty-eight clients so far. In spite of his fever, Toschi had been trying to run damage control and it was dragging him under.

Friday, Brad had a conference call with the lawyers who've been going through the *Zodiac* material. "When you make a movie based on actual events where some of the people are still alive," Brad explained, "you want to do all of your homework and see where you're legally liable. First, anybody can sue anybody for any reason. The meeting with the lawyers concerned more threat assessment if we were sued on certain things where we would be possibly in trouble." At the top of that list remained the prime suspect's brother and sister-in-law.

"Brad's talking to them has reassured them," Jamie said. "They are not asking for any money. The most amazing thing is that Brad got through to them at all."

Brad opened his files. The glow of the computer screen lit his face. Police reports from August 4, August 7, and August 9, 1971, filled the screen. As he read them, he reassured himself that if they failed to secure a sit-down with the couple, Fincher would at least have Inspector Bill Armstrong's interviews with the suspect's friends and relatives. He knew that they would not be enough for Fincher, who was looking for more of an emotional response, the director's final arbiter of truth. Unsettling quotes floated before Brad's eyes—"Allen is a sick man mentally," "hates his mother, threatened to kill her," "hates women," "woman says threatened by Allen, very afraid of Leigh," "some language in the Zodiac letters is consistent with Allen, also misspellings," "friends have complained of Allen molesting their children," "threatened to hurt or kill a woman and her new baby, but said in a joking manner," "Takes money from his mother for psychological help, but does not use it for medical help." "Psychiatrist asked if Leigh was capable of killing. He said, 'YES,'" "Said that the police had spoken to him feeling he might be a Zodiac suspect . . . thought it was funny," and says, "I have never hurt anyone in my life."

These statements danced before Brad's eyes all day. More sleepless nights followed. Finally, on Monday, March 8, Brad tried to run his luck up by securing an interview with Bryan Hartnell, the surviving Lake Berryessa stabbing victim who had demonstrated great heroism. In a letter to Hartnell he laid out the idea of *Zodiac* as a newspaper film and ultimate statement about the case. Time passed. He didn't have much hope Bryan would answer his letter. Yet, Fincher would not shoot *Zodiac* without speaking to Hartnell.

Time crawled. March 11, 12, 13, 14 came and went and still no answer. The pressure was killing. Brad felt boxed in. By March 15, Brad was still in the midst of ticklish, "even brutal," negotiations for the financing of *Zodiac*. Jamie could only hint at the bloody conflict behind closed doors. "I can't say too much," he said. "Look, we've been talking to them for a while. And we've been busy trying to make David's deal right now. David Fincher is so perfect for *Zodiac* and he really wants to do it." They expected an answer this week. Until then, they had to keep a lid on negotiations. Dana Harris of *Daily Variety* and columnist Mike Fleming learned something was in the wind and called Phoenix. Brad asked them to hold off. He knew what happened when revelations, accurate and inaccurate were released to the public. They were still interviewing witnesses who might shy away if they got the wrong idea what the film was about. There was another reason.

"The announcement on this movie hasn't been made yet because the deal hasn't been closed yet," Jamie added. "Right now I just don't know where we'll wind up." Fincher was the crisis of the hour, the day, the minute. Those minutes had begun to mount up.

"They're trying to make David's deal right now," Brad said. "Let's hope everything goes well. We'll know soon. Hopefully, it will be done this week."

On Wednesday, March 24, Brad discussed the situation with Jamie as they tooled along Hollywood Boulevard. "We are in the midst right now of negotiations which might or might not place the movie at one of three studios," he said over the noise of traffic. "It could still be Sony. It could be Warner Brothers. It could be Paramount or it could be a combination of any of those three."

"Co-financing the film where, for instance, Warner Brothers would take domestic, and Paramount would take foreign," Jamie said, "or vice versa. Something like that. They would all be great and we have great relationships with all of them."

"These things always get really ugly before they get pretty again," Brad said. "Fincher from his days at MTV knows exactly what he needs to make a movie. Hopefully, we'll get him and give him what he needs. It is the last hurdle. Once this is done we'll have a production commitment on the movie. Maybe it will be settled by next week."

Wishful thinking—it was not settled next week, so Fincher took a three month holding deal on a project called *The Curious Case of Benjamin Button* which Paramount was considering doing. Scott Fitzgerald's *Benjamin Button*, was a property that had been off and on for over ten years with different studios (Rastar, Imagine), different directors (Spike Jonze, Gary Ross) and different writers (Jim Taylor, Robin Swicord, Charlie Kaufman, and Eric Roth). The four and a half page short story, only the second thing Fitzgerald ever sold, wasn't original with him. He had appropriated the idea from William Butler's *Journal* wherein a man at age fifty begins aging backward. Complications ensue when he falls in love with a woman of thirty. Brad thought the fable probably attracted Fincher because of its high tech digital effects. In his hands, the material could be riveting and the visuals startling.

"You're going to spend one hundred and twenty-five million on *Benjamin Button*," Mike Medavoy told Lansing. "What are you thinking? If I were going to spend one hundred and twenty-five million or more to make a movie would I choose a story based on a F. Scott Fitzgerald novella about a guy who ages backwards?"

Yet, in the hands of Fincher who knew what miracles might be wrought? Medavoy had pulled off miracles himself. He had been one of the few who believed that Thomas Harris's spine-tingling novel, *The Silence of the Lambs*, could be made into a general-audience movie. Astutely, he had perceived *Silence* (a film reminiscent of the real-life Zodiac) as "a daring suspense thriller," with "moments of true tenderness." His intuition paid off. The film grossed more than $100 million in the United States, and won all five major Oscars in 1992.

Negotiations on *Zodiac* slowed to a crawl, then lay there like a beached whale. Brad's optimism now held a hollow ring. On March 31, Arnie Messer and Brad sat down with Josh Donen, a former executive at Universal Studios and lead producer for *Fight Club*. He had been the one who brought Chuck Palahniuk's (pronounced Pall-uh-nik) novel to Fincher's attention. "He's got a great client list, Brad said. "He's Sam Raimi's agent and David Fincher's agent." They were going to get a piece of paper with Fincher that formalized their understanding together. "This is all working toward getting the movie done. There's no question in my mind that David wants to do this movie."

You couldn't prove it by Jamie. He hadn't seen Fincher for a month and a half. "Things were going sideways by this time," he said. "Basically, I was doing the script for free. I made a handshake agreement with Phoenix and they got the rights and then I wrote the script." Jamie had had unfortunate past experiences with the endings of his scripts being changed. For that reason he agreed to write *Zodiac* on spec in exchange for more creative control. But because Jamie belonged to the Writer's Guild, Phoenix had to pay him a minimum to write the original screenplay for *Zodiac*. The Writer's Guild is the strongest of the creative guilds in Hollywood, a member pays a half-percent of his earnings and annual dues of a couple thousand. To join is a "Catch 22" situation. You have to sell something to a Writer's Guild signatory who is barred from buying anything from a non-Guild signatory writer.

Paid or not, Jamie kept to his routine, a regimen that has to have contributed to his great success. He rises at 9:00-9:30 AM, grabs a cup of Folgers Breakfast Blend Coffee, and after brushing with Colgate and shampooing with Herbal Essence ("Cause I'm a girl," he says) he goes right to work. His second floor office contains his Hitachi computer and an entire file cabinet filled with Zodiac documents. Jamie, who likes to write long, then bring the words down, writes from 10:30 AM, to around 3:00 PM, when he realizes he has no more blood sugar left and his stomach begins to complain. Then, he drags himself downstairs to cook something egg-based. The long, long kitchen had been remodeled and rebuilt as an addition when Jamie's fiancée, Amber, moved in last summer. It includes an all-wood breakfast nook, natural wood floors polished with polyurethane, a silver subzero refrigerator, a granite countertop, and a round table where Jamie and Brad go over the growing script at night until they can no longer stay awake. The house has French doors in every room on the ground floor. The kitchen is no different. Through them Jamie and Amber gaze out onto the backyard at a blue pool and spa.

Amber, lovely, blond, bright and supportive, is the daughter of Gunilla McDonough, nee Hutton, and Allan Freeman, a builder and real estate contractor who has constructed houses, condos, and apartment houses in LA for forty years. Whenever Amber and Jamie drive down the street, Amber can say, "My dad built that place . . . my dad built that place . . . my dad—" Amber's mom was a television actress on *Hee-Haw* and one of the three daughters on the first season of *Petticoat Junction*. When she left the show, Meredith MacRae replaced her. Amber's maternal grandfather is William E. Hutton of the Hutton stockbroker family.

"Oh, gosh, yeah," Jamie said as he banged about the kitchen like a bull, "I'm a terrible cook so if I'm cooking for myself, it's usually eggs, scrambled or 'omeletted' in a Teflon frying pan with a little Pam. It's lucky that Teflon was invented and that Amber bought nice pans otherwise I'd still be using the same crappy pan I got in college." After his eggs on very good days, he climbs the stairs and takes a second run at writing from 3:30 until 6:00 PM. On Saturday, April 3, Jamie broke his routine. He was out of the house long before three o'clock and headed for a more substantial lunch than eggs. By 2:45 PM, he was behind the wheel of the '99 Mustang convertible he had bought after he sold his first script, a comedy called *Independence, Mississippi*, two days after graduating from USC's Film Writing Program. "Before that I was driving a 1984 hand-me-down station wagon with the fake wood paneling," Jamie said. Though the script was never filmed, it still counted. "Hey, I've got the Mustang to prove it!"

By 3:30 PM, he was sitting outside the Chateau Marmont Restaurant in West Hollywood having a late lunch with a man he considers "a very good thriller director," Gary Fleder of *Kiss the Girls* and *Runaway Jury*. With all the lunches he's forced to endure during meetings, Jamie eats Cobb salads to manage his weight. "It's not really a salad," he said. "It's got lots of meat, bacon, chicken, egg, and cheese in it. I do the low carb thing, stay away from bread, pasta and rice." He is also trying to stop smoking. So is Amber. As traffic dragged by on Sunset Boulevard, Fleder and Jamie discussed a rewrite on a project at New Line called *Solace*." I wasn't working on it yet," Jamie said. "Eventually it got made by another director. At some point they actually thought about making *Solace* into a sequel to *Se7en*. All of these other thriller directors aspire to be David Fincher." Jamie looked up from his meat and egg salad to spot the man himself coming in to have his own late lunch. Fincher saw them, walked over, patted Jamie on the shoulder, smiled, and said, "I hope it works out," then walked inside without another word.

"Who's that?" Fleder asked.

"That's just Fincher," Jamie sighed. He was no longer hungry.

On Sunday, Brad read over the screenplay for *The Curious Case of Benjamin Button*. "We are probably going to make a deal with David Fincher where we will wait for his holding deal on *Benjamin Button* to be over sometime in mid-to-late summer. When that holding deal is over, if they haven't committed to making that film, which I think is unlikely at this time, then David will agree to do *Zodiac*, commit to *Zodiac*, and make *Zodiac* his next movie."

If that were to occur they could shoot *Zodiac* as early as late fall. While Fincher wanted to have the equivalent of summer and fall in San Francisco he could do winter and spring instead. "But if David decides to make *Benjamin Button*," Brad concluded, "we will probably move on to another director. As it stands now, I feel pretty good about *Zodiac*."

Brad knew that if the squabble with Sony could not be resolved, then Fincher would go to Paramount to do *Benjamin Button* and it would be a year and a half before he could devote his full time to *Zodiac*. By then it would be too late. They would have either gotten another director or the movie wouldn't be made at all.

On Monday, April 5, Brad attended an important meeting with

Medavoy, Messer, Richard Lovett, and Rick Nacita. Fincher's holding deal with Paramount on the f/x heavy *Benjamin Button* was to start shortly. Under this accord he was to get *Button* ready, prepare a budget, and conduct camera and special effects tests. "It's for three months— April, May, June to July," Brad said. "We would have to wait until mid-July or after. We're stuck in a holding pattern until we know if David hits his number on *Button* or we can move on to another director which I don't want to do." Tenaciously, he and Jamie clung to the roller coaster that was David Fincher.

"All those stories of David doing seventy-eight takes on one scene in *Panic Room*," Jamie said, "all that money adds up. He's not known for cost-cutting efficiency, but he gets incredible quality out of stuff he does that way. Fincher is much better at adding money than taking it away."

"He not only has to deliver a budget of $125 million [for *Button*]," Brad added, "but has to deliver an actor from an approved list. And I'm sure he can deliver the actor, but getting the budget down that much . . . It's so expensive because of the technology involved. Mike Medavoy spoke to David today. We told him we'll wait for him. We're not going to move on to another director. But we're not going to wait for him if he does *Benjamin Button*. If he does that we're going to go to someone else." Brad perked up at the next report. Now, Amy Pascal had lifted the restrictions on the turnaround so *Zodiac* would be free of Sony by June and Phoenix could make a deal with another studio. There was still a discussion of Sony splitting the movie. Brad suspected that Amy Pascal wanted to distance herself from the project. "I think she wants to wash her hands of it. We're not out any money. Sony's on the hook for the whole thing—for the *Zodiac* book, for Jamie's screenplay, and for our producing fee. It's in Sony's interest to have this film get done. We're going to get this done. There's no doubt in my mind."

In the late afternoon, Brad and Jamie gathered their energy for another long evening of screenings. Brad slumped in his chair in his new office on the third floor of the Frankovich Building. The loft-like, rectangular-shaped room was split by a wall jutting out from the long side of the room which still smelled of fresh paint. His desk faces an exposed brick wall, a coffee table scattered with magazines, a few thirties Big Little Books (was that *Alley Oop*? Was that *Orphan Annie and the*

Mysterious Shoemaker? Was that *Brick Bradford*?), and a little conference area. Jamie reclined on a comfortable couch as if dead, hands laced across his chest. To Brad's left was another coffee table and a second, less comfortable couch. The small office was a movie lover's room, a shrine to film and its infinite possibilities as art. Two movie posters filled one wall. "I am a huge, huge Stanley Kubrick fan," he said, "and *Full Metal Jacket* is one of his most brilliant films." The other poster was of *The Thin Red Line*, a film Medavoy had been intimately involved with and viewed with justifiable pride. In January 1995, he had just left TriStar and not yet capitalized Phoenix Pictures. Once Phoenix was formed, he rolled *The Thin Red Line* into their development inventory. Ultimately, it was nominated for seven Academy Awards, including Best Picture. "I was Mike's assistant when we were shooting *Thin Red Line*," Brad recalled. "I started in '98 when it was coming out of production and going into post." Terrence Malick, who had adapted the novel by James Jones and worked on several drafts of *Dirty Harry*, was the director.

"It gave Brad a chance to perfect his Terrence Malick impression," Jamie said laconically. He opened one eye as he lay on the couch, his long legs stretched out. Jamie had been the butt of several crank Malick impersonation calls from Brad. "No matter how high I did his voice," Brad said, "I could never get it as high as Terry actually speaks."

Brad and Jamie had one poster in common on their respective office walls—*Basic*, a film they had produced with Medavoy and Messer and which Jamie had scripted (it had been greenlit solely off his outline). Last year, three of Jamie's screenplays, *Darkness Falls* (his first produced screenplay), *The Rundown*, and *Basic* had been in theaters. "My producing credit on *Basic* is a bit of a tricky credit," he said. "I was not really a true producer in the sense that Brad was. Brad was co-executive producer, but deserved a full producer credit. He was with *Basic* from beginning to end. The set of *Basic* on the Cecil Air Force Base while they were shooting the bunker stuff—machine guns chattering, rain machines pouring, propellors spinning, and actors to talk to, was great, exciting—at first.

"Honestly, though," Jamie said, "after two hours if you have nothing to do, a movie set is the most boring place in the world. We had a director for a year, Lee Tamahori [of the Bond film, *Die Another Day*]. He was very wiry, with a kind of Malcolm McDowell-look." Tamahori held their daily story meetings at 4:00 PM, in a little seaside bar, Chez Jay, which encouraged patrons to toss their peanuts shells on the floor. "Lee, New Zealander that he is, would have a pitcher of beer waiting for us on the table. We'd drink pints of beer, bond, and talk about the script. The scene in *Basic* with the guy being pushed toward the whirling propellor, that's all Lee Tamahori. It ended up in all the previews and TV commercials and kind of made up for all the problems we had later. I thought Tamahori was fun to work with, though we didn't end up shooting the movie with him."

Brad and Jamie went through two directors and a threatened actor's strike on the production before they were done. "We'd get an actor and he would fall out and we'd get another actor," Jamie said. "Three years later, we were shooting—three years from the time I sold the script to when cameras rolled. The movie was in preproduction, then got shut down before it went up again, this time with John McTiernan who had directed *Die Hard*. Brad was on set every day enduring the full wrath of John McTiernan. If there was ever bad news to give to the director, they'd send Brad to deliver it."

"I was right in the eye of the storm," Brad admitted. "When we were working with McTiernan, we would sit there and riff about something that was exciting to us and he would just sit there silently. He'd have his arms crossed, look up, roll his eyes, and sigh. Then he'd just look at us and not say anything. This is a man who is not uncomfortable with long silences."

"At one point he said, 'I'd like to do this,' and threw out an idiotic idea," Jamie recalled. "'That's an interesting idea,' we said, trying to be very politic. 'That's one way to go.' Brad and I talked off and on for about five minutes back and forth and he's completely silent. Then we finished and he stayed completely silent. He stared at us for about a minute and finally said, 'Well, why don't you tell me to go fuck myself.'" During *Basic*, the movie's star, John Travolta, had flown them in his 707 jet. "Travolta flew everywhere," Brad said. "He would fly home, but lived so close we could see him take off, then land in the distance."

One of Jamie's girlfriends had once told him, "You can't write for women." The comment made Jamie angry, but he took it to heart. "And then we broke up," he said. "I cannot tell you how excited I was that Connie Nielsen wanted to play the female part in *Basic*; Helen

Hunt wanted to play the female part. I was sitting back and going, 'Oh, really. I can't write for women, huh. An Oscar winner wants to play the role I wrote.' At the time people thought, 'Wow, *Basic* got done really quickly from writing the script to being released.' I believe *Zodiac* will be quicker. With *Zodiac* it was easier to move faster on it because I had the book," Jamie said. "There's a good amount of dialogue in the book that I can take. *Basic* is something I would never do it the same way again. Because of all the things I learned doing *Basic* I was able to do *Zodiac*. Because of all the things I'm learning on *Zodiac* I'm going to be able to do my next screenplay. Its evolution."

Brad had one more poster in his office, five sheets that took up an entire wall. It was his prize—an original 1933 *The Most Dangerous Game*. This movie about hunting people as game had been Zodiac's inspiration to pursue young couples under the bright moonlight. The two men were thoughtful. The sun was sinking and they still had work to do.

"Remember what David said in San Francisco, Jamie?" Brad said.

Jamie lifted his head from the couch and replied: "Fincher actually put a percentage on the odds that we will make this movie—with him. He was pretty clear that if we couldn't get a meeting with the brother and sister-in-law, I think he said, 'There is a one hundred percent chance that he wouldn't make the movie.' As always, Fincher was up front. At the beginning of discussing *Zodiac* as a movie, he had said, 'The only way I can direct this movie is if we are able to talk to the only two people in the case who've refused to speak about it for thirty years, never given an interview.' It was as if he was saying, 'The only way I can direct this movie is if you shot put to the moon.'"

"If I were him," Brad said, "I would also want to have that conversation and sit down face to face with these people before going ahead because you want to know as many facts as possible. That no one has ever been able to get them to speak is what makes the challenge so great. Background is so important, the challenge itself is self-evident. Without it you can't responsibly move forward. Without being able to sit down with the brother and sister-in-law in the case, who have been silent for so long, there is a big black hole there. For us to do this we have to shine a light on it. As Fincher said, 'We can't posthumously convict a guy and then find out after the fact one of his relatives goes on CNN and produces a plane ticket or hotel receipt that he was in China on July 5, 1969 [the date of one of the Zodiac murders].'"

CHAPTER SEVEN

THE MOUSETRAP

APRIL 7, 2004, WAS a gloomy spring morning, freezing San Francisco cold. A dense fog bank two-and-a-half miles long and a couple of hundred feet high hugged the Baker Beach shoreline. The cliffside stood out like iron plate. The lack of sun was depressing for everyone in the city except Toschi who was too furious to be despondent. The *Chronicle's* front page headlines shouted in his mind like the biggest billboard in the world: "FILES SHUT ON ZODIAC'S DEADLY TRAIL; The SFPD renders 35 year case inactive."

Toschi read on. "Police have deactivated the case of the Zodiac killer," said SFPD Lieutenant John Hennessey, head of the department's homicide unit. "Given the pressure of our existing caseload and the amount of cases that remain open at this time, we need to be most efficient at using our resources. If we believed that there was a significant lead that hadn't been followed, we certainly wouldn't be doing this. The case has taken on cult-like fascination around the world. It is really hard to justify to the families of homicide victims from more recent cases—who you meet with every two months—the expenditures and use of resources for this case." Lieutenant Hennessey said that the Zodiac evidence has been locked away in a battered gray file cabinet kept in a closet across from the department's homicide office. "There are no plans to unlock it," he concluded.

Toschi threw down his morning *Chronicle* with disgust. "I find it unbelievable to read something like this!" he said. "Going all the way back to 1969, I think of all the people who have done so much work on this specific case. I'm upset because of the stupidity of it." Over coffee and lemon meringue pie at the Copper Penny later, he calmed down. "I'm feeling fine now," he said. "I just initially got very annoyed when they did that and whoever made that decision was very foolish." He finished his pie, put down his fork, and pushed his plate forward. He listened to the rumble of traffic on Masonic.

Toschi had another problem, not so much a problem, but a difficult decision. He had to decide whether or not to give permission for the filmmakers to use his real name in the movie. He had remained hesitant all this time about using his name for a very good reason. "My wife is just afraid I won't be treated right," he said. He had been treated badly on the front page of the *Chronicle* in the past. "On the other hand I did enjoy meeting those three fellows." He smiled at the memory. "They were good basic guys, straightforward about what they wanted. And this movie means lots of money for the Bay Area and work for lots of people." Toschi rubbed his forehead, obviously pained at the choice he had to make. "I just don't know," he said. "I just don't know."

In Los Angeles, Jamie read the same story that Toschi had read. "Conspiracy theorist that I am," he said, "I know that Brad went to see the Mayor and the head of the San Francisco Police Department and a month afterward they announce to put the case away and are not working on it anymore. The old journalist credo is 'You should never affect the story that you are reporting.'" Powerful people do not want this movie made. What other reason could there be?

In 2002, *Chronicle* reporters Jaxon Van Derbeken and David Parrish had stirred up a similar hornet's nest with their seven month-long investigation of the SFPD homicide unit. Their review of thousands of police and court records and 100 interviews may have had an impact on today's decision. They found that policies and police procedures within the SFPD had "significantly affected homicide detectives' ability to solve murders. They caught the killer in only half the city's murders, below the average of other big city departments." The *Chronicle* discovered murder cases in which investigators failed to interview key witnesses, neglected to pursue vital leads, and lost critical evidence. "Investigators arrived hours late to a murder scene," the newspaper wrote, "were ill-prepared for court and even went on vacation at critical junctures in an investigation." Even Mayor Newsom had shown up at crime scenes to demand that the department's success rate needed to improve.

Brad was at Phoenix Pictures waiting for the legal opinion on depiction and thinking about Toschi. He understood that the retired inspector wanted confidence that he was going to be presented in a good light. He called Jamie. "Showing Toschi the completed script," Brad said, "that's something we definitely want to do. I hope Dave doesn't think we have anything but the highest respect for him." The *Chronicle* front page of July 18, 1978, had been headlined: "Toschi Cleared by [Chief] Gain. 'He Didn't Write Letter.'" Duffy Jennings and Birney Jarvis's story said: "Inspector David Toschi did not write the Zodiac letter sent to the *Chronicle* earlier this year—but neither did the real Zodiac killer said Police Chief Charles Gain."

"We got to put that headline in the movie!" Brad said, slapping the newspaper down on his desk. If the film showed the charge refuted— and the Chief of Police saying, "We've done all the tests. Toschi did not write that letter," it would drive home his innocence once and for all. "When this movie comes out nobody will ever again think that Dave wrote that letter. But that works only if we use his real name. It's crucial."

On Thursday, April 15, Jamie reported good news. "We're getting there with David Fincher," he said. "It's probably going to be another week or so before things are firmed up. I think it's moving in the right direction."

"We could still stay on track for late fall or get pushed until a little bit later than that," Brad responded. "All of that still needs to play out. It's all going to depend on David." Everyone was on hold. Jamie had gotten other script offers, but needed to keep himself open. Then, he could go into rewriting on *Zodiac*.

"It's never easy, these types of things," Jamie said. "But everything is looking good, and David or no David, I'm very confident this is going to get done. Even if it's not David, it will still be Brad, myself, the script, Mike Medavoy, and everybody else involved."

"It's so hard to think about a second choice because David is so perfect for it," Brad said. "And when people ask why are we holding off on *Zodiac* and not doing it with someone else, that's the answer I give them." Fincher had called a week and a half earlier, but since then gone quiet—all because of *Benjamin Button*. "We're going to get there. There's too much enthusiasm and excitement for the script and this movie. David's agents are calling us every day because he doesn't want to lose this." Brad had personally held off the press announcing the movie even though he'd continued to get calls from *Daily Variety* and *The Hollywood Reporter*. First, he had to be certain everyone was on board. "It's a momentary hiccup because you're dealing with a bunch of different studios, with a very famous director, and a lot of money on the table," Brad said.

By May 5, Brad and Jamie were still waiting for things to shake out. Fincher's holding deal was to end in the summer.

"Things are sort of moving along," they said. Lumbering along was more like it. Medavoy was impatient, but Fincher was worth waiting for. "He's the guy who can do it," Brad said. "For this David needs the full budget. He said five to six months of shooting which is long. Usually it is three months." Fincher wanted *Zodiac* to be a classic, with special cameras and opticals, to make it look unlike any other film in history. To this he was going to use some of the techniques he had developed with film editor Angus Wall on HP commercials.

All over Hollywood everyone was buzzing about the quality of Jamie's script. It was a long script, growing as the fledgling detectives lost themselves further in the investigation and came up with more leads. Their discoveries increased the length of the script. If Fincher had his way the script would get even longer. What would people think then? Would they still love it? As it stood now Mike DeLuca told Jamie his *Zodiac* script was so good he wanted "to crawl inside of it and live there." DeLuca had a pirated copy. So did others. "This screenplay has been in such demand," Brad said, "people have gone to great lengths to try to get a copy of it." He had safeguarded against that. "Every script that we send out is on red paper to make it difficult to photocopy," he said, but admitted it was not foolproof. "You can make a copy. It's still legible, only darker overall. Hollywood scripts are always extremely well protected, especially the James Bond scripts which are printed on a special paper that does not photocopy at all."

As a further safeguard, Phoenix Pictures watermarked each page of *Zodiac* with the initials of the person sent that specific script copy. "If someone made a copy and it got back," Brad said, "we could see exactly who made it." But someone had taken their copy and cut out the initials by slicing a big rectangle into the middle of each page and then writing in what was missing by hand on each page. "Now, there's an illegal copy of the *Zodiac* script floating around on photocopied red paper with cutouts," Brad lamented. From now on, he decided to splash the recipient's whole name across the page. That should fix them. By May 18, he was exasperated and extremely tired. He still wasn't sleeping.

"We're still just waiting," he said wearily. "We've gone kind of back and forth and right now David's gone off to look at a couple of locations for *Benjamin Button* this week. We still just don't know. Right now, he's getting that script rewritten and he's going to look at it." A brief article in *The Hollywood Reporter* said that Warner Brothers had agreed to come onboard to co-finance *Benjamin Button*. "With or without David this movie is going to get made. I'd say that seventy to eighty percent of my time is focused on getting *Zodiac* made. David's heart is really with *Zodiac*. I really want to believe that." Fincher was so passionate about their movie and Paramount and Warner Brothers were so desperate to do it—that Jamie believed it too.

Paramount's business affairs people were talking to Messer at the same time Brad heard from people at the studio that they were making *Button*. "If *Benjamin Button* doesn't go," Brad said, "David said he'd commit to making *Zodiac*. David has been saying, 'I do love this project and I do want to stay with it. I care about it. I do want to direct it.' We've had interest from other directors—Ridley Scott, Michael Mann, Wolfgang Peterson." Joe Carnahan had shown interest in *Zodiac* after the option was released by Disney. "I ran into Joe not long ago working on *Mission Impossible 3*, which is hysterical because guess who used to be attached to direct *Mission Impossible 3*? David Fincher! Three months ago we could have said, 'You know, David, it's been nice to know you but we're going to go and get another director.' We didn't do that because we feel David has such a good grasp of the material." Besides, no other director had been so personally touched by the fear of Zodiac.

Over lunch at the Chateau Marmont Brad talked to Jake Gyllenhaal.

"What's going on with *Zodiac*?" the handsome young actor asked, honestly mystified. "I'm dying to do this movie. David didn't return my calls."

Deco building in 1930, had also designed the classic LA City Hall and the LA train station.

Brad was wearing a purple button-down shirt and black pants. Jamie was his usual disorderly self in gray T-shirt and jeans. He felt for his pack of cigarettes. The stress had gotten to him. He was smoking again. He had cut his long hair, but since the day Fincher took the holding deal for *Benjamin Button* he had worn a "rally."

"I will not shave this goatee until Fincher directs *Zodiac*," Jamie vowed. He raised his right hand Boy Scout fashion.

"David's been here a couple of months," Brad explained as he looked around.

Manila envelopes containing actors' 8 X 10 glossies were piled on the other side of a short gate. Bypassing all these hopes and dreams, Brad and Jamie headed down an alley to a high barrier. The electronic gate slid back and they turned right to the actual entrance.

"He may have bought the building," Jamie suggested, "all 11,000 square feet of it."

Fincher, dressed in a T-shirt and cords, was in the doorway. He greeted them and led them inside to a short staircase and from that to his office in the south-east corner. Fresh mail was piled at the foot of the stairs gathering dust.

"All the ceilings are twenty feet tall," Brad said in wonder.

"David, your office is a building," Jamie added. "Who else is in here?"

"No one," he said, "just me."

"It's a huge, amazing office," Brad said. From then on it was always to be the Amazing Office to them.

At the top of the brief flight, they turned right. Fincher dropped down onto a plush leather chair behind a wooden slab ten feet long by three feet wide. After confirming a fact on the Internet, he grabbed a Sharpie with two fingers and with his other hand selected some note cards. Jamie considered the vast ground floor workspace perfect. It was futuristic, spare, stylish, and jam-packed with high-tech equipment (mostly Sony, with an Xbox and PlayStation under the TV). Books on film filled a low shelf behind Fincher; *Freakonomics* lay under a Riddell red football helmet. Fincher read few books. His mind was a visual machine.

"David loves you, Jake," Brad replied. Gyllenhaal was excited hear that. His movie [*The Day After Tomorrow*] had just opened around eighty-million dollars—the same amount of money Fincher fe he absolutely must have as the budget for *Zodiac*. There were so man things acting against him making his dream film and possibly solvin the case or adding to the truth of the case—enough for several of Brad Fischer's famous lists.

On Tuesday, June 29, Jamie and Brad had a meeting at Phoenix with Fincher who had been up since 6:00 AM, a routine he followed even when he didn't have a film to shoot.

"David gets up at that ungodly hour," Jamie said, "because I guess he's crazy. He'll say for instance, 'Shall we meet in my office at 8:00 AM?' and I'll say, 'Can we make it 10:00 AM?' David's office is an hour from my house and I have all that LA traffic to battle. What time does he go to bed? I didn't dare ask.

"We all love David," Brad said, "and one of the reasons why is that he's such a straight shooter about what is going on. The position he's in right now is he's going to turn in a budget to Paramount on *Benjamin Button*. *Button* has about one hundred and fifty expensive 'face replacement shots' where they would 3D scan the map of someone's face and put another over it. Computer-generated, each shot cost within itself over $100,000."

"David loves the technical challenge, but what Brad and I came away with after a two-and-a-half hour meeting, David was very up front in saying this, is 'I'll deliver the budget to Paramount that it would take to make this movie, but I don't anticipate them saying yes to it.' It was very encouraging."

That night, Brad, who had been in various meetings all day, headed for a screening of *Spiderman 2* to relax. His day never really ended, but he got away from himself for a while, then stole a little sleep at home. The next morning, he had a very, very early meeting with Jamie at Fincher's new office on Hollywood Boulevard. The handsome alabaster structure, the former California Bank Building, was characterized by chevrons, zigzags, geometric ornamentation, and a soaring tower with a crystal pyramid. A tracery of dark tiles underscored the classic Art Deco building. Overall, this modern, very functional castle had the look of an icon. No wonder—the father and son architects who had built the Art

"Let's go check the Chronology," he said.

They rose from their chairs and crossed the cement floor to a group of couches and two chairs. Their footsteps echoed in the tomb-like building. A giant oval-shaped light twenty feet in diameter covered half the ceiling of the bare-walled conference room. Its high-tech A/V reminded Jamie of the war room in *Dr. Strangelove*. "You know that POV in movies of people waking up from surgery and there's that big kind of dome light over them," Brad said. "Its like that." The big low-tech board was pasted up with note cards and scotch tape. "Whenever you do a movie, everyone's always concerned with the studio you're going to work with because the creative team has a big influence on the script and everything else."

"There are certain people I've worked with in the creative side, executives who are very good," Jamie added politicly.

Fincher stopped him with a look. "Stop worrying about that," he said. "The creative side of *Zodiac* is in this room. Everybody else is just there to make the movie. The only thing I'm concerned about is who is going to be selling this movie." Fincher's experience with Twentieth Century Fox on marketing *Fight Club* and *Alien 3* had made him bitter. Last minute rewrites and studio interference had caused him to consider Fox as a venue with an "intense contempt for creativity," he said. "Take all of the responsibility because you're going to get all the blame."

"David believes," Jamie said, "that whatever studio makes *Zodiac* is there to fund the film and to release the film and that was all." He was still trying to unravel Fincher's complex character. "I think David has a tremendous ego in this business, but in a very different way most people in Hollywood have an ego. Most have very large egos. That translates into: 'They are always right.' Especially if it's a director working with a writer. What is amazing to me is that David's willing to collaborate in terms of, 'I like how you did the scene. Maybe this should go here and this should go here?' Ninety percent of the time he's so friggin' smart I go, 'You know what, you're right.' But the other ten percent, I'll say, 'But, what about this' or 'I think you're wrong about this.' At this point most geniuses would go, 'Get out.' He will listen and go, 'You know, that's a better idea.' The better idea always wins, no matter what. It doesn't matter if he came up with it, I came up with it or Brad came up with it. He gets you to bring something else to the table to enhance it."

"He's very open," Brad agreed. "It's always like a dialogue with him which is great. With David Fincher you really get the sense he's listening. Yet, he is someone who is whip smart and just has no patience for fools." This quality has also made him a great investigator as he drew new information from witnesses and detectives. What was the attraction of *Benjamin Button* for Fincher? Was it the technical challenge? Jamie didn't know and didn't ask the director over a late lunch of barbecued chicken and Cobb salad. He was too happy. The way Fincher presented himself today was all about *Zodiac*. Under no circumstances did he and Brad want to break that positive mood.

On the Fourth of July, Jamie invited Brad to his home to celebrate. "We'll cook some burgers and hot dogs," he promised, eager to try out his new grill.

"That's a lot more than a grill," Brad said. He circled the gleaming machine which took up a good chunk of the backyard. "This thing is suitable for travel in outer space."

The smell of sizzling hamburger, not too fat, not too lean (a seventy-thirty mixture), filled the backyard. They talked as they ate. *Zodiac* was never far from their thoughts, no matter where they were. Jamie's mother was still "very, very scared" about Zodiac and had asked him, "You have an unlisted number, right? If Zodiac's still around he might come after you."

"I think I can make it to the door." Jamie told her.

"My mother was never concerned," Brad said.

"My mother was very concerned," Jamie said.

"My number is listed, so if I disappeared—"

"But what a great ending for the movie, Brad, I get married and you disappear."

"Anything to heighten the drama."

The topic changed from grim, to one of absolute joy. How could it not? Throughout the many-windowed house there is a sense of hopeful anticipation that pervaded every room. Jamie and Amber are to be married on May 7, 2005, in Santa Barbara.

"AMBER IS FROM SANTA Barbara," Jamie explained. "Her father was an Air Force guy, but that's not why they were in Santa Barbara. In my freshman year at USC, I had dated this girl named Alisha who had been best friends with Amber in high school. All of my other friends met Amber before me. We just kind of missed each other. On January 22, 1999, during my senior year at USC, my friends and I went to this bar called St. Nick's in Los Angeles on Third Street off La Cienega. We'd been going there for years. One of my friends said, 'We're going to this party tonight. One of Alisha's friends is having her twenty-first birthday.' I wasn't interested. They said, 'Oh, its at St. Nick's Pub.' I said, 'Ah, ha! I will definitely go because that's my favorite bar in Los Angeles.' We went down there Friday night and there was this beautiful girl there. All of us had many drinks. Alisha had a disposable camera with her and persuaded Amber to start kissing the boys in our group at the bar and she would take pictures to celebrate Amber's birthday. So she kissed a couple of our friends and then she kissed me, and I liked to think there were sparks! Alisha said, 'I only have one picture left. Who do you want to kiss again?' 'I want to kiss that guy,' says Amber. So I got a second kiss. Then, they had to leave and I pulled Alisha aside and said, 'I kinda want to see your friend again. She's really kind of cute.' Apparently, Amber said the same thing to her after they left."

"The next morning, I woke up," Amber recalled, "looked at my best friend from high school and said, 'This boy will be mine.'" The next night at the same bar, there was another birthday party for someone and Jamie found out Amber was going. "So I went. We started dating and the rest is history. What I like is that I still have photographic evidence of the last time she kissed other dudes." Amber was "completely in love" and deduced Jamie felt the same. "She was like, 'You know you're in love with me,'" Jamie said. "Before I proposed to Amber, I wanted to ask her father, Allan, in person. I had called him the night before and figured he would know why. I had been seeing her for almost five years and we got along extremely well. Things were moving in that direction and it was fairly obvious."

"Hi, how are you?" Jamie asked Amber's father over the phone. "Can I come up and see you tomorrow?"

"Is Amber fine?"

"She is. Just don't mention to her that I'm coming to see you."

"Are you sick?"

"No."

"Is Amber sick?"

"No, Allan, don't worry. It's a very good thing. I can't tell you over the phone. It has to be in person. I swear to you it's a good thing."

"I'm not going to sleep tonight," he said.

"Allan! Sleep tonight. I promise it's a good thing."

It never crossed his mind why Jamie was coming to speak with him. Amber was going to be out for the day and Jamie pretended he was driving to a meeting, but drove to Palm Desert in the center of the Coachella Valley, a two-and-a-half-hour drive from Los Angeles. Heading east on Highway 10, he passed through Riverside and Palm Springs and along the northern edge of the San Bernardino National Forest. Rock formations leaned to one side like stacked bricks and impossibly tall palms swayed alongside the highway. In the distance came the wail of a locomotive passing over a chasm on a metal bridge.

"What is it?" Allan asked as soon Jamie pulled up in front of the house.

"I want your permission to ask for your daughter's hand in marriage."

"Oh, Thank God!" he said. "I thought you were coming here to tell me you were leaving her."

"I wouldn't drive 140 miles only to have you punch me in the face," he said.

When Jamie gave Amber the engagement ring, Amber repeated, "Really?" for twenty minutes. Finally, Jamie stopped her and said, "I'm going to need a 'yes' or a 'no' here."

THAT EVENING, BRAD ARRIVED home from Phoenix Pictures late. "If I was doing something that was more nine to five and it was just about the money," he said, "I would be really depressed. Producing is something I'm really passionate about. You know that. I love it. If everything goes as I hope it will, and the other film does not happen right now, and Fincher's out of it, then in August David and I will go up to see the brother and sister-in-law." He wanted to get Fincher with the SFPD and the VPD so he could really start "getting into that stuff."

"We know we don't want to move off of David," Jamie said. "If he ended up going into this other film I would be sad that he was leaving us, but say, 'Good luck, man. It's going to be a bear.' A lot of people in

Hollywood, even my agent says, 'We should go get another director and get the movie made.' Either we operate from the point of view that this movie is going to get made and I'm going to get paid, but the question is 'Is it going to get made *well*?'"

The next day, Amy Carr of Phoenix Pictures found herself doing two jobs. She left her scripts behind to check the JFK Center in Vallejo for any Zodiac stories. This was more backbreaking research for the movie. She had to admit this was more exciting than dealing with scripts. The University of Texas grad found she enjoyed sleuthing as much as Mark J. Arneson, the detective the studio had employed along with private investigators from Wilmore & Associates and Thomas Dale & Associates. Arneson, an operative with the Quest Group, was a thirty-year LAPD veteran who preferred being a private dick to being a cop. He also performed off-duty body-guarding, surveillance, and home security work for Hollywood stars. Brad knew Arneson through his wife, Jody who had transcribed the Don Cheney interviews for him. Arneson arrived at Phoenix at 3:00 PM to confer with Brad, Jamie, and Lou Phillips about locating Mike Mageau. It had been over a decade since the only other surviving Zodiac victim's last sighting. In the meantime, Mike had become a street person and was suffering horribly.

"Well, we've got all we can get on Mageau," Brad said as he looked over his dossier in another three-ring binder. "We'll send Mark off to get the rest."

This nearly impossible task only encouraged the iron-hard Arneson who began rumbling up and down the Pacific Coast like a freight train, looking in every hostel, and under every overpass determined to locate an invisible man who didn't want to be found. Nothing had changed for Mageau since 1969. Psychologically, he was still in fear of his life.

By phone, Captain Jackson at the VPD arranged for Brad and Jamie to see their Zodiac files late the next day, Thursday, July 15. "I left a message for Sergeant DiStefino to brief you," he said. The filmmakers, who were connecting some of the evidentiary dots, still wondered why the department hadn't brought charges against Leigh Allen.

"If anyone knows," Captain Jackson said, "George Bawart does."

"We trust George implicitly," Brad said.

In San Francisco, Toschi was still running North Star Security, but the strain of doing his job as well filling in for his ailing boss was telling. The following day, he drove to San Leandro to meet a new loss prevention director, but first answered a call from Brad and Jamie.

"What we're going to do is go up and speak with George Bawart, and start talking to the VPD and SFPD about seeing some of the stuff they supposedly have," Brad said. "What does SFPD have that we should ask to see when we visit?"

"You should look at the bloody swatches," Toschi said, "the seventeen crime scene photos from the cabdriver shooting taken at different angles, the 9-mm casings, and the 'unidentified' letter the crime lab had supposedly tested for DNA. Frankly, I don't know why Zodiac would lick the back of a stamp after all those letters to us. If it's true, that's the only time he did that. The only Zodiac letters you should trust for DNA are those containing a bloody swatch from Stine's shirt. If you see all this with your eyes you will see all we saw on October 11, 1969." Toschi told them to say hello to Bawart for him and hung up.

"We are to meet at the restaurant for lunch," Bawart told his wife, Jan. "They are coming in two cars 'cause Jamie doesn't like to fly and he and his girlfriend drove up.

"My fiancé, Amber, and I went by car because of my crippling fear of flying," said Jamie who had also driven to the San Francisco Clift Hotel meeting in January. "They didn't have any lower end cars because we were renting so late, so they gave us a price break—a luxury SUV, the Infiniti QX-56. We liked it so much we ended up renting it for five days, much to the great chagrin of Arnie Messer. It was more expensive than all the flights put together. So we have this boat that we drove up at night in less than six hours with the newest GPS navigation, the whole nine. Yes, we're very spoiled now. Amber drove most of the way because she's much tougher than I am and got us into Vallejo at 3:30 AM."

The Vallejo film commissioner had put them up at a Holiday Inn by the Marine World where they missed a nearby shootout with police and men in gray Buick automobiles by only two days. Jamie made a mental note to not rent a gray Buick next time they visited. "So we ended up waiting and waiting at Denny's Restaurant. This time the airline hadn't lost Brad's luggage—his bag was the third one out. This time it was Brad who was lost."

At Denny's, Jamie looked up to see Brad rushing in the door. He looked haggard.

"You can't find the Denny's that is right next to the highway with a twenty foot sign?" Jamie said in amazement.

"I saw the Denny's," Brad said, "but the exit was different on the other side. Besides, you have the directions with you in your pocket. By the way, what's that?" He turned and pointed an accusing finger at the gleaming Infiniti parked outside. "Jamie, why did you have to rent the most expensive super-pimped out version of the SUV available?"

"I was going to get the less expensive one," Jamie said, "but it didn't have a CD player."

Brad's cell phone jangled. It was Bawart. "The two of us were going to meet at the restaurant for lunch and go directly to George's place, but then he called me and I told him we were both there."

"I'll just come by Denny's," he said. His was a rough, powerful voice filled with humor and enthusiasm. Brad went outside to wait.

CHAPTER EIGHT

BIG MAN INTERROGATION

WHEN BAWART ROARED UP five minutes later in a storm of dust and exhaust, Brad was on his phone speaking with Toschi. Brad thanked him and jumped off. He had seen old photos of Bawart, but barely recognized him now. There was a spring to his step, his hair was cut close, and he was slightly tanned. His thick-lensed, wire-framed glasses glittered madly in the sun. Bawart's hearing aid was barely perceptible. This morning, he was dressed in ultramarine-blue trousers, and a powder-blue polo shirt, but the big change in the detective was invisible. His doctors had cleared his arteries of plaque, whipped and beaten his blood pressure until it was under control, and persuaded him to eat healthier. Visibly, George's exercise in his backyard pool had resulted in a trim silhouette. He had slimmed down an amazing sixty pounds!

Bawart's weight loss had been beneficial to their search for the truth in an unexpected way. His sleek new shape had allowed him, for the first time in years, to squeeze through the tiny opening into his dusty attic where, basking in 110-degree temperatures, he had sweated off a few more pounds as he rummaged through boxes of papers. Managing to wrestle this hidden wealth downstairs had been even harder and probably worth the loss of a few ounces. Bawart had taken the time to dust off these forgotten treasures and arrange them to be presented to his visitors. Right now, they sat just offstage of the kitchen ready to be presented to the filmmakers in a grand manner as befitting their importance.

Brad greeted the ex-motorcycle cop, and they hurried into Denny's to join Jamie and Amber in a quiet back booth. Once more, through fate or habit, Jamie and Brad were dressed in identical Hollywood uniforms—black jeans, black shoes, black T-shirts. The only difference was that Jamie's T-shirt was a V-neck and Brad's wasn't, and Brad's shirt was pressed, and Jamie's wasn't. It was rumpled and wrinkled as befitting a serious writer. Bawart noticed the screenwriter's highly shined boots had a big hole in one sole and the cuffs of his trousers were frayed. How does a guy who's one of the Vanderbilts go around like that? "That's how Jamie is," Bawart decided, "not pretentious at all, just a nice, nice guy, a really likable guy. Doesn't try to tell you how much he knows or doesn't know—likewise, Brad. I was predisposed to think fairly highly of Brad and Jamie because Captain Dave Jackson had called me up about them. We talked cop-to-cop. He told me these guys are good people. 'These aren't guys who are trying to exploit you, and take advantage of you,' he said. Not that they could. I don't know how they could! So I thought they might be pretty good folks and they turned out to be absolutely nice people, just regular folks. They asked questions, weren't mean-spirited, didn't say, 'How come you didn't do this?' 'Why did you do that?'"

They ordered club sandwiches, Brad's staple breakfast, dinner, and supper. Jamie had already had breakfast so he ordered fruit and tried to look healthy in between frequent trips outside to smoke. Bawart, who had given up smoking, yearned to join him and did. He eyed Jamie's cigarette wolfishly and sniffed the air, but that was all. Back inside, Brad and Jamie begin by talking to him about the movie and what their goals were. Bawart listened carefully.

"From what I see now," Bawart said, after he had heard them out, "we weren't getting a lot of reports from San Francisco, nor were they getting reports from us. Anyway, I went to San Francisco to look through their evidence and see what Stine's shirt looked like. Have you guys seen the shirt from Paul Stine, the cabbie Zodiac murdered?" Brad and Jamie shook their heads vigorously. All they had seen was Brad's stand-in shirt which Fincher had almost ripped to pieces.

"I had a horrible time finding it," George continued. "It turned out it was in Questioned Documents. It's a good thing I did find it.

It wasn't what I had in mind. All the reports say is that it's a striped shirt. The reason I wanted to find it is that we were serving a search warrant on Arthur Leigh Allen's house. Let's say that he has ten striped shirts and they've been through the wash and they've got bloodstains on them and part of them cut off, I want to make sure I know what I'm looking at." Bawart had gone to San Francisco to look through SFPD's evidence in order to see what Stine's shirt looked like. "When I went into the evidence locker they had lost half the stuff or didn't know what it was," he said. "I finally found the shirt in a box in the corner in the Questioned Documents office. It's a good thing I did. It didn't look at all like what I had in mind. It's got big stripes and little stripes and was just rumpled up like you took your shirt off in the morning and threw it in a box and let it sit there for twenty years.

"So I say, 'Could we cut a little piece off so I can take it with us?'"

"They said, 'Oh, no! That is evidence.'"

"'Jesus Christ,' I said, 'it's been in the trash and now that somebody's interested in it, you won't give it to us.'" Now Brad had a question for Bawart.

"Was the fabric that it was taken from cut or torn?" he asked. This was another of Fincher's questions that he needed answered.

"I don't know," George told him. "It's got bloodstains all over it." He paused and took a sip of coffee. "Next, I went to Napa and they had all their evidence together, better than anybody from Vallejo or San Francisco and it was well-preserved. So I went through all their evidence. The only guy still left around from that era was Ken Narlow. Next, I went to Narlow's house, a home not too dissimilar to mine, in a tract area in Napa, and they've got like a shrine to this case. I went and talked to him. I told him I had this search warrant I was going to do on Leigh Allen's house. He said, 'O.K., great.' He was getting ready to run for sheriff and this would be good press. This was in '91. We had just served the warrant on Allen and the news came out in this little throwaway newspaper. We were trying to keep it hush-hush, but other papers picked the article up and now it became a big deal. But, this unwanted publicity actually did me a favor. The various articles brought forward the woman who knew who 'Robert Emmett the hippie' [a name mentioned in Zodiac correspondence] was. He's a little sawed-off guy, really bubbly. He was a mime and was on the *Ed Sullivan Show*.

Tracking him down involved a long trip and we got very little from him. He wasn't involved. At VPD, they had beaten the Zodiac case to death," Bawart continued, "and they had to have somebody field all these calls. Everyone would retire or die, so I turned out to be that guy by attrition." He paused and looked Brad and Jamie in the eye. "Who have you spoken to so far? And who are you going to speak to?"

Bawart leaned back in the cushioned booth, watching their lips intently as not to miss a word. Occasionally, he adjusted the volume on his hearing aid. George was certainly a more relaxed and humorous man these days. He had worked homicide for almost twenty years, but been forced to retire in 1989 because of his hearing loss. He had gotten into police work in an odd way. While working in a paint shop and training as military policemen as a reservist, he and a friend had applied for a job with the force on a lark. He passed the test. His friend failed.

"George isn't at all guarded about the case," Jamie noted, "very candid, but very genuine, a warm, funny guy."

George explained that the Zodiac case was unlike any criminal case he had ever encountered. He gave an example. "When the topic of a serial killer came up back when it all began," he said, "I wondered, 'What? Does he kill people with cereal?' Cause to my knowledge we had not had a serial killer in Vallejo or anywhere else that I had even heard of. I knew about Jack the Ripper and don't remember him ever being called a serial killer. Just a guy who killed prostitutes in London years ago. It was really strange to me how one guy could kill people for no particular reason."

Bawart also thought he knew what had caused an increases in the Vallejo murder rate and tried to make sense of it for Brad and Jamie.

"Before the heavy dope started happening," he said, "the VPD was like every other police department: eighty-five percent of the homicides were solved and probably three or four unsolved within a five year span between 1966 and 1971. That's the way homicide was in those days. You didn't have unrelated people killing each other. You might have a guy doing a stickup and the gun goes off. He wasn't drug-crazed and going in there to do the stickup and just to kill somebody too. That happened in the eighties. Before that it was marijuana, heroin and LSD. Heroin addicts were mellow. They weren't crazy. The only time they went crazy was when they needed a fix and needed some money. All they wanted to do was have sex, eat, and listen to music. Then the crack and crank came in and people got so violent that they'd kill somebody over nothing."

After lunch, everyone started out for Bawart's home some distance away.

"Sometimes it's a little difficult out here in the country to locate addresses," Bawart explained as he slid behind the wheel of his car and peeled away toward Vacaville, his hometown. Coming straight up 80, he swung off on the Alison Nut Tree Road Exit, crossed over the freeway, and sped past a shopping center and a Bed Bath & Beyond outlet. His visitors followed swiftly as they could through a Byzantine maze of bumpy country roads, grasslands, and beige houses hidden behind cinder block walls that encroached upon farmlands. Streetlights and stoplights gave way to larger trees, more puzzling turnoffs and more secretive cinder block walls until Bawart finally wheeled onto a dusty road. With little warning, he accelerated onto a gravel driveway leading to a low, Western-style house which took up several acres. Brad and Jamie almost lost him. Bawart had no sooner pulled to a stop at the end of the long drive than he leapt out and bounded toward them as they were hesitantly entering the drive. Brad and Jamie heard the crunch of gravel as they climbed out.

"When I bought this house in '80," Bawart said, extending his arms to encompass his dream home, "my credit was good and I was married to a different woman at the time. Though we made fairly good money, the best rate of interest we could get was 17 3/4 per cent. For the first year we paid on the first mortgage, then the rates went down. Since then I've refinanced it a number of times. The place is in flux." Bawart's cheery home had polished wood floors, new carpet, and a varnished oaken barrel inside the front door which on rainy days held a single umbrella. Right of the entrance, a hall led to tidy bedrooms, immaculate bathrooms, Jan's tidy office, and Bawart's desk where he had been assembling his radio-controlled airplane. A travel book (George read voraciously) lay open on the bed. Turning left, he escorted his visitors around into the living room.

Even if a visitor had been to the Bawart home many times before or if it was their first visit, George never failed to show off the living room centerpiece—his magnificent 300 pound throne, a chrome-plated barber's chair with a full-grain leather headrest and metal chrome foot stand. He sat there most evenings, hydraulic chair tilted, feet up, to watch *Jeopardy,* and its current unstoppable contestant, Ken Jennings. On weekends, George watched Nascar or football, but always from this remarkable chair.

"Jan wasn't here when I bought this house," George said. "She didn't particularly care for it or that wall down there with the fireplace. The brick used to be all brown stucco stone which I thought was fine. Jan thought it was ugly. Two years ago, I flew down to visit the son of another cop in Costa Rica for a week. First thing I'm out the door, Jan ran down and rented an electric jackhammer, jackhammered everything off that wall and asked a guy to come in and put new fireplace brick in. The problem was that when I got back the brick guy hadn't come by yet to install it. I walked into my house. The wall was gone! Only a nut like my wife would do that." He smiled broadly. "And then she ripped everything out of the back and put new carpeting in."

It was the kitchen which most exhibited Bawart's high mark as an accomplished cook of healthy dishes and sometimes unhealthy yet tasty dishes. George could whip up an unforgettable bacon-wrapped burger in fifteen minutes—cheddar, parmesan, onion, ketchup, Worcestershire sauce, and crispy bacon, secured with toothpicks. It was tricky. Guilty pleasures always are. The bacon had to be pliant. His dishes were created in an unspoken competition with Jan who made sure he kept to his diet with healthy food. That the kitchen was Jan's bailiwick was demonstrated by the mix of modern appliances and the antique throughout the nook. Under a huge bonnet, hunched a "Depression green" cast-iron stove. It wasn't for cooking. Jan had crowded the top with ferns, flat irons, canisters, a breadbox, and an antique wire toaster. Light streaming through the wide window illuminated cane-backed chairs arranged on a tile floor. A row of delicate cups dangled under rosewood cabinets. The wallpaper design was of poppies, lilacs, and long twisting vines. On the counter were gold-framed pictures of Bawart's granddaughters.

"Wait here," Bawart told Brad and Jamie as he left the kitchen. He reentered with two battered boxes under each arm. Brad estimated they weighed about six pounds each. Bawart placed one box on the floor and hefted the other onto the kitchen table. Looking over the contents strewn on the white tablecloth table top—four thick blue binders, a Xerox paper box strapped with aluminum tape, three fat manilla file folders, and six thin legal envelopes, the two filmmakers recalled what investigator Arneson had told them. "The one thing about cops is that cops keep stuff," he had said. "Not because they're collectors, but because one day they might go through all of it."

"There's a treasure trove of stuff on that kitchen table," Jamie said in awe. "George has all the original color photographs from when they searched the Allen house on Fresno Street in 1991. There is a photograph of the drawer pulled out from the desk in the basement and six handguns lying on the desk and pictures of Allen's pipe bombs."

"We were amazed at the amount of stuff on his kitchen table," Brad said.

"Yeah, I found all this stuff I had forgotten that I had," Bawart said. After his full-time duties had ceased, the VPD hired George back as a consultant. "Just before I retired, some new information came in [on Zodiac] and we started to 're-look' at the case, started to really look at the case heavily, probably the way it should have been looked in the first place. This is the deal here, I had these binders made up [in 1991] in anticipation." He tapped each with his finger—one, two, three, four, then ran his finger along the black edges. "If we were going to file on the prime suspect, Arthur Leigh Allen, they had to have copies for the DA and some for us to keep. I had one of the secretaries, one of the community service officers, put it all together and put it all in those envelopes." He indicated the legal envelopes. "What you have in front of you is the whole of everything that Vallejo's got." Years ago, Bawart had kept a credenza at VPD that held all his reports and a copy of all the stuff they were working on, "Notes, junk, everything." After he retired, he couldn't come down to the station every day. One day he was told, "Get all that stuff out, get all that stuff out." Bawart asked, "Today?" "Yes," was the reply. So he scrounged two large boxes, threw all the stuff from the credenza in, went away with it, and never looked at those copies again—until now.

"One of the problems is at the time Zodiac was going on," Bawart continued, thrusting his jaw forward bulldog-like as he did when intent, "was that I was doing all the other work that was going on. I didn't get intimately involved with the investigation until much later on." He pawed through an envelope and shook his head. It was incomplete. He shrugged, turning his palms up as if he couldn't believe it.

As Brad rummaged through the salvaged papers, Bawart said, "Those are all copies of Bill Armstrong's handwritten notes." In 1991, when [Captain Roy] Conway was trying to revive the case, he requested copies of Armstrong's affidavit. "Listen," Bawart said. "Conway was a guy who was gonna be the brass. He was always gonna be the brass. He was gonna be Chief of Police—that's what he wanted. He was not a guy who is down in the trenches."

"Obviously," Jamie told Brad, "you take a look at George Bawart's face and here's a guy who is down in the trenches. And he likes Conway and respects him. George is a smart guy, a tough guy, but back in the day you probably didn't see the smart before the tough."

"Conway and I put the file away after Allen died and the government declined to proceed further. When Conway retired a couple of years ago, he and his wife bought an RV and took off to travel the country. Bawart didn't know where he was, but said he could talk to friends and friends of friends and find him if Brad and Jamie wanted.

"We want," Jamie said.

Next, Bawart poured out a gray envelope marked "Quality Photofinishing." There were a number of photographs taken during the 1991 search of Leigh Allen's basement which depicted an open desk drawer with six handguns. Color pictures showed four pipe bombs in a box, two bombs police had laid out on brown paper in the driveway, and a bomb, fuse extended, balanced on top of a pink cinder block. "I've got bombs in my basement," Zodiac had written the *Chronicle*.

Then, Bawart slammed a brown plastic Rolodex down on the table. It was a real beast and heavy as lead. "What do you think of that?" he asked. "Well, that's Leigh Allen's Rolodex which contains the names of everyone he knew. I saved that from the scrap heap too."

Brad sat straight up, immediately interested. He noticed that there were little turquoise tabs with white lettering designating *A* through *Z*.

Under *A* was "Ace Hardware, on Tennessee" where Allen had once worked." Breathlessly, Jamie thumbed to *Z*.

There was nothing under that letter.

"Look up Darlene Ferrin," Brad said urgently.

Jamie thumbed to *F*.

There was nothing under *F*.

Then, he skimmed back to *D*.

There was no "Darlene" under *D*.

Next, Bawart lifted out Allen's black, boxy General Electric tape recorder, so old it was held together by a piece of yellowed masking tape. One end had curled up like a rattlesnake about to bite. The detective inserted a red plastic Maxell audiotape that Allen had made, closed the lid, and solemnly depressed the white play key. Bawart probably should have warned Brad and Jamie what was on the tape. There was a second or two of static before piercing, heartrending screams of a child being beaten filled the cosy kitchen. It was a horrifying contrast.

Brad slammed the audio off with his fist.

"It's the same all the way through," Bawart said. His voice was strained. "You don't want to hear more."

No one did. The sounds were unbearable.

Two nondescript boxes containing reel-to-reel tapes and video cassettes tumbled out onto the tablecloth next. Then, came a white box marked "econosource," which held two Maxell VHS tapes, the 1967-68 CHIA membership roster, and a copy of the book, *Zodiac*. "I've got these two videotapes," Bawart held them up by the corners, pinky extended, "and I think you will find them very interesting." The shorter tape was a Channel 6 report, but the second was over an hour-and-a-half-long.

"What's on that tape?" Jamie asked.

"It's a 1991 videotape of Conway and me questioning Leigh Allen at VPD," said Bawart, "the only copy in the world. Would you like to see it?"

Jamie and Brad looked at each other and then at the tape and both mouthed at the same time, "Holy shit!"

Bawart slid the low-tech police videotape from 1991 into his VCR. There was a hollow "*thunk*," some streaking, and then a concrete interrogation room came into focus on the screen. The camera, mounted high between the corner of two walls and the ceiling, showed Allen seated right front and center. From this angle Conway and Bawart were not visible. "I had Allen in the interrogation room at 9:30 AM, sharp," Bawart explained. "I turned the camera on before I brought him in. Allen is a smart guy and I knew if I suddenly reached under the table and flicked a switch he would know he was being recorded. If Allen was just an intellectual crook that didn't have these other motivations we wouldn't have spent two minutes talking to him. I asked Leigh to come in voluntarily for some innocuous reason, but the real thrust was to sit him down, get him on tape being interviewed, and try to coerce him into a polygraph examination. The suspect was there of his own free will which is mentioned on the tape. Just that morning there had been something in the papers about him."

Any criminal interrogation is conducted under impassioned and volatile tension, but adheres to certain basics—an uninterrupted span of time, a private, soundproof room and a seated subject. Bawart and Conway kept Allen sitting because a seated person is more likely to disclose subtle physiological changes—ear pulling, foot tapping, or arm crossing, than a standing person. Bawart was an expert in reading body language. First, he had studied Allen's eyes. Were they shifty? Was that a quick look to the left or right? Was there dilation or contraction of the pupil? Bawart had no difficulty telling Allen's mouth was dry. The suspect kept swallowing. As much as Bawart wanted his suspect to lose his cool, he had to keep complete control of himself and exhibit every measure of self-confidence during the interview. On the tape, Bawart comes across as self-assured, placid, a man with a sound, fundamental knowledge of physiology and practical psychology. Brad and Jamie had earlier seen Allen on the KTVU-Channel Two Oakland news performing for veteran crime broadcaster Rita Williams. On Bawart's tape the suspect was performing again, but this time for the police.

"Allen starts out with these little *faux* tears—'all the years of being through this,' that kind of speech," Brad noted. "And talking about how, of course, he'd thought of suicide. It's Allen talking a lot without saying very much."

First, Bawart appealed to the subject's ego, speaking clearly, slowly, commanding respect. He was so highly conversant on the Zodiac case that if he bluffed Allen, he was not likely to be caught. He went through items the police had discovered during their search of Allen's basement home on February 14, 1991—a Ruger .22 revolver Blackhawk, a .22 automatic clip with three rounds, a Marlin .22 rifle with scope, an Inland .30 caliber rifle, a hunting knife with sheath and rivets, a Stevens Model 835 12-gauge double barrel shotgun, a Winchester Model 50

20-gauge automatic shotgun, and a Zodiac "Sea Wolf" Watch. They
had also recovered and photographed four pipe bombs, one primer
cord, blasting caps, seven railway torpedoes, and bottles of potassium
nitrate, bottles of sulfur, half a can of black powder, a formula in Allen's
handwriting for making a bomb using ammonia nitrate, stove oil, and
gravel.

"You know, Leigh," Bawart said, "there are also some formulas for
nitroglycerine here."

"Yeah," Allen said. "I might have written down some formulas,
but I don't know what's in nitroglycerine."

"If you were to write a formula, Leigh, what would be in there?"

"Well, nitric acid, but I don't know what else."

"You studied chemistry, didn't you?"

"Well, I minored in that [at Sonoma State College].

As Jamie watched the screen, he whispered to Brad, "George is a
really great interrogator."

When Jamie wrote *Basic* he had boned up on interrogation and
was practically an expert on the subject. Watching the tape, he saw how
adroitly Bawart paid it out—"Oh, really? That's interesting—it's funny
you mentioned that because we found this out which totally blows
what you just said. So what do you have to say to that?"

"This guy's a talker," Jamie said, "so let him talk. Let him hang
himself. He's playing with the cops." It amazed Jamie that in 1991,
with all the TV shows on the air where people won't talk to police
without their lawyers, Leigh goes in and sits for an hour or more when
he doesn't need to and all the while talking about Zodiac. "Whether
you are Zodiac or not, if the police came to me and said, 'We want you
to come down and talk about this murder case you might be involved
in,' whether I'd done the crimes or not, I'd think, 'No friggin' way!'
Leigh pretty much volunteered to come down. That fits in with the
'Wile E. Coyote, Super Genius persona' theory of Fincher's."

Leigh was also aware of what the cops were up to. He hung out
at the police station, ate lunch where the cops did, bought books on
disguising handwriting and wearing disguises, and researched no
differently than Fincher did in preparing a film. It harkened back to
Allen sending a typewritten letter to Toschi saying, "Is there any way I
can help you catch Zodiac?"

"It's almost like, 'Let's just check in and see where the police are on this,'" Brad said. "'I am obviously smarter than them. I'll be able to ferret out what I need.'"

When the tape played out, he asked Bawart what Officer Dick Hoffman was like. Hoffman was the responding officer the night Zodiac shot Darlene Ferrin and Mike Mageau at Blue Rock Springs.

"I can do better than that," Bawart replied. "I can give Dick Hoffman a call and see if he's around." Hoffman was around and came right over. In detail, he went over the events of the night of July 4, 1969. "When I got the call—'Teenager shot at the Blue Rock Springs Parking Lot!' I didn't know if teenagers had been shot at or teenagers were shooting off guns."

Bawart filled in a few administrative blanks. "Back then Conway and I weren't really on the case," George said. "Mulanax was dealing with Armstrong and Toschi. When I started working on the Zodiac case later on I was investigating Blue Rock Springs, Berryessa, and Paul Stine. Conway had theorized that these three were the only true Zodiac murders. Which, I tell you, is not a stupid idea. I like Leigh Allen for these things and we know these things are the Zodiac."

He paused, took a step back, and looked the guys up and down. He had suddenly become serious. "I am going to let you take the interrogation tape and copy it, but you have to swear to give it back to me."

"We swear," Jamie said. Bawart meant this. George's tough side was showing at the edges. "Mr. Fincher is nothing if not precise and wants to make sure he has everything. We're going to be on the set and David's going to go, 'O.K., if we can figure out this and that,' and now we have this." He clutched the video cassette to his chest. "George, It's been a great day," Jamie said, as they shook hands all around. "We'll see you tomorrow."

Outside, the sky was tinted pink. Now they had to work the labyrinth backwards. Soon they were again speeding by Bed Bath & Beyond and beyond that. Brad looked over. Jamie was glowing. Bawart had loaned them the Rolodex to take along too. He trusted them.

"George was great and Hoffman was fantastic," Jamie said.

"We've still got plenty of detecting in front of us," Brad said, his eyes locked on the road and the many adventures still ahead.

The next morning, Friday, July 16, Brad, Jamie, and Bawart kept their ten o'clock appointment with Sergeant DiStefino at VPD. The officers in their black T-shirts, some working out in a new gym, were fit, muscular, intense, and very respectful of Bawart.

"What's that?" Brad asked, indicating a sad little binder on DiStefino's desk.

"This is the Zodiac file."

"That's it?" Jamie said. For some time VPD had been battling to get three Zodiac letters back from the SFPD, and had even considered legal action to regain their property so they could send it to Sacramento for DNA testing.

"Honestly, I can't believe it," Brad said. Physical evidence included Darlene Ferrin's blouse and patterned slacks, a bayonet with brads and rivets, and a typewriter taken during a search of Allen's house. The font of the typewriter, though a similar model to the one Zodiac may have used in a Riverside letter, did not match. No tests had been done on the bayonet which resembled the knife used at Lake Berryessa. Nor were there any photos of the Blue Rock Springs crime scene in their file. It would be up to Fincher, Brad, and Jamie to find those pictures—if they still existed.

"After all these years it's definitely clear that everyone's stuff is all over the place," Brad said with a shake of his head. "I think Vallejo even has some of San Francisco's stuff." The few Lake Herman Road photos in existence were in the custody of Solano County and Benicia PD. It surprised Brad that DiStefino didn't know about the 3 X 5-inch "Zodiac" postcard to Sergeant Lynch mailed in an envelope from San Francisco at 3:00 PM, on August 10, 1969. The typewritten card began: "Dear Sergeant Lynch I hope the enclosed key helps . . ." Tucked inside the envelope was a sheet of paper bearing handwritten letters and symbols beginning A-G-S-(backwards)." Brad knew the card existed because it was mentioned in the list of DOJ Zodiac correspondence alongside a photocopy of it. Fincher would want that. After lunch, they returned to Bawart's home to sort the last of the material. Under Jan's watchful eye, Brad and Jamie carefully spread out the evidential copies on the floor. "I was afraid to mess anything up because I'm a fairly messy guy," Jamie said, keeping a wary eye on Jan. "We could tell she wanted to clean up. Anything we weren't using she would come along right behind and organize. We were driving her crazy."

"I think we still have some Diet Coke," Bawart said. He disappeared into the kitchen and came back with the flattest Diet Coke Jamie had ever had. "I think they have Diet Coke from the seventies," he whispered to Brad, but sipped it anyway. Every time Jamie went out to smoke a cigarette, Bawart trailed after him, eyeing his cigarette wolfishly and sniffing the smoke before the wind carried it away. "I'll take second hand if you don't mind," Bawart said, moving downwind. By visit's end he was asking Jamie whenever he got up, "Are you going out to smoke?"

"I was really just getting some more water, George," Jamie would say, "but we can go smoke if you like."

Next, Brad and Jamie came to four boxes containing seventy to eighty homemade videotapes seized from the suspect's basement home along with Allen's RCA video camera which sold for $300 back in those days. This was another indication, along with the expensive Zodiac Wristwatch the suspect had been given just before the Lake Herman Road murders, that the family had money.

"I watched thirty to forty percent of the videotapes," Bawart said as if recalling a bad dream. He sounded tired for the first time. "But when Allen died, I stopped going through them. The tapes were interspersed with episodes of *Star Wars* and other programs. I've seen more episodes of *Yan Can Cook* [on KQED Channel 9] than are known to man."

Brad inserted a tape in the VHS player and scanned a copy of Carl Sagan's astronomy documentary *Cosmos* (which ran in the Bay Area between 1980-1981). As he watched, he thought of Zodiac and the stars. Just then, he saw something flash by on the screen.

"There are people on those videotapes!" he said, getting to his feet. "Rewind! I saw some weird friend of Allen's in his basement and he was zooming in on the guy's crotch, smiling and saying, 'What a handsome guy you are.' Then his dog gets up on the bed and he starts cooing at the dog and the dog looks so scared."

"Did you ever try to track Leigh's friends down?" Jamie asked Bawart.

"Never even tried," he replied. "You'd think somebody who had a video camera would have more tapes of whatever he does daily, but they were just copies of programs."

"Look, he clearly has recorded over stuff," Brad said. He paused on a freeze-frame. "See! There are a couple of seconds of things, then it veers off to something else. At the end of one tape there's a kitchen for five-seconds, brief flashes of other things that might bear more scrutiny. Some are only two or three frames long."

What could be hidden in those microseconds, perhaps a universe worthy of Carl Sagan.

"See," Bawart said. "That's probably what I missed because when I was going through them, if it wasn't something I was interested in, I'd fast-forward." Bawart still had fifty more tapes to look at. "Do you want them today?" Then, for the first and only time during their visit, Bawart became deadly serious. "Listen, guys, you can't screw me on this. If you do find something you have to come back to me." Brad and Jamie understood. They would be obstructing justice if they failed to report anything they discovered on the tapes, and so would Fincher. By phone, Brad filled Fincher in on the material Bawart had loaned them. He said he could have duplicates of the tapes made at Sony on Sunday. "David was really thrilled," Brad said as he hung up. If Fincher wasn't sure he was going to shoot *Zodiac*, he might change his mind after seeing what treasures his sleuths had uncovered.

FRIDAY NIGHT, THEY DROVE to San Francisco and once more checked into the Clift Hotel. Inside its placid exterior, Brad was still badgered by calls from every direction—budget negotiations, casting, and the long wait for Fincher and all the legal ramifications of competing studios. Jamie had his own battle to wage—the long, long script. Brad and Jamie ate club sandwiches and were so exhausted that they dropped off to sleep still dressed and clutching pages of the voluminous script.

At 11: 30 AM, Saturday, July 17, they entered City Hall Room 473, to see Mike Billington of the San Francisco Film Commission. The trim, dark-haired young man was excited about the opportunity to have a major movie shot on city streets. A supervisor told them, "Our arms are wide open." A single film like *Zodiac* could mean an influx of millions of dollars for local performers, technicians, set builders, carpenters, lighting and sound personnel, and caterers when it was shot on location. Presently, there were only two full time film office workers and a handful of unpaid commissioners to attract filmmakers to San

Francisco. The situation had changed drastically since the 1990s.

Back then, Robin Williams made four movies inside Treasure Island's huge 140,000 square-foot hanger. Filming on San Francisco streets brought in $460 million a year and millions more in tax revenue and payroll stimulation. Don Johnson's TV show, *Nash Bridges*, netted the city $25 million a year. In 2002, local film spending abruptly dipped to $138 million and the Bay Area became a wasteland for films on location with a loss of 155 production companies, prop and camera rental concerns, and grip and lighting equipment houses. The following year, *The Hulk* shot only B-roll exteriors in the city and filmed 90 percent of the show elsewhere. San Francisco, with a cinematic tradition going back to Charlie Chaplin's studios in southern Alameda County and film noir classics like *Dark Passage, Bullitt, Dirty Harry, Jagged Edge, Basic Instinct*, Hitchcock's *Vertigo, The Laughing Policeman*, and Fincher's *The Game*, had become expensively uncooperative. The city offered no tax incentives and film location managers had to budget $90 an hour for each police officer assigned to their shoots. In contrast, New York City provided free police and a ten percent tax credit on production costs, a five percent tax credit on lodging, car rental, and airfare, and zero sales tax on production goods and services.

The time was ripe for Brad to get some major tax incentives for *Zodiac*. Confronted with a projected $97 million city revenue shortfall over the next eighteen months, Mayor Newsom might make a sweet deal to shoot on location and bring money into the cash-strapped metropolis. The Bay Film Alliance prepared a 180 page package to enable the Mayor to attract filmmakers by offering rebates up to $600,000, including an unexpected windfall of $350,000 from hotel tax revenue allocated to them. Not only that, but Newson would abolish a fourteen percent "administrative fee" added to the cost of fire, public works and police services. He would offer "rent givebacks" to filmmakers in return for facility improvements on Treasure Island and the conversion of existing stages into state-of-the-art sound stages. Within months, director Chris Columbus, a San Francisco resident, would bring *Rent*, a $40 million musical, to Treasure Island and the San Francisco streets, the first of several projects intended to employ local workers. "Everybody had left," Columbus said. "We want to bring them back in a big way."

The Mayor replaced eight of the eleven Film Commissioners and named Stephanie Coyote as Executive Director. Dark-haired, with startling blue eyes, the former location scout and liaison between production crews, city officials, and residents, had contributed to sixteen Bay Area feature films, including Fincher's *The Game*. Coyote, who has a BA in Communications from Pennsylvania State University, would be invaluable to Fincher in securing film permits and as coordinator with SFPD. The rapid downturn in local filming over the last four years had helped derail her career. "I went from turning work away, to no work," she said. "We as a city need to present a united front to Hollywood making it very clear to them that we in fact do want them here."

Billington arranged dinner reservations for himself, Brad, Jamie, Amber, and George and Jan Bawart, then contacted Inspector Kelly Carroll to arrange a brief meeting with the filmmakers. "What are you going to need?" Carroll asked. "How can we help?" Carroll, who had gotten the Zodiac case in 2000, had added considerably to the case by recovering three lost letters which had fallen into private hands and gotten them tested. "I work in Hollywood where *everyone* wears black," Jamie laughed, "but Kelly Carroll showed up looking like Al Pacino— black pants, black button-down shirt, and black blazer. He looked more Hollywood than Brad."

"We got to talking," Brad said, "and I asked, 'Did you ever see a composite profile of Zodiac?'"

Inspector Carroll had not seen one. Neither had Toschi and Armstrong. As for seeing Stine's shirt and the Zodiac letters, that would be possible only if the filmmakers gave the police advance notice which Brad had already done. "When we were sitting with Kelly Carroll," Jamie said. "He was telling us about DNA. He showed us the *Exorcist* letter with the palm print on it. He said he didn't know which letter they got the DNA from. "I completely understand the demand of current cases," Carroll told *Chronicle* reporter Charlie Goodyear, "but the Zodiac always stood to me as symbolic of SFDP's commitment not to give up on unsolved homicides." And now they had.

"Were there palm prints on other letters that were genuine Zodiac letters?" Jamie asked.

"Yes, there were," Carroll said. "Did we match the palm prints on the other letters to the palm prints on the *Exorcist* letter? I don't think we did. They got enough of a partial DNA signature to rule out somebody, but not enough to match somebody." He was cautious. He told them he was "not eager to propagate the myths and misinformation on the internet." Neither were they. Nor was Fincher.

"If they had one partial DNA profile from one stamp, four out of nine marks," Brad said. "I don't know how significant that is, certainly not nearly as significant as it would be if they had more than one sample on more than one letter. If they found matching DNA partial or a full DNA profile that they were able to develop on more than one letter they wouldn't have kept it a secret." Right now that was another mystery.

"Thirty years later," Fincher said of the partial DNA fingerprint, "I don't put a lot of trust in the DNA studies these fucking tabloid television shows are doing, all this nonsense. I don't believe 160 IQ Leigh Allen would do such a thing as lick a stamp." Even in the 1970s saliva spoke volumes through a simple ABO-PGM test. More worrisome was the chain of evidence. Which letters had been tested and who had had them all this time and where? Most importantly, were the letters tested actually from Zodiac?

That night, Brad, Jamie, and Amber arrived at the Ferry Building Terminus. They entered through a long continuous double front arcade bounded on the northeast by odd-numbered state-owned sheds and on the south by even-numbered private piers. Boxcars were rocking in the rising wind on spurs of the Belt Railroad. The 240-foot-tall Neoclassical clock tower above showed 7:30 PM, as they followed a rear walkway to the Slanted Door restaurant and met Bawarts inside. Everyone was led to a huge round table in the center of the room. Bawart sat down at Amber's left. "I put my wife Jan on my bad ear side," he said impishly, then took a sip of hot green tea flavored with jasmine and lychee flowers. Mike Billington joined them. Five minutes later, Mark Arneson, the detective hired by Phoenix Pictures, arrived and sat down to Brad's left. Arneson was muscular and with his bare hands could probably twist horseshoes into knots and the horse along with them. He also had an unusual way of speaking. As he answered Brad's many questions, he was alternately humorous, grim, cynical, and cryptic. "Maybe I did and maybe I didn't," was his typical response. Arneson had not only been locating people, but speaking to them. Brad furrowed his brow at this information. "Speaking to them?" That was troubling. Arneson could be abrasive in his zeal. On the plus side, nothing was going to stop him from finding Mike Mageau who had seen Zodiac without his hood. If Fincher could put Mageau on camera he would have more than a movie; he might have a solution. Mageau had by this time identified Allen to Bawart as the man who shot him at Blue Rock Springs. Fincher wanted to hear that for himself.

Jamie and Amber excused themselves to have a smoke. They stepped onto the pier overlooking the glitter of the Bay Bridge. In the night, ferry boats were battling choppy waves and backwash was spilling coldly onto the walkway. Jamie broke open a pack and lit up. George Bawart, who had trailed behind, leaned in to inhale any residual smoke before it was whipped away. A wave swept up to his feet. All three listened to the *chug chug* of diesels and call of klaxons in the darkness until Amber looked through the big lit window and saw that dinner was being served. Famished, they returned at full gallop to a table groaning under a couple dozen plates. What a menu! At each place setting was lemon grass tofu and sugar snap peas with *maitake* mushrooms. There was green papaya salad, crispy Imperial rolls with shrimp, glass noodles, and barbecued Niman Ranch pork spareribs with honey-hoisin sauce.

Against the crash of waves outside, the conversation was lively and warm, though they were all companions on a grim mission. They ate their fill and were content for the first time in days. Finally, the tower clock above struck eleven and everyone pushed back their chairs to go the, . George and Jan left to cross the Bay Bridge, and Jamie and Amber climbed into their rented Infiniti QX-56.

"When Amber and I drove back to LA, with the confidential police VHS tapes from George Bawart," Jamie said, "I was terrified that we would drive over a cliff and lose those irreplaceable documents."

Jamie had to live long enough for Fincher to see them.

CHAPTER NINE

JAMIE'S CLUE AND BRAD'S TOO

BY SUNDAY AFTERNOON, JULY 18, Jamie was home again and sitting cross-legged on his beige living room carpet. He rubbed his back, still aching from the six-hour drive back from San Francisco. He rested his chin in one hand, tugged at his rally goatee, and thought. There was so much material to take in. Where to start? He dared not miss anything important. Bawart's borrowed material was strewn before him like so much pirate booty. "Honestly," he recalled, "it was one of those situations where I was completely alone and actually sorting through stuff for Brad to come over and pick up."

Patiently, Jamie worked his way through another pile, but from time to time had to stretch and ease his muscles. He could sit cross-legged and put his head on the floor. "All that tennis I played as a kid has made me ridiculously stretchy," he said. Jamie, facing toward the French doors, gazed dreamily into the backyard. The kitchen, a self-enclosed room, was to his right as was the table where he and Brad had spent so many productive and unproductive hours trying to crack the case. The day waned. Jamie yawned, got up and turned on the lights. "I can't do this on so little sleep," he complained.

One hour melted into another. The house was silent because even music was distracting to him. In the background he heard the pleasant *burble* of two fish tanks. A flash of tan, brown, and white, proceeded by a tiny black nose, scurried across the beige carpet into the circle of light. As Jamie was reminding himself that their little dog, Sophie, needed a trim, she scattered the carefully organized pages as she chased her white ball. "Sophie El Diablo Vanderbilt!" Jamie cried. He got up and rearranged and re-stacked the pages. He'd been drinking ice water since morning, but around midnight took a sip of his only rum and coke of the day. Jamie lifted a page as if it was heavy and made a light checkmark in the corner so he would not read it again, though he knew he would. In the shadows he could barely make out his faint pencil marks. Though he was handling mere copies of copies, he was loath to damage the pages in any way.

Underneath the next page was a drawing on wide-lined paper such as a student might use. He tried to focus on it. He rubbed his eyes. His head was throbbing. He took another look. In the center of the page was a kidney-shaped outline. At the top was the letter N and at the bottom of the shape was an S. He got it then. It was a map someone had drawn in a reedy and consistent line. In the center of the free-form shape was the word, Berryessa. It was a map of Lake Berryessa and it was signed.

"This can't be what I think it is because that would be too crazy," he told himself. "There's no way this page has been sitting in a box of Vallejo files and nobody has picked up on it." He held the drawing up to the lamp and asked himself, Is this Bill Armstrong's hand drawn map of Lake Berryessa? What else could it be? But, Jamie had discovered the map among prime suspect Leigh Allen's papers. That made no sense to him.

"It occurred to me that Allen could have drawn it, but for a good five-to-ten seconds I tried to talk myself out of the fact that he could have done this. Leigh doodles on his papers from time to time. So, I'm looking at it and I realize that his name is in the right hand top corner: 'Leigh Allen.' So I'm still thinking to myself, 'O.K., hold on, maybe Inspector Armstrong was thinking about Allen when he drew the map and jotted his name down.' The thing that did it for me was that if it was a crime scene map, why were there no markings where the bodies would be?" In the upper lefthand corner the artist had marked "Mt. St. Helena and Knoxville Road." Interesting—whoever had drawn the map had made a notation that Knoxville was a dirt road that becomes a "one lane asphalt" just before it reaches Lake Berryessa." Notes for an escape route? There were initials on the map too, but they made no sense where they were placed. *M*, and *SF* (San Francisco?), and words, *Hotel*, and *Lo Rd*. Obviously, *N*, *E*, *W*, and *S*, were directions. Jamie sifted through everything again as he waited for Brad who had been too hyperactive to sleep to drive over and lift a few of the leaden pages with him. He saw the lights of a car entering his driveway. He hurried to the door and let Brad in.

"Look," Brad said, kneeling on the rug, as he studied Jamie's discovery. "Leigh Allen has a little note on the map that reads, 'Ask about permanently fixing slides' (amber resin etc)' and it matches his other handwriting exemplars from class notes he took." Brad knew that Allen was good with a steel-tipped arrow when he hunted chipmunks at Lake Berryessa for pets and to study. He also went fishing with his chum, Don Cheney, about one hundred yards from the murder site. The same day the students were stabbed, Allen told two coworkers he had been at Lake Berryessa that afternoon and later confirmed this in a letter from prison. Fincher would want to see that document.

As Brad and Jamie examined a folder marked "handwriting samples," they learned Allen often drew cartoons. One, a crude handmade greeting card to his mother, said: "Happy Muther's Day: This is hoping your Muther's Day will be a day to remember. And this little poem is especially for you: Roses are 'Red' Violets are 'Blue,' [then a black line] (That part had been censored!) So we'll just say—Fuck You! May your vices be as hard + long lasting as this one."

Brad reread the last line: "as hard + long lasting as this one." A plus (+) sign for the word *and* was unusual. The second cartoon depicted a boss with a bullwhip shaking a ruler at a sweating little man playing with a yoyo. "Eegads, late again!" the boss is saying. A third, captioned "Little Al," showed a downhill snow skier looking over his shoulder at a billboard advertising "Visit Florida." When Zodiac mailed three altered greeting cards to the *Chronicle* on November 8, 1969, April 28, 1969, and October 27, 1970, he had shown artistic talent by rearranging one of the dancing skeletons on his threatening card to Avery and given it a rollicking, animated expression. Whoever Zodiac was, he was a cartoonist who perfectly aligned his pages of code using a T-square, lined paper, triangle, and a light table—the tools of an artist, student, or architect.

Brad and Jamie rose from the rug, massaging the base of their necks, and went into the kitchen. They usually worked in the little nook which adjoins the living room so Amber could watch TV undisturbed, but tonight she had long been asleep. Like Fincher, they wanted to make *Zodiac* into one of those "great, long classic movies." Their shoulders slumped. The seriousness of the case had sunk in and would not lift until they were done. The cries of a beaten child on audiotape were still ringing in their ears. They wondered how many more there could be.

As Brad went through Bawart's massive file of discarded copies, he came across a traffic ticket mixed in with samples of Allen's hand printing. "It is not a particularly good example [of his printing]," he said, "but I guess the police kept it because his signature is on it." He squinted in the subdued light and made out the number, "Ticket No. D929636, Section 2210." The traffic officer had listed Allen as a student at Sonoma State and his vehicle License number as "WDB 151, 1957 Volkswagen black." As Brad read, he observed that at Broadway and Columbus, at 1:35 PM, on March 13, 1971, Leigh Allen had been ticketed for an illegal left turn at Columbus and Broadway in San Francisco's North Beach section. Brad studied the ticket. He knew it meant something, but couldn't figure out what. Since it was so late, he decided to take an armload of documents back to his lonely apartment for a second sort-through. As he drove, Brad glanced at the stat of the parking ticket on the seat next to him. It was practically worthless as a handwriting exemplar. Once he got home, he threw himself onto his living room rug as Jamie had, arranged the papers, and got to work. Around 4:00 AM, he tucked the ticket into a binder he had just created and decided to sleep on it. Instead, he dreamed about finding Mageau, the Zodiac victim who did not want to be found. Wherever he was, Brad knew, suffering on the streets or in an alley somewhere, screams must be ringing in his ears too.

On Monday evening, Brad returned to Jamie's home to further organize the material. They lugged the box into the kitchen, arranged the contents on the table, and began plowing through it once more. First, they went through the way Bawart had the files organized. "Well, George didn't really do the organization," Jamie said. Much of what Bawart had given them was in envelopes with contents that did not always match up to how they were catalogued. "A secretary at the VPD who had been organizing his files had done that. Frankly, it was a little haphazard. We have to figure out what page goes with what. What's this here? It looks like a class schedule for Leigh from this year. Then, what's this?" When they were done Brad created another organized binder.

"When Brad needs to get his mind around things," Jamie said, "usually a binder is made which he then gives to David Fincher."

At this point, everyone had a huge binder which Brad called "the Murder Book." Several hours later, Brad left to prepare the final details for their meeting with the brother and sister-in-law, one of the most important in their search for emotional truth. Brad was in the midst of figuring which questions to ask when the answer to the ticket enigma suddenly came to him. It wasn't the handwriting or the location on the ticket that had significance. No, it was none of those. It was the date.

Brad thumbed through his binder and took out a page. That day, "March 13, 1971," was the first time a Zodiac letter had been mailed from a zip code *outside* San Francisco, the Pleasanton zip code. Now, the question was, "Why?" Leigh's father, Ethan Allen, had been admitted to a hospital in that zip code. While visiting his father, Leigh may have mailed the letter. Sadly, his father died three days after.

On Friday, July 23, Brad was on the phone telling a director he wouldn't be able to see him.

"How about Monday?" the director asked.

"Jamie and I have to go into a lunch meeting on Monday."

"Who are you having lunch with?"

"David Fincher."

"Oh, David Fincher—" the director said, "he dates a lot, but doesn't do much fucking."

Fincher had committed to many projects in the past, but moved on from them for various reasons. The deep and sensitive artist in him compelled him to look for a reason to walk away. "Of course, David Fincher really wants to make a lot of films," Jamie explained, "but he wants to make them on his own terms. I think that he sometimes is at first unwilling to do anything unless it's his way completely; secondly, he looks at it and says, 'I know I'm going to be judged for this and if I feel like there's no way to control it I'd rather opt out of it.' That's what's tricky. We've come to him in a really interesting time. He's getting to the point where he knows he needs to make another movie. Not for any commercial reasons, but just because he's desperate to go shoot a movie. Like The Beatles, he loves the act. My dime store analysis of him is this: The Beatles in their prime put out two albums a year. I mean two albums a year! Nobody does that. Why? Because they love the act of making music." Jamie indicated a film director like James Cameron who was just now maybe going to make his first film since 1997s *Titanic*. By the time his movie comes out, if he starts shooting this year, it will be nine years since his last movie. It begged the question, "Why?" He didn't feel like he could top himself. With certain artistic people there is the need to be bigger and better. Tod Browning, embittered director of such classics as *Dracula* and *Freaks*, gave up filmmaking and meant it. "When I quit a thing," Browning said, "I quit. I wouldn't walk across the street to see another movie."

"One of the things I like about David just as a person and hopefully he likes about me," Jamie continued, "is he doesn't get his self-confidence or his life out of Hollywood and his place on the totem pole. He's got a kid. He's got his friends. He has a life outside of all of that. He's a regular guy. For God's sake, he says, 'Thank you' to waiters! David's considered one of the touchiest and weirdest directors by executives, but as a writer I consider him the nicest and most normal of them all. But maybe the same thing that is wrong with him is wrong with me. Everyone who ends up being artistic either has a problematic family life, or at least imagines they did."

The next day, Brad swung by Beverly Hills to see Arnie Messer's son, Scott, with whom Fincher had entrusted the Leigh Allen police interrogation tape. His job was to transfer it onto a permanent digital DVD format at Sony. Though D-1 transfers cost around seven hundred dollars, they never diminish in quality and last virtually forever. "Have you ever seen a D-1 cassette before?" Scott asked.

Brad shook his head.

"It's so huge it comes with its own briefcase."

ON MONDAY, JAMIE AND Brad, the heavy valise under his arm, arrived at Fincher's office. They ordered food in. "I had the club sandwich—what else?" Brad recalled. They ate, then examined the D-1 transfer inside the case.

"It's the size of a seat cushion!" Jamie said. "It looks like a prop from *Honey, I Shrunk the Kids*." They moved to the conference area which was equipped with Fincher's sophisticated AV equipment to watch the D-1. "When you watch the interrogation tape that we have you are kind of slowly gauging the amoeba," Fincher said thoughtfully. "I thought it was very effective. The interesting thing about him is that he's a guy who seems to be at turns and at moments aware of the fact that he's not as smart as he thought he was. And he gets upset. What he does (which is interesting in that most people speed up) is start going slower, cause what he realizes is you have to give yourself time to get three more moves ahead. It is obvious that they are trying to coerce him into a polygraph examination." Captain Conway later assured them that it wouldn't have mattered. "Arthur Leigh Allen," he said, "would have passed that polygraph test [Psychopathic individuals or people on drugs can pass lie tests]. The difference between him and other sociopaths is that Allen is super-intelligent. Now, the personality type that allows for the kind of complete denial of their actions to exist is the classic sociopath."

After they had fully analyzed the tape, Fincher buzzed his assistant. "We need a locked room somewhere in this office," he told him, "no heat in there, very little air conditioning, just to preserve everything and nobody else can get in to the tape but me. And I want no markings on it." After that, their short working lunch became a fast-paced, "Amazing meeting" that went from 1:30 PM, until 6:45 PM, when Fincher sent Allen's reel-to-reel audio tapes to a sound guy up north for further study. One of the director's techniques for sleuthing was to hire experts to do the analysis. David is on the Zodiac case, Jamie thought as he left, and there was no shaking him from the trail. But would he be on the *Zodiac* movie? "My feeling is that David definitely wants to do this movie." He scratched his *Zodiac* goatee and considered the situation. "If it was a perfect world for him, we would wait for him as long as it took him to get to it. We're tied to him until Paramount says 'yea' or 'nay' on his other project which is gonna happen within the next five or six weeks. If they say 'yea,' he's contractually obligated to go off and do that film. If they say 'nay,' he's making *Zodiac*."

On Tuesday, Brad Fischer got "really great news." Fincher was to set a firm date to go up and see the brother and sister-in-law. That would probably be in a week or so. Then, he practically tripped over another snag in the schedule that he had not anticipated. "Baron von

Vandypants," he complained, "is heading off to Europe between August 4 to August 25, so a follow-up meeting with the family will have to be planned for late August or early September when Jamie can be there too." Perhaps this was for the best, he thought. By then, Fincher would know about his option and have finished up everything he had to do with *Benjamin Button*. All the director would have to do was wait for the special effects tests to come back from the lab before he showed them to Paramount.

Unbelievably, another step backwards—the visual effects took longer than expected—a long time to come back, and a longer time to be approved. *Button*, the story of a man who ages backwards, called for unprecedented visual effects which Fincher not only had to specifically create, but test to make certain they worked, and see how cost effective they were. The visual effects shots he needs for aging alone will cost $15 million before he shoots a single frame. "Each time some new effects technological innovation comes along," Brad pointed out, "motion pictures become more about the spectacle than story and characters. *Jaws* and the *Star Wars* and the *Indiana Jones* movies altered the film industry. Before then they had films for kids, adults, couples—after *Jaws* came out, everybody wanted to see the Big Event movie." He slumped in chair. This had been the longest three months of his life. "David's giving such special effects a huge budget number," he told Jamie, "I suspect that will make them say, 'no,' at least at this time. The *Button* budget doesn't even have casting yet. If David gets Tom Cruise for the movie the cost could be astronomical."

"From what I understand," Jamie replied. "If he got me to star in it, it would be astronomical."

"A budget depends who the director is," Brad said. "It will take one guy half the number of days to shoot the same script." *Fight Club* had a schedule from June to December, two hundred and seventy scenes and thirty takes of each fight scene which was brutal on the actors. A director with a big movie realistically takes from full preproduction to final cut fifteen months. Fincher worked longer.

"With Hollywood budgets," Jamie explained, "money comes out of the amount of days you shoot for and the longer the script the more days you shoot for. My script clocks out to about two hours and forty minutes of screen time." His experience had been that Hollywood responds to good stories in a good way. "I remember when we first started talking about *Zodiac*, before the script was written, and I made the deal," he said. "People said that's like a *CBS Movie of the Week*, or an HBO movie at best. We said, 'No, it's not,' and went away and did the script and told the real story." Jamie couldn't imagine not shooting the bulk of the movie in San Francisco, though it was the most expensive city in the United States to shoot in.

"Let's say David delivers a budget for *Button* of $167 million," Brad figured. "If they say they will make it for that amount, he's got to go do it. That's the deal. I don't know what number he's going to deliver to them, but I do know it's going to be a lot higher than what they want. They want it at $125 million." When Jamie heard this, he said, "With David it's always good news/bad news. Good news for us and bad news for them because he's the kind of guy who gets the best people and says, 'How much is it going to cost to do this effect and shoot this camera and for this amount of time,' and he goes back and says, 'This is how much it's going to cost.' The studio says, 'Can you do it for cheaper?' He says, 'Well, I'm not going to do it for cheaper because I'm going to work with the best people and make the best movie. The ball's in your court.'"

When Fincher gave them the number for *Button*, he was going to say, "Seventy-two hours, Let me know." Right now, everything was going to depend on lead actor Jake Gyllenhaal's schedule more than Fincher's.

The reason this has taken so long," Brad explained, "is because we like David for this film so much we can't move off of him. We could have very easily a couple of months ago moved on and been farther along in the process. We want to make sure it's the right guy doing it. We're coming to a point where it's going to be him or it's not going to be him. We just want to get going. As for the script, I think it's mostly taking a lot of the stuff that's in *Zodiac Unmasked* and expanding the context of the original *Zodiac* book." Fincher wasn't interested in the back story of any of the *Zodiac* characters. He just wanted to know what each did regarding the investigation.

To Jamie, as a writer in Hollywood, the interesting thing was that the amount of work on a script is always different depending on who the director is. If it's Fincher there are certain things he would want done, but that another director would not want to change. He'll want other things changed. "There will always be more work to be done on the script," Jamie said, "but that's something I would be doing concurrently with preproduction."

At 1:00 PM, on Wednesday, July 26, they met Fincher for lunch to try and figure out what they could do on *Zodiac* while he was considering this other film.

"The script keeps getting bigger," he said.

"How big is it right now?" Brad asked.

"Two hundred and forty pages."

"Two hundred and forty pages? How the hell are you going to . . ."

Fincher cut Brad off and said, "How am I going to stuff sixty pounds of shit into a three pound bag? I don't know."

"I'm assuming David was exaggerating," Brad said. "He's got this two hundred and forty number that he likes a lot. He also thinks *Zodiac* should run two hours and forty minutes, the length of his benchmark film, *All The President's Men*."

"It's a script almost like that," Jamie admitted (he had a recent version at 190 pages) "where you have three or four central characters who take up almost all the screen time, but there is the background at the newspaper and the Hall of Justice. The amazing thing about *All The President's Men* is that it is half a movie. It just ends in the middle. William Goldman, who wrote the movie, said he wouldn't have done it the same way today because everybody knows that Woodward and Bernstein eventually took down Nixon. He wanted to end the movie with something surprising so he ends it with them messing up, knowing that the audience is going to fill in the blanks."

If Fincher went elsewhere in September, did they have a backup director? They had been talking to Joe Carnahan the most. Carnahan had won at Sundance for his film, *Narc*.

"When I first met Joe at a party at Las Palmas after this whole thing happened with David, he put me in a headlock," Brad said. "He turns to his sister and says, 'These are the guys who took *Zodiac* from us.'" Carnahan had just fallen out of *Mission Impossible 3*. Since he and Jamie had the same agent at Endeavor, Jamie had asked her to talk to him about *Zodiac*. She hadn't yet, but said, "Listen, he loves the book." Carnahan had been in competition with Phoenix and five other bidders for the option to *Zodiac*.

"And he definitely has a copy of the script," Jamie said. When Medavoy had an annual Golden Globes party, Brad introduced Jamie to Carnahan. "This big, big guy with a shaved head," Jamie said, "not the kind of guy you want to run into in a dark alley, sees me and Brad, spreads his arms and puts me in a bear hug and goes, 'You motherfucker!' But a really nice guy."

"Joe also pointed out that he'd be cheaper," Brad said.

"There's very, very serious interest if David doesn't work out," Jamie said. "We're working hard, but it's all hurry up and wait. Brad and I are going to walk to Hell and back to get this thing done. We could have done this faster if this was going to be a cheaper 'knock-offy' movie. We're not going to let that happen."

"We'd rather wait longer and do it right," Brad said. "Everyone who's read the script says this is an Academy Award film." Maybe that's why Brad's phone had been ringing all day. Gyllenhaal's agent had called him that morning. Jake was still very eager to do the movie.

On Wednesday, August 25, at 7:30 PM, Jamie returned from his two and a half week long vacation with Amber. First, he'd been to see his parents in Connecticut, then gone to London, Paris, and the South of France to attend the wedding of one of his best friends in high school. "Being in a town next to Monaco," Jamie said, "I felt very James Bondish. Amber and I have this tradition that any place we go we find the world's tackiest ashtray with the region written on it." This time they brought home a tin ashtray with a stamped impression of the Eiffel Tower, some French jellies, and a sketch of the Arc de Triomphe that Amber picked out from a Montmartre sidewalk vendor. He still wore the goatee he had vowed not to shave until *Zodiac* was greenlit. A week earlier, Brad's assistant, Diego, had left for a job at William Morris. He was replaced by John who was also from William Morris.

"I was having some drinks with some of the other assistants," John said, "and somebody said Jamie Vanderbilt's name. I said, 'Oh, that's my boy. He's writing some projects for us.' One of the other assistants goes, 'Oh, no, no, no, that's my boy! He's writing projects for us.' Somebody else goes, 'No, no, no, Jamie's our boy. He's writing for us.' Jamie's writing for everybody! The guy is a hit. But I knew him just by name and that he's writing *Zodiac*.

"The first time I saw Jamie, he came to the office and I didn't know he was going to be there. I was waiting in the hallway and this guy gets off the elevator. He's wearing the regular black leather jacket, jeans, kind of has his hair 'grunged,' sort of unassuming, just looking around, looking at the poster. While I'm waiting for Jamie Vanderbilt, I lean over and say, 'Can I help you find something?' 'Nah, I'm Jamie Vanderbilt.' 'Oh! I'm John and I'm waiting for you. Right this way!' I've never seen anybody more unassuming." Jamie liked John too, "But, I gotta be honest with you," Jamie said. "Brad is a tough boss. I try to be the funny guy who calls on the phone to John. I try to make him laugh and we make fun of Brad a little. He's such a smart executive. In fact, it's a good mentorship."

On Monday, Mike Medavoy and Brad had lunch with Michael Mann at 1:00 PM. A week earlier, his Tom Cruise/Jamie Foxx thriller *Collateral* had come in at No. 1. Mann, a quiet, introspective man, was coy, but obviously interested in *Zodiac*. "You'll see me again," he said as he left. Fincher's Bay Area visit to see Bawart was now set for September 10 or September 11. On Thursday, August 26, two days before his birthday, Fincher met with Paramount Chief Sherry Lansing and Alan Horn on the *Benjamin Button* project. Friday, he conferred with Donald DeLine, Lansing's head of production, and on Monday spoke with Jeff Robinov, Warner's head of production. "Robinov is very soft spoken, very smart," Brad said. "A lot of studio heads have more of a business mentality about things, but Robinov, a former agent, is very good creatively and very good with talent." Friday, Fincher presented the visual effects and budget to Paramount for *Benjamin Button* which will be extraordinarily expensive. It was back to more waiting. The answer came on Thursday, September 9.

"It seems that *Benjamin Button* has gone the way of the pelican," Brad said as he announced the news. "I'm not sure exactly what that means, but it's at least postponed. It looks like we've got David Fincher!"

"We just left a meeting with him to get everyone back on the same page, 're-strategize,' and figure out the next step," Jamie added breathlessly. "David looks very happy and eager to start moving on *Zodiac*." On the business side they still had to figure out which studio will end up doing the movie."

"We're definitely a big step closer to making it," Brad noted. "Joe

Carnahan and Michael Mann are . . ."

"Definitely out of the picture," Jamie interjected. "We were definitely interested in them. Ridley Scott was definitely someone that was discussed."

"Ridley's agents were chasing us," Brad added. "The fact is we were chased by many different directors or their representatives, but for Jamie, Mike, and me, there was really one guy for this movie—David Fincher. Well, for the rest of the day I'm going to field a lot of phone calls."

"And I'm going to field a lot of phone calls—from Brad," Jamie said.

And both would be talking to Fincher.

CHAPTER TEN

GUN PLAY

ON THIS BRIGHT MORNING, Brad was more energized than usual.

"David is really pumped up and excited," he said, circling his desk, phone tucked under his chin. "We're going to see George Bawart in Vallejo tomorrow and meet with the brother and sister-in-law the next day. They'll be coming to see us in San Francisco at the Clift." The meeting was to be an exploration of emotional truth. Brad carefully packed the hand drawn map Jamie had discovered in the dead of night. He planned on springing it on George without any warning. After all, the veteran detective had given them enough shocks for a lifetime.

Friday morning, David, Brad, and Jamie arrived at LAX wearing jeans and cargo pants, a limited but functional wardrobe for their Bay Area visit. Jamie had nervously agreed to fly. "I never had a fear of flying as a kid," he said. "I developed it as an adult. I now have a very nice prescription for it. The problem of flying to San Francisco is it's not like flying across the country, because if I fly across the country I can take a full Klonopin tablet, an anti-anxiety pill. Basically, it's a Xanax. You can't really do that for the short flight because you'll be zoned out all day. I took a third of one on the way out to San Francisco. It wasn't enough so I ended up sort of white knuckling the whole way."

From SFO, Brad, Jamie, and Fincher drove across the Bay Bridge to Vacaville to see Bawart. The detective greeted them warmly at the door and ushered them inside. Behind the door was a varnished oak barrel filled with umbrellas. Left of that was the living room. They entered and took chairs around George's reliable chrome-plated barber's chair. Bawart kicked out the footrest, sat down and tilted the chair back for a pleasant hour of jousting with Fincher over ballistics.

"David, I only met him this one time," Bawart later recalled of their first meeting, "didn't know much about him, but he was very pleasant. The thing about it is, I've dealt with the media many times on many cases, and when they want something from you they can be real nice, when they don't want something write you off like you are some kind of nobody. I didn't get that impression of these folks at all. If you say something that's contrary to what their thoughts are like—for example, David was here and we were discussing ballistics."

"You know," Fincher began, "if you're really going to plan a killing," he said, "you probably wouldn't use a .22. You'd use a bigger caliber like a .38."

"You know," Bawart said, "I disagree with you. So many killers use .22s because the ballistics aren't there. They're cheap guns and you get rid of it and you're not throwing away a five hundred dollar gun, you're throwing away a fifty dollar piece of junk." Then, I thought to myself: Oh, no, this is a high and mighty director I've disagreed with and all of a sudden he's going to say, "Who's this guy?" When I saw that Fincher was receptive I changed my mind. This guy is pretty cool. He doesn't seem to have any preconceived notions when he is talking to somebody who has actually done the work.

"A .22 is like playtime," Fincher continued, "unless you're working for the Chicago mob and you are going to get right behind the ear. With a .22 you are asking for trouble. People have been shot in the face with .38s and gotten up and testified. If you are an evil genius, and you're going to fire through a 1967 Corvair, that's a lot of glass and metal and a very small round. If you add a .22-caliber at Lake Herman Road to the docket of Leigh Allen, then you're not talking about evil genius, you're talking about quick study. I get the whole reload thing and I understand having thirteen rounds and all that stuff makes sense. But if you can get a 9-mm Browning it just seems to me, if your whole thing is to get away with the shooting, and you've thought about it in advance, it's not too quick."

"What you have is probably a pretty good theory," Bawart said, "but the fact is if you are really smart and you're going to commit this kind of homicide—.22s you can dump a lot easier and .22s pack a potent round."

"A .22 through a window?"

"We had two male cops killed with a .22 short fired out of a pickup box derringer in 1966."

"My point is," Fincher said, "if I know I'm going out to look for stragglers, I'm looking for the slowest sheep in the flock who just happen to be on the outskirts of humanity. No one is going to hear it. I want as much stopping power as possible because I'm going to want as much lead time as is possible. Yeah, I want thirteen or fifteen rounds at my disposal, but I won't have to use fifteen rounds. And we're talking about cars in the mid-sixties. You're talking about a .22 that isn't going ninety degrees into a Corvair with a curved windshield. You're talking about a lot of deflection and room for error. That a .22 is used is inconsistent with the evil genius. It's a gut thing. Maybe he is that smart, but if he has a 9-mm (which we know he has) you bring the 9-mm cause you get as many rounds."

Fincher knew that getting different types of people with different eyes looking at a problem makes you see it in a different way. He asked Bawart a crucial question.

"Do you think Zodiac was Leigh Allen?" he asked.

"Oh, hell yeah!" Bawart said without missing a beat. His eyes lit up. The barber chair kicked up. "I'm 95 to 99% sure he did it. There are so many coincidences. I think Leigh was very lucky as we're just discovering."

"Did you know that Arthur Leigh Allen got a traffic ticket in San Francisco on March 13, 1971?" Brad asked.

"Really?" Bawart said. "Arthur Leigh Allen got a ticket in San Francisco on the day one of the Zodiac letters was mailed?"

"You know who we got the ticket from?" Brad said.

"No, who?"

"You."

"No kidding! I don't think anybody put that in the report. I probably looked at this thing, didn't look at the date and thought, 'Oh, there's an old ticket.' And this is an SFPD ticket."

Brad had tried to make out the name of the officer who had issued the ticket, but it was an indecipherable scrawl. "It looks to me," he continued, "as if Zodiac had been in the habit of dropping his letters in San Francisco and let's say that Leigh Allen is Zodiac, he's got his letter with him and he's driving around San Francisco in his VW and he's going to mail it from a particular box. Then, he gets pulled over and ticketed for making an illegal left turn at Columbus and Broadway [at Big Al's sign], a heavily trafficked tourist area. Now that a record exists of him being in San Francisco in that area at 1:35 PM, on March 13, 1971, maybe he's thinking, 'I'll drive a couple of counties over and mail the letter from there where there is no record of my being.'"

Fincher discussed the notion that up to that date, Zodiac had mailed all of his letters (except four which had no postmarks) from a San Francisco mailbox. The day Leigh Allen was ticketed, Zodiac broke his pattern and mailed a letter from Pleasanton 94566 where Leigh's critically ill father, Ethan Allen, lay dying in a hospital. Sadly, the father would succumb three days later.

Solemnly, Brad thumbed through his binder until he came to their second find.

"George," he said, "did you see this hand drawn map that Allen made of Lake Berryessa and signed?"

George took Allen's map from Brad and studied it. On the right side of the map was an elongated kidney-shape which Leigh Allen had labeled "Berryessa." He had even written "north," "east," "south," and "west" on its perimeters. Starting at the bottom, George slowly traced what had to be Knoxville Road from south to north. Knoxville Road was marked with abbreviations and he needed to know what those meant. He went to a drawer and fished out the printed map he had used the last time he was at Lake Berryessa, and returning to his barber chair, compared it to Allen's hand drawn map. He started at the first word, "Hotel." He was not as knowledgeable as Captain Narlow, but as far as he could tell, "Hotel" stood for Steele Park Resort. The next abbreviation was "*S F.*" That was easier. "This stands for Spanish Flat Resort," Bawart said. Next, he moved his finger upward until he came to "*M.*" "That would be Monticello," he said. He went higher, his finger moving slowly until he came to "Putah Resort."

"That's a park," he said. Higher up Knoxville Road was marked "asphalt," and then higher north still, "dirt." He continued upward following the contour of the lake.

"This is showing a continuation of the road," George said. Suddenly, his face grew ashen. "This is right where Narlow and I are going to take you," he said. His voice had grown husky. "This is a windy mother that ends up at Mount St. Helena." He paused and stared into space. "I have never seen this map. What did he draw this for?"

"Just drew it for himself," Brad said. "The map says something about fixing permanent slides, amber, resin. Maybe, he was planning on trapping chipmunks there."

Or marking escape routes, Bawart thought. He reconsidered the notations—"dirt road," "asphalt road," "one lane road," and an unmarked road that would take him west from the crime scene. At an intersection with Knoxville and another road, Pope Canyon Road, were three triangles filled in with black ink. They were turned on their sides.

"This is where Leigh Allen used to take Don Cheney," Brad said.

George's brow furrowed. He adjusted his glasses and gripped the arms of the barber chair. It was incomprehensible, he thought. Lake Berryessa, the largest lake in Napa County, is three miles wide with approximately 165 miles of shoreline. Yet on Allen's signed, homemade map, he had marked a specific site with a line and three black triangles. This could not be a coincidence.

"This is where the murder took place," Bawart said after a minute. "Perhaps his original intention was to stab the three college women. Until now I had been 95% sure we had the right man. Now I'm 100% sure."

And the killer had even signed his map.

The Compass Rose on the real map was a crossed-circle.

About 5:30 PM, the three filmmakers thanked Bawart for a lively discussion. They had all learned a lot but were exhausted. They still had a lot to do. As long as there was daylight left, they decided to take a stab at locating the Lake Herman Road murder site. In the darkness, the empty fields were unsettling as they drove the long curving road. Around one bend, they made out the silhouette of an iron gate and gravel area and beyond that the gray sweep of Lake Herman. When it is dark on Lake Herman Road, it is pitch-black. Headlights from an oncoming car on such a road would be blinding. Unnerved, they decided to come back in the daylight. Turning on the gravel inlet, they

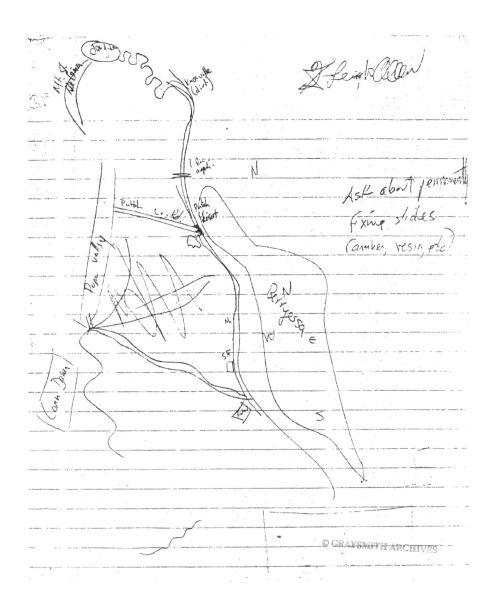

Arthur Leigh Allen's hand drawn map of Lake Berryessa.
(*Courtesy of the author's collection*)

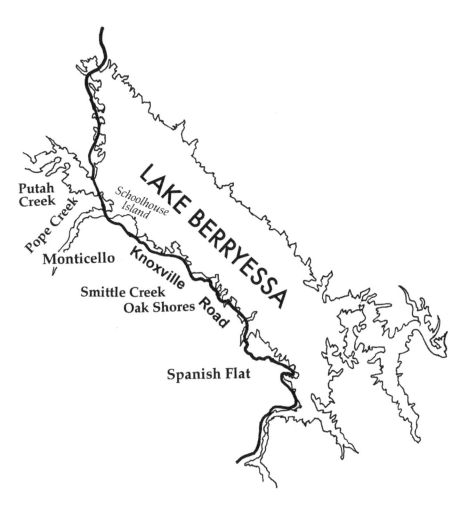

Accurate map of Lake Berryessa.
(*Illustrated by the author*)

hurried back the way they had come. On the way they saw no other cars which underscored Lake Herman Road's solitariness.

That evening, in preparation for the morning meeting, Fincher went over Toschi's earlier remarks about the brother and sister-in-law so he would know what questions to ask. "You spoke to Leigh Allen's brother in 1971 and '72," Fincher had asked Toschi in mid-January. "I'm trying to imagine the kind of concern that I would have if I felt in his situation. When a sibling calls the police because they believe that this person is a danger to society or a danger to themselves, it's such a big deal."

"Very, very difficult," Toschi had replied. This was one of the most heartbreaking cases he had ever encountered.

"So would you characterize the brother as beyond sadness?"

"As any brother would be. He was frustrated and he was concerned that his brother was still killing," Toschi had replied. "He's disturbed by the possibility."

"Tell me about the brother," Fincher had asked him.

Toschi recalled trying to size the brother up during their first conversation and finding him to be "very, very sincere, a very decent person." He'd discussed the problem and thought about it. Toschi had heard that in his voice. That's why Toschi asked him, "Can you talk to us now. Tomorrow might be too late. Somebody's going to drop a dime." The brother agreed. "Oh, my God," Toschi told his partner, Bill Armstrong, after he hung up, "this is our chance!" They jumped on what sounded like a major, major breakthrough right away. But the brother's dissatisfaction with the Vallejo police had put the SFPD in a difficult situation. Sergeant Jack Mulanax, the Vallejo officer on the case, kept telling Toschi, "I checked this out, I checked that out," and this annoyed the brother who must have thought, "But you haven't gone all the way—you may have done steps eight and nine, but you didn't go to ten." Toschi and Armstrong would have to go into VPD's backyard again to interview the brother and his wife together. Mulanax thought Leigh Allen was "good, a good suspect," but had done as much as he could. "I talked to the brother," he told Toschi as if being insulted.

"Oh, my God," Toschi had told him. "This is a courtesy call."

No matter what any other jurisdiction had done, the murders had been dropped in San Francisco's lap. They couldn't walk away. Too much was at stake. On August 4, 1971, Toschi and Mulanax questioned the sister-in-law, who earlier had attempted to induce the suspect's boss to report that Leigh needed to be gotten off the streets and into an institution. Toschi and Armstrong had listed the conversation in their police report.

"The brother and sister-in-law have seen this cipher," Fincher had told Toschi. "They've seen him with his weird collection, dead chipmunks and squirrels, keeping small animals organs in the freezer, living in the basement. They get together and the brother and Cheney are better friends than Leigh and Cheney. And Sandy Panzarella and Cheney and the brother are better friends than Sandy Panzarella and Leigh are. So they've discussed this and come up with a plan of action, sort of supporting each other in what must be a really difficult thing. So when you describe the brother's frustration about Vallejo not doing anything, is there an element of this that is also fear? Is there a fuse on this not only because no one will listen to him and that his brother might kill again, but partly he wants the police to tell him he's wrong?"

"Yes," Toschi said.

"We have two outbursts from Leigh Allen," Fincher continued. "— one when he's called on the carpet for touching children. He says, 'I did it. I did it! I can't help myself. I know I've got a problem!' and he loses that job then. It's spring, so he's three-quarters of the way through the year. No teacher, no matter how mediocre, loses their job three-quarters of the way through the school year. It doesn't happen." In September 1968, before the Lake Herman murders, Leigh was fired from Valley Springs, he told his friends it was just politics and moved back in with his parents. "But they suspect," Fincher continued, "there's something deeply, fucking wrong with him. He is a pedophile. His world crashes in around his fucking head. Now he's got it pretty much under control until the next time, when the cops come to get him in the basement and he's covered with squirrel shit and screaming. Now this guy knows he's being finked on by his brother and very likely some acquaintances."

"The sister-in-law really wanted to talk to big city detectives," Toschi recalled. "They just thought we'd listen a little more intently. And we did. But the brother never found anything to give me when he searched the basement. I never liked that a civilian had done the search for us. Later, I felt the case was solved when a search of Leigh Allen's basement lair uncovered bombs."

"Forget bombs," Fincher said. "This guy is a convicted felon. You've got five handguns."

"I was in disbelief," Toschi said. "Why didn't they arrest him?" He underscored each of the words in the air with his finger. "When they told me what they found during the 1991 search of his home I thought without question that was enough to make an arrest."

Guns and pipe bombs recovered from Arthur Leigh Allen's basement.
(*Photos by Vallejo Police Dept.*)

"Certainly enough to detain him and toss every fucking thing in his basement."

"If it was my house and I had unregistered handguns, I'm in real trouble, but with bombs in the basement we're past the point of no return."

"Why didn't they arrest him? Why didn't they tell him they were going to fuck him and send him back to Atascadero? Leave this guy's fat ass! It seems so unbelievable. Even with the circumstantial evidence you have to make a case; it's going to take a combined effort of all these different law enforcement agencies. Have you ever in your experience heard of anyone at a federal level say, 'You know what, it's O.K. to let him go, put a close on this.'"

"In all my years, NEVER!" Toschi had said angrily. "We were getting bits and pieces in, but trying to give everything we had out so somebody could make an arrest—anybody, any cop, any citizen who says, 'I know who the Zodiac is.' O.K., Let's arrest him." Fincher put his notes away and turned back to Brad and Jamie.

"It's really a tough thing to take in and accept certain things your brother has done," Brad said, "especially when your new fiancé is fearful about him. As a pedophile, he wreaked a certain amount of havoc on the family. It was not hard to imagine the difficulty of the situation then—a woman whose whole life is entangled in protecting children in a child social center comes into the family of a child molester. A fierce advocate for children's rights, she compels her husband to confront the school principal who fired Leigh for child molesting."

"She had disliked Leigh from the first night when his remarks about kids had set off alarm bells," Fincher said. He had gleaned this information from Armstrong's interview and from various VPD reports. "She didn't like Leigh. Leigh didn't like her. And the brother was caught in the middle." The director decided they would not cause more strife by bringing up the subject of Allen's molesting during tomorrow's interview. To them, it was so much in the past. The brother and sister-in-law had laid down strict ground rules for tomorrow morning's meeting. "Listen, we'll speak with you," they had said. "We just want our lawyer to be there."

"I'm sure they want the lawyer there to make it clear they want no money," Jamie said. "All we had to do was pay for the lawyer's time."

"And you are to repeat nothing that we say," they concluded. Agreed. Agreed, all around.

BRAD WOKE EARLY THE next morning, barely able to contain himself. On the darkest of dark days, the third anniversary of 9-11, he had granted Fincher's make-or-break wish. "We got the meeting!" he told Jamie, who was still not fully awake. "And you made fun of me for the letter, all those drafts, and calls, didn't you? And look what happened. Look what happened! We got the meeting." Brad had "shot-put the moon," as he had expressed it. George Bawart hadn't talked to the family at all during his Vallejo investigation, but now the three amateurs were about to. "I remember the brother's about my age," Bawart had told them. "I think he took out my sister one time or was friends with my sister. He was not a real outgoing guy, but always a nice guy, a standup guy." The morning conference was designed to provide Fincher with a more profound psychological perspective by looking the family members in the eye and seeing if he believed them.

For Brad, the meeting was about opening up a dialogue and seeing what type of people they were and letting them know what kind of people the filmmakers were, what they were after, and what their plan was. Every first meeting held so far in their search for truth had been tailored to prove that the filmmakers are good and honorable people who are not looking to exploit their pain or disrupt their lives to make a quick buck. "You know when you sit in a room," he said, "you get a sense of the person you're interviewing, whether they're credible or rather they're trying to lie to you." He didn't expect any of their witnesses to deliberately mislead, but after all it has been thirty years. "The scariest thing in the world is somebody calls you up and says, 'We're doing a movie about the darkest period in your life.' No, the scariest thing in the world is the unknown."

For Jamie, the forthcoming meeting was to establish the truth of his script. But the last vote would be Fincher's. The film will be his opinion of what he thinks. Whatever he decides to focus on in his film will be what it will be. "It is an extremely difficult thing to make a movie that posthumously convicts somebody," he said. Fincher intended to be upfront with them that he was going to use the name Arthur Leigh Allen in his film. "Our position is to tell a newspaper story," he planned to say. "Our job is not to do *JFK* where Oliver Stone is working to prove historically that this is what really happened. We're telling a character story. We're telling a story about the city of San Francisco at this time and the effect on it." Jamie, normally the sunnily optimistic one of the three, predicted the family might not be forthcoming at the conference. He expected them to say, "Now, we're done. We've said what we wanted to say, what we believe and what we believe the inconsistencies are. Thank you for your time. Don't call us again!"

"They have to be nervous about meeting," Brad said as he checked his watch.

Fincher had another question he might or might not ask the couple: "If one person could put him somewhere other than the murders on one of those days, it would go away, wouldn't it?" All these thoughts were racing through their minds before the meeting. Finally, it was time. At 11:30 AM, the family and their lawyer rode the north elevator up to Fincher's small suite. His regular room was booked. This morning, they would have use of the hotel's conference room tables. The sister-in-law seemed reluctant, as if dreading the meeting. The brother looked nothing like Leigh who was predisposed to being a big guy. "When we met with the brother before the meeting," Jamie said, "he was very relaxed and calm. He wasn't an angry guy at all. What was interesting was that I don't think he and Leigh travel in any of the same social circles. He didn't want to know Leigh's friends. He loved Leigh as a brother and looked out for him, but they led very different lives." Their memories would be challenged. Everyone entered the conference room and the door closed behind them. The meeting was to last five hours including a break for lunch and that was all anyone outside that room would *ever* know. Brad, Jamie, and Fincher had given their word.

One could only speculate. Fincher was probably going back and forth following different paths and returning to the same questions again. Producer Laura Ziskin, who first worked with him on *Fight Club*, called the director "just scary smart." He considers each answer, takes it apart and builds on it to pose the same question in a different way. Like his films, he will do as many takes as necessary to get the answer to a question. His interviews always range far and wide—the journey of a director trying to dope out his film. Five hours later, the door opened, the elevator doors closed, and the family and their lawyer had gone. The meeting had been so productive that the three detectives looked at each other and said, "Wow!" Through the briefly open conference room door, the empty cups, plates, and scraps of paper on the conference table suggested the aftermath of an emotional battlefield in which the family had set the record straight. The chairs were still pulled out. The lunch scraps suggested Jamie and Brad had sat at the head of the table, Fincher to Brad's left. As promised, the Hollywood detectives never repeated a word the brother and sister-in-law had said.

Real men kept their word.

"We were kind of reeling at this point," Jamie said, "so we took an hour nap, then went to have dinner. David loved the meeting! It went really, really well. We got some really interesting information and could have gone longer, but we could sense they were kind of flagging."

At 8:30 PM, Brad and Jamie felt their way through the dark, alley-like entrance to Hawthorne Lane. Fincher trailed behind, contemplating the meeting and visualizing a film that might or might not be. The director wasn't closing the door to the idea that Leigh knew Darlene Ferrin, yet for now that had to remain mere speculation.

"What really stood out for me," Brad said, "is that they are good people. Sitting next to the brother, I felt that he is a solid person who turned out very well, an upstanding guy. I was just really pleased to see that he survived this. Obviously, he comes from a home and a history that's terrible. There is a certain amount of guilt in dredging this stuff back up when you're sitting with actual people, but at the same time I think they understood that we're not trying to hurt them in any way."

They entered the restaurant, sat down in a booth on the northern side, and ordered from waist high menus. As they ate, Fincher had news for them. Earlier, he had spoken to Robert Ressler, the FBI profiler of violent sociopaths. Fincher had found it fascinating that Ressler knew nothing about the Zodiac case. When they spoke, Fincher had gotten right to it.

"Talk to me about the tenuous connection between a rage killer, which is basically what David Berkowitz was," he had asked Ressler. "Shooting children on lover's lanes in the back of the head with a .44 is sociopathic. It's striking out against society. There's a specific kind of thrill. It's not only reading about it in the papers. There's a psycho-sexual component of the act of discharging this weapon into the backs of people's heads, hunting people down, shining flashlights in their faces. Talk to me about the relationship between that and a pedophile."

"There is none," Ressler had replied. Now he had a question for Fincher. "Tell me about the pedophilia in this case," he asked. "Is it somebody who lives down the street who takes a kid into his basement, then strangles him and threatens to kill him and/or his parents if he tells?"

"No," Fincher had replied. "He is a seducer. He is the money. He befriends them. He befriends their parents." Fincher was still refining his ideas as he spoke, following the twists and turns of a dark mind. "He molests little girls. He molests little boys."

Overall, Ressler had been shocked that Allen was a cross-gender molester. "There's no relation between this," he said. "These, from a psychological standpoint, don't exist in the same person."

"Ressler concluded that it is rare that you have a pedophile who is molesting both boys and girls," Fincher told Brad and Jamie.

"There's no exact science to his bullshit," Jamie sniffed.

"And he says that," Fincher agreed. "But my point is that so much of what we actually know about Arthur Leigh Allen is a conundrum. He's already a unique individual, taking Zodiac out of the equation entirely."

Fincher was referring to Allen's continuing association and misadventures with children apart from his schoolteaching which was well documented. From June to September 1964, he had been the pool manager for the Watsonville High School Swim Pool. He managed one hundred and fifty grade school children and supervised a staff of six assistant lifeguards and one attendant. He did this from 9:00 AM, until 5:00 PM, and the Family Swim from 5:00 to 6:00 PM. Near the end of his contract, he hurt his leg in a motorcycle accident and was forced to quit. On April 10, 1968, he took a seven year old girl and her sister on an "outing" to the San Francisco Maritime Museum at Polk and Beach Streets. Leigh had instructed the girls to stay in the building while looking at the exhibits, but at 1:00 PM, he noticed the seven year old was missing. Responding SFPD Officers George Cloney and Robert Hooper searched unsuccessfully for two hours. They were worried because the museum was on the water. At 3:40 PM, the Bureau of Inspectors put out a teletype. Sergeant Mattox, Juvenile Bureau, Central #10, arrived at the Museum and widened the search. At 8:30 PM, he contacted the children's parents, but by then a stranger had brought the little girl home.

Brad noticed that Fincher was only picking at his food. So far, he had been subdued on this trip. From the expression on his face, he was still turning over Ressler's comments in his mind and pursuing his theory of Leigh Allen as a seducer who flattered and bribed children. Aloud, he enumerated the evidence: the live chipmunks Allen kept in the trunk of his car to entice youngsters, the audiotape of the screams of a child, and the quarters he pressed into the sweaty palms of two small victims. He once had charmed a mother to gain her trust and enlist her unwittingly in his victimization of her child. Technically, Zodiac, excluding his murder of Paul Stine, was a lover's lane shooter. Fincher's big question was, "How does a guy like this go from being a pedophile cross-gender, which is admittedly odd in and of itself, to a rage killer. Is it a psychotic break? He's growing out of his pedophilia in his thirties. That would make sense."

"He's still got it in him enough to be sentenced to Atascadero [prison]," Jamie said.

"But there's nothing after Atascadero," Brad said. "At that point he's a convicted pedophile. Now, if you discount the idea that Leigh might have done the 1966 Riverside murder that would make Lake Herman Road his first murder a couple months after the closest person in his life discovers his horrible secret." After dinner they returned to the Clift, grabbed a few more winks, then left for a 7:00 AM flight back to LA. "We left so early they hadn't even blocked off the roads for the big bike rally that morning," Brad said. "I'm just exhausted."

"Once we met with the family and David saw what they had been through," Jamie said, "he was O.K., with changing their first names at their request. The sister-in-law would appear in only one scene in the movie, the scene where Inspectors Toschi and Armstrong, and Sergeant Mulanax see her at her home after they interviewed Leigh Allen at the oil refinery. In that scene she says [as she told Toschi] 'The way he spells Christmas as *Christmass* [as Zodiac did in his letters to the press]. I think I got a Christmas card from Leigh.' She doesn't deny that meeting and that is enough in our movie to get us going on Leigh Allen. We don't have to go in and put in more scenes with them she claims didn't occur and other people claim did occur. We don't even have to get into a fight about it."

Brad and Jamie returned to thinking over the budget.

"David Fincher knows what shit costs," Brad said. "This guy's not like you or me going, 'It should maybe cost about fifty-million. I don't know. I've never worked with a grip company.' It's not like if it costs less it's going to go into a Grand Cayman account. There are two cardinal sins: going over schedule and going over budget. The guy who says the movie is going to cost sixty-million dollars gets the money and starts shooting the movie and the movie ends up costing ninety-million dollars—that's the guy they don't want to hire again. You're going to have helicopters over San Francisco following school buses. Now there are buildings in San Francisco that weren't there thirty years ago that you have to have a visual effects artist go in and take out. That stuff costs money. Now, it becomes finding the right studio, finding the people who will give us the most freedom and money. The idea of the grass always being greener or keeping up with the Joneses was never more alive than it is in Hollywood."

"In a situation," Jamie amplified, "where one studio says, 'I really want to make this movie, but it's too rich for my blood.' The other studio says, 'I also want to make this movie, but it's too rich for my blood.' It's like two roommates renting a place together. 'We really love the space, but I couldn't front the rent all on my own.' It's sort of risk versus reward, fear verses greed. If we own all of it, if it hits we'll get everything, but if it doesn't hit . . ."

In five days, they received their answer. After all their setbacks, it was still a stunning moment.

"We've got David!" Brad reported as soon as he heard.

"The movie is in turnaround from Sony. We control it again. If, and this is zero-zero-point one percent of this happening, every single studio in town says, 'We don't want to make this movie. We want nothing to do with it,' he's no longer connected." April was the earliest they could start shooting because now it was all about the actors' schedules. "Let's say its Jake Gyllenhaal, God willing," Jamie said, "and I say April because Jake's free in April. On March 22, Jake had wrapped Sam Mendes' *Jarhead* [the name for a regulation Marine haircut]. For that film he had shaved off his thick brown hair to play twenty year old Anthony Swofford, an elite Marine Gulf War sniper.

After lunch on Tuesday, Brad felt a bit under the weather. By 1:00 PM, he was feeling queasy. By 3:00 PM, he felt like someone else entirely. By 5:00 PM, he felt horrible. "I felt really tired," he said. He wanted a coffee, but then his stomach started doing flip-flops. "I wonder if I have some kind of viral thing. Whatever it is just hit me really fast and really hard." For the next two days Brad was sicker than he had ever been. Thursday morning he felt a little better, but it was hard to tell. He always felt bad in the mornings; he was a bear in the morning. "There's nothing worse than food poisoning," he reported. "I felt so washed out. My whole body was weary, but I did get a call from David Fincher's agent, Josh Donen, today and that lifted my spirits. Essentially, we're waiting on these guys to make their final proposal. Sherry Lansing had a call in to Josh today to discuss this. These things are never simple, but I feel like things are headed in the right direction." When you start dealing with business affairs people things go very slowly and even more so at Paramount and Warner Brothers.

"The last vestiges of the other project are gone," Jamie said on September 28. "It was just they weren't even going to start talking about *Zodiac* with us until they got the message that project wasn't going to happen with David right now. That's honestly what's been going on the past week or so is them going back to David and saying, 'Well, what about this?' and 'What about this?' and he's saying, 'No.'"

Then, with Brad Pitt's renewed interest in the project, *Benjamin Button* struggled to its feet again, rosy-cheeked and full of life.

"Its like a vampire that won't stay down," Jamie groused. "No one thinks it's going to happen, at least now, but if Brad Pitt wanted to take one more stab at trying to make a deal work at this time, who knows?"

Brad Fischer had afternoon coffee with Brad Pitt, whom he had met before and found to be "a regular guy, a very down to earth guy." He liked that Pitt showed up on a motorcycle at the Beverly Hills Hotel. "A lot of movie stars seem very affected and don't have the same grasp of reality most of us do. I didn't get that sense of him at all."

If it were up to the two studios, Brad thought they would want to do the other film with Fincher because then they would get Brad Pitt. It was just business. "At the studios people are so insecure they're afraid of taking chances, everything is about movie stars because in a business that's clearly defined by risk which is really much greater than other businesses. Anything that you can grasp on to that gives you some sense of control and where you're hedging your bet, they'll jump on it. It's all about actors. They make the foreign guys comfortable, but there's no way they're going to make *Benjamin Button* right now at the price. Initially, it was thought *Button* was going to be around $125 million, but the budget Fincher delivered was $160 million, which is tremendous! That's a lot of money! It's the same problem as with

Zodiac, but a bigger problem on *Benjamin Button*. The problem with Sony was that the *Zodiac* budget wasn't enough money, but to a smaller degree of difference. If they don't give David the amount of money he needs to make that movie, then David Fincher's not going to make that movie."

Brad found it "quite a little game," but a game with a maze of possibilities. Warner Brothers and Paramount, the two studios that really wanted *Zodiac*, also happened to be the same two studios that had *Benjamin Button*. "David thinks it's ridiculous and just wants the whole thing to be over. We're still waiting for this to drag out. Mike Medavoy is getting very impatient and really wants to move this thing off the center." Brad was caught in the middle as the days grew longer, the nights shorter and more sleepless. On Monday, his run of bad luck persisted. "I had a car accident earlier today," he said. "I'm fine, but about two o'clock I was coming from lunch and was making a left turn out of the driveway. This other guy was making a left from the opposite side of the street. I was coming around him and he kind of smashed me on the inside driver's side a little further back. I got shaken up. John, my assistant, was in the car with me, and so was Christine, Mike Medavoy's assistant. The other guy was fine. My BMW 330 is really screwed up, so I need to bring it in and get a rental." Brad, who had learned to drive in New York, could be a "very aggressive driver." He recalled driving Medavoy from breakfast at his house back to the office. "He's the worst backseat driver," Brad said, "and he's constantly yelling at me, 'Stop!' 'Go left!'"

Now that Brad had recovered from his food poisoning, it was Jamie's turn to be under the weather. Even "Iron Mike" Medavoy had a stomach flu of some kind. On Thursday, Brad had dinner with John Landis at Ago, but felt "so disorganized that it was ridiculous." He had been looking forward to a trip in Egypt, but canceled it because of the bombings there. Instead, he decided to go to the Bahamas to recharge. When Brad got back to his desk, there was an envelope there. Fincher had sent over a picture of a guy he wanted to play Leigh Allen. "He's perfect," Brad said as he held up the glossy photo to his assistant. "He's the lead singer in a band called the *Pixies*, a guy named Frank Black." Coincidentally, "Frank Black" was the hero's name in the series *Millennium* which had featured a pretty accurate episode on Zodiac.

Brad understood the way Fincher wanted to handle the material. If Channel 2's ace reporter Rita Williams' interview with Leigh Allen was included in the film, he would use the actual interview rather than dramatize it. In the televised version, Allen's face was obscured so there wouldn't be any problem matching the actor. He also considered having different actors play the same part.

In San Francisco, on Monday, October 11, the thirtieth Anniversary of Paul Stine's murder, Toschi's granddaughter rode on a decorated float as Queen of the Columbus Day parade. That same day Linda Del Buono, Darlene Ferrin's sister, died of brain cancer. Linda, a Mare Island cook in Vallejo, had been an important witness in the case. She had provided information for *Zodiac* in 1980 from French Camp Women's Prison outside Stockton. Amidst this tragic loss, Brad had a different kind of news.

"Again, in the great words of one James Vanderbilt," he reported "'*Benjamin Button* is dead, Long live *Benjamin Button*.' Yeah, I think *Benjamin Button* is finally, finally gone until *Zodiac* is gone and then we wish it all the luck in the world. We are expecting an offer from Warner Brothers and have been told it will be for $70 million. That figure's within striking distance, but Fincher still feels like he's going to need $80 million to make *Zodiac*, but I think he really wants to get moving. He wants to make a movie. He wants to make *this* movie. We're going to make this movie. My head has been filled with so many things, mostly *Zodiac*."

In the meantime, they were losing opportunities for other films. After *Basic*, John Travolta had asked Brad to produce *A Love Song for Bobbie Long*, but he couldn't because of his situation at Phoenix. Brad did attend the premiere screening, and party and had dinner with Travolta and his wife, Kelly Preston, at Kate Mantilini Beverly Hills. "Travolta," Brad noted, "had a larger security presence than he normally did because of a bomb scare,".

At least Fincher could now think wholeheartedly about *Zodiac* again.

"David Fincher wants the movie's opening sequence to be the Zodiac letter arriving at the *Chronicle*," Brad said, "the cameras following the letter into the newspaper." Fincher visualized the locked canvas mailbags on a flatbed truck, its squeaky wheels and scrape of metal, as it is trundled into the tiny wood paneled elevator—*clang*! *clang*! The *whoosh* of doors and the torturous, creaking climb to the third floor. First, he needed to know where Zodiac had posted a letter to the *Chronicle* in time for its next edition. He called the always reliable Amy Carr.

AT PHOENIX, AMY CARR was going through the postmarks on the Zodiac letters. Fincher wanted her to match them to a specific mailbox and clarify what certain markings meant. The delivery units most often repeated on the authenticated Zodiac envelopes were 1A (5 times), followed by 4A (2), 6B (2), 1B (1), 8B (1), 940 (1), Pleasanton (1), and H (1).

"I cannot figure out what 1B, 4A, and 1A mean," Amy said. "Do they represent sorting machines, various post offices, or zones? On one Zodiac letter I noticed the markings '11A/900.' I assume that '11A' means 11:00 AM, but what would the '900' mean?"

By phone, she verified that letters processed between midnight and noon are postmarked AM; those handled between noon and midnight are postmarked PM. During the Amerithrax case of 2001-2002, US Postal Inspectors had tracked the path of anthrax-laced letters from mailbox to mailbox to their origin through a system of magnetic encodings in bar codes, and sorting and canceling machines. No such tracing technology existed when Zodiac letters were flowing through the Bay Area mail stream. In all likelihood, Zodiac used the same postbox in San Francisco to mail the 1A letters. Amy considered that a viable theory. She suspected that Zodiac so enjoyed the thrill of placing himself in jeopardy he might choose a mailbox offering the greatest amount of risk. Such was a mailbox directly in front of the *Chronicle* at Fifth and Mission Streets. The Main Post Office at Seventh and Mission Streets less than two blocks away from the *Chronicle* provided the fastest mode of delivery. His letter would be collected, processed immediately, and be in the mail stream before mail collected from other parts of the city reached the downtown processing center. A busy newspaper like the *Chronicle* picked up its editorial mail twice a day directly from this post office. Zodiac's constant admonitions of "Rush To Editor" demonstrated his frantic dash to have his message heard and printed.

Amy learned that the main office, the geographic unit, was designated "1A." Next, Amy began plotting the locations of prime mailboxes on one of her Amazing Maps for the Amazing Office. Soon her maps would cover entire walls.

ON THURSDAY, NOVEMBER 4, the deaths of important people in the Zodiac investigation shook the city. Two San Francisco police chiefs involved in the case passed away. Less than seven hours after a former police chief, Richard Hongisto, passed away at age 67, Chief Donald M. Scott, who had replaced Chief Al Nelder in September 1971, died at age 89 at Marin General in Greenbrae.

Brad was having lunch with Jamie and Jeff Robinov. "You probably read Sherry Lansing has announced that at the end of her contract she'll be leaving Paramount Pictures," Brad said. Lansing, who's "had that job forever," was not forced out as much as it was her own decision. She had wanted to go out on a high note and felt that *Benjamin Button* was going to be another *Forrest Gump* for her. "She was so invested in getting this movie made that that's why it stayed alive for so long."

"She wanted her swan song to be *Benjamin Button*," Jamie added. "With Sherry Lansing gone, Brad Grey, who used to be Brad Pitt's producing partner, is running things."

"Warners seems pretty excited and we're in negotiations," Brad reported. "But there are always touch and go moments and still going to be because David has been consistent about the money he needs to make the movie." Brad had other news. He paused dramatically. "So, guess what? I bought a house," he announced. Brad had other news. He paused dramatically.

"So, guess what?" he said.

"What?"

"I bought a house—Spanish-style, two stories. It's got 1900 square feet. It's got two bedrooms, two baths and the original fireplace. There's a good-sized yard and two levels to the yard. One room opens endlessly into another as you ascend and descend and ascend and come back around through the patio from a different angle. Isn't that awesome! I saw it on Tuesday, the very first day it was offered, They were asking $749,500. I offered $739,000. They countered with $744,000. I got it for that and with closing costs it was $759,000. Houses in the neighborhood are at the same level and are all more expensive. I loved it when I first saw it and when the realtor said Boris Karloff used to live here in the thirties I was sold. There is still a stained glass window in the room where Karloff conducted his seances. Anyway, I snapped the house up and we closed it yesterday, Wednesday. 'What's wrong with the house?' I asked the owner. 'Well, my roof leaks a little bit,' he admitted. When they did the home inspection, the inspector said, 'This place needs a new roof,' and got very indignant with the fellow and said, 'You can't sell him a place that needs a new roof.'"

They reached an agreement—the owner would give Brad half the money for a new roof.

"Now Brad being Brad," Jamie said, "he can be a little cheap toward himself. Instead of going and getting a new roof, he says, 'Well that can wait.'"

On Saturdays the *LA Times* Real Estate Section has a "Hot Property Listing" which usually shows celebrities when they buy or sell their homes. "My real estate broker says this is the kind of thing the woman who does that column really likes. It's got celebrity history." The headline read "Big Shoes to Fill Karloff Digs."

Brad counted all 107 steps up from the street. The long flight of wooden stairs were treacherous, especially at night "They go up almost vertically, really high," Brad said. "The owner said he lost forty pounds living there. I obviously have a Jewish mother who worries constantly about every little thing. She is very upset because she has a bad knee and all these steps from the street up to my house are the only way to get up there. And her cousin said to her, 'Gosh, I hope Brad doesn't break his leg or anything.' If I break my leg how am I going to get in and out of my house? And she's very concerned about it, but says, 'O.K. as long as you're happy.'"

When the first big wave of winter storms arrived, Brad called Jamie and said, "Oh, I'm so mad."

"Well, the guy told you," Jamie said. "What did you do with the money?"

"Well, I kept it."

"You kept the money for the new roof that everybody told you were going to need and then it rains torrentially and you're shocked?"

"I didn't really think it was going to leak."

"You're not going to be worried about your roof until it comes down on your head."

Remarkably, during LA's torrential rains, triple those ever recorded, the Karloff house persevered like *Benjamin Button* and shed water like a duck. It was preternatural.

"Jamie and I have decided the house is haunted and I end up disappearing somehow."

"Brad's just planning on disappearing," Jamie said. "He's just trying to cover his tracks." Jamie kept annoying Brad by calling his new place "Bela Lugosi's house."

"It's Boris Karloff's house!"

"Same difference," Jamie said.

In retaliation, Brad began to refer to Jamie's place as "Castle Dracula," a dig at Karloff's costar Bela Lugosi's famous role. At the end of the day, he went out onto the patio and sat down on the top step. He folded his arms and put his elbows on his knees. He took a deep breath of the cool evening air. It did not lift his spirits. He looked out at the vista. You could see forever. His new home by the Hollywood Bowl faced the west and south, and offered amazing views of the Hollywood Hills, the city, and canyon. "If you look northwest," he said, "you can see the green belt vistas of the hills with all the sparkling lights and then to the south is the city, the LA basin."

After a while, he got up and trudged down all 107 wooden steps. He had another meeting to attend and another battle to fight. He looked back up at his new home, knowing he would have to climb those 107 steps all over again.

AT 5:30 PM, FINCHER, Jeff Robinov, and Lynn Harris, the executive vice president in production at Warner's, a position she had held at New Line, sat down for dinner. Harris, as one of the producers on *Se7en* had worked with Fincher before. "So she's been very helpful," Brad said. "Fincher and Robinov had a very good meeting. Jeff basically says he thinks he can get this done." Then they went back and forth on the cast even though Bencio Del Toro and Jake Gyllenhaal were both pre-approved. When Fincher saw *The Assassination of Richard Nixon* he was turned off of doing *Zodiac* with Sean Penn. Jamie wasn't surprised. He had never visualized Penn as Toschi. "You know who's not on that list," he said, "who I think would be interesting to play Paul Avery—Kevin Spacey." Fincher even said that Kevin Spacey needed to be in their movie at some point, but they ultimately moved away from him.

"Jeff is going to get final approval from Alan Horn who is the boss of all bosses at Warner Brothers," Brad concluded. "He's in the Amazon right now on vacation with his family, but will be back on Monday." Brad and Jamie were waiting on the money side and very encouraged that Fincher had a standing appointment to meet with them three days a week—Mondays, Wednesdays and Fridays. The first Wednesday, Brad and Jamie wanted to start reworking the script so that they didn't lose another beat. Such a schedule would also allow them to continue their research as they poured over clues and unbroken ciphers. The case was burrowing deeper under their skins and that rabbit hole was beckoning. They dared not fall.

"David is doing all this work in anticipation that he's making this movie," Brad said. "If they make a deal then he'll get paid. All the work we've done over all these months has been speculative on everyone's part. We will all get paid at the same time. Nobody has gotten anything. Jamie's yet to cash his option check from *Halloween* of two years ago. I know there's a $7,000 check floating around that's driving the Phoenix legal department crazy. Either cash it, Jamie, or endorse it over to me." The check was made out to "Mob Front, Inc." For tax purposes Jamie is a corporation. Whether he writes an original script or adapts a book like *Zodiac*, Jamie gets paid the same amount.

The problem of the budget still loomed. "David, if nothing else," Jamie said, "is a technician who knows what every lens does and what every day of shooting will cost."

"He obviously is still insisting on more money," Brad said. "He wants $5 million for music."

The budget was at $75 million now. David Fincher wanted $80 million. He needed $80 million. He hungered for $80 million. He had walked away before when he couldn't get the money he needed and was ready to walk away again.

CHAPTER ELEVEN

SKEPTICISM AND AMY

IN HIS AMAZING OFFICE, David Fincher was considering new facts and disputing the old. He made speedy progress until he turned his attention to Kathleen Johns who had claimed that Zodiac had kidnapped her and her baby on March 22, 1970, and taken them on a terror ride. If this was true, then she had seen Zodiac up close without his hood. She had heard him speak. Fincher printed her name on a note card with a Sharpie, then put a question mark next to it. Was she telling the truth about Zodiac? If so, was Zodiac telling the truth about her?

Take One: In Zodiac's July 24, 1970, letter, he boasted that, "I now have a little list, starting with the woeman + her baby that I gave a rather interesting ride for a coupple howers one evening a few months back that ended in my burning her car where I found them." Zodiac had uncharacteristically delayed claiming responsibility for John's abduction. Yet, Zodiac had done that before with Lake Herman Road, mentioning it almost as an afterthought many months later. Fincher knew John's account by heart but read it over anyway. At 3:00 AM, forty minutes after Kathleen escaped from her kidnapper, she filed a report with Stanislaus Sheriff's Deputy Jim Ray Lovett. *The Modesto Bee*, a McClatchy paper, picked this up and printed Johns' story immediately afterward on March 23, 1970, on p. A-1—"Woman Says Zodiac Killer Captured Her."

What evidence was there to either rule in or rule out her story? Fincher found it suspicious that Zodiac only mentioned three bits of information in his letter. There was nothing about the spit-shined shoes Kathleen said she had noticed her abductor was wearing. He wondered if Zodiac had used cues from *The Modesto Bee*, the only newspaper which included in their story the three main details that Zodiac mentioned: "Her car was found totally burned at Byrd Road and [rarely used] Highway 132 where she thinks she stopped when her wheel fell off." Fincher assigned Amy Carr to find out where Zodiac might have read that story.

She began with the *Modesto Bee's* circulation. "The thirty-four year old report is not very detailed," she told Fincher. "The woman I spoke with could not tell me specifically where in San Francisco those papers were delivered—newsstands, individual residents, racks, etc . . . Also, she was not able to release a copy of the annual internal report [of March 31, 1970] as it is confidential. I asked her three times." Amy, always resourceful, eventually got her hands on the report. The *Modesto Bee's* circulation was 48,000 daily copies and 50,000 Sunday papers distributed throughout Stanislaus, Merced, and San Joaquin Counties. Only a few individual copies were trucked to San Francisco County where Zodiac may have seen the article. Dorothy Harrison, who wrote the original story about Johns, freelanced for the *Stockton Record* which had decided out of caution not to run the story, though most *Bee* papers did. Zodiac might have seen the Johns story in a *Sacramento Bee* article since he had responded to their positive Sunday profile of state handwriting examiner Sherwood Morrill instantly. In doing this, he broke a three-year letter writing drought. Next, Amy turned to Bay Area newspapers. The *San Francisco Examiner* of March 23, reported only that Johns' car "was found on Highway 132 burned. Somebody had put the torch to it." The *Vallejo Times-Heralds* of October 20, and November 22 wrote: "Woman Believes She Fled Zodiac."

And what of the *San Francisco Chronicle?* Zodiac's favorite daily had not run the Johns story. This omission might be explained because *Chronicle* crime reporter Paul Avery had received a threatening card (PEEK-A-BOO, YOU ARE DOOMED) from his "secret pal," Zodiac, on October 28.

Eight days later, Avery wrote to Dave Smith, his colleague at the *Los Angeles Times*, about the threat:

"I feel like Cinderella. I was Queen for a Day Friday night through

Sunday afternoon. The biggest fucking thing since the discovery of pasteurized peanut butter. Your story which made not a few papers contributed to the sensational feeling of being, albeit briefly, a celebrity. Sunday night the seriousness of the whole thing began to sink in and I've been On Alert ever since. Paul."

Eleven days later, Smith wrote Avery back to say his story, "Evidence Links Zodiac Killer to '66 Death of Riverside Coed," was splashed across Page A-1:

"So here—a bit later than I'd promised. But God am I glad to be able to enclose the high school [bus] thing. Thought I never would get that Goddamn thing off my soul. Still no word from the editor on your file. As of this morning, he still hadn't got to it, and I don't want to harp on it to him too often, or he'll maybe get irritated and take it out in his reading of your stuff, so I'm just trying to play it cool. I am going to be out of town visiting family in Tucson, so I will leave my number with you in case anything should pop."

Ten days later, the *Chronicle* ran its first story on Johns. Two days later, Warren Williams, *Modesto Bee* Valley News Editor, wrote Avery to fill in some blanks in his story:

"Am sending this along in case it will help you. This is from our Patterson stringer, twenty years with us and very reliable. I thought you would be interested because of the method of operation. Very beguiling way of 'helping' a person about to be in distress—the wheel-wobbling bit—and thereby setting them up to get in the car when Zodiac (or whoever) returns. As to why he did not kill her if he were the Zodiac, perhaps it was because of the baby?"

As Fincher perused Amy's report, he told Brad and Jamie, "One of the things I got [about Johns] is that she had just broken up with somebody and was on her way to Petaluma. Whatever happened during the abduction, we have to take her word for it. She jumped from the car. There's no police report of scrapes, cuts, and bruises, so she didn't jump from a car at high speed."

Johns had explained this. "When my abductor inadvertently drove up a freeway off ramp," she had reported, the car came to a full stop and I was able to leap out." After that she had been taken to a

Highway Patrol station where she saw a Zodiac bulletin on the wall, and yelled, "That's him. That's the guy!" Unbelievable! But, what would Kathleen's motivation be to connect her abduction to Zodiac? The maniac was no longer Page One news. Her kidnapping had occurred at a location a distance from San Francisco, and she hadn't capitalized on the publicity. When Zodiac became active again in the early seventies, Kathleen went into hiding for a decade.

A few more doubts about Kathleen emerged when she embellished her story on tabloid television in the late 1980s. In 1990, George Bawart and Captain Roy Conway conducted a breakfast interview with her at Denny's.

"Roy, do you remember she had that lipstick on that came up over her lip?" Bawart said. "She was really a mess, and seemed to be enjoying the attention."

Filmmaker Tracy Torme conducted several interviews with Johns for a documentary. Shortly afterward, *Primetime* television director Harry Phillips' stringer located her. Just as he arrived at her address to interview her, he saw an ambulance out front. Johns had just died of coronary thrombosis.

As Fincher mulled over the Johns' abduction conundrum, he again considered casting a different actor to play the part of her kidnapper each time he cut back to the shadows. "In that way," Fincher said, "you can't get as much a physical read of his face."

Brad and Jamie liked that idea.

What had triggered Zodiac's letter months after the Johns abduction? Did he feel neglected when his June 1970 letter was delayed in the mail? Had he tried to inflate his frustrated ego with wild claims? Fincher thought that might be the case. So did the SFPD.

"Zodiac is claiming responsibility for crimes he hasn't committed," police said. On Friday, June 19, 1970, at 5:45 AM, Patrolman Richard Radetich, twenty-five, had been sitting in his patrol car writing a traffic citation for a car with an expired tag when someone fired three shots at him. He was found with a .38 slug in his left temple, his service revolver holstered, and the microphone still clutched in his hand. Six days later, Zodiac claimed to have shot "a man sitting in a parked car with a .38." Homicide Inspector Walter Krache publicly called Zodiac a liar and said police knew who the shooter was. But charges were dropped against their suspect in January and the Radetich case remained unsolved. The lasting effect of the cowardly attack was this: Before the murder a police officer rode patrol in a one-man car; afterward the department announced they would use only two-man patrol cars from now on.

On Tuesday, November 9, Brad sent Josh Donen an email, then waited for official word from Warners. Late last week, he had spoken to Lynn Harris. She and Robinov would be speaking to Allen Horn at Warners, about approving the $75 million budget plus an additional $5 million for music. Donen sent his typical shorthand response to Brad's email: "Spoke to Jeff on Friday. He told me that he and Allen Horn would meet on Monday, yesterday, to discuss. Am in New York traveling to LA. We will get into it this afternoon. Josh."

Fincher told the studio he didn't need a composer. Instead, he would purchase an armload of popular songs—"Sky Pilot" by Eric Burdon and The Animals, "Soul Sacrifice" by Santana, "Hurdy Gurdy Man" by Donovan, and Three Dog Night's cover of "Easy to Be Hard," a song deeply ingrained in his memory as being "the sound of the Northern California summer of '69." Their score or "scource," as Fincher called it would be forty signposts guiding them through nearly four decades. To fill out the *Zodiac* soundtrack Fincher wanted to use clips of AM radio (KFRC-San Francisco), and advertising sound bites ("Top of the Hill, Daly City"). The studio agreed.

"As of now, Warner's and Paramount in the negotiations will be splitting *Zodiac* between them," Brad said. "In terms of '*Benjamin Button* is dead, long live *Benjamin Button*!'"

Jamie held up his palm. "We decided we are not allowed to say that anymore," he admonished.

"The fact that Paramount has now forded *Zodiac* at least in the negotiation capacity of a partner with Warner Brothers is a first signal," Brad said.

"It's a little bit like running to stand still," Jamie said. "With us we need to run even faster to get the movie made."

Brad had to deal with conflicting memories and misinformation which they had to reconcile for Jamie's script. In an office below Brad's, Amy Carr was slogging through the VPD reports to locate all references to Darlene Ferrin's Vallejo painting party where Zodiac might have been seen. Brad knew the painting party would be part of their all day discussion tomorrow. "We're looking forward into sitting down and getting into that guest list," he said. Amy still had eight more of Leigh Allen's homemade videotapes to watch. Exhausted after tracking mailboxes, she trudged up the narrow stairs to Brad's office to deliver the first part of her index describing every part of every tape Leigh had made. It had been a mind-numbing task, one that had daunted even the indefatigable Bawart who was tough as a junkyard dog.

At 2:00 AM, Jamie stepped off a plane from Washington, DC, bleary eyed, disheveled, suffering from jet lag and prepared to plunge back into *Zodiac* after a short break. His *Zodiac* goatee was ragged, but still there. "Amber likes it now," he said. Over three straight days, he'd worked with former Counterterrorism Czar Richard Clarke and his deputy, Roger Cressey, adapting Clarke's bestselling book, *Against All Enemies*, for Sony. "I liked Clarke. Very serious, very smart and very opinionated and dedicated which is good considering he was in charge of counterterrorism for twenty years. The film is about the rise of Al Qaeda and almost a history of counterterrorism for the last twenty years." He looked at his watch. His lunch meeting with Brad and Fincher was scheduled for 3:00 PM, and this left him time to get more work in on Zodiac. He arrived at the meeting with new pages. Going page by page, Fincher excitedly talked about different ways to "textualize" things and change some detailed material. The Paul Stine scene was not as big and all inclusive as he wanted it to be.

"What David would like to do," Jamie explained, "is finish this next pass on the script in light of everything we've learned in the last year." One eyebrow-raising fact that amazed him was that Leigh Allen drank two quarts of Coors before 10:00 AM, every day. "And I've never met anybody who has a specifically cut out beer jug. It's a little Uncle Jesse out of the *Dukes of Hazzard*." They battled through the script for hours but had only reached page 32 before they quit at 6:30 PM. From now on their meetings would average at least three hours in addition to all their other duties and movie projects. Script length remained a serious problem.

"Jamie is very reclusive," Brad noted the next night, "it's almost impossible to get him to leave his house."

"It's just that I really, really like my house and I have friends in all the time," Jamie said. "Witness Brad in my kitchen right now. I love hanging out here. Luckily, I'm marrying a woman who likes all my friends. Amber's not like: 'What are all these people doing here.'"

The pizza arrived—the third night in a row they'd ordered pizza.

"It's a zoo here," Brad said. "Twenty dollar pizza from Fabrocini's, a great Italian place, the best."

According to Jamie, Brad ate more pizza than he had ever seen any human being consume. "I don't know how he stays so thin," he said, then shouted over the din, "And Brad, you have another pizza from Lamonica's sitting right here!" Brad ignored him and bit into the new pizza. As he munched, he was busy thinking about their Friday meeting with Fincher.

"In case the movie goes over budget," Brad found out the next morning, "they want the overages to come out of Phoenix and Fincher's back end. A normal over-budget penalty would be fifty percent of the overage out of fifty percent of the back end. This time they're insisting on one hundred percent out of one hundred percent which is pretty egregious. Everyone is unhappy. We got to figure out how to make it work. David is extremely uncompromising since *Zodiac* seems like such an obvious commercial bet, in addition to being such a great film that can really last for ages. Zodiac did all the marketing for us. This is a story that you can tell once and for all. In addition to not giving David all the money that he wants, it is also saying if you go over then we're going to penalize you like we don't usually penalize directors. I see the Warner's side of it also because they're saying, 'Look, we stretched to get from seventy to seventy-five which is our cap on the movie. If you want seventy-five you got seventy-five, but not a penny more. If you go over, then you're paying for it.'"

Jamie was conflicted. He thought they were both right and both wrong. He and Brad met with Fincher at 2:30 PM, and went through the script again. "It seems like it is going to expand because the context of the story that David wants to tell," Brad said, "which encompasses a lot of what is in the books *Unmasked* as well as *Zodiac*. To do that it's going to expand the page numbers. If anything, the studio wants it to be shorter. It's never a situation when you're developing a screenplay and everyone's really on the same page. It's really more of a back and forth dialogue discussing how we can improve the scene."

"This is really what I'm looking for here," Fincher said, describing a scene.

"Oh, O.K.," Jamie said, "that's a really good idea. What if we did this?" He riffed on that. "It's different with every script when you go in to change it. We haven't even started talking about the details and changes in the script that Fincher will want to do. As a screenwriter you're always sort of nervous what a director's going to say. 'I love this part,' 'Love this part.' 'Love this part.' 'What if we tried it this way,' and then he gives you an idea that makes you think that's a better way to do it." Jamie felt that incorporating what they'd learned on their research trips was making the script more truthful and longer, getting these new facts in, and making sure the structure of the movie still worked. "Sometimes you need to put in everything but the kitchen sink and you cut it back down to fighting weight, but you don't necessarily know which scene is more important. You have to have them all in there and sort of lay them out. Then you can go, 'Oh, we don't need this.' It's like if you're working out a lot, you actually end up gaining weight."

Sometimes a really good dynamic exists among producers, writers, and directors. Other times creative conflicts can tear a movie apart. When the star and the director have conflicting ideas the power generally tends to shift to the director and the star, the two stronger entities. The producer, depending on his relationship, can have a great deal of influence, the writer less so. That evening, just as Brad phoned Toschi, Mike Medavoy called on the other line and Brad had to call Toschi back. Then, Fincher called Brad. Finally, Brad was able to tell Toschi they hoped to come up to San Francisco again in mid-December and he could walk them through the Stine scene. When Brad's phone rang, he had to go again. Puzzled, Toschi looked at his phone. Was it possible for anyone to be that busy?

On Tuesday night, November 23, Brad and Mike Medavoy had drinks with Christian Bale from the new *Batman Begins*. Bale, very interested in *Zodiac*, had set up a meeting with Fincher.

On Sunday, November 28, Jamie and Brad spent the day at Jamie's house discussing the progression of time from *A* to *B*. The script was chronological, so they focused on the progression of the Kathleen Johns abduction and how the Riverside incident played into Paul Avery's downfall. At what point did Avery get the gun he almost had to use? At what point did he start to lose it? Was the Halloween card death threat he got from Zodiac the breaking point for him? Was the card a result of the article he wrote? Was it one specific article or just a cumulation because he was the guy covering the story?

"When and how did Toschi hear about Riverside?" Fincher asked.

"He read it in the *Chronicle*."

"If I were Toschi," Jamie said, "I'd be pissed at Avery."

"Reporters say, 'Hey, we got this great letter.' The modicum of civic pride in them doesn't say, 'Let's run this over to the police so they can keep it.' That letter goes into that paper to make sure no other paper is going to get it. Avery's letter to the Attorney General requested he be placed officially in charge of the Zodiac investigation, in effect taking the investigation away from Toschi and Armstrong."

"Give me a gun and a badge," Brad said. "Was there any tension between Avery and Toschi?"

"No, Toschi loved him."

Once, Avery left his briefcase in Toschi's office with a running tape recorder inside, but it was discovered. Avery got in Dutch with every detective on Homicide—except Toschi. "Paul had such a great, great newspaper career," Toschi lamented. "At the end, Paul was doing cocaine, was on a machine, and in really bad shape. He called me before he passed away. He and I had become very good, trustworthy friends."

"That's what Fincher was talking about today," Jamie recalled. " Toschi really wanted everybody to be friends and sort of cooperate at the Riverside conference. It seemed like their one chance: 'Well, finally we're getting together. Napa didn't send us the thing about the Wing Walkers [the exclusive Navy shoes Zodiac had worn at Lake Berryessa], but now we have a chance.'"

"But the first thing that happens," Brad said, "is that they look at Avery who had come on the same plane and then look at Dave Toschi like, 'Oh, you brought your press agent.' Dave's look is, 'I didn't know anything about this,' and to Avery, 'What the hell are you doing here?'" Another question: by the time they had the Riverside Zodiac conference, Sherwood Morrill had already made a handwriting match with Riverside. "Police were like, 'Aha, we've finally stumbled onto something. Zodiac didn't take credit for the Bates' murder and thus might have made a slip down south.'"

Fincher was thoughtful. In hindsight, he thought this could have been Zodiac starting to take credit for something he didn't do.

THE NEXT DAY, BRAD had a long conversation with Jake Gyllenhaal's agent. "We were talking about the price," he said. "Jake is obviously being sought after. We have a very tight budget for *Zodiac*. We're trying to figure out exactly how to put all the pieces in place so we don't get held over the coals. He got one and one half million dollars for *Jarhead*. If it is Jake and Benicio we'll try to do a favored nation deal where both get the same amount of money which we can justify because Toschi's part doesn't work as long." At 6:30 PM, Christian Bale met with Brad and Jamie at the Bel Air Hotel. He heard Jamie was doing more work on the screenplay so he brought it along with him.

"This is one of the best scripts I've ever read," Bale said. "As soon as I finished reading it, I wrote one word on the cover." Bale dropped the heavy script on the table and pointed to the word he had written: "Phenomenal."

"We would have both *American Psycho* and *Donnie Darko* [Bale and Gyllenhaal's most famous roles] in our movie," Jamie said. Both actors were represented by Endeavor so Jamie knew their respective agents were going to sit down and talk. "He wants to play the Graysmith part, but we have him in mind for the role of Avery. You know, Jake lost out on *Batman* to Christian and Christian is going to feel like he lost out on *Zodiac* to Jake."

The following day, a Warner's executive called Brad about the budget. "They flinched a little bit, but we'll see what happens," Brad reported. "We may have found the perfect director for this movie, but he sure isn't the easiest guy to get a movie made with. The ironic thing is that everyone is so nervous about David going over budget and he doesn't go over budget. David needs the full budget. He said five to six months of shooting which is long. Usually it is three months."

"Not on purpose, David gives people the impression he's more hands off in terms of studio executives than they would like," Jamie added. "Studio executives like to feel like they are part of the creative process and they're buddies with the director and the actors. Frankly, David is somebody who is like, 'Yeah, no, you're not. We make movies. You pay for them. We'll see you at the theatre.' Studio executives don't like hearing stuff like that."

"If you have a difference of opinion," Laura Ziskin said of Fincher, "he'll listen politely, then tell you in no uncertain terms how completely wrong you are."

MEDAVOY AND MESSER'S PEOPLE were accustomed to having staff meetings every Tuesday in the main conference room on the second floor at Phoenix Pictures. Now, they scarcely recognized the room. It resembled a police Homicide squad room. The walls were blanketed with Zodiac flowcharts, timelines, and chronology—lines and arrows leading everywhere, down the halls, and up and over door frames. This technique was so low-tech that thirty-four years earlier the police of multiple jurisdictions had similarly covered their walls on the same case. To Messer's knowledge this was going to be "the most extensively researched script, the most meticulously accurate representation of actual events consistent with dramatic movies ever. I've been producing thirty years, and I have never been involved with a movie that has been this close to the truth and the amount of research and energy put into it. The guys went into the books, the raw files, the ten thousand pages of transcripts. It was really impressive the work these guys did to make sure they were in line with the facts."

The flow charts were Amy Carr's greatest contribution. "Many days, we worked on the time charts lined up in the hallway," she said, "looking at them, lining them up and making sure everything was in order." As rain poured outside on December 1, she industriously constructed two versions of the timeline. One, from 1963 to present day, had branches going up into blocks of text. The second was a calendar twenty-five feet long—the months of the year and the major events that happened on each day of each month. Amy inserted the last of Allen's homemade videotapes and pressed "Play." Her eyes glazed over, but her ordeal was finally over. There were nano-seconds of scenes that had been erased except for a frame or two and those were tantalizing, but finally she pressed the "Stop" key. After nearly five years in the Phoenix Pictures story department she was leaving to work at NBC-Universal. "I've got to. Its time," she said. "I need to just move on. I might do that for a year, but I want to go into marketing. I like that research. I like studying people. Applying some of the stuff I'm good at. I like dealing with people and I like stories, but I'm not good at just negotiating things and cold-calling people. But *Zodiac* was the most fun of all my projects for Phoenix."

The next day, Brad called Bawart. "Our story editor, Amy Carr, has finally gotten through all the Allen videotapes," he said. "We had her watch them straight through, every single one, and catalogue them and make a log of every tape."

"Did you tell her there's about fifty more of them here," Bawart said.

"Yes, and she left the company."

Brad drove the chronological flow chart over to Fincher's Amazing Office where it would form the basis of his war room display, an odd combination of no-tech and cutting-edge innovations. Fincher needed to have a sense of what happened chronologically. "I am reworking the chart," Brad said, "but it's a lot harder without Amy's help." He enlarged the note cards and tacked them to the wall in David's conference room to create a comprehensive Zodiac timeline.

"Let's just make sure that didn't happen before that," Fincher said on the way to his desk. He wanted to date and time each beat, like a musical score, to see the spaces between where nothing happened. As in music, the spaces between the notes are as important as the notes themselves. "As a visual aid for David and I," Jamie explained, "we are able to step back and look just at the concrete stuff we absolutely, positively know is attributable to this case and the people involved."

"What I'd like to do is sort of a variation on that," Brad suggested as he recrossed to the wall. "Let's lay out everything we know for sure that we think and then color code it like bright red when every letter from Zodiac comes in."

"Right. Then, we can focus on one aspect at a time during our fact-checking pass." Jamie hadn't started the rewrite; he was still combing through the script section by section with Fincher. Before writing the changes, Jamie got all the notes together. Brad and Jamie each kept binders, though there was no doubt that Brad remained the undisputed "King of Binders." They wrote down notes with the script open in front of them. "We got to put something different here," Fincher said and drew an arrow or applied a Post-It there. "We're going to pull this scene to move this scene later." It was fun to see the master of high-tech working with such basic tools as felt-tip pens and Post-It Notes. Soon, they could start incorporating the changes they had documented. "The length of the script is still at 169 pages and we're making it larger," Jamie said. Days passed. At last, Fincher thought Jamie was ready to start working on the material they'd covered so far.

That night, Brad did the final walkthrough of his new house and closed escrow the next morning, Saturday, December 4. After a month, he officially owned the Karloff house. Monday morning, moderately refreshed, he was back in the thick of the negotiating process and the over-budget issue with Donen, Robinov, Horn, and Lynn Harris at Warner Brothers. "We're just going back and forth on all that stuff," he said. At 3:40 PM, Brad attempted to reach Toschi to brief him about their January trip up to San Francisco. He was unsuccessful. He then called George Bawart about locating surviving Zodiac victim Mike Mageau. "Mageau's parents are deceased," Bawart explained, "but Mike's twin brother might be in a town near the desert."

"We were to have another session with Fincher," Brad said, "but he's in the middle of shooting a Super Bowl commercial." Fincher's Super Bowl spot, "Heineken Beer Run," sets Brad Pitt inside a dark cityscape where, in a series of aerial views, he is seen eluding the Paparazzi, buying beer from Ron's Market, and safely returning to his room.

"David has a very lucrative career with television commercials," Jamie explained, "and that's one of the things that makes him so frustrating to studios. He can do television commercials the rest of his life and put his grandkids through college."

"It's two or three million just for doing a commercial," Brad said. "*Bam*! He gets it just like that. He doesn't need to make films to make money. That's why he terrifies studios. He won't compromise." Fincher believed that commercials could be great art, not the fine art of the surrealistic painting or the Elizabethan sonnet, but art nevertheless. Commercials gave him time to choose his next project, negotiate some control over his next film, and experiment with the new technology he loves. Right now, he was still eager to cut a picture in high definition. "Tape is stupid," he said. "It's just not reasonable to have a 4:4:4 camera that goes to any kind of compression/tape format you couldn't play back." It reminded him of an electrical outlet with too many plugs: "You need a DNC cable that goes to a NTSC deck to recover the videotape so you can have VTR playback." Earlier, he had discussed shooting

HD with Angus Wall, his brilliant film editor. Wall, cofounder of Rock Paper Scissors, had designed the titles for *Se7en* and collaborated with Digital Domain (DD), the special effects house, on *Fight Club's* opening title sequence. Recently, Wall had worked with Fincher on his BMW and Nike ads. When Fincher shot *Panic Room*, his thriller of two years earlier, no reliable HD ready to shoot a feature existed. Avid technology did not allow editing in HD with Apple's Final Cut Pro which Wall preferred. But when he and Wall met in Venice, California in February, Wall had exciting news. "We are finally in a place where we can cut in HD," he said. This meant a simple, efficient, uncompressed, entirely tapeless HD workflow path through production, post and delivery could be posted as data with no tape media except for backups on vaulted LTO data tapes. Fincher could shoot his next film, put it on a drive, and send it to DD.

That night, Brad took a break from budgets, casting, and leaky roofs to enjoy himself at the premiere of *The Aviator*. In the morning, he rang Toschi to get an answer to a question he had been loath to ask. "How many times had Cecilia Shepherd and Bryan Hartnell been stabbed," he asked. There was silence at the other end, so long he thought he had lost the connection. Finally, Toschi consulted his small black notebook, and replied tonelessly: "Six in the back for the boy and fourteen all over for the girl." Brad thanked the retired inspector and hung up. It was information he would rather not have known. It was information Toschi would rather have given. Next, he reached Captain Ken Narlow who agreed to take Fincher and his team around Lake Berryessa during their visit and invite the original investigators, Dave Collins, John Robertson, Rangers Dennis and Ray Land, and William White, to join them. Brad's eyes roved to the top of his list. For the last ten months, he had been waiting for a reply to his letter to the lone Lake Berryessa surviving victim, Bryan Hartnell.

John, Brad's assistant, was at his desk when a call came in. John was pulling for Brad. He knew how hard he had been working to secure that interview. But it was not Hartnell. It was a youthful voice. "Who's calling," John said.

"I'm Benjamin Hartnell," he said.

John could hardly contain his excitement. "I've got Bryan's son, Benjamin, on the line," John told Brad. "He's calling on behalf of his father."

Brad feared that the son was calling to say his father was not interested, but steeled himself and picked up.

Brad said, "Hello," and put the phone up to his ear.

"My father is considering talking to you," Benjamin said, "and I'm just calling to get more information."

A grin spread across John's face. His was a practiced ear, and he considered this call to be more than information gathering. "Just in my personal background of trying to get people for interviews," John ventured, "they don't ask those kind of questions unless they've already decided. If they are really truly on the fence, they have a different set of questions that put us on the defensive. This easygoing call from Benjamin is, I think, pretty positive."

"I hope your dad doesn't think I've been a pest over the last two months," Brad said, when Benjamin finished speaking.

"Not at all," Benjamin replied.

Bryan, a probate lawyer, hadn't needed a letter of introduction. He knew exactly who David Fincher was, and on the basis of his reputation, was agreeing that he might come up to Lake Berryessa with them and walk them through the scene. Benjamin said his father had done that for him and told him the story.

"Well, this is an opportunity to set the record straight," Brad said, then said goodbye.

"Maybe Bryan's just been thinking about it all this time," Brad told John. "We've been working for so long on getting Hartnell."

He could not wait to tell Fincher who was at that very moment in Hawaii vacationing with close friends, Brad Pitt and Jennifer Aniston, and his partner, Ceán Chaffin. With her blue-gray eyes, broad smile, and shimmering shoulder-length blond hair, Ceán was sunny and open, the perfect counterpoint to Fincher's darker nature. David first met her when she produced a Japanese Coca-Cola ad he was directing in the early '90s. They married soon after. The consummate professional, Ceán was a master of budgets and production. Whenever David needed to make a crucial decision about which film to make or what scene to shoot, she was the one whose opinion he most valued. The few times he hadn't listened to her were the few times he had been wrong. Fiercely protective and loyal, she was wary of anyone who might attempt to take advantage of him. "I don't see how they could."

"This week has been so insane," Brad continued. "I'm exhausted, but David really wants this film to be the last word on *Zodiac*. The deal is almost closed with Warner Brothers." He transcribed his calls, typing swiftly and error-free in spite of being completely worn out. He needed a vacation from *Zodiac*, from Jamie, Fincher, and himself and from the haunting riddle of the "Cipher Slayer." He yearned for a tropical island and a respite from the driving rain peppering the streets outside and the honeycombed Karloff House roof which amazingly still refused to fully yield to the downpour. On Saturday, Brad called Judy Colbert, the agent for Frank Black, lead singer for rock group, The Pixies.

"And this would be for the role of the Zodiac killer, right?" she asked.

"I'll say it's the part of the primary suspect," Brad replied.

"O.K., he's very interested and he's dying to meet with David," the agent said and hung up. Brad knew Black was excited. To the best of his knowledge *Zodiac* would be his first film role.

On Wednesday night, Brad and Jamie ate at a new Japanese restaurant. "They have the most amazing lobster rolls at this place," Jamie said, then looked at Brad and put the menu down. "Now I am very dubious of Brad's sushi-picking abilities because he got sick at a poison squid place," said, "but we'll have sushi anyway."

Brad and Jamie met with Fincher the whole of the next day, discussing dates and letters and expounding and exploding theories. They followed Fincher's rule. If something couldn't be proved, it did not go in the movie. This included Lake Herman Road, and possibly the Kathleen John's abduction which still troubled the filmmakers.

Fincher kept the Amazing Office really cold. He likes it chilly. His assistant, also named Jamie, was bundled up in a wool sweater. Finally, she broke and walked in during the middle of the meeting. "I'm turning on the heat," she said decisively. Fincher hardly noticed. Nor did Jamie who kept going back and forth from room to room, sitting down getting up and running in to check on stuff in the binders, going out and coming back. "O.K., we can move this here," he said. "This really happened here." "We're macro instead of micro," Brad reflected.

Every time Jamie turned up his collar and stepped out to the parking lot to have a cigarette he would have a thought, snub out his butt, rush back inside and say, "If we take a step back, how does this affect this?" Resting the *Zodiac* book on his left knee, Fincher tilted his head back and looked at the open book from a distance as if to take the whole story in at once. He was great with expanding and contracting.

As Jamie walked in again, Fincher halted him. "You can't go in there!" he said. "You'll see the Big Board."

"Its great to go through every scene, but I need to see the overall flow of the thing too," Jamie protested.

"All right," Fincher said, rising from his chair. "Let's go into the flowchart room" which Jamie found to be a very 'Dr. Strangelove-esque' room. The script's new shape was finally taking form. They now had a running time they needed to hit, but would Warner's give Fincher the money to shoot a 240 minute movie? Jamie hefted a huge sheath of papers as if weighing them. It was his script. "More like three hours," he calculated.

"I'm hoping we can close the main points of the deal that are left over, relatively small all things considered, before the holidays," Brad said.

"The problem is not to close . . ." Jamie said.

"The deal itself," Brad chimed in. By this point, they were finishing each other's sentences. As they immersed themselves more deeply into the mystery, they began finishing Fincher's sentences too which usually elicited a glare from the director.

"To relieve stress, I go to the gym," Brad said.

"Not true," Jamie said. "To relieve stress, Brad calls me."

Brad called Jamie so often and so late that Amber finally asked him, "Is Leigh Allen dead? "Yes," Brad answered. "Well, Jamie's sleeping. It's not like you're in a race against time to catch the guy," she said and hung up.

The next morning, Fincher bounded down the wide staircase to the high-ceilinged lobby. His "baby" had just been delivered. Still wrapped, it lay to his left on a little table at the foot of the stairs. He picked up the long package and carefully unwrapped it from its brown paper. Inside was a spade-shaped head—inclined, small, quick, efficiently designed, and primed to strike like a rattlesnake. Fincher lifted the lightweight camera in his arms and carried it up to the Amazing Office as if it was the most precious object in the world. It might be. It was a magnificent moment. He believed he could make his new camera sit up and do tricks. But first, he would have to break its back.

In the beginning, Fincher had considered two high resolution imaging systems—ARRI D-20 (Arriflex) and Dalsa Origin. Instead, he had chosen another three-sensor camera design, a light, relative newcomer to the field. The Thomson Grass Valley Viper, an HD video camera, captures data raw and shoots with little to no light. He had already tested the high speed, high capacity FilmStream/S.Two system on a few 30-second and 60-second Nike and HP commercials and liked the process of working digitally. He enjoyed the work flow of the S-2 because he didn't have to go to the lab or wait for pull takes. With no irreversible video manipulation, or compression, what the lens sees is what the camera delivers.

"Because of the random access and ability to review what I just shot in full resolution," he explained, "we could shoot, select a take, and go 'That's the one we want.'" Fincher was on uncharted ground, potentially dangerous ground. No major studio feature had ever been shot and produced digitally without the use of videotape or compression. His next movie, whether it be *Benjamin Button* or *Zodiac*, would be historic—the first motion picture ever shot entirely in the uncompressed digital format (except for traditional high speed film cameras for a few slow motion sequences).

Everyone was tired. Though there was no loss of interest in *Zodiac*, they needed a vacation.

On December 18, Jamie and Amber traveled east to visit his folks for Christmas. "This vacation is really to take time apart from Brad," Jamie said. "It is tough enough for him and I not to speak for one day. We've spoken almost every day for the last four years. It's been such a long process for us. Sometimes, it seems like two steps forward and three back."

MEANWHILE, HORN WAS GOING back and forth with Fincher's agent about terms.

"Phoenix would like Warners to close the deal and start cash flowing!" Jamie said. "A lot of the stuff we need to do is expensive. I'm not on salary, though Phoenix pays my travel expenses. One perk is that if I travel for any reason on a project, the company is required to fly you first class." Earlier, when Phoenix was talking to Sony, Jamie began an annotated draft for legal purposes, citing on each page where each item originated. Legal would have to be able to look at the script and be able to say where the information came from.

On December 20, Brad moved the rest of his possessions into the Karloff House, then left for the Bahamas. In San Francisco, Toschi was busy scheduling security people for Christmas and New Year's Eve. In Vallejo, Detective Mark Arneson was steadfastly searching for Mike Mageau and asking questions. So was George Bawart.

"Mike and his father," Bawart learned, "had been estranged. When the father died in 1998, they tried to locate Michael to come to the funeral and were unable to do so."

When Jamie and Amber returned from New York, three of her older brothers drove up from San Diego to celebrate New Year's Eve with them. After the holiday, Brad returned home to find the electrical wires in the Karloff House screwed up because of the rain. "Everything was a mess," he said. "My television doesn't work now. My telephones weren't on until yesterday when the telephone company spent the entire day hooking things up. I have absolutely no idea what's going on in the world." A week passed. Still no word on the budget. Everything was grim and gray. In his loneliness, Brad trudged down all 107 steps seeking the sound of human voices.

"We have made progress as far as the budget goes as far as getting the studio invested in making the film," Jamie updated. "It's a combination of companies, but Paramount has let Warner Brothers take the lead and set the terms in the negotiations. What Paramount doesn't want and Warners doesn't want is us trying to negotiate with both studios and playing them against each other. We've put ourselves on the block for David. Brad doesn't talk about it, but he has taken a lot of flack for sticking with David. It's been a really tough week for him. He's gotten beaten down by Mike Medavoy a little just because this process is taking so long. We're in really uncharted territory here because we're not asking Warner Brothers to buy the project. We're asking them to buy it and make it. It's having to make those three or four decisions at once. We're not just talking about them just paying me, we're talking about them giving us $75 million to make the movie in a situation where they don't really have much control over what the content of the film is going to be or the length.

"Part of the deal is that David has to turn in a theatrical version of the film that is no more than two hours and twenty-five minutes. David is comfortable with that. He says he wants the DVD cut of the film to be two hours and forty minutes, so they're talking about the differences in that. It's not such a leap of faith for Warner Brothers, but more of an investment. Either you're all in or you're not in at all. David won't take anything less. We won't either. The nuts and bolts of it is this question of overages. They've agreed on $75 million. David's agreed he can make the movie for that. I think he can too. David rarely goes over budget, but at the same time he doesn't want to be penalized for things that are out of his control."

Anytime you're shooting a movie with any scenes outside, bad weather can cause you to go over budget. Fincher did not want weather delays to come out of their back end. Ironically, if you are trying to shoot outside in a rain scene, you cannot have it really rain. In *Basic*, the one preproduction experience Brad and Jamie had shared, all the rain was man made—wind machines, flash machines, and rain towers with pipes like a huge shower. They had all the interiors in an aircraft hanger, two locations in Florida and a jungle in Panama. Preproduction takes a long time, especially on a film with many unique locations like *Zodiac*. "A movie like *Zodiac*," Jamie continued, "we're going to have to go to Washington and Cherry, and Lake Berryessa. We're going to have to build a lot of interiors—the *Chronicle* may be out on Treasure Island. We might have to double Vallejo in Marin somewhere." Two weeks of rain could force Fincher to change the shooting schedule, cover the sets, move the cast and trucks and shoot interiors at enormous cost. Insurance companies no longer cover "weather days." Studios have to cover them. Fincher wanted to make certain any overages did not completely come out of his pocket. "I'm not in the business of financing movies myself," he snapped.

"How's the rain in the Bay Area?" Brad asked Bawart on Monday, January 10, 2005.

"Three inches behind LA."

"The weather is just horrendous. I hope it clears up."

"We have to make offers to actors Jake and Benicio, their availability is this summer," Brad said. Jake Gyllenhaal had just completed *Proof*, based on David Auburn's Pulitzer Prizewinning play, wrapped *Jarhead* in LA with Jamie Foxx, and was doing the stage work at Universal. A tangential mention in an article about *Benjamin Button* revealed Fincher's interest in *Zodiac*. It was picked up by people on the message board. Now there was worldwide interest in the movie.

"We're headed up to San Francisco Wednesday morning, so everything looks like it's in shape, but we might be having a little trouble with one of the witnesses in the Stine shooting. Earlier, Inspector Kelly Carroll expressed relative confidence that it wouldn't be a problem, then I got a call that it is a problem. Kelly who spoke to the witness didn't sound very positive. He will be having dinner with him and press the subject then. The Stine witness is really important. David is so precise and getting his perspective is extremely important. When he's shooting that scene, he wants to have a sense of what specifically was seen from an upper floor across the street."

Brad called Jamie next.

"Jamie, did I tell you I spoke to a cop who knew Darlene. He said he'd love to meet with us, but we've got to pay him something— surprise, surprise, surprise. He wanted money, a significant amount of money. The only reason to talk to him is that he had a romantic relationship with Darlene as opposed to anything salient to say about the actual crime scene."

"Is Toschi excited about the meeting?" Jamie asked.

"Toschi's like the tide, excited one moment, shy the next."

Each time they dug into the case there was more to learn. Every little thread led to something else in the Zodiac Labyrinth. "We're looking into the Mike Mageau situation," Brad said. "Where the hell is Mageau?" Arneson, their private investigator, was on Mike's trail. He had turned up some interesting information: Mike's twin brother has a son who might be living in Las Vegas. Arneson was right behind Mike, but just kept missing him. He discovered some homeless people in the city of Highland who recognized him, but hadn't seen him around in a couple of weeks. "The two leads we've got are Temeculah south of Riverside, and Vegas," Arneson reported. "I'm trying to work a trip to Vegas." Arneson said with a laugh. "Brad's going for it because he says he wants to go to Vegas too."

At 2:30 PM, Brad and Jamie went over the final itinerary for their

Bay Area trip with Fincher. They were to visit each of the Zodiac crime scenes in chronological order with the original case detectives who might see something more this time than they did thirty-six years earlier. That night Brad attended a small dinner at the home of Barbara Davis, Marvin Davis' widow, who was honoring Mark Forster who had directed *Finding Neverland*.

Davis's son, John, was a producer at Twentieth Century Fox, a company Fincher had had a horrible experience thirteen years earlier while making his first film, *Alien 3*.

"It was a bloodbath to get made," Fincher recalled.

"David," Jamie asked him, "do you hate everyone at Fox?"

"Well, no," Fincher answered. "I haven't met everyone at Fox."

CHAPTER TWELVE

HOMICIDE PANCAKES

WEDNESDAY MORNING, THE TOWN car carrying the guys plunged into a driving rainstorm, the strongest storm of the new year so far. Fincher, Brad, and Jamie couldn't recall the last dry day. Damp and tired, Brad scanned the dark skies. For weeks a record breaking downpour had pelted LA with an astonishing seventeen inches of rain. Nevertheless, they splashed their way to LAX and by 7:30 AM, were strapped into seats 3A, 3B, and 3C on United Flight #976. "Jamie is going to fly—reluctantly," Brad said. "He tried to get me to drive. He really did. I just sort of sighed."

As they landed at SFX, Brad glanced at the heavy silver watch on his wrist. It was precisely 8:50 AM. For weeks, the Bay Area had been ravaged by the same storm system striking LA. As the filmmakers disembarked, it stopped raining as if a switch had been thrown. The sun wasn't far behind. It burst through gray thunderheads as they crawled across the Bay Bridge in their rented SUV, pushing against the morning rush hour traffic. It had become a lovely day. The sunny skies would stick with them throughout their crucial fact-finding trip, though it would be gloomy at Lake Berryessa with some precipitation there and back with wonderfully windswept blue-black skies in between. Soothed by the feminine voice of the NeverLost system, Brad entered a parking lot at the IHOP Restaurant in Northeast Vallejo. It was just off the freeway.

This morning, Fincher was dressed in a long-sleeved brown sweater, brown trousers, and running shoes. As a cool wind rose, he tugged a green wool fisherman's ribbed hat down over his ears. Brad wore a turquoise shirt under his immaculate zipper jacket. Jamie was attired in a blue sweater and sunglasses carelessly hooked by an earpiece into the *V* of his collar. The goatee he had vowed not to shave until the movie was greenlit was now scraggly and unkempt. As they crossed the wide parking lot, Jamie tossed his head back to rein in his long, windswept hair. His demeanor was so intense he could have been "Wild Bill" Hickok on his way to tame a Kansas town.

Inside the restaurant, the smell of buttermilk pancakes and hash browns assailed them. George Bawart and his former boss, Captain Roy Conway, were already there and waiting for them. Conway, a commanding figure in a sage jacket and light green sweater, looked every inch a chief. His thick dark hair was silvering at the temples. Bawart shook Fincher's hand, and slid into the red leather booth after him. Conway sat opposite, a bit remote, back pressed against the leather seat, reading Fincher as policemen do. Fincher was doing the same, just as directors do. Very early on, Fincher makes a decision about a person and asks himself: "Is this person even worth talking to or paying attention to or not?" Once he has decided you are, he will listen to you and respect your opinion. If he decides you are not, he can be dismissive. "He does not suffer fools lightly," Brad said.

"Let me brief you," Bawart began, placing both elbows on the Formica table and fixing his eyes on Fincher to his right. He wanted to be able to read the director's lips. Bawart's azure golf shirt perfectly matched the blue carafes scattered about the table. "Officer Howard 'Buzz' Gordon can't come," he began. "Neither can Officer Dick Hoffman [dental appointment] nor Ed Rust. A guy named Mike Travers out of Fairfield is going to meet us for lunch." Detective Sergeant Travers was in charge of the investigation division for the Solano County Sheriff's Office. "Afterward he's going to take us up to Lake Herman Road. I couldn't do that, I've never been there. I don't think Roy has ever been to the exact location." He looked across the table to Conway who was silently studying a tall, acetate-covered menu.

"Thirty-five years ago I was on Lake Herman Road in Solano County jurisdiction," Conway said brusquely without lifting his eyes. "Yeah, I was there."

"Was there ever a discussion," Fincher asked him, "where the DOJ or the DA said to you, 'It's not worth pursuing because Arthur Leigh Allen is going to be dead?'"

"Absolutely!" Conway said, suddenly animated. He laid down his menu and leaned forward, eyes bright with interest. "It was Jim Lang who had that conversation about pursuing the case. He was second in command in the Vallejo DA's office and had he pushed the case for filing it would have been filed. But, there was no practical reason to pursue this because if Allen's going to die shortly there is still all the stuff we would have to gear up because it was a death penalty case."

"Where is Jim Lang?"

"He's in the grave."

Conway and Bawart had good memories of Lang, a meticulous, conscientious man, who worked easily with them because of his varied background. Before Lang was a deputy DA, he was an LA cop and, after that, an LA homicide inspector while putting himself through law school. Since the LAPD had a flat twenty year retirement at the time, Lang went into private practice. When that didn't work out, he came up to Northern California and was appointed by the then-governor to be DA of Shasta County, a small county up north. Ultimately, he left the public defender's office, came down to Vallejo, and was hired in the DA's office as another grunt DA. It worked out real good." Lang was there seven years at most, before he was made Chief Deputy DA. He was assigned to work with Conway and Bawart because he could talk their lingo. Whenever the two detectives went off on a tangent, Lang would say, "Slow down here."

"Do we have a problem," Fincher asked, "if we have a scene in the movie where somebody says, 'He's gonna be dead in six months. We're not spending the amount of money that it takes to get a Grand Jury and get everybody hooked up.'"

"That's major paraphrasing, but what do I care?" Conway said. He shrugged. "My import doesn't have any meaning one way or the other."

"Sure it does." Fincher said earnestly. "You have at your fingertips more facts about this than most of the others, certainly SFPD. We'd like to work with you to reconstruct at least a facsimile of the moment where somebody says, 'We're confident that you have the answer or confident that this is the correct answer.'"

"The whole point is my personal satisfaction in convincing a guy like Jim Lang so that he is willing to put his career on the line," Conway said. "Jim Lang was assigned by Mike Nail to assist us in this case. This is unusual. They usually assign the police senior. There was a long, ongoing involvement almost on a daily basis. At one point I heard the words, 'I'm going to get the DA to file this if he's not hung up about Allen's dying.' But the DAs are politicians. They're not about to take a case that would ruin their career, because if something goes wrong— Not Guilty or whatever. So, the way they deal with guys like us, they say, 'Well, O.K., I need to have some followup on this particular point. Go find that information and come back to me when you've got that.' So we make an appointment two weeks later. 'Well, O.K., now you've got that, now I've been thinking you may need to follow up on that.'"

"They run you around," Bawart added. Conway explained that, as one of the biggest cases of their careers, there were so many politics involved that they're just not going to move.

"My question is this," Fincher said. "There's the practicality of it and then there's the perceived justice of it."

"When you're talking to DAs all they care about is the practicality of it," Conway said.

"Two million bucks to go forward and the guy's never going to get to the witness stand." Aloud, Fincher imagined the scenario: "The State of California finally got him—the manhunt is over. The guy may be in a fuckin' pine box, but the good guys won." He slapped the table enthusiastically.

"I worked for two chiefs of police," Conway said. "Both were kept apprised of how the investigation was going. Both of them were absolutely, in private discussions, satisfied: 'You solved the case.' 'O.K., then why don't you go tell the world?' 'Oh no, I couldn't do that. Are you kidding me?'"

"Why?" Fincher asked, feeling like he was in Wonderland.

"Because they'd be inundated with reporters and guys like you for the rest of their lives and just consume all their time for nothing. I got sick of it. There's a television special about Zodiac at least once a month and every time that comes up there are phone calls to us." During Conway's last five years at VPD, right up to his retirement in 1997, he spent a third of each week talking to somebody about Zodiac.

Fincher rested his elbow on the table, supported his chin with his hand and waited. He tried again, speaking in a calm voice. "We'd like to work with you to reconstruct at least a facsimile of the moment in time where somebody says of that critical juncture, 'We're confident that you have the answer or confident that this is the correct answer.'"

"Jim Lang is the one I got the biggest satisfaction out of saying that to me," Conway said and smiled.

"And part of the ramifications of this is that Mike Nail, the DA at the time," Bawart added, "was headed for a judgeship and could care less about the DA's office."

"And he wouldn't think of a trial on the Zodiac without somebody of the highest caliber he could find and he'd probably get a third or fourth opinion after that," Conway said.

"And so," Bawart said, "we had this two-fold meeting with myself, Roy, Mike Nail, Jim Lang, and DA Paulson, the present DA. That's where this list of reasons why we think the Zodiac is Arthur Leigh Allen came from. I was the author of that and we compiled that so we would have something to—." "That was a joint effort," Conway interrupted, proprietary about that list. "There's a couple of inaccuracies on the list that we found out after we made the list that I said, 'Uh, oh. We can't sustain that.'"

"We left those in there specifically because we can't sustain them," Bawart said with a big grin, "Let them figure out how to do it."

"At the time I was making the list, I didn't think it would ever be a public document. We knew the politics of Nail wanting to be a judge. We're working our ass off and there's nothing funny about it. That was when he turned down our filing on both of them. It was all 'tee-hee,' a big joke."

"The worst case scenario with Arthur Leigh Allen is this," Jamie interjected from the far end of the booth where he had been listening silently, "'What if we filed on him, it got thrown out, and then he dies. We look like morons. We know he's gonna die, better forget him.'"

"The real worst case," Bawart said, "is if you file on him and you get a Not Guilty and you've spent $1 million of the county's money prosecuting this case—"

"And then you're not the DA anymore," Conway said. "That's the worst case."

"This is also a guy at Valley Springs School who molested as many as two children that were under his supervision," Fincher said. "He kinda embroiled the parents. He worked as a classic sort of seducer-pedophile. When push came to shove and the principal of the school brought him in and sat him down and said, 'You fondled and maybe orally copulated with one if not two of the kids in your class. This guy burst into tears, confessed everything and lost his job in the same hour. How does that guy drive this kind of bizarre kind of—"

"I have a simple answer," Conway said. "He was a sick genius." During the service of the 1991 search warrant on the suspect's house, Conway spent nearly an entire day speaking with Leigh Allen. They had sequestered him upstairs to restrict him to one spot in the house so he would not be wandering around. "Upstairs, O.K., fine," Allen had said.

"Lieutenant Hauser here is going to be sitting with you, Leigh," Bawart told him that day. Hauser, about six foot-four inches tall, weighed two hundred and fifty and had played for the Houston Oilers. "Just a huge man, he'd make mince meat of Arthur Leigh Allen. They sat up there and just chatted back and forth. I wanted to make sure I put somebody there who was intimidating enough, although Arthur Leigh Allen at that particular point was pretty sick. He had diabetes, walked with a cane, had difficulty seeing. People would say to me, 'How come you're leaving this guy out on the street?' The answer is that I don't know if he's a threat anymore."

"The most convincing thing about Leigh Allen," Conway continued, "he would never admit that he was the Zodiac. He always denied all kinds of things, but when we played that recording that we found in his room . . ."

"Of the screaming kids being spanked?" Fincher asked.

"The kids being spanked. I instantly saw what happened to him when he was confronted by something he couldn't deny, something he couldn't walk away from . . ."

"Couldn't explain away, couldn't cry away—," Jamie said from the far end of the booth.

"That was the moment that I knew that we had him," Conway said. "Though he would never admit it." When the police found the tape, that slowed the tempo of his conversation.

"When we started playing that tape he knew what was coming,"

Bawart said. Before then Allen's general conversation had been joking, messing with you, and misusing words in conversation. "His English was good. He was a teacher, but when he was talking to me, he'd say, 'done did' or something like that, screw up his English and screw up his pronunciation. He would write 'eggs' as 'aigs.' He liked to screw with you like he's putting something over on you. He was shocked that we caught him in a lie, because he was bragging that he was not worried about anything and could explain away anything we bring up to his face. Leigh was big into puttin' something over on people."

"When was it you brought it to Jim Lang?" Brad asked. "That point where he said, 'You know what, I would feel comfortable doing it or I would be uncomfortable doing it.'"

"After the second search warrant," Bawart said, "enough evidence against main suspect, Arthur Leigh Allen, developed that we went to file the case. Two weeks later, [August 26, 1992], Arthur Leigh Allen failed to answer his upstairs neighbor's knock. A young woman renting the upstairs peered into his basement room, they are on a rise there, and saw him lying on the floor. VPD Officer Jerry Durrand determined he was dead and called the Fire Department. Paramedics arrived and they confirmed he was deceased. Durrand called me at home and said, 'Hey, George, I'm in Leigh Allen's living room here and he's dead on the floor. And he's bleeding from a wound on his forehead and it looks like its still kind of fresh.'"

Bawart had rushed there and descended into the basement. "I could see where he hit a coffee table when he fell and cut his head," he said. Bawart had insisted they have an autopsy because Leigh Allen had accused him and Conway on TV of trying to kill him. "'They're trying to kill me, the skunks,' he had shouted," Bawart recalled, "and I wanted to clear the air on that. When Coroner Jimmy O'Brien arrived, I told Jimmy, 'We have to have an autopsy.' I also wanted to collect DNA so they would have it if something new came up."

Bawart had seen Allen's computer glowing in the dark. Information about Zodiac was on the screen. "It was something innocuous," Bawart recalled. "I saw the computer, but that's not illegal. It's in plain view. You can do that. But if I wanted to look at anything else I would have to write a search warrant. Now, I don't know what expectation of privacy he would have after he's already dead. The family would raise that.

That's the only reason I wrote that second search warrant. We put an addendum to the search warrant. There was enough that I thought I should look at the other stuff—such as a posthumous letter from Leigh Allen." Because he had been a notorious pack rat, the VPD knocked holes in the drywall and tore the place apart "pretty good." They searched the crawl spaces under the house, rumored to have a hidden room, and found nothing, only rusted car parts. The brother, who owned the house as part of the trust and had dispensed it to Leigh, was never paid to repair the damage or given an apology—standard police department policy.

"I would have liked to have seen this go through the court system," Bawart said. "I would have liked it solved by a jury of twelve. Unfortunately, there's no vehicle to do that once you die. There's no way to file on a dead guy. O'Brien ruled that the death was due to natural causes."

As Fincher sat rigidly in his seat, taking in Bawart's recitation, he glanced past the bright red Valentine hearts stuck to the plate glass window. Between two pink cupids, he saw a tall, square, young man in civvies and coatless, climbing out of a green Ford. His blond hair was set off by a fresh white shirt and rainbow-colored tie. His holster and badge were plainly visible at his belt. Detective Sergeant Travers was eager to get into what was a new case for him. Fincher waved to him through the glass. He headed inside.

"There's somebody," Conway said, "that Allen told, 'I want to be the Zodiac.'"

"Don Cheney," Jamie and Brad said together.

"We talked to Don Cheney," Fincher said. "He literally says that Leigh took him in a car and took him to Lake Herman Road . . ."

"He told you guys that?" Conway said.

"This is the problem with Cheney who is by all accounts, as Leigh's brother will say, unimpeachable, absolutely," Fincher raised his voice above the clatter of the crowded restaurant. "If Don says it happened, it happened. Don Cheney is extremely reliable from all sources. Again, it is like everything with this case. Eighty percent of it that you go, 'O.K., that makes perfect sense,' and twenty percent of it fuckin' makes it wiggly and hard to get your hands on."

"What you're telling me is that he's embellished the story over the years," Conway said. "But the point is at the time Cheney told us about Leigh Allen, there's no logic for him making it up."

"There is good reason to believe that a lot of people involved in the case have children that had been molested by Leigh Allen," Fincher speculated. "I believe that Don Cheney acted prudently and the way that he describes his fears. His three year old says to him after a boating trip while he was living over in Walnut Creek or Orinda, 'Uncle Leigh, touched my bottom.' From that moment on, and Cheney knows him for a good, eight-nine months . . . and they're fraternizing, he never allows his children to be in proximity to Allen. And what he says, and I buy it, as a fairly neurotic parent, I buy it. What he did was he just refused to bring his children or his wife, who had issues with Leigh. So again, seventy-five percent of what Cheney says, if you'd only stop there, I'd have something great. You had to go the extra mile."

They pushed aside their cups, got up, and crossed the street for more of a substantial meal than coffee and diet cola. Outside, Fincher extended his arms upward as if asking for strength. "I tend to believe them, especially when thirty years has passed. The truth is somewhere in the middle with people forgetting certain things. When you honestly look at history and any kind of group of people who all see the same event or participate in the same event and describe it exactly the same, then I think you should be suspicious."

As they reached the door to the Black Angus Restaurant, David, Brad, and Jamie recited their mantra.

"I believe Dave Toschi.

"I believe Don Cheney.

"I believe the family.

"I believe that thirty years have passed."

FACING PAGE: 1) Capt. Roy Conway and David Fincher. 2) David Fincher and Detective George Bawart. 3) Jamie Vanderbilt and Brad Fischer.

CHAPTER THIRTEEN

SPINELLI

LIGHT BOILING THROUGH THE colored window in the steam-filled backroom of Black Angus created a stained-glass effect. Like grape shot, overly solicitous waiters assaulted the detectives and filmmakers on all sides. Their apparent mission was to sidetrack any cogent discussion and derail any train of thought just as Fincher was about to learn a new fact: "Is everything all right?" "Can we get you anything?" "Is everything O.K.?"

"Yes. Yes," Fincher said. "But could you turn the music down?" The director had to yell above the clink of dishes and booming music. Focusing his thoughts, he began once more: Take 2. "You got a guy who's two years, three years removed from Atascadero. We know that he's deathly afraid of serving any more time and he's a convicted felon who has a box full of pipe bombs. You tell me—why didn't you squeeze his nuts then? Why didn't you say to him, 'We're not fucking around. You'll be in San Quentin,' cause we know this guy blubbers like a baby when he's confronted with hearsay? The word of two children in Valley Springs and he doesn't miss a beat. He doesn't deny a fucking thing. These are third graders. Why do you listen to them? No, he goes, 'You're right,' he says, 'I have a problem.'"

"When you throw in the fact that he's a fucking genius on a scale of anybody's standards," Conway said, "ambidextrous, and has a factual knowledge of all kinds of obscure information, then we look at the books and his writings in the house that day. He's just extraordinary whether he was the Zodiac or not. He just grew out of being a pedophile and his satisfaction in life became taunting people."

"It's interesting," Fincher said, "because the thinking is consistent with the notion that here's a guy who in the spring of 1968 loses everything." Fincher paused, seeing parallels in his own life. "He's worked his whole life to be a teacher. He has certain sublimated urges that are part of his reason to want to be around kids, but he, on the day-to-day, certainly cares for them. He overly cares for them, and all of a sudden he's discovered to be this monster. He moves back into his parent's house. He soft-pedals the whole thing to his brother, Cheney, and Panzarella. He's living in Southern California, and he says, 'You know it's politics and I lost my job.'"

Fincher explained to the detectives that his movie was about a time, a place, a process and a series of events that shaped California in an interesting way. "Certainly Graysmith came to his conclusion," he said, "and it was good enough for him. He felt like he knew who the guy was and he knew the hardware store he worked at. When Leigh died, he felt like it was put away. That's what we want to present. We also know there has to be a scene in it where the Department of Justice says, 'This is all really interesting stuff. I wish we could follow through on it, but the reality of the situation is that we can't put this guy on trial so if there's not going to be that kind of public satisfaction there's no real upside. And we want to talk about the politics of that. The case against Leigh is a good one. I buy it. I look at it and it's incredibly compelling. But it's circumstantial and we have to kinda present that and go, 'We think everyone can rest easy.'"

"Circumstantial cases are the best cases," Conway snorted. "Most people think there's something derogatory about the word 'circumstantial.' A fingerprint on the windowsill, that's circumstantial; having bombs in your basement is circumstantial."

"This is a convicted felon with bombs in his basement and guns. They would have filed on that in a hot second. Why didn't they?"

"Because he's going to die!"

"What I'm saying is that I'm working backwards from lots of conclusions that the books draw," Fincher said. "What I think is interesting is, because I do not buy Kathleen Johns. I don't buy Riverside. I think it's interesting in both cases—Kathleen Johns and

Riverside in writing, in irrefutable Zodiac evidence, we know that he's taking credit for something that he probably didn't have anything to do with. So we know that's a mechanism, that's one of the things that he's comfortable doing. If Lake Herman Road is not the first Zodiac [killing], then it's a problem for me. If I'm to accept the idea of an evil genius, I don't see a lot of genius work in the notion of going out to hunt people with a .22." Conway agreed that Zodiac took advantage of the Lake Herman Road thing because it was there. Fincher thought that made sense. "But now, it's contextualizing the thing in a whole different way. You've got somebody who's a loner . . .

"Who's never had a relationship with a woman in his life," Conway interjected.

"Except when he was working as a diver over at the JC," Bawart added. "She was one of the girls on the high school JC diving team and dumped him for one reason or another. She's always said it was platonic, but she's the one who witnesses him beating up the sailors and she's one of the reasons he goes to fuck over [Ralph] Spinelli."

"Never had a relationship with a man that wasn't based on some sort of weird duplicity," Fincher said, "we know that the molestation that sent him to Atascadero was a boy. So, there's a homosexual leaning there to begin with."

They sat in silence trying to gauge their suspect. Bawart sipped his Diet Coke. Fincher lifted his cup of decaf coffee. "When Leigh gets upset he writes a letter," he said, motioning to Brad for the black binder. "Take this one. It's brimming with suppressed anger and racism." He showed Conway and Bawart a copy of a note that Leigh had written to a friend while incarcerated at Atascadero. "This might provide some insight into his mind. When Dee Brandon of Ward 4, Atascadero, was hit by a patient in the food/diet line, Allen submitted a formal complaint to assistant director Dave Hamilton:

> My reason for writing is to affirm that the incidents do happen when the black woman, Kathy, is on the diet line. Her crew (all Black, some very obnoxious) is noted for shorting patients on food so servers can take more 'leftovers' with them when they leave. I believe that Kathy is very racist. I can clearly remember being shorted on my meat, while the black behind me on a lower calorie diet received a double portion when he answered 'yes,' to 'want some more, brother?' I believe

myself to be objective and non-prejudiced in racial matters. This may be verified by Mr. Tueban Tarver, the hospital x-ray tech and his son, Mike. They are both good friends of long standing. Mike works here in food services. Less than two months ago I complained of being shorted (which has happened several times on Kathy's shift) . . . The server became extremely indignant and followed me out as I left with my tray and threatened me in the hall. Staff from a passing ward intervened before he could hit me. As I am diabetic, I could ill-afford this action.

"We also know," Fincher continued, "that six months prior to Lake Herman and a year prior to Blue Rock Springs, he not only loses his job as a teacher, but under particularly interesting circumstances. His motivation is to get back at society."

"That's not his motivation," Conway said firmly.

"You don't buy it?" Fincher leaned forward, alert, interested. "Then what is it?"

"His motivation is to satisfy his urges to taunt the police. You attribute criminal revenge to his motivation. The several hours I spent with Leigh Allen, he could have, logically speaking, said, 'O.K., fine, I'm the Zodiac. So what? I'm going to die in a few weeks. I wouldn't mind the publicity. My confession would put the topping on the cake and everything. Why would I do that when I get a lot more satisfaction out of taunting you guys on how much of a genius I am?' That's what I came away with from that conversation. The shooting of people was not a revenge on society or anything any more than molesting a kid."

"Molesting a kid," Fincher said, "is the only outlet for a bottled sexuality that has existed for years."

Conway believed Allen's genius had to have an outlet—writing recipes, glorifying himself on being a master sailor and archery expert, and a hundred other things. The veteran detective believed the whole idea behind the Zodiac killings was to do something heinous and write letters about it.

Fincher nodded and elaborated—"That is consistent with somebody who is writing the *Chronicle* and *Vallejo Times* and Vallejo PD and saying, 'I'm responsible for this,' and they're saying, 'If you are, give us some more information.' It would be consistent with the self-righteous, 'I did do that, God dammit, and I'm taking my place in history. You cannot deny me my ink!'"

Fincher replaced the letter in the three-ring binder. "That would also be consistent with a man who knows he's got five, ten minutes before he hears sirens going to Washington and Cherry," Fincher said, "after shooting Paul Stine and knows not to run. If you're smart, you know that running is: A: going to draw attention and B: leave you open to all kinds of slipping and falling and hurting yourself. So he calmly walks around—we still don't know what he was doing at Washington and Cherry. What was Zodiac doing all that time?"

Conway brought up the jurisdictional issue. "If there would have been a task force formed like we did in later years, it would have been a slam-dunk." He explained that every law enforcement agency in the world now immediately forms a task force. "The chief of police calls up the chief of police of someplace else and gets people assigned. They've had marvelous results when they did that."

"That's what Graysmith was doing," Fincher said.

Conway turned in his seat to gaze down the table at Brad and Jamie. Brad had something to say.

"So Graysmith was going and talking to Vallejo." he said, "and then to Toschi and telling him things he never knew and back and forth."

"George," Jamie asked, "you said you didn't know they had searched the Santa Rosa trailer until the book came out . . ." Arthur Leigh Allen had lived in that trailer as a student while attending Santa Rosa JC and Sonoma State.

"Yeah," Conway interjected, answering for Bawart, "that's a fact."

"If the SFPD had done a search of Fresno Street at the same time as the trailer the case would have been solved on the spot," Bawart added. "I was scared off by Toschi after the bad publicity surrounding the 1978 Zodiac forgery letter. At the time, I didn't want to get information from him that would taint my search warrant, so I went to Armstrong in 1991 instead. He maintained that Allen was living full time in his trailer in Santa Rosa."

"So they were misinformed," Fincher said.

Allen had other trailers: Roy's Used Cars & Wrecking Yard between Vallejo and Napa, and Tall Trees Trailer Park in Vallejo. Other trailers might be hidden in a tract of deep woods at Dillon Beach or Morro Bay where he had close friends, or at Bodega Bay where he often sailed and dived.

"Allen still maintained a house in his mother's name," Bawart said. "I can't get into their mind what they were thinking back in 1971."

"Did you ask Toschi why they didn't serve the search warrant in Santa Rosa and Vallejo at the same time? Conway asked.

"Yeah, we did," Fincher said. "I think they couldn't get one."

"Nonsense!" Conway snapped. "With that search warrant information, cause we piggybacked it ourselves, you could have served that search warrant in Atlantic City if you wanted to."

"The DA's office wanted everything done by them," Bawart added. "But if you got all this legalese bullshit, I would write a search warrant, take it directly to a judge, circumvent going to the DA's office. San Francisco—they don't make an arrest; they don't do anything unless they have someone from the DA's office. In Vallejo we never operated that way." Bawart once had a suspect living down south in Hawthorne. Having never even seen the house, he wrote a search warrant, had it signed in Solano County and personally served it in LA County. "You can serve a search warrant from one county to another. The only thing you have to do is let the city you are coming into know you're there." Everyone focused on their lunch and silently considered past mistakes and missed opportunities. Finally, Conway looked up.

"What was the name of the guy who took up all of our time?" he said and looked to Bawart. "Oh, yeah, Harvey Hines." His face lit up with a big smile. "Now if you guys took the time to have lunch with Harvey Hines, an Escalon police officer, you'll have a whole different movie. Very articulate. I spent hours with Harvey Hines—unfortunately." Conway considered him obsessed, a man who went to more lengths to find out facts than he would have ever done. Conway found Hines's theories interesting on the face of it. "The problem was when you start digging into it—"

"Yet," Bawart interjected, "keep in mind that Hines started our motor going again. In the middle of our digging, Ralph Spinelli came up. He was the key to the whole thing. Spinelli claimed that [in 1969] he had a conversation with Arthur Leigh Allen in which Allen told him several days before Stine was shot that he was going to go to San Francisco and kill a cabdriver. I'm completely convinced he was telling the truth about that."

"Really? Interesting," Fincher said. "Why is that?"

"It had credibility because it was a way to convince somebody like Spinelli that he's credible," Conway said. "Because Spinelli, knowing him, would say to Leigh Allen, 'Oh, you're full of shit. I don't believe a word you are saying. Get out of my face.' And he says to Spinelli, 'Well, I'll prove it.' 'How you gonna prove it?' 'I'll go do this and you'll see it in the paper and you'll know it was me because I told you in advance.'"

"Yes, that goes to the notion of somebody who wants to claim credit."

"I'm telling you, I was convinced. George and I had some pretty interesting conversations with him. Spinelli got us to reinvestigate the whole case and things the department had not done. The search warrant, the whole thing came from Ralph Spinelli. If it wasn't for him we wouldn't have bothered because we had already given up, finished."

"But my question is if Spinelli, who is characterized as being—"

"A lowlife crook," Conway said, "Lowlife crooks are the ones we deal with."

"Why does Allen want to impress Spinelli? Just because he's a hard guy?"

"I'm generalizing, but Spinelli was considered as close to low Mafia as you could get."

"Is there a Mafia in Vallejo?" Fincher asked with a grin.

"Some gambling, a few whores," Bawart said. "But two whores do not a Mafia make."

"Spinelli never plea bargained," Conway said. "George and I went to him two or three times and tried to cut a deal with him."

"Remember," Bawart said, "he called us back and we ended up in that goddamn cell and he said to us, 'Hey, I gotta have a deal on this. I go free on all this.'"

"What Spinelli wanted was the deal before he would give us anything. We went back and forth, two or three meetings. The way it was always left with Spinelli the last word was 'Fuck you!' and he said, 'Fuck you!' to us."

"I've got them coming at me," Spinelli said later, "and I'm thinking if anyone is using his head I'm going home. Robbery vs Zodiac Killer— that gets a little heavy. Who's not going to make a deal on this? I had a conflict lawyer, Pat Kelly, and he didn't want to get involved in the Zodiac stuff. Kelly told me that Bawart and Conway went to Mike

Nail, the DA, to make a deal. He said, 'I can't do anything with it.' People need to know, the families need to know these people had another agenda. When I was arrested on the Oregon case, they came at me with just a herd of cops—Solano County DAs, Deputy DAs, Solano County Sheriffs, Fairfield PD, California CI&I, and federal. Just a herd of cops. I had just taken money for my lawyer out of the safe and I'm walking out the back door of the Crazy Horse Saloon, when I hear, 'Ralph.' I look and around the corner of the building is Mike Nail pointing a gun at me."

"Spinelli got sentenced to Pelican Bay which is a bad, bad prison," Bawart told Fincher. "He was of the impression Conway and I caused him to be sent to Pelican Bay, cause we wanted to jack him up. And we fathered that. But we had nothing to do with it. A cop can't say who gets sentenced to XYZ prison." Conway and Bawart saw Spinelli for the last time at the state's ultra-maximum security prison some 280 miles north of San Francisco where he was serving a ten-year stint.

"I had clean sheets last night and a nice dinner," Bawart told him. "How about you, Ralph?"

Spinelli laughed in his face. "George, you're telling me like it doesn't happen to you very often." A pause. "OK, what is my sugar here? What do I get out of this deal?"

"We'll put in a word with the Parole Board."

"George, I don't go to the Parole Board. Convicts don't go to the Parole Board. I have a parole date already. The only people who go to the Parole Board are lifers. There's nothing you can do to help me. You're too late. You waited too long." The judge had the discretion to bring Spinelli back and change his sentence, but lost that discretion after ninety days. Bawart and Conway had waited one hundred-plus days. Shocked by Spinelli's revelation, the detectives asked some guards to verify it. "When you tell the guards I was connected to Zodiac," Spinelli said, "that is not a good thing for me at Pelican Bay. Why are you doing all this kindness for me?"

"We're giving you a chance to clear your conscience," Bawart said.

"All right fellas, take off. I'm not prepared to deal with stupid."

"You're full of shit, Spinelli," Bawart told him, "I'm putting a letter in your jacket. When you're convicted every time you come up for parole they going to open that jacket and see 'Has information, major

murder cases, refuses to divulge information.' The parole board's going
to look at that and say, 'O.K., fine. Go back and think about it another
twenty-three years.' And that's what's going to happen."

"You're threatening me," Spinelli said. "You can't legally do that."

"Yes, we will," Conway said.

"Did you tell anybody about what you knew at the time?" Bawart
asked.

"Yes," Spinelli said.

"Well, we'd like to talk to them."

"Well, you can't talk to them until I talk to them first to see if it's
all right with them and I'm not going to do it over the telephone. You
know what you have to do, fellas. Here's the deal: I go home and I'm
there for you. I'll do this."

"It's not going to happen on your terms," Conway told him.

"Well, in that case it's *not* going to happen, fellas," he said. "Let's
just call it a day. I'll go do my time. I'll do what I have to do and you go
and do what you have to do."

"Let me ask you this," Fincher asked when Conway and Bawart
had finished their story. "Arthur Leigh Allen—has far too much contact
with children. He lives in a fucking basement. He's kind of a closet case.
He's not a guy who frequents strip clubs. We know that he beat up some
people or had been in physical altercations with a couple of people on a
couple of different times when he was younger, but by the time Zodiac
is happening, by the time Spinelli would have had this conversation
before Paul Stine [was shot], he's not a guy who's fraternizing with
anybody. So how did Ralph Spinelli come into contact with Arthur
Leigh Allen?"

The racket inside the Black Angus Restaurant had grown louder.
Bawart adjusted his hearing aid. Fincher leaned forward, Brad and
Jamie moved closer. This was going to be interesting.

"We told Spinelli, 'You corroborate and we'll see what kind of
deal,'" Conway said, "He said, 'I want the deal and then I'll give you the
corroborating information.' What we wanted from Spinelli was very
simple. People that would corroborate the conversation, that saw him
with Arthur Leigh Allen."

"Just physically in the presence," Bawart said. "We didn't even
need to corroborate the conversation—just physically in his presence."

"One name," Fincher said. That would be the case breaker. There was such a person.

CHAPTER FOURTEEN
THE WITNESSES

RALPH SPINELLI'S EARS HAD to be burning. Some thirty-five miles from the Black Angus where Fincher was praying for a second witness, Spinelli was seated in a booth at the Daily Grill being interviewed. The restaurant was only two blocks from the Clift Hotel where Brad, Jamie, and Fincher had stayed in January. The focus of the story was his published memoir of his time at Pelican Bay "the toughest joint anywhere." What showed of him above the tabletop were a pair of broad shoulders and powerful arms, a thick white mane, and a strong, square chin. His eyes were penetrating, daring. Since his release from prison earlier, Spinelli had become an award winning nonfiction writer and earned a PhD.

"I recently learned that my story, 'House Cleaning,' he began with a smile to the reporter, "is required undergraduate reading at St. Mary's College. That pumps my head up a little."

The word on the streets back in the '60s was that Spinelli "was Italian organized crime." His father had paid him to commit his first serious felony at age fifteen. "He knew I would never rat on him," Spinelli laughed. "My dad and uncle were thought to be the local gangsters. They all drove new Cadillacs and owned bars, and were involved in gambling. Dad was also in the vending machine business which encompassed slot machines." Back then, Spinelli had commonly carried $50,000 in his pocket, what he called "walking around money." After his release from prison at age fifty-nine and a heart attack, his life was a far cry from those days. "By the way," he said, "all the information Conway and Bawart ever got was given backdoor by my public defender who told them, 'O.K., he wants to cooperate.' As soon as they knew I was in custody they went right to Arthur Leigh Allen and told him what I had said. He and I had an unspoken understanding that I wouldn't tell anybody. You can imagine how that went."

On July 19, 1974, Zodiac mailed a threatening letter to *Chronicle* columnist Count Marco Spinelli, asking that Spinelli be "put back in the hell hole whence he came." "I took it to be a veiled threat against me," Spinelli said. "After all, Pelican Bay is known as the '*Hell Hole* of California.'

"It was 4:00 AM, the summer of 1958, when I first met Leigh Allen. I was asleep in a small detached room at the rear of my father's house on Manzanita Street in Vallejo when a knock sounded at my door. Still in my boxer shorts, I opened up to see some guy I barely knew."

The teenage intruder leaped into the room, slammed the door behind, and within seconds they were battling. Ralph, a 190 pound football player, was very strong in those days and got his attacker down on his knees. The teenager grabbed Spinelli by the balls and was holding on for dear life when the door imploded in the center and a huge man burst into the room. "This was a heavy door, no lightweight thing," Spinelli said. "He hit it hard. I figured he was a friend of the guy I was tussling with, which was the case. He wasn't at the party I had just left so they must have been friends. He must have got him and said, 'I've got a guy I've got to go beat the shit out of. Come on, I want you to help me.' The fact that he obviously hit the door with his shoulder and was coming in behind it, saved my bacon. He stumbled in."

The stranger was carrying a huge hunting knife and the fight suddenly got serious. "It was clear to me he was on a mission and this man was possessed. My instinct told me this guy is not in touch with his immortal soul. He has no contact with it at all. This man doesn't care. I could see that in his face. If it's lights out for him right now, it doesn't matter. He was putting it all on the line. That's a very dangerous type of person. I've often thought I may be the luckiest guy in that he hit that door with his shoulder and fell into it. If it had been me, I would have stood back and kicked the door." Spinelli snatched his baseball bat from the corner.

"I cracked him with it. The bat hit him in the front of the forehead." Spinelli made a quick diagonal slice with his hand across his left eye to show the exact spot. "I would have continued to hit him if it were necessary, but by that time my father was out there and everything was under control. The cops got there and said, 'This is Ralph Spinelli, Jr., and Ralph Spinelli, Sr., but who the fuck is Leigh Allen? Who gives a shit?' All we knew was we didn't need this kind of grief—. It turned out Allen was arrested, taken into custody and, as I understand, later discharged from the navy because of this. Too bad he got so stupid. It wasn't any of his business. His mother asked my father not to press charges. Dad said, 'I don't want to press charges.' So we didn't press charges. Now, because we did not press charges, Allen thought we were great guys. Allen, who was eighteen or nineteen years old at the time, ultimately paid for the door and charges were dropped. One fifteen-minute incident in my life and it meant nothing to me, but it meant something very big to him.

"When Leigh was in the Navy stationed at Treasure Island he got caught with weapons concealed in his car, a gun and a knife. The gun, which was Navy property, had the serial numbers filed off. Leigh's father, a former Navy officer, got a big shot lawyer to represent Leigh and used his juice to avoid a dishonorable discharge for his son. So 1969 comes along. I'm in my office at the Crazy Horse Saloon in Fairfield [the former Fire Plug 2]. The intercom rings and it's Preston [a young Fairfield vet]." Spinelli had hired the clean-cut, respectable twenty-four year old airplane mechanic from Travis AFB as a vending machine business manager for S&S Vending by day and a bodyguard by night at the Crazy Horse. Preston, an Armijo High grad who had been drafted during the Vietnam War, had worked on Travis AFB in 1965-66. Spinelli said that Allen had worked on the base at the same time and only two blocks away, but doubted that Preston had known him then. His reaction when Allen showed up at the door pretty much proved that."

"Some guy out here wants to see you," Preston said.

"Some guy? Who is it?" Spinelli asked.

"I don't know."

"A cop?"

"No, I don't think so," said Preston, who had gotten a close look at him.

"'Tell him I'll be there in a few minutes,' I told him. So I go outside, and there's this big guy out there."

"What can I do for you?"

"Why," he said, "I'm Leigh Allen."

"Well, help me out, Leigh. Who the hell are you?"

"Can we talk somewhere?"

Spinelli was hesitant, but asked Leigh to step outside anyway. Around this time some prosecutors had been sending people into the Crazy Horse to entrap Spinelli because they considered the bar a "stepping off place for organized crime on the West Coast." "They would come in with an offer to kill somebody," Spinelli said. "You can't imagine the stuff they would try. So by this time I'm really cynical. Leigh Allen makes a brazen proposal to me. He suggests he can provide a service for some of my friends to kill people and take the heat off of us. He'll misdirect."

"Get away from me!" Spinelli bellowed and pushed at Allen, really just to see if he was wired. "Get out of here! I don't know why you would come to me with something like that. The answer is no!"

"Well, he came back a second time—well after Blue Rock Springs, and Preston admitted him and stood by in case he was needed. 'Dude, I don't want any of this,' I told him. 'I don't want to talk to you about this. I don't believe you. I want you to get away.' It was the third time that he came to me with the same proposal that he told me he was Zodiac. He didn't say, 'I am *the* Zodiac.' He said, 'I'm Zodiac.' I thought to myself this guy is looney-tunes. He's certifiable. Why would anybody, at this time, make that statement? And I told him that, 'I don't know why you would tell that. Look, I still don't believe you. Stay away from here!' Then he said, 'I'm going to prove to you who I am. I'm going to kill someone in San Francisco. You'll know it's me.' Two nights later Paul Stine was killed and there was no doubt in my mind when that happened—that's not a coincidence. A guy doesn't come and say, 'I'm Zodiac and I'm going to do this,' and then this guy gets killed and Zodiac takes credit for it.

"I did go to my lawyer immediately and talked to him about what I knew. He said, 'Don't tell me anything about this.' I talked to my dad and I talked to my Uncle Phil about it. My uncle never wanted any notoriety. He was really old school. 'I don't want to hear anything about this. Keep that to yourself.' My dad was trying to think of some way we could turn the information into money. So I talked to three people about what Leigh Allen told me—my dad, Uncle Phil, and my lawyer. At the time, it never occurred to me for a second that I should give him up so that I could give the families of the victims some peace. I didn't give them any consideration. Didn't even think about it. Now, I would like to say to those people I am sorry. But I'm different now. I'm smarter than I was then. My priorities are different now. My values are different and I realize that may have made a difference."

"Later, after Leigh's visit, an interesting thing happened. We played a lot of pool at the Crazy Horse. We had some really good shooters. Nobody could beat Preston if he didn't want to be beat. We had a world champion in there one night. We took all the money he had and shooting one-handed. We were that good. So anybody that was in there on the pool table we'd watch them to see how good is this guy. Well, Leigh Allen came in and is shooting pool by himself and he had a shot where a normal person would have taken a bridge for going behind his back. He just switched hands. Well, I had a stepson who was ambidextrous and I said to Preston, 'Look at that.' A very important part of shooting pool is how you leave the cue ball. If you don't have a shot you want to make, then you leave it bad for your opponent. If you've got a guy who's ambidextrous it's much more difficult to leave it bad. So I just filed that fact away in my head and told myself I'm not going to play this guy for money. So that's how I knew Leigh was ambidextrous and when the police started saying this handwriting doesn't match—No shit, really! Tell me again. I'm trying to remember which hand he held the knife in that night when he broke through my door. Somehow in my memory the knife was in his right hand, but I can't swear to that— that was nearly fifty years ago." Spinelli inclined his head so that his thick white curls fell to one side. He thought some more. "It was his right hand," he said, and stood. Seated, his wide shoulders and large head had made him appear formidable. Standing, he was a very short man, and though stocky, a sense of frailness clung to him.

"I could have made the case for them," he said sadly. "I could have given them Zodiac. I wish I had spoken sooner." Shortly after the cabbie's murder, Spinelli had gone away for a long stretch and taken his knowledge with him, leaving behind someone who could place him together with the prime suspect—Preston, his bouncer and manager, a standup guy who was now a successful mechanic. Since then, he had thought little of the big man who often visited Spinelli and shared hushed secrets with him.

CHAPTER FIFTEEN

THE LONELY ROAD

"ONE NAME," FINCHER SAID over his lunch at Black Angus. He pushed his plate away. He had hardly touched. "Just one witness physically in the presence of Spinelli and Allen." His expression said, "Now is that so much to ask." He looked Conway and Bawart in the eye. "We didn't even need to corroborate the conversation." Fincher was both perplexed and suspicious at the same time. "But it doesn't make sense that he tells Spinelli this thing, only because I'm not as steeped in it as you are. It didn't make sense to me that he brags to Spinelli."

"Again," Bawart said, "working backward from aberrant behavior is not the best way to figure this out. There's little or no risk from driving around golf courses if you know that's where teenagers are out petting and shooting them. There's a big, big risk to shoot a cabbie in San Francisco . . ."

Conway and Bawart agreed that Zodiac almost got caught at Washington and Cherry. They had concluded that because Allen told Spinelli he was going to do a certain thing, "He had to follow through to have credibility with Spinelli who was so-called connected and is either going to have a hit man or a strong arm somebody. *Arthur Leigh Allen is applying for the job.*"

"According to Don Cheney, Allen's fantasy was to be Mike Hammer," Fincher said. "He wanted your job. One of the things we know about Leigh Allen is that he's thorough. If he is Zodiac he is extremely thorough. So if he's bragging to Spinelli that these are the kind of things I'm capable of and what I'm confident doing. There's no follow up. Ever."

"The reason I don't know is that Spinelli wouldn't cooperate with us once he went to prison for all those robberies," Bawart said. "He's out now."

"There was some evidence-handling problems with the robbery," Conway added, "and he'd be in jail to this day if they hadn't screwed that up. The saddest thing of the whole case, was that had there been the slightest bit of coordination with the SFPD and Napa, the case would have been solved instantly."

"The case would have been solved in ten minutes if they had had a cellphone back then," Bawart said.

"Let me ask you something," Fincher said. "It seems to me like San Francisco is a tangental adjunct to the case. It's the easiest pickings there are, aside from prostitutes. You raise your hand and the cabbie stops and you get in the back of the car. The only thing you've got to do is get into the trees before the cops show up." He hooked his thumb as if hitching a ride.

"Arthur Leigh Allen was a zealot," Conway said.

"Zealotry of any kind is always the scariest thing," Fincher agreed. "This is where the beauty of Hollywood comes in. So if you want to get to a sociopath, get to them through their agent. What was Allen a zealot about?"

"A way of validating his life by proving to people he's smarter than anybody else. Sociopath by definition means they don't have any conscience."

"But it's not even about conscience. I don't believe at his marrow—with O. J. Simpson, it's not the same guy who killed those people[1], is not the same guy who got into the Bronco, or the same guy who is playing golf in Florida right now. I guarantee you this motherfucker was not there at the killings, and yet he killed both those people with his bare hands. I do believe that there is a sociopathic multi-channeled nature to O. J. Simpson, though I don't believe that he is a classic multi-personality. You give that guy a polygraph, he could pass it, give him

---

1 O. J. Simpson received a not-guilty verdict in his criminal trial on October 3, 1995. In a separate civil suit, he was held liable for the wrongful deaths of Nicole Brown Simpson and Ron Goldman.

Sodium Pentothal. If you woke O. J. Simpson up in the middle of the night, he would go, 'Absolutely not. I don't know what happened.'"

"His was a crime of rage," Conway said. "Arthur Leigh Allen had nothing to do with rage."

"I think Paul Stine had nothing to do with rage. I think Blue Rock Springs is not rage. I think that the multiple stabbing at Berryessa, of a girl that is rolling away from you, or attempting to roll away from you, is probably as full of rage as Arthur Leigh Allen ever got."

"His whole motivation for being there and being in his costume was rage."

"No, no, no—it was power," Fincher said.

"It wasn't a snap decision to do it," Jamie added. "It wasn't as if he were strolling around Lake Berryessa with his costume on at night."

"It was, 'I will either hunt gophers or people,'" Fincher said. He paused. "Where do you sit on Darlene Ferrin being an object of Allen's affections?"

"Nonsense," Conway said. "That was hyped as a theory."

Yet, there was one question he and Bawart had never been able to answer. "Sergeant [John] Lynch wrote a memo [on August 4, 1971] that has Arthur Leigh Allen's name in the body of it, the first time in my life that I ever heard that name. But it doesn't say *why* Lynch went there."

"That's the biggest question mark of the case," Fincher said. "'Why did you go out to a school to interview a janitor about a shooting?'"

"You guys don't have an answer to that?" Conway said.

"We didn't have an answer while Lynch was still alive," Bawart added. "I would like to know why Lynch got ahold of Arthur Leigh Allen in the first place. I talked to John Lynch a number of times, but I was never in his house. He would meet me at the front door and you'd talk to him at the front door. That was his thing. He never, never showed up drunk at work, but he would go home and soon as he got in the house would turn out the lights and start hitting the sauce. I went over and knocked on his door. 'Lynch, why did you speak to Allen?' 'I don't know. I don't remember. I don't know how I got Allen's name in the first place,' he said. You know, the way things were going then there were so damn many people to talk to and we were getting so many phone calls and letters and clues. Some of those reports left a lot to be desired. That was the way they hid things in those days. There is nothing in any of Lynch's reports."

In an interview, Lynch eventually remembered that the anonymous tips had come by phone from an unknown woman who said Leigh told friends he was going to be up at Lake Berryessa on Saturday, September 27, 1969, the day of the knife attacks. There had to have been other calls because Lynch was interested enough to seek Allen out in person and talk to him "at great length a number of times within one or two months of the Blue Rock Springs shootings." On October 6, 1969, he visited Leigh Allen at the Elmer Cave School where he was employed as a janitor. "I went up to the school," Lynch said. "and told him someone thought you might be the Zodiac killer and reported you. His response was 'I was with three or four other guys on the Fourth of July.' I got so, I almost looked at the guy and said to myself, 'that's not him.'"

Detective Sergeant Les Lundblad of the Vallejo Sheriff's Department verified that Arthur Leigh Allen had been a suspect "right from the beginning." Lundblad had driven over to see Allen three weeks after the two teenagers out on Lake Herman Road had been murdered. He had not shared the interview with VPD because the Vallejo Police and Sheriff's Departments were independent units. "I was out at Fort Point near Big Sur scuba diving," Allen told Lundblad.

"The other side of the coin," Bawart continued, "is the person I never asked—Ed Rust. Now Ed Rust was working under Lynch and may know the answer to that question. I never have asked him." The identity of the female tipster remained unknown. Lynch's informant could have been Linda Del Buono, Darlene's sister, or Sue Ayers, a public defender who spoke with Blue Rock Springs survivor Mike as he recuperated in the hospital, and may have learned something. It could have been Bobbie, a young swimmer who rebuffed Allen and feared him, or victim Darlene Ferrin who said she knew the two kids out on Lake Herman Road and said she knew who had murdered them. Or it could have been some other woman.

As the detectives sped along winding Lake Herman Road, Fincher leaned from the window, feeling the cool wind and peering out over rolling hills, grassland, cows, and rusted gates. Beyond, and out of sight, lay isolated ranches and water pumping machinery. His mind was aflame with questions. The more he found out, the less he seemed to know and the more he wanted to learn. Near the murder site was a small pink house belonging to an early suspect who was never fully investigated. The man had not been home when sheriff's deputies went to question him and they never went back—a promising lead lost in time. They came to an extreme turn in the road. The detectives parked at an angle off the road. Conway climbed out and walked to one side of the white padlocked gate to Pump House #5 where some footprints, possibly those of Zodiac, had been found the day after the double murders. Brad joined him.

"It took Conway some time to really warm up," Brad recalled. "When Fincher was doing his thing, pacing off distances and testing the gate and its padlocks, Conway and I were talking separately. He said, 'I've been in a room with a lot of really horrible and nasty people—rapists, murderers but the one and only time where I really and truly felt like I was in the presence of someone who was just deeply evil was with Leigh Allen.'" Brad repeated the comment to Fincher. "That is so important," said Fincher, who was interested in hearing what people's instincts are when they are in the room with someone, what kind of vibe they got. Going to the crime scenes with these detectives was invaluable to him. He couldn't make the film he wanted without them and as a matter of principle wouldn't. Fincher joined Conway, leaned back against the painted metal gate, and spread his arms along the top rail. Together, they breathed in the fresh air and appreciated the beauty of the site in spite of its horror. The fog was burning away.

"At some point I was at the Lake Herman Road murder scene," Conway said. "I was a patrol officer and wasn't working with anybody then. Ultimately, George and I thought that case had nothing to do with the Zodiac."

"Lake Herman didn't?" Fincher said, fixing his eyes on him. This was important. It might help him to decide whether or not to include the Lake Herman scene in a film he might not make. "Tell me about that. How do you account for the details that Zodiac provided of the crime scene, the Super X ammo, the position of the bodies?"

"Because it was in the newspapers," Conway said.

"Who put Lake Herman with the Zodiac?"

"He did!" said Conway and Bawart together. Brad and Jamie weren't the only ones finishing each other's sentences.

"Zodiac wrote a letter that said, 'In answer to your question about more details,'" Brad interjected, "and compiled this list for Blue Rock Springs and Lake Herman Road describing the caliber and ammunition, what the victims were wearing and the position of the bodies." He passed a copy of the letter to Fincher who scanned it. "Interesting," he said, "because the Super X ammo is very much a congealing of all five murders."

Travers popped open his briefcase and withdrew Xerox copies of the crime scene photos and diagrams. The originals were too valuable to be allowed out of the office. Fincher studied the three pages as cars passed in the daylight and curious faces peered out at them. Could these pitiful sheets be all that was left of the Lake Herman investigation? The first Xeroxed photo depicted an open passenger door and a cop, his back to the camera, shining a light onto the front-seat. The second was, for all the director knew, the only existing evidence of the slain teenagers. It depicted a wide stain and two long octopus-like arms of blood flowing down the slight incline from where the male victim's head had fallen. "So there are no crime scene photographs of how the bodies are aligned," Fincher said, wondering how Zodiac could have had access to photos that the Vallejo police did not. He knew enough about procedure to know there had to be many more shots of the scene. Brad handed Fincher a copy of Zodiac's letter so he could compare facts to image. "The car was pointed toward the east," he said, and looked up. "He got that wrong. The boy's body lay north to south, according to the police drawing in his hand. Zodiac wrote, 'the boy's body lay heading to the east.'" If Zodiac had appropriated facts, his source material might have come from the *Fairfield Herald's* young reporter, Thomas Balmer, whom Max Daly, Fincher's slender, dark-haired researcher, had located and questioned.

"The night of December 20, 1968," Daly reported, "Balmer was cruising around Lake Herman Road listening to his police scanner. A squawk came over his radio: a driver on his way to Reno had been robbed and stabbed." Balmer got to that scene just as a second bulletin crackled. "The first report that came across about Lake Herman Road," Balmer told Daly, "was that it was a suicide-killing. The victim was so small police thought a little girl had been shot and because she was in a station wagon they thought, 'Oh, it must be a family murder-suicide.'"

At the scene, police kept Balmer at a distance. When the coroner showed up they lifted the blanket and he took a flash picture. When they removed the other blanket, Balmer snapped another. That's when police confiscated his camera and film. "They can't do that!" his editor back at the *Herald* shouted. Within twenty-four hours Balmer got his film back. "So Balmer only has two pictures," Daly concluded. "He doesn't have any of the negatives because on January 2, 1969, a week and a half later, he was shipped off for basic training in the Air Force with no idea it would be such a big case." Balmer agreed to email a high-res scan of the two photos for Fincher to see. Next, Daly would contact the Benicia PD to see if he could get their photos of tire tracks in the frozen, fine mesh gravel at the gate.

Fincher handed the Zodiac letter back to Brad, then frowned. "I have yet to see conclusive evidence that the breadth of information that Zodiac had in his letter wasn't publicly available," he said. He felt the *Chronicle* did a major disservice to the case by printing the actual letters and mentioning the blue ink. "They made everybody's life difficult with that." He turned to Conway and Bawart. "So you guys are fairly confident that Lake Herman is not Zodiac—"

"Listen. Listen," Bawart said, holding out both palms, "there's always that possibility."

"So it's interesting that you talk about your skepticism about Lake Herman Road," Fincher said, "because I think it goes to the core of the notion that this is a premeditated use of jurisdictional borders, the 'Wile E. Coyote: Super Genius' concept. I don't buy it, certainly if it's Leigh Allen." Fincher thought Blue Rock Springs was more likely because it reinforced the notion of somebody trolling. "It supports the David Berkowitz, Son of Sam idea of somebody who's got a gun and is fuckin' angry and is looking for stragglers to pick on."

"The killing of people was just a mechanism for playing mind games with the public, the police and the newspapers," Conway said.

"So you discount Lake Herman Road," Fincher said, stroking his chin. "Take Lake Herman off the menu. It's .22 caliber and doesn't fit any of the others. If Zodiac sees the ink being spilled on this and goes, 'Here's my way to get back at society. The world's fucked me over' and he goes out and . . .'"

"Can I run something by you here," Travers asked, "and to be honest with you I only had like half an hour to review the file before I came."

"But you solved it, right?" Conway grinned.

"Could Lake Herman have been a trial run for Zodiac and his homicides?" Travers said. "This might be a favorite place for him to go, to be alone and contemplate, read pornographic material, masturbate—and all of a sudden he gets there and there is this car with these two kids in it." It was true that this was the same spot where Leigh Allen used to go and drink beer in his own custom-made jug in the morning. "He uses a .22, disposes of the gun, and then goes to the Blue Rock Springs and that's when he starts."

"If Lake Herman Road is not his first foray," Fincher said, "but simply a template for him to follow, then what you're saying makes sense."

"On the other hand," Conway said, "George was convinced we had two other really good suspects for Lake Herman."

"Tell us about that," Fincher said. He leaned forward, eyes intent.

For ages the VPD had looked at the Lake Herman Road double murders as being a Zodiac crime. That all changed when a man rushed into the VPD one morning and sought Bawart out. Back in the day, Bawart was a young rookie sergeant, "tough as forty dogs." "I'm a property owner on Carolina Street," he fumed. "Some Navy guys living there moved out. Now somebody I don't know has squatted in there."

"Come on, I'll go with you," Bawart said. He got his coat. At the house he banged on the back door, got no answer and said to the owner, "Well, it's your flat. Nobody is renting it. Open the door." The owner unlocked it and they stepped inside. A half dozen men and women spread out on the floor were doing reds (Seconol, the drug of choice then). Babies and bundles were everywhere. Bawart started rousting the squatters. They didn't have portable police radios then, so he got on a working phone in the flat and dialed headquarters. "Send me some cover to whatever address I'm at," he said. "All the while I was talking, the men are restless and moving around. It's getting a little hairy, because I don't have a gun out. 'Stay over there,' I told them, but no one was listening and they were advancing." Against his back, Bawart felt the property owner cowering behind him and the door—a further impediment to his mobility. Finally, he heard "*thump! thump!*

thump!" Oh, shit! Bawart said to himself, I called for help and the front door's locked.

Finally, he heard the door splinter. Cops rushed into the room and arrested two hopheads, a black woman, a woman called "Mollie-something," and two wackos, one named David Magris. "They were wired on reds and screwy as bedbugs," Bawart said, dismissing the pair as "sniveling little punks."

"I changed my mind less than a month later. That's when Magris, the hophead I had arrested, started taking people out and mowing them down with a semiautomatic M-1 carbine and a 9-mm." Magris, accompanied by two brothers, started robbing gas stations. Magris was out celebrating his 21st birthday when he hit a Standard station not far from Lake Herman Road, then a Texaco station at the corner of Highways 29 and 37. Both stations were open late at night and operated by lone attendants.

At the Standard Station, they took the attendant, Steve Tompkins, out into a field and pointed the M-1 carbine at him. "O.K., run!" they said. Tompkins took off, thinking he was going to get away. That's when they shot him in the back and killed him.

Magris drove across town to another Texaco station. On the pretext of using the bathroom, they robbed the attendant, twenty-six year old Dennis Tapp, made him open the safe, got the money and then decided to lock him in the back bathroom. Changing their minds, they shot him twice with a 9-mm, and paralyzed him from the waist down.

"Oh, shit!" Bawart said when he heard about it. "If they had had that M-1 carbine or that 9-mm the day I went into their apartment I wouldn't be here. They are bad, bad crazies." After they were captured, convicted and sent to Death Row, rumors started filtering back to Bawart. "Magris and his partner is the snitch information I got who killed the kids on Lake Herman," Bawart said. Soon after he arrested a woman in an unrelated case.

"Oh, please don't take me away," she told him. "I've got my kids. I'll tell you who killed the kids out on Lake Herman Road."

"Please, you're just trying to wiggle out of a beef."

"Magris and his buddy did the Lake Herman Road thing, I swear."

Bawart got other snaps and grabs of intelligence, but was not one hundred percent convinced. "I was semi-convinced Zodiac didn't do it, but took credit for it," he said. "So I talked to some other people. They wouldn't confirm it, but they wouldn't deny it either."

"Magris and his partner," Fincher said, hefting the padlocks on the gate to see how sturdy they were and how easily the gate could be opened, "are just sociopaths, thrill killers. The thing that I'm interested in is the sociopath who shoots at close range. It's a different thing from Charles Whitman on the Texas tower to two guys who rob a filling station and tell the guy, 'Here's your chance to run,' and shoot him in the back."

"The fact it was two kids made it unusual for the Vallejo area," Bawart said, "but not as unusual as when some wacko starts writing letters about it and killing people."

"To me," Fincher said, "the notion that Lake Herman Road is something that Leigh Allen hears about and then goes out and does Blue Rock Springs suddenly makes more sense. To me, it makes more sense than a lonely, beer-guzzling pedophile who decides, 'Fuck it, I'm gonna go out to Columbus Parkway, cruise around. I'm going to be Son of Sam. I'm going to go out there and shoot people on a lover's lane too.' That doesn't make as much sense as somebody who looks at the papers and sees all this ink that is being spilled on these two kids, shot in the back of the head and it explains why there's a correlation between 9-mm at Blue Rock Springs and 9-mm in San Francisco! Again the description of the gun would be consistent with a 9-mm and it would have to be an auto because of the number of rounds fired."

"An M-1 carbine and a 9-mm are efficient ways to dispose of humanity," Brad said. "A 9-mm was used at Blue Rock Springs, at Washington and Cherry, and, we think, at Berryessa."

"He got 'em down with that," Bawart said. "What Bryan Hartnell described seems like a 9-mm."

"Nine mill or a .45," Fincher said, kneeling and examining the rock-strewn ground. "There's tire marks of somebody exiting and there's a body been shot in the back. All right, well this makes sense. However deranged they are, two hoodlums come in and they riffle through, and steal the cash. They let the guy go and shoot him. That's a different thing than two kids, teenagers, who are just fondling each other."

"I don't believe those two wackos were Zodiac," Bawart said, "only thieves who would have taken the kids' wallets [neither the boy's wallet nor the girl's purse were taken]. While I don't excuse them, I think dope led them to do what they did. When Magris was six his mother put him in ballet. Then, he got caught up with this guy who was just a yahoo, a high school dropout, and got involved in the drug scene. By eighteen, nineteen, he was as bad as the rest of them. However, Magris, of all things, proved to be a renowned ballet dancer."

"Stay with ballet, kids. Don't ever stop . . ." Fincher said. Magris, who was paroled in 1985, turned his life around just as Spinelli had and had become an inspiring lecturer who helped other reforming convicts. The director leaned both arms on the swivel gate and gazed toward the lake—listening. He could hear the crunch of gravel, the sound of running feet, the rasp of frosty breath in pitch blackness. He no longer had to imagine where the bodies fell on old Lake Herman Road. He turned. The teenagers' car had been parked precisely where Travers' green Ford sat now. Fincher walked around the auto, running his hand across the metal. It was still hot to the touch. "The boy was on his back with his feet to the car . . ." he said aloud, "the girl was on her right side feet to the west—her feet are to the west which puts the blood downhill."

"Why did they conclude a flashlight was attached to the gun?" Conway said.

"Because Zodiac said it in a letter." The light-gun was Zodiac's explanation of how he could aim and shoot so accurately in the blackness.

"Nonsense."

"Zodiac describes the black splotch right in the middle of the light," Brad said.

"You would have a black splotch where you have a parabolic reflector because what you get is the shadow of the bulb," Fincher said. "You've got to do that if it's on axis with the gun. It won't do it if it's at an angle. Again, the flashlights of the period would not allow you to be able to hit somebody at twenty feet. The light of the period is like a silver bullet with a little nipple on the end. It works if you are illuminating something three or four inches away. Any further and it's not going to do jack shit . . . We'll do the research, but I guarantee you, you could not mount the penlight of the time to a gun."

"Theoretically you could tape something to a gun," Conway said.

Brad agreed. He believed in the electronic gunsight. "The .22 used at Lake Herman Road, a J. C. Higgins 190, has an ejector and you can see how a small light could be attached to the back."

"It's like Abbott and Costello with the penlight," Jamie said, as he watched them debate the physics of reflected light.

"I argued with David vociferously," Brad said, "over whether there was a sufficiently strong enough penlight in 1968 to do what Zodiac claimed. It's not like rocket science that they would have the technology to have a powerful penlight then." The only way Fincher would believe that was if Brad produced such a penlight from 1968 from a penlight expert.

"Yes, there are experts on penlights," Brad said.

"And Brad will speak to them all," Jamie said.

"As to finding the right penlight, there is a guy."

"There's always a guy," Jamie said. "You never cease to amaze me, my friend." The penlight would become a test of wills between David Fincher and Brad. "This will end with us back at Lake Herman Road and probably conclude with someone being shot, either Brad or David," Jamie said in mock disbelief. "We're going to end up standing here at 11:00 PM, with this flashlight."

"EverReady was the biggest maker of penlights of the 1969 period," Fincher said. "The [EverReady 230 Heavy Duty model] penlight is exactly the light I am talking about. It has no parabolic reflector and subsequently will *not* create the little dark spot in the center of the beam. It is also in my experience, useless for accurate targeting at the distance Zodiac fired on the running woman. The dark spot is present with a number 222 bulb, but may not be pronounced. One may call it a dark spot. Another may not. I just cannot see the 1960s technology of penlights as being strong enough." Yet, there was one penlight, light as a feather that projected a beam of light fourteen feet with a dark spot in the center, a four inch-long, green plastic Dick Tracy Toy light from 1962.

But Fincher had decided. He would *not* include Lake Herman Road in the film he might or might not make.

CHAPTER SIXTEEN

THE PHONE BOOTH

TWO CARLOADS OF DETECTIVES poured into Blue Rock Springs. At 4:00 PM, the shadows of cypress were lengthening. Iridescent green and blue shapes moved among the trees and shrubbery. Feathery eyes and a long train of plumage marked with eyespots peered back at the searchers. At first, Fincher was puzzled, then he saw two magnificent peacocks strutting arrogantly across a well-kept lawn. In the uncertain light, Fincher saw that long ago Fourth of July night come alive again, shimmering before his eyes—the '63 Corvair, ignition on, transmission in first gear, radio playing, handbrake not set, left blinker flashing front and back, and periodically lighting up the parking lot. "Mike Mageau's aligned with his head toward the rear of the car," Fincher said, as he made a mental note. He was getting his facts straight for a filmed scene that he might or might not make. On the hottest night of the summer, Mageau had been wearing three pairs of pants (green slacks, blue cords, and brown slacks), a white T-shirt, a long-sleeved brown shirt, and three sweaters (a yellow sweater, a red sweater, and a white sweater). Possible protection for an attack he suspected might come? Fincher thought so.

"Was he lying here face up?" he asked Conway as he strode to the side of a car that wasn't there.

Conway nodded, then zippered his white jacket which was no match against the chill now rolling off the waterlogged hillside to his right. Across the road, wind stirred a grove of oaks where Officer Hoffman had once held a Zodiac stakeout for several days. In 1969,

Conway had just been promoted to sergeant and was working the swing shift when all of this came down. "I automatically got out of the car with a flashlight 'cause it was so dark out here that night," he told Fincher. He knew that the director was interested in the quality of light and how it changed a scene and how he could make it get up and dance for him. "It wasn't a battery block [light]. We never had those."

"So you can see [Mageau]," Fincher said, his eyes a camera, his mind a time machine. "So he can see you. He's pale. So you pass him." Now, in the empty lot, in the lowering light, in the long ago world that Fincher hoped to vividly recreate with a new technology he was still inventing, he asked Conway to walk to where he had found Darlene. Conway did so, then stopped on the empty tarmac and spread his arms to fill the width of a phantom Corvair.

"Darlene Ferrin was in the front-seat, shot in the side, slumped over to her left," Fincher said. He looked to the pages of notes in his left hand to confirm it. The report was incomplete. "Were her eyes open?"

"Her head was back against the back of the seat and looking out the driver's door window," Conway answered. "I leaned into the car and tried to talk to her. There were noises coming from her, like gurgling."

"Are you talking about sucking chest wounds?" Fincher said.

"I'm talking about her making some noise which can't happen if she's dead" Conway said sharply. After all, he had been on the scene and Fincher had not.

"But obviously if she's been shot through the ribcage and has a sucking wound you didn't hear a moan. It's not vocal."

"No, it wasn't vocal. Instinctively, I knew that she was going to be dead in a minute so there was nothing to lose by trying to see if she would say anything."

"Are you here twenty minutes before she died?"

"Yeah, she was still making those noises. The [medics] didn't treat her as a dead body."

"You come back in. You kneel to talk to Mageau. What did he hear?" This was important to Fincher. It was said that he had "an almost psychotic attention to detail when it comes to sound."

"He said that he had heard a muffled sound . . . sounded like a gun with a silencer on it. He felt a pain in his back and around his neck area, then heard more muffled sounds . . ."

George Bryant, who occupied the caretaker's house on a slight hillock 800 feet from the site, had been home that night, and never heard a thing. He had never heard a shot which supported the theory that Zodiac's gun was equipped with a silencer.

"When the report says, 'lights on, doors open,' does that mean all four doors were open?" Brad asked.

"Corvair did not make a four-door," Fincher said matter of factly, and plunged back into the past like an Olympic diver. Thumb to thumb and index finger to index finger, he framed the scene. "Darlene's in the driver's side and she's slumped over," he said to Conway, "shot in the chest a number of times. So you come on the scene and as you pull in you're seeing the back of the car and both doors open and there's a kid lying in this very awkward and strikingly similar position. It could be that he got out of the car, was shot and fell backwards."

"Mike later told me," Bawart recalled, "that he saw the person coming towards him had a flashlight and he thought it was the cops. And Mike turned toward Darlene and said, 'They're going to check our IDs.' The window was down already. It was a warm evening, hot evening. All of a sudden the guy started shooting. Shot a number of times into the car from Mageau's side. He said, 'It caused me to go up into the air . . .'"

"And kick back into the backseat," Fincher said. He visualized Mageau's brown hi-tops flailing out against the backdrop of an 18-hole golf course, parched tan hills, and a night sky filled with blue and gold skyrockets.

"He was trying to get away from the bullets and was moaning," Brad said. He handed the director a police diagram of the scene. Fincher mentally placed the car in its proper spot, facing northwest close to the curved southern rim of the lot. He had a sharp eye for measurement and estimated the rear of the car was three times as far from the lot's west side.

"Zodiac was walking away, then he came back," Brad said.

"And shot him some more in the car." Fincher said. "O.K., it's a bench seat. So it doesn't have a headrest cause it's 1969. He flips over into the back. Now he's got to extricate himself from this. That's some serious doing, especially if your knees are over the back of a bench seat. If you propel yourself into the backseat, he probably didn't get that far.

To get shot in the knee, he's got to be up here." Fincher gestured with his right hand to show the height. "The guy tries to shoot him here and it goes into his knee. Now he's got to get most of his body weight up through the backseat and back out here where he stumbles and falls."

"Is there or is there not a report that says the assailant at Blue Rock Springs said, 'Hi, Dee' before they're shot?" "Dee" was Darlene Ferrin's nickname.

"Mike Mageau from his hospital bed says that," Toschi said.

"The clincher is that if Mageau has someone with a flashlight and a gun at the scene, says, 'Hi, Dee,' and opens fire on the car, that is all you need to hear in order to be certain.

Had Leigh Allen ever used the name Dee in one of his letters.

Letters that Leigh had written while incarcerated at Atascadero provided insight into his mind. Had he mentioned anyone named Dee as a jibe at the cops. The jibes, the mention of the names of victims, and hints of violence against people who might have knowledge of his activities. When Dee Brandon of Ward 4, Atascadero, was hit by a patient in the food/diet line, Allen submitted a complaint to assistant director Dave Hamilton. When Leigh got upset he wrote a letter, this time brimming with suppressed anger and tinged with racism

"Another thing," Conway said, "why would Arthur Leigh Allen leave them not knowing for sure they were dead?"

"He wouldn't," Fincher said grimly. He stroked his goatee and thought. Such pauses were rare. When Fincher spoke it was a clear, confident flow of words without a stroke of hesitancy that went on until his point was made.

"They were clearly alive when I got there," Conway said. "A half hour later they were clearly still alive. The question is: did he honestly think they were dead or he didn't care whether they were dead or not."

"His gun held sixteen, one in the pipe," Fincher said. He began to count them off on his fingers. "Sergeant Rust and ID tech John Sparks discovered two spent 9-mm casings on the right rear floor of the Corvair," he said. "Hoffman found seven more. That's nine. At least nine copper jacketed 9-mm bullets had been fired." Fincher consulted Brad's copy of the police report. "Sergeant Lynch discovered three more slugs—one behind the left front-seat, one on the seat under Darlene Ferrin, and one where Mike Mageau had been lying on the pavement.

At the hospital doctors extracted one slug from Darlene's right second rib and another from her left rib between number seven and number eight. Wow! Mageau has to be hit multiple times, four at least." A slight pause, a tug at his goatee. "Now it starts to make sense. Does he go back to his car to reload? Yes, he goes back to his car to reload. Yes, he hears them groaning—*bang*! *bang*! *bang*!" There came a resounding clap of Fincher's hands in the still evening air in the darkened parking lot. Jamie and Brad expected it to be followed by, "Take One," but it wasn't.

"O.K., that answers that question," Conway said. "He was trying to confirm they were dead."

"Remember, he talks about 9-mm," Bawart added.

"There's a 9-mm parabellum [semiautomatic pistol]," Fincher said. "Nine millimeter is a 380 round. Was this a 9-mm Luger?"

Conway reminded him that the Luger is a true 9-mm, that's it's a not a 380. "The 380 and the 9-mm are the same thing, one is a short one, one is a long one." No one asked if a 9-mm could be fixed with a silencer. Silencers are illegal in California, but can definitely suppress a 9-mm handgun and are slender enough to leave the iron sight visible for the shooter. The silencer could have been a good lead, but seems to have never been followed up.

"So this is a Browning," Fincher said. "Nine millimeter is not as high velocity as a .38 and it doesn't do the same kind of damage."

Conway said it depended on whether it was a soft point or hollow point. "But, I'm still mystified a little bit on this light and window reflecting business," he said.

"What's that?" Brad asked. He wanted to get every detail down. Jamie was listening with intensity.

"We were so skeptical about showing Mageau a photo array because he said he couldn't identify the guy in the first place. That's why I was so shocked when he actually picked Allen out of that lineup. How could he do that? From everything I heard at that time, there's no practical way Mageau could have seen the face or identified the face of the shooter."

"That's why I didn't think he would pick out anyone from the photo lineup I showed him years later," Bawart said. "And he picked out Arthur Leigh Allen."

"Mag-lights didn't exist," Fincher said to Conway. "My point is that the lights that existed at the time would not have been powerful enough to blind anybody. If you're standing at a car like this, [he stood, and acted out lifting a light] and you have a much more powerful flashlight and you shot somebody here. Say you're holding a flashlight in your right hand cause you're left-handed or you're ambidextrous. The thing that we always have to fight in cameras—[he put down the make-believe light, and turned back to the detectives] whenever you put light at the camera, it bounces off the front of the lens. So what you get is illumination off glass. You shine a light into here, you're going to illuminate the person because ten percent of the light isn't going to go through the glass, it's going to reflect off. So it's possible if the light is bright enough to actually blind him it's also. . ."

"Bright enough to reflect back onto his face," Brad said.

"And illuminate the shooter," Fincher said.

Bawart thought to himself that no one mentioned the Corvair's headlights and blinking directional signal flashing front and back.

"The DA never was impressed," Conway complained. "'Oh, yeah, he confessed. We got the guy. We got the bomb. We got the costume. We got everything.' 'O.K.,' he says, 'Let me give it some thought.' The frustration is that those kind of facts never impressed the DA."

"The great news about being us is we don't have to," Fincher said. He turned to Bawart. "Did you ever see *Dirty Harry*? It was based on Zodiac."

"It was?" Bawart said.

"Oh, yeah," Fincher said. "They called him the Scorpio Killer in the film. The Scorpio Killer is going to shoot kids on a school bus." Fincher found the parallels to Don Siegel's *Dirty Harry* and the Zodiac story compelling. "You have people in real life who aren't willing to be part of the fascist state and do all the things that are done in the obviously invented movie at the expense of the Zodiac story. There's an intensity of the push-pull of a murderer who's killing people and you have this public outcry and you have the *Chronicle*, whether they wanted to or not, feeding the sense of injustice."

When *Dirty Harry* came out, Toschi did not know it was a Zodiac-type movie until he got to an invitation-only screening. As the movie was unrolling someone behind him said, 'Hey, Dave this is your case. How does that make you and Armstrong feel?'"

"Actually, my partner didn't come that night," Toschi had explained. "He was kind of divorced from the case. It had affected him deeply. I felt flattered they were doing a movie that turned out to be kind of a classic of detective work, even to the point where Harry throws his star away." When Toschi and his wife were walking out, Chief of Inspectors, Charlie Barca, had called out, "Tahs-kee! They did a damn good job on your case. When are you going to solve it?" "'Dirty Harry' Callahan can do it in an hour and a half," one of his fellow inspectors hooted.

"Don't they know how hard you're trying, Dave?" his wife said, clutching his arm tighter.

"Sure they do," he said. "Bill and I have been trying since the first night to the point where we get sick over it we stress out so much."

"I didn't see *Dirty Harry* when it first came out," Fincher told Bawart. "I remember being really upset because I didn't understand that people could hunt other people and that they could get away with it. I remember at the time being very disturbed by the Zodiac case. I remember four o'clock Halloweens and going, 'Mom, we can't do this now.' I saw *Dirty Harry* in about '74, I remember when I saw it I was kind of appalled that somebody was making light of something that seemed so serious—it seemed cheap. I loved that scene in Kezar Stadium, good stuff, but I remember even at twelve years old, thinking, 'People, this is not fun and games.'"

"I wonder if Toschi had had any sense that Hollywood gets to come in and pick and choose the things it wants to deal with. We don't have to deal with thinking, 'Well here's Mike Mageau who's homeless now.' And what must it be like to be seventeen or eighteen years old and be in a car for whatever reason, then you are shot in the face and a kind of psychic terror is visited on you in a very short period of time. Somebody chose to take out that kind of anger and hostility, forever change the course of your life. In *Dirty Harry*, they got the vengeance that Toschi couldn't, as a law-abiding police officer, possibly get. When I went up to Marin and saw the trestle, rock quarry and Larkspur Landing [scenes in *Dirty Harry*], that was sort of exciting and I knew the places where scenes were being shot. I had been to Kezar Stadium. But I also couldn't help but feel that they had kind of just raped the facts to make this kind of very easy, salacious thing . . . putting the ideas out there that this [case] is even possible to solve." When ardent, Fincher cups both hands to his heart as if to offer it. He did this now. "Quite honestly, this is the failing of movies, they are in such a rush to get to our vengeance that we never show the difficulty in getting to Justice."

"The wheels of Justice turn slowly," Jamie added. "Somebody says to Toschi in late '71, 'I know you're going to get him. You're Dave Toschi.' He says, 'Pal, they're already making movies about it.' It's the idea that entertainment has caught up with real life."

Just then, Brad remembered that he needed the exact date that *Dirty Harry* was released and dialed their executive contact at Warner's, Lynn Harris. "I'm sure she was expecting us to say, 'David Fincher and Brad Fischer calling. Here's what we want to do with the deal,' a really serious business question. Instead we are asking, 'Lynn, can you please find out the exact date *Dirty Harry* was released, dates of any press screenings, and the premiere.'" There was only a moment's pause before the answers came back. "Tuesday night, November 9, 1971, 8:00 PM, at the Golden Gate Theatre in San Francisco," she replied. "This was a screening. The premiere date was on December 21, in San Francisco. The day after that the film opened in Los Angeles and New York City."

Brad thanked her and hung up. "As David says," he explained, "one real benefit of being at Warner Brothers is that we would have easy access to their film *Dirty Harry* and can use the footage for free." As it turned out, Clint Eastwood's lawyers held an opposite view. If any *Dirty Harry* poster or standee was used in *Zodiac*, they said, it would be without a head so that the camera couldn't accidentally stray upward and show Eastwood's face. Irritated, Fincher suggested they take the severed head and put it on Eastwood's pillow, like the horse's head in *The Godfather*.

Fincher turned to Conway with a question. "Mageau was pretty incoherent," he asked. "He tells you his name?"

"I talked to him and he answered some questions and gave me a description, for God's sake."

"The statement Mike gave me later," Bawart added. "He said he saw the car pull up, saw the person walk toward him, thought it was a cop, come to check their IDs. Cops do come through here. But it never would have happened on July Fourth 1969, cause we were all out doing business."

"Tell us about that," Fincher said.

THE NIGHT BLUE ROCK Springs came down it was a sultry 95 degrees without the faintest breeze. Everyone was down at the waterfront watching the July Fourth boat cavalcade and absorbing the coolness off the Mare Island Strait. In 1969, Bawart, a motor cop until he made sergeant (sergeants don't ride motorcycles), and his partner, Howard "Buzz" Gordon, were on overtime. They had been assigned to lead the parade and keep the crowd off the road. As Bawart headed west, he raced his cycle, feeling the wind dry his sweat-soaked uniform. To make the siren go, he had to lift his left foot and put it back on a little pedal, like the generator on a bicycle that would rub against the tire. To get the siren really screaming, he had to stand up and put all his weight on the pedal. Later, Bawart drove a '57 Chevrolet, like the rest of the VPD, but it was not much better. To activate that siren, he had to push a button run by the battery. It would draw so much juice that when Bawart was chasing somebody going sixty miles an hour and his siren would go on—suddenly he'd be going forty-five miles an hour. "So," he said, "you'd try to stay off the siren as much as you could 'cause it would kill the car." For a light he had to reach behind for a pole he'd shove up in the air three or four feet.

As Bawart rolled down Tennessee Street that night toward the waterfront, a message crackled over his radio. "Somebody's had a heart attack," it said. "The fire truck can't get through because the roads are blocked. They will be coming down the parade route—push the parade off to the side." Bawart gunned his cycle, signaling and shouting as he rolled. "Get over! Get over!" he shouted. "A fire truck's coming!" Ahead, in a marching band of cub scouts, a ten year old with a bass drum panicked and ran right into Bawart's motorcycle. *Boom*! He's on the ground.

"Are you O.K.?" Bawart asked.

"Jeez, I didn't see you," the kid said. "No, it's not your fault. I'm fine."

After the fire truck passed, the band reformed, the kid picked up his drum, and the parade continued. An hour later, Bawart was down at the Marina where the VPD kept a boat, *Police 50*, which was going up and down the sea wall. The fifty footer had a little cabin at the bow and a long flat deck at the stern covered with lawn chairs. Bawart decided to take a ride. "So it turns into the dock," he said, "this guy Roger is running the boat and Howard Gordon and I get on and we go out to where all these boats are anchored to watch the fireworks. There's all these women there." After a while Bawart and his partner wanted to be brought back in. Roger pulled the big boat into the Marina, Gordon jumped off and grabbed the bowline and Bawart jumped off to the side. "Well, the boat starts drifting off." Bawart said, "Roger says, 'Give me your hand.' Like a dumb shit, I give him my hand. I can't pull this huge boat in, but it pulls me. So I go into the water. I'm hanging on the side of the boat and I can't get up, guns in the water. I got those motorcycle boots and they're full of salt water."

"Goddamn it, Roger," Bawart had hollered, "pull me out of here. I'm your boss and your ass is in trouble." They got the boat in and pulled Bawart out. He tugged off his boots and poured out a cup of water from each boot. His uniform was soaked so he went out onto Interstate 80, spread his legs out, cranked the bike up to about ninety miles per hour, and got dry. "Which is O.K.," Bawart said, "except everywhere the pants are double-seamed, the salt dried. So I got white lines around my fly and my pants, and because the butt in those things were heavy duty—I got a big round circle of white salt on my butt."

A cold wind gusted across the lot, so unlike that blazing July day in 1969. Crickets were sounding across the road. Peacocks were strutting in the bushes. The filmmakers moved away from the phantom Corvair, having gotten all they could from Blue Rock Springs. It was time to move on to the next site, the phone booth.

"Because it was July Fourth, no one's making a run out here to the golf course," Fincher said. "Zodiac knew that, but how did he know that? Somebody knows something about the workings of the Vallejo PD."

Bawart nodded. It was an interesting question and one he would think about. He got behind the wheel of his car. As he sped away from Blue Rock Springs, he discussed Zodiac's call to the police the night he shot Darlene Ferrin. "If I were coming along here and gonna look for a phone," Bawart said, indicating the dusky Vallejo street, "this is where I would go cause the police department is down here a short ways. I feel in my heart of hearts that Zodiac made this phone call close enough to the VPD that he could pull up just a little bit of ways and see the cars screaming out of the police department 'cause you got to get some thrill out of it. You can't make a phone call right where a crime's committed."

Bawart pulled up to a 76 Station and shut off the engine. "Right up there, past that chain-link fence, is the bar," he said, pointing across the street. "This is Springs Road and Tuolumne Street where the phone booth was. The reason I didn't bring you guys down Springs Road is that most people come down Florida if they're going to come right into this area. The route I took from Blue Rock Springs is the route in my mind that Zodiac would have taken." It was also the route that Leigh Allen would have taken to his house on Fresno Street just off Tennessee.

Ahead, the others had already gotten out of their cars and were milling about, the roar of traffic so loud they could barely hear each other speak. "Left on Tennessee, right on Fresno," Fincher said, his voice rising above the others. "From Tennessee, Allen's home on Fresno is one half a block on the right. O.K., what is your theory on the phone calls to the Ferrins, who are in the phone book, and the phone calls that were made a thousand feet from each other at different phone booths at different times within an hour and a half after Darlene's murder. Here's my question—does Arthur Leigh Allen know his victim?"

"No," Conway said.

"So then the crank phone calls, the breathing on the phone is happenstance? Three family members receive calls. Official reports say the calls are 'taunting' in which some words were exchanged, though no transcript exists of the call.

"If it was Arthur Leigh Allen, it had to do with the grand theory that he had in his mind of getting satisfaction of his behavior," Conway said.

"I understand, but you can't have it both ways. It's not that three random people received phone calls from a guy who was breathing. Three relatives, all of the same name, all listed in the phonebook in Vallejo, receive phone calls long after a polite telephone hour, after 12:30 AM. Now this is an interesting thing, within an hour and half of the murder, being pronounced DOA, Dean Ferrin, Darlene's husband, receives a phone call from somebody who just breathes. Dean's father receives a phone call from somebody who just breathes. These people don't know another family member has received a phone call. Whoever was responsible for that crime knew Darlene . . . "

"I see," Conway said, "that's where you draw the connection

between her and the Zodiac. That theory I heard from the get-go."

Fincher wondered if anyone ever asked the family, "Do you get phone calls like that every night like that?"

"The Ferrin family was not the most stable family in the world," Bawart added, "and might have wackos calling them all the time."

"As evidenced by Darlene's behavior."

"Twenty years later," Conway said, "I concluded it didn't have anything to do with it."

"But if you buy that those phone calls weren't just happenstance or that they are not just being made up by family members," Jamie said, "Zodiac, Arthur Leigh Allen or not, has to know Darlene by sight or not. He could have been 'bang, bang, bang!' oh, shit, that's Darlene Ferrin.' Otherwise there's no other way he would have called."

"Everyone knew her name," Bawart said. "Darlene was kind of promiscuous."

"There was absolutely no known connection between her and happenstance," Conway said. "He didn't know her." Bawart pointed to a cream-colored building by some palm trees at the intersection with Tuolumne and Solano, then indicated a building with a blue awning. It was an old car dealership which Brad recognized it as the one used in the movie, *Tucker*. "That building wasn't that tall in 1969," Bawart said, "but the county building's always been there. You turn right and the Police Department is about two or three blocks up. My thinking is Zodiac makes the call from where we are, dumps the phone, and goes up to that intersection so that he can see cars come screaming by."

"So you pull into the filling station, the phone is in the back," Fincher said, turning back time with his actions and words, "you make a phone call. He came the way you said, or he could come down Springs, he could make the phone call . . ." Fincher rapidly sorted the possibilities in his mind and walked to where the booth had been.

"You would almost have to drive up to that filling station because there were a lot of buildings on that side," Bawart explained.

"Zodiac got from Blue Rock Springs to here [four miles] in about ten minutes—tops," Jamie said. "The phone call to the police from Tuolumne and Springs was made at 12:40 AM."

"If Allen walked from here to his house you're talking at least fifteen minutes," Conway said.

Phone booth used by Zodiac, midnight, July 4, 1969,
to call police and victim's families.

"He calls the police to say, 'and I shot those kids.' He didn't leave
the phone off the hook like he does in Napa," Fincher said. "Here, he
hangs up the phone." Fincher doubted that 1969 technology allowed
the phone company to trace a call once the party had hung up.

Brad sorted through his black binder until he came to Sergeant

Lynch's supplemental report of July 5, 1969. It stated the opposite. At 12:47 AM, "Mrs. Johnson, PT&T operator reported the call was traced to a coin operated telephone at Joe's Union, Tuolumne and Springs Road by operator Betty Main and her supervisor." Good to know.

"So," Fincher continued, "Zodiac pulls in either off Springs, or he pulls into the filling station because it's not open. In those days there was no self-serve."

"The station would have been closed downtown," Bawart said. "If this was a highway it might have been open, but it was closed that night." He and Conway had come by before 2:00 AM a few nights earlier and the station was already closed then.

"It's less likely it could have been open because it was the Fourth of July," Jamie said. "Besides, why would Zodiac have pulled into an open station?"

"So, then he's on his way to his house," Conway said.

The detectives returned to their cars and drove to the house on Fresno Street where Leigh Allen had lived. Standing in front, Fincher surmised what the cops must have said to each other the day after the shootings: "'Do you know Darlene Ferrin? Somebody fucking ventilated her and that skinny kid. . . Wow, there's going to be an investigation into who's been sleeping with Darlene.'"

"Does someone say, 'Oh, shit! That's the girl so and so the cop was fucking." Jamie added.

"I was tight with that guy," Bawart said. "That's the honest to God truth. And he never told me he was screwing her till years afterwards. Shortly thereafter, he got fired because he got involved with a fifteen year old chick, fifteen, looked like she was thirty."

"Yeah. That's always the excuse," Fincher said sarcastically. "'She's not a day under seventeen.'"

"In 1995, Vallejo had fifty-sixty murders in one year. But in 1969?" Conway said, "It was mostly husbands and wives, but it still would have been unusual. Three years later it was more common." Fincher pointed out a gang of kids having a fight down the street. They could hear their shouts. "If there was a shooting and one of those kids got shot, people would say that's just what happens in Vallejo. If it wasn't for the so-called Zodiac element in that whole thing, it would have just been that. There were no leads and no other witnesses. The case would never have been solved. We would have forgotten about it and moved on to something else and we wouldn't be standing here on the street in the dark talking about it. If it wasn't for Zodiac taking credit for Blue Rock Springs, it would have been a closed case."

Just then, Brad's cellphone trilled to life again in answer to his earlier request to attend a *Chronicle* editorial meeting. He passed the phone to Fincher who eagerly accepted it. It was hot to the touch. "We don't want to impose," the director said politely. "We just want to get the lay of the building. We don't want to wear out our welcome." Fincher nodded, then hung up.

No one said a word, only stood quietly in front of Allen's house, and gazed at the darkened window to the basement where he had lived for so many years. Then, they looked to the Ace Hardware store barely a block away where he had worked. The IHOP Restaurant, where Darlene Ferrin worked and Allen often visited with Cheney to watch her, was only sixty paces from his home. His visits had upset her so much she quit to work at Terry's Restaurant much further away and he followed her there too. Now an odd question as dusk completely claimed the day and silence fell.

"At Lake Berryessa," Brad asked, "did anyone scream?"

"Lake Berryessa is incredibly open," Fincher said. "Would anyone have heard the screams?" Bryan Hartnell, crawling for help, heard white noise from the highway above, a doctor and his son target shooting into the water heard shots, but had anyone heard screams?

Jamie turned up his collar and shook his head. "I would think that Zodiac in his first pass punctured her lung," he said. "She couldn't make any kind of sound, but she would scream while Bryan was being stabbed first. When we go up, we should have someone stand at the murder site and scream and someone go a distance away."

Brad and Jamie looked at each other with foreboding. Tomorrow, they would find themselves back at Berryessa and discover just how far a scream at the lake would carry.

CHAPTER SEVENTEEN

HELL GATE

AT 7:00 AM, THERE was the slightest shimmer of rain and fog as Brad, Jamie, and Fincher crossed the Golden Gate Bridge on 101 North. An hour and a half later, they were in North Napa, out of the elements, and inside the Lyons Restaurant enjoying hot coffee, and studying the lined faces of retired Napa investigators seated around a long table, really two tables pushed together. Ken Narlow of the Napa Sheriff's Department hadn't yet told the men they were going to be tied up all day at Lake Berryessa. His plan was to wait for breakfast, then see what they had to say and if they were agreeable. Narlow's hip was bothering him a little because of the weather, but otherwise, he looked fit. White-haired and white-mustached, he was dressed in a white striped shirt, leather jacket, tan pants, and Hushpuppies. Bawart, in a sea-foam jacket, blue shirt, and brown pants, was in an exuberant mood this morning. At 8:10 AM, he was on his way into the restaurant when he ran into Ranger Dennis Land who had coincidentally been eating breakfast there and was on his way out.

"Hello, Dennis," Bawart said brightly, "Goldurn, good to see ya! By the way would you mind hanging around? You look like you need another breakfast. You seem kind of hungry, kinda gaunt. Have a seat." Bawart couldn't persuade Land to stay, so he went inside and sat down next to Narlow—two old warhorses, two old pros on one big case on their first visit to the lake together. Brad was sitting across from Dave Collins and listening to him speak touchingly of holding Cecelia

Shepherd in his arms as she was dying. "She kept saying, 'I'm so cold. I'm freezing,'" Collins said. "She was going into shock, so I put my coat over her and she wore it until the ambulance came. She was crying, injured so badly. She kept saying, 'I hurt all over. Give me something for the pain.' But I didn't have anything." He recalled trying to get her to describe the man who had stabbed her and Bryan Hartnell. She had seen Zodiac in the distance without his hood. "Was he as tall as that tree there?" he had whispered. "How about in relation to that bush?" he said softly. Cecilia would not let me leave her for a moment. You could look at her and tell she couldn't hurt a soul. She was a pretty, fragile little lady . . . He didn't take anything. He just wanted to kill."

Sitting to Collins' right was venerable Hal Snook of the Napa Sheriff's Department, the forensics expert who had done what he could at Berryessa with "a non-crime scene" which someone had thoughtlessly tidied up. Snook was not up to today's trip to the lake and would stay behind.

At the far end of the table, John Robertson, big, beefy, jovial, rosy-cheeked, and up for anything, was describing with great sweeping motions his adventures taking crime scene photos from fixed-wing aircraft. In a booming voice, he enumerated a dozen close calls with distracted pilots. "Excuse me, but do you see that other plane there," Robertson would say to the pilot. But it was Narlow, who always took the toughest jobs, who had snapped the famous aerial photos of Zodiac's escape path at Berryessa. From the air, the killer's heavy tracks had been delineated by protective cardboard boxes placed over them by Narlow and his deputies.

This morning, Fincher was wearing a dark blue navy-type coat, blue jeans, and Nike running shoes, but not his wool ski cap. In the open light, his sandy hair showed a few traces of gray. The strain was beginning to tell. Quiet and thoughtful, he sat to one side and listened as Brad explained their mission to the detectives. "We are here to meet the real people whose lives this movie is about," the producer said, "and visit the places where they lived and where they died. We are here to tell the true story and verify everything in the script!" When Brad completed his talk, Narlow looked over at the director and concluded that he was taking pains far beyond those any reasonable filmmaker would.

"He's hooked," he said to Bawart. "If he doesn't make the film, he'll solve the case."

Another sip of decaf and Fincher was ready to leave for what promised to be an exciting and informative day. Jamie accompanied Bawart and Narlow in one car to Lake Berryessa. Brad drove Fincher in his SUV. The other detectives, for multiple reasons, couldn't be persuaded to come. As Brad drove, the NeverLost GPS electronically guided him: *pok—pok—beep—beep—*.

"If you're going to put on an executioner's costume and a hood," Brad asked Fincher over his shoulder, "why would you wear a wig?"

"Very good question," Fincher said from the backseat. "There's a lot of things you can say about Leigh Allen, but long-haired is not one of them . . . aside from Jeffery Dahmer who really had no interest in the person while they were alive, they were just useful once they were dolls. If you're going to stab someone, then you know you have to get close to them. If you're just going to shoot them, then you don't make the costume. I'm not working backwards from Leigh Allen as much as I'm working forward. We do know the guy takes credit for shit he has not done. But the key is we've got to find out what was publicized."

"Turn right at Capell Valley Road 128—*pok—pok* . . ."

"In an effort to get a script that's under 200 pages," Fincher continued (the record breaking length was still difficult to believe), "the stuff that we can easily discount or we can't corroborate with enough credible witnesses we have to discount. And then the stuff that we don't know what to do with, I think we have to see the characters struggle with that. The stuff that we know, we have to present the strongest version of that."

He stared gloomily out the window. There was so much to do and all for a project that was very much in doubt. The sky was overcast, a grayish-olive color, with high sweeping clouds. They passed a row of high tension towers striding on four legs right out of the climax to *Se7en*, Fincher's "unrelentingly bleak" thriller. Another mile passed and so did the present. Fincher's thoughts were now on the past. There was silence in the car as the director recalled long ago summer days when he, his parents, and his sister, Emily, paid a dollar for a pail of cool cherry cider along this same road. Fincher is not a sentimental man, but there is a wistfulness about his demeanor at this moment which Brad had not noticed before. At eight, David had been inspired by a video documentary on the making of 1969s *Butch Cassidy and the Sundance Kid*. His dad was a voracious film buff. He and David often attended the local Novato and Sausalito revival theaters where they saw *2001* and *Rear Window* and, at the Coronet on Geary in San Francisco where they saw the first showing of George Lucas' *Star Wars*. In 1972, Lucas became their new neighbor when he moved into the big white Victorian two doors down. One morning, the director shuffled out in his bathrobe and slippers to fetch his *Chronicle* and David realized that Lucas was "just a regular guy like the rest of us." That moment made him understand he could make movies too.

Back then, it seemed like everyone in San Anselmo and Mill Valley was working on a script. The signs were everywhere. Beneath Park Way runs a larger thoroughfare—Red Hill Avenue which enters San Rafael to the southeast as Fourth Street. That is where Fincher saw Lucas shooting *American Graffiti*. Further along, Fourth becomes Second Street where the production company had roped off the street to shoot *The Godfather*. His second grade classmates had shaved their heads for Lucas' *THX 1138* and been extras in Phil Kaufman's *Invasion of the Body Snatchers*. *Dirty Harry* had been filmed at the Larkspur Landing.

In 1976, the same year Toschi's partner, Bill Armstrong, retired from homicide, the Finchers moved from tiny San Anselmo to little Ashland, Oregon. Right after high school graduation, David blew off college and, with the blessing of his parents who constantly encouraged him to follow his dreams, escaped back to Mill Valley. Fincher's eyes grew distant as he remembered the long, lonely trips up to Oregon to see his parents. In Mill Valley, he loaded cameras for John Korty Animation, did special effects on *Twice Upon a Time*, and within four years had progressed to second unit camera work and visual effects for Lucas's Industrial Light & Magic (ILM). He shot blue-screen on a motion capture stage, loaded cameras, pulled focus, and for *Return of the Jedi*, was first assistant cameraman. He mastered every aspect of special effects from high-tech to matte painting. His matte photography on *Indiana Jones and the Temple of Doom* earned him his first screen credit. After co-founding the advertising and production company, Propaganda Films, he made commercials and music videos with Madonna, The Rolling Stones, Rick Springfield, and Michael Jackson before he turned to feature films.

Brad drove past a desolate open field along a winding road. It was sprinkling now. The sky was solid gray with a tint of green. "What's interesting is seeing the Zodiac myth develop," he said, "seeing it in its chronology as it happens. Even in going through the police reports, reading what was put down without the benefit of hindsight, and then demystifying it."

"Let's be honest," Fincher said, taking his eyes from the roadside and dragging his thoughts back to the present, "we got a guy with a pistol and a knife who knows how to sew a little bit who gets high and writes not very legibly with a felt-tip pen and we're still talking about him thirty-five years later."

One of the things the *Zodiac* book accomplished was to create imagery that made the case unforgettable. After all, they were still talking about Jack the Ripper a century later. After the Ripper's murders in Mitre Square, legend said police were so close on his heels that the water in an outdoor sink where he had washed his hands was still swirling with blood. That story was a myth, but the image was captivating enough to entrance. No surprise, Fincher was a "Ripperologist." He had gone on the Ripper tour, though the sites were mostly gone now, wiped out by redevelopment and the enemy shelling of World War II. What was left of the Ripper files at Scotland Yard was a nearly empty folder—a handful of letters, only two definitely from the Ripper. Fincher recalled the London Bobbie who stepped off the curb and onto the corpse of one of the victims.

"There's some crack forensic work," he laughed.

"Go approximately seven point six miles past the Napa Field Office," piped the guide. As they approached the Oak Shores entrance, Brad asked, "Was Zodiac on drugs?"

Fincher thought about this possibility. "Henry Lucas was kinda fucked up during his nefarious activities," he said evenly, "[Jeffrey] Dahmer almost always had a couple of drinks." Though multiple personalities had become a cliché with serial killers, Fincher believed there was a compartmentalization that happened with the true antisocial. He brightened. His mind was back on the movie where the future offered endless possibilities. "This is the exciting time of it—up to casting and rehearsal, and then it's all over. It's less exciting the more you embrace the sweat and toil of it. Then, it's just fourteen hours a day of dealing with the ninety people who all need your attention for reasons other than support." Fincher was not one to dispense hugs. He was there to get the best performance he could out of his team, no matter how long and how hard, and how many takes it took. He compared location shooting to a wild west show. "Supervisor says, the mayor says, the film commissioner says, as soon as you go, 'I want to shut down this lane of traffic.' 'Well, when?' 'I want to do it on Saturday.' 'All day?' 'We're making a fucking movie.' 'How about Sunday morning 3:00 AM, to 3:15 AM?' 'Whoa! Whoa! Whoa!' It's impossible. It's like Paris. One of the reasons Paris is so picturesque is it can't be shot."

"It's surprising that any books can be written," a writer once told him. "Years of research, writing, editing, lawyers picking at the manuscript."

"It makes more sense than film making," Fincher had replied.

"A writer likes being the boss," the writer said.

"I like pretending to be the boss," Fincher had retorted, "and spending somebody else's money." A frown crossed his face. "We don't have enough money to make this film," he said to Brad. This was a legitimate concern. Without enough money, Fincher had no intention of shooting *Zodiac* no matter what they learned today.

"Dude, the fact that we got as much as we have with the cast that they're letting us make the movie with is fairly astonishing," Brad said, as he took a sharp turn.

"It's a tribute to my vindictiveness," Fincher said slyly. "In *Fight Club* we went to every location, took photos in every place and took those photos back and edited the movie in advance, then turned it over to our storyboard artist and then we shot the storyboards exactly." Fincher did not think he would use that approach with *Zodiac*. "I've been thinking, 'Oh, we'll shoot in Vallejo, we'll shoot in Berryessa, we'll shoot in San Francisco.' I think Berryessa and San Francisco we can shoot. I don't know if Vallejo is shootable. It doesn't look like it did in 1969. It needs that period gas station on the corner. You've got to see him go into the phone box and do that thing. You've got to see him walk out and look down the street and see a police car, a 1968 Dodge Fury . . . Maybe it's Bakersfield, maybe it's Pomona. Pomona was really good for us on *Dogtown* and *Z-Boys* when we were looking out there. What do you hear, Brad?"

"About the movie?" He shrugged. "I haven't heard anything."

The swipe of the wipers was sluggish now, as if keeping time with a dirge. Fincher consulted Brad's binder and saw that the fifth and sixth paragraphs of Sergeant Lynch's 1969 supplemental report contained all the information Zodiac had provided in his letter. Had he somehow seen a copy of that report? If so, how?

"Now, in Sergeant Lynch's report," Fincher continued, "Lynch tells how he talks to Arthur Leigh Allen and Allen says, 'Never went to Berryessa. Went to Salt Point. Gave up on Berryessa. Didn't go there.' Allen told me he was at Berryessa the day of the stabbings, his friend Jim had told. 'Yeah, I was at Berryessa. I was there, but I left just before the stabbings.

"Leigh told me he was at Lake Berryessa the day of the murder," his friend, Jim, had said, "hanging around hunting for squirrels. He told me he was there—flat out! There's no question about it. And he had gone to an area of Berryessa that was with trees, but it was also kind of open and it was remote. It wasn't a high visibility area so that nobody would have seen him up there in that area of Berryessa. He would have been all alone. He did say it was the same day the kids were attacked. And he said that if anyone had seen him they would have seen he was off in a different area of the lake and had left before the murder happened. And he had hung around for a couple of hours and then decided he had either had enough or couldn't find what he went for and he decided to come on home.

"It wasn't long after that the police showed up [at his door] and he said, 'Oh, I've been home for an hour and a half' and they said, 'Do you have a witness telling that you've been home an hour and a half?' So he went down to the manager of the trailer court because she would have seen him come in. And she apparently had suffered a heart attack and later died. So, she was unavailable. There was no doubt he was up at the lake because that's why he was all upset when he'd tell me these things. The reason he was upset was just because he was there and he came home. It was all circumstantial, but there was no question that he was there. I never understood why the police would come to his house that same day just hours after this had all happened. Why would they be looking for Leigh in the first place? To me that sounded like a lie, like 'That's a big story, Leigh.' He never invited anybody to his house. If he had, I probably wouldn't have gone anyway. He was an odd character. My wife never trusted Leigh at all, just didn't like him. He'd do some of the damnedest things like be waiting on a customer and of all sudden you'd turn around and Leigh was gone. But he never told anyone where he was going. He'd just disappear."

The lake was just ahead. Fincher closed the binder and stretched. He was on familiar ground here. "In 1972 and 1973," he said, "the site had five picnic tables, a couple of trash cans and that was about it." Torrential rains had swollen Berryessa and remolded its miles of shoreline. The trees were nearly leafless, yet the grass along the shores shone bright green, an odd combination of winter and springtime. The two carloads of amateur and professional detectives got to the lot several minutes apart. Fincher piled out and headed downhill from the lot, dodging rattlesnake holes and red rocks. Energized, he was ready to do another take. He shouted to Jamie who was further down on the peninsula.

"Hey, Jamie! Scream!"

He did.

"Noise travels over water like this pretty good," Bawart said, coming up behind the director.

"Can you imagine a girl screaming," Fincher said.

"A much higher pitch."

"You would hear that for a mile. With only nine people out here, you have a lot of privacy, but as soon as you hear that . . . [Jamie screamed again]. I lived next to a playground and was not accustomed to hear children scream because I was single. When you hear children scream, the hair on the back of your neck stands up. You go, 'What was that?'"

"The only people in real proximity to this place are the father and son out there on the water in a row boat," Jamie said as he trotted uphill to join them. Brad saw he had his camera with him. "They heard the screams. They came closer and then thought, 'It could be a trap. We don't want to go in there. Maybe it's someone screaming to get us over there to rob us.' So it wasn't like fifteen minutes later when they shouted to shore and Bryan said, 'We've been stabbed.'"

"Then they're not too far from shore," Fincher said. "The thing is, if someone were standing on the other side of this tree your attention would be . . ." The south wind carried away his words as a gaggle of geese flew overhead. Fincher was already making decisions. Sound to him was half the movie experience. If he shot *Zodiac* he would use the sound of their *honks*.

Narlow pointed out that in September you could walk twenty-five to thirty feet further out on the point. "When Cecilia first saw this guy, he was over here," he said. He pointed. "And she had to see him standing watching them and she put her head back down. The next time she heard a noise, he had gone from here over there to behind an oak tree. She said, 'Oh, there he is again.'"

"Now," Fincher said, "he went behind those trees?" He looked doubtful.

"There were two large oak trees. I'm not sure if it's the one closer to them."

"But, if the incline is the same on the other side as it is here, if it's greater, then you've got a problem. The blanket would have to be on a fairly flat area. As sloping as it is here . . . Were they over the edge?" Fincher was puzzled. Something did not fit. Something was not right. Narlow explained that they were on the far left edge and pointed to a little grove of trees in the area. The grass was tall and foliage was on the trees.

"So, if I'm Zodiac," Jamie said, assuming the part, "and I walk down, by the time I get down here, you can't see me."

"And the car's there," Fincher said and looked back uphill.

"Could you see them down on this island?" Bawart asked. Narlow didn't think so. Zodiac had to have seen a single car and come down to investigate as he had done earlier with the father and a son with a rifle two miles away.

"He wasn't going to mess with that rifle," Narlow said.

"The lake ends right there?" Fincher asked.

"Oh, no, the lake goes on around this bend, a 21,000-acre expanse. There's two huge bridges up there and it goes another ten miles."

"Obviously, they weren't followed to this location," Bawart said. "It was a random-type deal. Zodiac couldn't see exactly where they were from the road. He had to do some squirreling around to find them." Fincher agreed. Bawart had not been up to the lake for a couple of years. Luckily, Narlow had been here the day the stabbings happened, September 27, 1969, and he could ask him.

"Communications called me at home about 7:00 PM that day." Narlow explained to Fincher, " I was at the hospital within half an hour to see the victims, and up at Lake Berryessa by 10:00 PM. When I saw tracks by the boy's Karmann Ghia, I decided to seal off the area rather than work in the dark and risk destroying evidence. I left two deputies up there to spend the night and the next day got a good tire cast of two different size front tires, one a little wider than the other. We collected soil samples and performed a compaction test in the sand with Deputy Bob Leahy who weighed 225 pounds."

"His footprints didn't match the depth of the prints," Bawart added, "so they estimated Zodiac weighed more than that. They photographed the footprints and enlarged them back at the office, but it took a while to match the footprints to a particular shoe."

"How would one do that?" Fincher wondered. "Did somebody come in and go, 'Oh, this looks kind of like this boot I own?'"

"That's exactly how it happened," Narlow said. "Sergeant Snook had put aside the plaster cast of the footprint design to process a green bottle found near a stump for latents, when Probation Officer H. B. Schotte saw the cast, he said he knew of a similar sole design and could take us to it."

At 9:00 AM, on October 1, Sergeant Lonergan, OSI Special Agent Donald Santini, and Narlow drove to Travis AFB to consult Air Force Master Sergeant Bassell M. Jones. Jones, who was employed at the base as a flight line mechanic, recognized the design.

"Most of the personnel and many of the civilian workers at Lackland AFB, Texas," Jones told them, "have to wear this type of static free, naval issue boot for aircraft called Wing Walkers."

He determined the size of the cast was 10 1/2 R, the military equivalent of 10 1/2 D.

Next, they took a sample shoe to Colonel Bender, Officer in Charge of Base Security.

"This shoe is government issue," Bender had told them. "The Travis Base Exchange store stocks these special boots and requires anyone buying them, from enlisted men to dependents, to present a military ID card, an issued purchase requisition, and sign a form. One hundred pairs of Wing Walkers have been sold at Travis AFB and many more at Lackland."

"Then, we've got him," Narlow said. "All we have to discover is who bought a 10 1/2 D pair of Wing Walkers. We hurried to the Travis BX, but when the documents were brought out, we discovered that the signed forms on file didn't indicate size and some were not signed at all."

Narlow finished his story and leaned back against a lightning-shattered tree (his hip was still troubling him). "That was thirty-five years ago," he told Fincher, "and those records are long gone." Because of lack of sharing between jurisdictions, Narlow did not have Leigh Allen's name until much later. Thus, he was unaware that Allen's shoe size was 10 1/2 D, that he worked as an occasional teacher at Travis, and had an ID card and access to the Exchange where he could purchase Wing Walkers. "Bryan Hartnell's Karmann Ghia had been parked up on the highway," Narlow continued. He gestured toward Knoxville Road above. "It was on an incline in a wide area covered with shore gravel, maybe one hundred feet wide where cars could pull off the road because there was no parking lot there in 1969. A fence lined the road. On the side, in a direct line with a little ridge, was the service road and gate. When the father and son were shooting on the other side of the island, they heard the victims screaming for help, rowed down-lake for two miles, and alerted the park rangers. One ranger went up in the boat and the other, Dennis Land, came up this road in his county vehicle to the service entrance and saw Hartnell lying on his belly halfway toward the highway."

"He crawled the whole way. A half-mile?" Fincher asked.

"We figured five hundred and some yards," Narlow said.

"Fifteen hundred feet. Man!" Fincher indicated the road above and visualized the scene. "If you're driving along and driving this way and the Karmann Ghia is facing that way—."

"He pulled in behind them," Narlow said.

"So he turns around and pulls in behind them," he said. He sorted the possibilities. "The kid and father were hunting up here and they see somebody, allegedly our suspect. He then gets in the car and comes down here and finds the Karmann Ghia, turns around and pulls in behind them. That means he didn't see the Karmann Ghia on the way up. They've been here for an hour. O.K., he's not coming from Napa initially."

"Before the attack, three girls at the A&W saw somebody staring at them."

"But, that's miles away."

"The girls described a man thirty years old, six feet tall, stocky, black short sleeve sweater shirt paunchy in front, dark blue slacks and straight dark hair neatly combed."

"Wigs are normally built with parts," Fincher said. "They said the suspect had 'medium-colored skin.' I love that. That's the most idiotic description—sounds like an ad agency. 'Can we get someone who is kinda medium-colored.' He had to have gotten out of his car because then she wouldn't have seen him in his trousers."

"She saw a white belt around his back," Brad added, "but it might possibly have been his T-shirt hanging out."

"When they say T-shirt hanging out, are they saying it's a T-shirt that's been removed and is stuffed into a back pocket or tied around his waist or is it just a long T-shirt, the tail. Even in the late sixties, early seventies, with white patent being as popular as it was at the time, that whole Joey Heatherton thing, it was hard to believe he would have worn a white belt."

"They say the man 'was fairly nice-looking and had a round face.'"

"Nice-looking?" Fincher said in disbelief. "It's not like Zodiac is pleasant and smiling, just that he has a windbreaker on so he looks 'kempt'. So perhaps when they say 'nice looking,' they say he looks like a post office worker, somebody who's put together. What they are not seeing is a knuckle-dragging fuckin' Haight-Ashbury fuckin' degenerate. So that's what she means by 'nice-looking.' So he comes up the road. We know the Karmann Ghia is parked there and has been there for at least an hour. They have come from Napa and they park there and he has either passed them by, gone upcountry, stopped, seen the doctor and his son—that's a mile that way?"

"Two miles."

"That's a pretty good distance. He turned around and came back, saw the Karmann Ghia, pulled in behind the car, wandered off and figured there's got to be somebody from this car within walking distance. So he comes a little way down toward the lake, comes up over this bluff . . . I remember as a kid that this was here. You had this kind of wooden picnic table, not the steel ones, in and around here—none of these tables were there then. It was only virgin soil, uncut grass, and grazing land then. "Did the grass get as high as this?" Fincher held his hand at knee level.

"It did," Narlow said.

Fincher returned to earlier inquiries, smoothing them out and simplifying, getting the facts right. "From the attack to phone call—."

"He put '6:30 PM,' on the car door," Narlow said. "And the call [to Napa PD] came in about 7:15 PM."

"That 6:30 on the car door could be there to throw us off. We know he's wandering when he runs into them, if he's the same guy . . ."

"Probably was. They described him pretty much the same— heavyset guy with a blue windbreaker and baggy pants."

"O.K., so he runs into them and then he goes back and gets in his car or he continues walking along here, goes down, does this deed here, comes back, has to walk all the way back to get his car and drive over. There's a possibility that he doesn't, but he's not actually prepared. He doesn't park his car until after he's attacked them and he's said, 'My Karmann Ghia is up on the road.' So he goes back, pulls his car around, writes on the door, then takes off."

"The crime can't be too much earlier," Jamie said, "just because they're alive."

"The odds are that he pulls in behind their car and that's what leads him to go find them," Fincher listened to the wind. "It's not like they were making a lot of noise. They don't have a radio. It's going to take you five or ten minutes to go from the scene. He's not running. We know that from his footprints. The footprints you have or they headed that way or headed back?"

"The footprints on the island are going toward the victims," Narlow said.

"Moving toward his victims," Fincher said, then paused, visualizing the scene. "So that is cautious, predatory-taking steps. He doesn't run at them. He just walks up to them and he's got the gun so he knows he has control of the situation. You don't have prints of him running back." Narlow nodded and said he wasn't running in either direction. "They're going to be more stealthy and cleaner . . ."

"Because he's taking his time," Jamie said. "Trying not to make any noise."

"Why did he come down to the lakeshore to walk to here, not

knowing what he was going to find?" Bawart asked.

"The question is," Fincher said. "Did he see them from over there?"

"You've got a car by the road and the people with the car can't be too far away," Brad said.

"So he either has rope for five, if that's what it needs to be. He's setting the table, right? Before he gets there he's got a gun. He's got a knife . . . a man and a woman. Well, if it's consistent with Blue Rock Springs—they're a couple."

"But can you say he was stalking the girls that he saw by the A&W?"

"They didn't have anything that resembled a Karmann Ghia," Narlow said, "so he would know right away it wasn't the girl he'd seen."

"But, if the girls reported this weird guy watching them, then saw him again."

"Working backwards," Jamie said, "he's not looking for Bryan and Cecilia specifically. He's looking for somebody out there—"

"He's looking for lovers!" Fincher said.

Jamie was too excited to film. He had hung his video camera around his neck again and crossed his long green muffler over it to hold it in place. Narlow pointed to the road above which went all the way into Lake County. "He could have gone twenty-five miles up the road," he said, "come back and found the Karmann Ghia, which doesn't necessarily have to be here the first time."

"They are there for a while."

"If you can believe Allen, he probably had his skin diving gear and all that stuff," Bawart said. "People don't really skin dive in this lake. The visibility of this water is poor, murky, and probably not three feet deep—unless you want to dive down and look at the old city of Monticello."

Further up, underneath the dam, is the Devil's Gate, a deep sandstone notch carved in a high rocky ridge at the narrow point of Putah Creek. To build a reservoir for agricultural, industrial, and drinking water as far away as Vallejo, they first bought everybody's property, moved them out, flooded the town, and left the buildings way down deep. Back then, men could get risky jobs removing bodies from the Monticello Cemetery to the higher ground of Spanish Fly ten to twelve miles down the road. Not too long ago, the lake had gotten really low and five feet of the buildings were exposed. People dove in and collected all kinds of artifacts. At the high-water line the lake's elevation is 440 feet but it doesn't often reach that. Near the dam, there is a 1500 foot log barrier through the narrows, past the rock slide, and northeast of where the detectives stood.

"Have you ever seen a Glory Hole on a dam?" Narlow asked. "They don't have spillways per se in this dam." He described a big round pipe 30 feet across that went down some 400 feet, came up and stuck out of the water. If the level got too high the water went over the edge and was drained off. As water gravitates to the top of the Glory Hole, all three of the Monticello Dam's powerhouse generators release 100 cubic feet of water into Putah Creek. "Ten years ago a woman committed suicide, Narlow continued. "Witnesses saw her hanging on the Devil's Gate, before she jumped and fell 440 feet to the bottom."

Fincher gazed out to the center of the lake where it was 200 feet deep. "I want to go back to the precut lengths of rope," he said abruptly, "you didn't come with a big skein over your shoulder and measure that out. What the three girls saw in his back pocket would have been the hood or the rope. We know he's got a gun. We know he's got a knife. We know he's got rope, and we know he has a hood. Those are the four things that we know."

"Is he carrying a bag?" Jamie asked.

"No one sees him with a bag."

"Is he wearing the gun and the knife already?"

"Under the windbreaker," Fincher said. "So you stuff the rope into your windbreaker, zip it up a little bit. You got your hood which is maybe this thick." Fincher measured out an inch with his thumb and index finger. Was this the paunch the girls had mentioned?

Narlow had not known the killer was Zodiac from the dates scrawled on Hartnell's car door. "I wasn't that aware of the dates in Vallejo," he said. "I had enough on my desk to worry about. A crime in Vallejo didn't really interest me unless they'd say, 'Hey, Narlow, up in Napa we've got this going on.' Then it would have got my attention."

The wheels were turning slowly, Fincher suggested. Again, he assumed the role of the killer and visualized himself looking for a way to go. "Zodiac was trolling this side of the lake. He can't go over to that side cause he's spotted here, then he's spotted there and in the middle. It's just kind of an odd thing to do. You know there are people that way even if they're two miles up." He pointed. "You know that there are people that way even if it's four miles." He pointed the other way. "You know you have some time."

"But it's also getting later," Jamie said. "The sun's going down. Time is running out."

"In July," Narlow said, "you'd have three hundred cars parked along the road, but in September, after Labor Day, the kids go back to school and it's empty. Still, he probably didn't use a gun, but a knife because the report of a gun would have gotten somebody's attention. The clock is ticking faster and faster."

"And you can't kill two people with one shot."

"But he's got the rope cut," Jamie said. "So unless he cuts the rope in the car all of a sudden because he decides that the gun—."

"That makes no sense to me," Fincher said. "I think the knife is the key because the gun is there to subdue them so you can tie them so you can kill them—intimately. The only reason he makes a hood is so he can terrify them. The gun itself is probably in most cases enough to frighten. 'Get on the ground,' Zodiac says, 'I'm going to have to tie you up.' But he's selling an exit the entire time too. It's 'I'm just going to rob you. I have a stolen car and I have nothing to lose. I want your money and your car keys. I'm an ex-con from Deer Lodge, Montana escaping from prison and on my way to Mexico.'"

"I didn't want to mention it in front of John at breakfast this morning," Narlow said, "because I know he's embarrassed over it, but he inadvertently instilled the word 'Deer Lodge' in Hartnell's mind." At the words, " Deer Lodge," concern crossed Narlow's face. He was thinking back to what Detective Sergeant John Robertson had written in his report all those years ago.

The day after the Berryessa stabbings, it had been stifling in Hartnell's Queen of the Valley Hospital room. Sergeant Robertson had begun questioning him at 12:30 P.M., aware that he hadn't much time before Hartnell went under again. Hartnell was stammering, kind of struggling around.

"He said he broke out and had to kill a guard getting out," Hartnell said. "But I can't recall the name of the prison. Fern or Feathers? It's some double name, like Fern Lock or something. Mountain Lodge Prison or something of that nature . . ."

"Could it have been Deer Lodge?" Robertson suggested.

"Yeah, it could have been Deer Lodge," Hartnell said.

"I faked dead," Hartnell continued. "I didn't want him to come back and give me some more."

"So you were pretty sure he thought you were dead when he finished working on you?" Robertson said. Hartnell nodded.

"He said he was going to go to Mexico and he was flat broke."

"Did he search you after he—?" Robertson asked.

"Heck no! Very unprofessional. He didn't even end up taking that loose change and didn't even take my billfold." Robertson could not understand why he stabbed Hartnell since he wasn't fighting him off.

"I couldn't have fought him off!" Hartnell said. "Even if I'd have wanted to. I was laying on my stomach . . ." Hartnell added that the man was rattled because he was "very, very nervous. His hands were shaking . . ." Hartnell's voice trailed off.

"Well, you're getting kind of sleepy," Robertson said. "I'll ease up on you."

"Remember, he said he was headed for Mexico."

"I'll leave you my card. It's right up here. I'm going to go down and talk to your mom and dad." Hartnell's eyes came open again.

"You say you have a guard out there?" Hartnell asked.

Robertson nodded. "Don't worry," he said, and then left.

"I think," Fincher said, "one of the most compelling gems in this case is that in separate statements Bryan Hartnell gives Napa PD at his hospital bed, 'I'm too chicken,' that's actually verbatim, 'you need to do me first, I'm too chicken.' That Leigh Allen at the Pinole [Oil Refinery questioning] offers this choice tidbit unbidden to Armstrong, Toschi, and Mulanax: 'I killed a couple of *chickens* and I have knives with blood in the backseat.'" There was silence on the shore as the investigators took in this information.

"I know I took a long time sewing this hood," Fincher said, becoming Zodiac again as his fingers moved nimbly in pantomime, sewing.

"It's a guy stepping out in an executioner's costume going, 'O.K., nobody panic!'" Jamie said. "Cecilia Shepherd was bleeding, but she wasn't covered in blood. That says to me that the knife is extremely slender—a much larger version of a letter opener. What would you say is the median depth—six inches, eight inches?"

"Nothing like that," Brad said. He consulted his notes. "The coroner's report gives the measurements of the wounds in centimeters."

"Zodiac sees these girls," Jamie said, "'Maybe that could be something,' he thinks. 'Nah, I don't think so. I'm going over here. The doctor and son down by the shore have got a .22. Definitely not interested in getting involved in gunplay. It's getting late. There's a car on the side of the road. I'll just take a look.'"

"Now, you've got a guy who's taken the afternoon searching and now the sun is going down," Fincher said. "He's got somebody parked in a Karmann Ghia up on Knoxville Road and he comes down here and sees them looking up over the ridge. Actually, he doesn't see Bryan."

"He sees the girl. She's the one who looks up," Narlow said.

"He doesn't see Bryan because his head's in her lap."

"So he's here," Fincher continued, "within seventy-five yards." On his long legs Fincher paced off distances as he tried to get deeper inside Zodiac's head.

"He was more down on the water's edge when she saw him looking across over there," Narlow said.

"Something draws her attention . . . " Fincher paused in mid-sentence. He looked at the rocky ground and the steep slope of the tree as if was seeing them for the first time. Without a word he wheeled and walked some distance around to the adjacent peninsula. The investigators watched openmouthed as they saw the director follow the curve of land and circle to a little inlet on the other bank. Fincher's head was down as he took long strides, hands clasped behind his back. Suddenly, he knelt and studied the ground. Then, he stood and looked up at the road intently, then back at the tree. He tossed a few rocks in the air.

"He's a pretty smart kid," Narlow said, gesturing toward the small figure on the distant bank.

"He really is. He's a really smart guy," Brad and Jamie said together. They watched Fincher sorting facts in his mind, gesturing as he walked, and talking to himself in that way he had. Meanwhile, Bawart asked Narlow if he had learned anything from the knots in the rope Zodiac had tied the couple with?

"There were no knots when I got there," Narlow said.

"Of course," Jamie said. "Because the victims untied themselves."

Fincher returned from his scouting trip and made an announcement. "The other side of the little island out there is much more vertical than this side," he said. "I think that is the actual murder site."

"Let's go over and take a look," Narlow said and quickly started north. "I'm not 100 percent convinced this is the place."

Lake Berryessa attack site.

"You want to make sure," Jamie said, scurrying after Narlow so fast his long coat flew out behind him and the camera hanging around his neck banged against his chest. "So in September this gets shallow enough that you can cross the little inlet?" he asked Narlow.

"In September, it's bone dry," he replied. When it doesn't rain, it completely changes the configuration of the lake." When Narlow reached the other side of the inlet, he clapped a hand to his head, then hailed Fincher and Brad across the water.

"My God!" he hollered, "I took you to the wrong spot."

The lake contours, which had been drastically altered by the relentless downpours, and Narlow's initial nighttime visit so many years earlier had led the seasoned detective astray. The correct site, as Fincher had figured out in some magical way, was actually on the finger of land to their left. As Fincher walked around the inlet, he explained how he had figured out the right spot. "I was having doubts about that being the spot," he said. "I was just walking on this shale to see if it was not too rocky to receive a print. I analyzed how far Zodiac's boot compressed the ground." Then, he had compared vantage points. How much of the couple would Zodiac have been able to see from up there? The only way for somebody to see someone would be from this point. The other side would have taken too long and made the couple too suspicious for him to come up on them. I was just trying to work that out. I tossed some rocks and to see how sound carried. I listened for the echoes. That makes a lot of sense. Illuminating the fact that we were in the wrong place. You start asking questions. You always have to ask unexpected questions such as how sound carries over water and land. It was a thing that kept coming to mind. In Jamie's script, Zodiac starts stabbing Hartnell and Cecilia starts screaming. I was like, 'Oh, this would be great. You just hear the screaming coming from everywhere bouncing off the mountains . . . I get it, it's a big place. Everybody's spread out. There's no one around. The fact of the matter is a woman's scream is unlike anything from a DNA standpoint that we're programmed to respond to."

"The only thing I'm thinking, if I'm Zodiac," Jamie added, "is if I'm going to bang it out, then I'm going over to where nobody can see me."

"This is like power-fucking somebody," Fincher said. "The thing that was interesting about Lake Berryessa to me is that you have this weird push-pull going on. You have a guy who is going to get off coming out of the woods looking like an executioner. He doesn't have confidence in his physical presence. He's got a gun, but as we all know with hijackers now after 9-11—a guy gets on a plane and goes, 'Nobody move. I'm taking over this plane.' One hundred and fifty people are going to charge and suffocate and beat him! This guy gets ripped limb from limb an hour before the plane lands." They walked a few paces more. "It's the end of the day, so if Zodiac's gonna do it, he's gonna do it now."

Fincher expanded on Jamie's theory by abruptly changing places with the killer. It was unsettling when he so convincingly slipped into that role. "You go and you troll Berryessa which is a place that you are familiar with. And you see a man and his kid. They have a rifle and you go, 'Nah. It's more trouble than it's worth.' And you find three girls and you go, 'Mmmmm.' You kind of diddle around with them a while. And then you go, 'Enough of that.' Then you're driving home and going, 'Ah, shit. The sun's going down.' Come upon a Karmann Ghia and go, 'What if.' Then you head down the road. There's a sense of urgency. Didn't bring a flashlight. It's 6:00-6:30 and by that time the sun is low. We're a little high up. The sun's behind the hill, there's not direct sunlight any more, probably pre-twilight by about an hour." They reached the actual murder site. Lightning had splintered the top of one oak and it had fallen to the south. Its tangled roots had ruptured the ground and were bleeding into the lake. Fincher plunked himself down on the muddy earth and imagined himself to be one of the kids on the blanket. He felt this side was a much more romantic spot; the other side was not as graded, not flat, not even as gradual as this.

"This is a much better prospect," Fincher said. "You can see much better." He scooped up the brownish earth with one black-gloved hand and allowed it to trickle between his fingers. "It's more of a sand front. In and around that area there's no footprints. Where you have the darker gray, pieces of rock, there's no way to pull a print. But you could leave a print in here where the earth's brown."

If Fincher shot *Zodiac,* the shore and hillside would have to be landscaped, re-sodded, regraded, and rebuilt for the cameras to look exactly as before. Fincher considered the tremendous expense of time, money, and logistics. Production Designer Don Burt, a big, sensitive bear of a man who had worked on Fincher's *The Game,* would have to fly in twenty-four oaks, several weighing 13,000 pounds, by helicopter. Then, he would have to plant clumps of grass. "The trees are a critical part of the story," Fincher said, "because Zodiac hid behind them and Cecilia saw him there." Since the trees were protected California Oaks, Burt would have to construct an underground irrigation system to syphon lake water to their roots and keep them alive. When all was done, he would have to fly them out and restore the site to its present state of disrepair and decay. Fincher looked up the steep slope from his new angle and saw that due west over a ridge was something that looked like a road. "Could that have been the road as it existed?" Narlow didn't think so, but Bawart pointed to a pole up there. "See that truck passing on the road," he said. "If we can see it—you can ostensibly see down here. Of course, we're here in the winter time and the trees don't have that many leaves on them. Who knows what it was like then."

"Nah, there's a lot of foliage on the trees in September," Narlow said. He explained that in September they would be dried out, and not as mature or high as they are now. If there had not been much foliage on the trees, Zodiac could easily have been seen coming up over the rise. Brad asked which tree Zodiac came out from behind.

"That one," Fincher said decisively. Narlow agreed. He ran his hand over the stump of a seventy-five year old tree which had been standing there when he was here in 1969. Back then, the site was primitive and undeveloped—no driveways, asphalt, buildings, outhouses, or barbecue pit. "There was no nothing then," Narlow said. Bawart found a name carved into the picnic table.

"1987," Fincher read it off. "Something TINA."

"Tina was here," Bawart read.

"That slut!" Jamie said. "I thought she only had eyes for me."

"Well, let's walk it back," Fincher said, eager to work out the kinks in his muscles with a spirited climb up the cliffside, the same way the killer had gone. They began to climb. Perhaps from above, they could see more than they could on the shore. Perhaps they could see the truth.

FACING PAGE: 1) Lake berryessa. 2) Filmmaker's footprint. 3) Brad Fischer, Jamie Vanderbilt, Detective George Bawart, and Capt. Ken Narlow.

CHAPTER EIGHTEEN

GOT A LITTLE LIST

WHILE THE OTHERS DROVE to the top, Fincher and Jamie scrambled up the hillside, recreating the killer's escape route. As they climbed, Fincher craned his neck. He could see a bit of the road above. Then, he looked back over his shoulder at the lake. He was amazed at how much of the shoreline he could see from his vantage point. The two dead trees were plainly visible. He smiled, very pleased, his mind open to the sky. He enjoyed being the smartest guy in the woods.

"Yes, that location makes a lot more sense," he shouted above the wind to Jamie.

"Remember, if we're talking about Leigh Allen, this is a guy who is familiar with Berryessa," Jamie said. He recalled the signed, hand-drawn map of Berryessa he had unfolded on his living room rug. That map was one of the big discoveries of their private investigation. Not only that, but Bawart had color photos of the prime suspect in a formfitting, skin diving outfit at Lake Berryessa and possibly at the very spot on the road they were climbing toward. The original evidence photos (in one photo he was impishly showing his bare butt) had been recovered from Allen's basement.

"There's a picnic table in the period photo," Fincher said. He tented his eyes. "I'm just working backwards. You lay out a blanket. If you know there's that little inlet or a little peninsula there, you know there's a picnic table there. Now, it's starting to make a little bit more sense. But, in any case, the car parked by the side of the road has to in some way shoot you down. You have to go make that leap because otherwise, you're going to spend an hour and a half trying to find the fucking people. At what time does he see the guy with the son?"

"Five-ish," Jamie said.

"That's all I need to know," Fincher said. He grinned.

Halfway to the top, they were stymied by a chain-link fence, stands of high grass, and a wet, slippery slope swarming with larvae-like insects.

"I don't think we can get to the road from here," Jamie said. Zodiac would not have been similarly impeded because the fence and the huge water processing plant behind it weren't there in 1969.

"Three hundred yards from the island is not much past that little outhouse, maybe twenty yards past," Fincher said. He had no trouble climbing.

Jamie's fingers grasped the chain-link fence to keep from sliding in the mud. As the wind caught his thigh-length coat, it swept out behind him. He was losing the battle on the slick surface and running in place.

"There had to be an access road if there were park rangers," Fincher continued matter-of-factly as if he wasn't in danger of plunging down the cliffside, "but if there's an access road which I am thinking is a dirt road, why don't they pull down onto it and then walk down there? That's where the park ranger came down."

"This is getting dangerous," puffed Jamie, the serious cigarette smoker. He and Amber had pledged to quit in December. At this moment, quitting sounded like a magnificent idea to him. Jamie balanced on the steep muddy slope and grasped a thin branch with one arm to save himself. As he flailed about with his other arm, Fincher finally asked if he were okay.

"Sure," he said.

"Come on, there's a light at the end of the tunnel."

At half-past noon they finally reached the top, climbed over a fence, fought through some high grass, and joined Brad, Bawart, and Narlow who looked relaxed and cool on the shoulder of Knoxville Road. Fincher immediately began pacing up and down the road and darting from side to side more energetically than a foxhound.

"What is he doing," Bawart asked.

"He's establishing the exact location of the victims' car," Brad said.

"It could have been there," Fincher muttered, "because I remember the photograph of Land and Snook. It doesn't look like it's on a hill. You think it's on this side of the road?"

"Definitely," Narlow said. "I think the photo was taken from that way shooting from here." He stretched out his arm.

"Then Bryan's Karmann Ghia is facing camera left. So we got to work backwards. Now, a little geometry," Fincher said as he stopped at what must have once been a pullout and speculated that Zodiac almost had to turn around. "At three he's down by the root beer stand first. Four o'clock he's over here. He's driving back and sees the Karmann Ghia—'What luck!' Does a U-turn over here, parks behind the car. He has to back up . . ."

"It's more level here," Narlow said, pointing further up the road. Fincher questioned that. Narlow explained they had done some highway work since 1969 and bulldozed dirt over that area.

"The photographer was taking his photos from where Brad is standing," Jamie said. "But the writing was on the passenger side of the door and the car was facing that way so the camera man would have to be on this side of the road."

"You wouldn't want to write on the driver's side," Narlow said. "If a car came by they would see the writing and you'd have had a witness. This way you could crouch down and write and a car coming wouldn't see you." At the Napa PD Crime Lab where the actual car door was stored, up close one could see how neat and straight the lettering was. Written after a vicious double stabbing and a swift, steep climb, the printing showed coldness, precision, and nerve. Zodiac, as advertised, had been in complete control.

Fincher asked Brad to drive the SUV back down to the crime scene and play his radio as loud as possible so he could further see how far sound carried at the lake. Brad was gone for some time. From their vantage point, Fincher and Jamie could see that he'd lost his way and parked off the mark. Finally, Brad got to the right spot and they heard his radio.

"Whatever it is, it's bumping," Jamie said, waving both arms and jumping up and down to signal Brad to drive back. "We heard it as soon as you turned it on!" Jamie yelled as Brad rejoined them and climbed out of the car and into the weeds. Another list began to be made. Fincher added Dennis Land to their list of people to speak with in depth. Brad remembered him as the ranger leaving the restaurant that Bawart had been unable to charm into a second breakfast so he could talk him into coming up to the lake with them.

"Dennis is a slow talker," Narlow said.

"Goldurn, he is," Bawart said.

"Not very excitable," Narlow amplified. "I see him once in a while. I'll work on him a little bit. He could really hold the key to this whole thing."

"There you go," Fincher said with a big smile. "Land is the linchpin."

There was hearty laughter all around, a fitting end to a glorious, instructive day among new friends.

"All right, Ken, thank you so much," Fincher said to Narlow.

"This has been so exciting," Jamie said, extending his hand. He exhaled in relief. The hunt for clues was almost over and he needed a cigarette. He fought the urge. The detectives began the drive back as Brad followed in the SUV. Fincher was in his customary place in the backseat. Next to him, Jamie gazed thoughtfully out the window. In the front-seat the never-resting NeverLost beeped as its female voice told Brad the way back to Napa.

"Lake Herman, Blue Rock Springs—we'll take it piece by piece," Fincher was saying. In the shadows, his eyes began to glitter as he laid his plans for a film that existed only on paper at this juncture. "We need to get all these guys here. Buy them a fucking weekend, show them a good time and pick their brains cause I think there's so much stuff that's slid through the cracks." He grew more excited. "And make it like a ten in the morning until four in the afternoon and everybody can go get a fuckin' facial or do whatever they want to do. But do it for two days, maybe three days because there's so much valuable information—we've got to come back out here with Hartnell . . . a Zodiac Conference with all the detectives. We've got to do it right. We've got to do it the way we know how to do it as opposed to law enforcement. The problem with law enforcement is they're underfunded."

"As opposed to Hollywood," Brad said as he sped by the old A&W (now a bait and boat shop) near where Zodiac had stalked the three college women back in 1969. They passed Park Headquarters just as Fincher decided it was very important he speak with Inspector

Armstrong too.

"Narlow knows where he is, but would not let anybody find him."

"I can completely understand that. I do not want Arneson to find him. I don't want him to talk to him. I think we can find him ourselves." Brad shifted uncomfortably behind the wheel.

"I think Arneson already did find him," Brad said hesitantly.

"He did?"

"Arneson contacted Narlow and sounded like he was interrogating him about where certain things were that were no longer in evidence. Something to the effect of, 'So, Napa PD is missing a lot of Zodiac stuff,' he says, 'Hear you might have some of it.'" Fincher sighed audibly. The big detective had been assigned a straightforward task of locating a witness, not questioning him.

"We need Armstrong," Fincher said, repeating his new mantra. Brad beat his palms on the wheel in time to "Toschi, Toschi, Toschi." The homicide inspector was so much the public face of the case it had obscured how much Armstrong was involved and what a great contribution he had made. Jamie's impression: Armstrong was "the workhorse and would do the due diligence" and Toschi was "the good cop, the one who's going to go, 'What about this?'" He also thought that Armstrong took the Zodiac case more arduously than Toschi and in the first few years was hit "really, really hard" by the investigation.

"We've got to get Armstrong because his fucking notes are so good," Fincher said. He visualized Armstrong's pages of precise longhand—neat, flowing script like copperplate, the product of an orderly, searching mind not too far removed from his own. "We need a reputable, clear thinker. Armstrong is definitely someone we have to interview. Where is Armstrong now?" Armstrong, three years older than his partner, had retired about seven or eight years before Toschi and walked away from homicide. Armstrong used to tell Toschi that if he retired with twenty-eight and a half years it was better for your pension. "He had gotten a little bitter about the job and wanted to forget everything about his police days," Toschi had told them in San Francisco having initially heard about Armstrong's transfer from Homicide from another cop as he was passing in the hall. "When he got out," Toschi amplified, "he and his wife moved away. He had a little boat he sailed in a homemade lake around the houses. He and his wife just sort of drifted away from each other."

"Armstrong's ex-wife knows where he is," Fincher said decisively. "All ex-wives know where their ex-husbands are." He smiled. It was silent in the car now except for *"pok-pok—beep"* and rain stippling the windshield. It was hard to see now. All three were exhausted, yet eager to complete the last leg of their investigation, analyze what they had learned, and get back to the script and contract negotiations in LA. One problem— all this new information was sure to make the script even longer. Jamie held his head at the thought. Fincher finally spoke. "What we need are as many law enforcement officers as possible."

"We need the Land brothers," Brad said as he completed a tight turn, squinting his eyes against the rain. "Robertson, John Robertson, the guy who interviewed Hartnell, Dave Collins, the Benicia Police Department—Waterman, Butterbach, and Rust, the guy working with Lynch."

"Rust we got to talk to," Fincher agreed, "and we got to talk to him re: Lynch. We know that Lynch had problems. He had gotten a tip from some woman." That mystery was still unexplained.

"Can you guys get Hal Snook?" asked Jamie. Snook could speak in depth about processing the phone booth that Zodiac had used.

The director wiped the steam from his side window and peered out. "So that seems like that's it for law enforcement. We want to get the two victims. We want to get Mageau right here and Hartnell." Fincher dragged out his cell phone, punched out some numbers, and began discussing possible locations with his production team for a movie he might never make. "I would endeavor to put that in LA," he was saying. "Would that be cheaper? I'm not talking about San Francisco. I'm talking about Marin or—we're on our way to Napa to take a look and see what that looks like. I just want to maximize what I can get here. Understand? Like I say, we'll know so much more when I get back. The Lake Berryessa scene is really doable. San Francisco is gonna be pieces of it. Any of the wide shots of the bay are gonna have to be digital . . ." Fincher used digital for background effects more than any other director. "Vallejo now doesn't look like it did in 1969. We could shoot all the *Chronicle* stuff on the newspaper stage in Pasadena." He ended his call abruptly.

"You're just like the Wizard of Oz behind the curtain," Brad told him, "only more irritable." Brad changed the subject. "We haven't even talked about Napa yet."

"Let's get an estimate," Fincher said.

"Let's go to Napa," said Jamie who was hungry.

"I mean for our MUST list," Brad said.

"Let's go to Napa," Jamie said.

On the road ahead, Bawart's car had taken a series of hairpin turns as he barreled down the mountain. A few minutes later, he realized he had lost his companions. He pulled over to the shoulder to wait for them. When Brad eventually caught up to Bawart, and stopped, Bawart ran to their car and rapped on the window. He needed to give them better directions to Napa and suggest a place where they could grab a bite. Brad got out and stood in the rain with Bawart, map open on the steaming hood, so that they could read by the beams of the headlights.

"I would go back this way from Napa," Bawart advised, turning up his collar. "This way you won't have to go all the way back to Vallejo—."

Brad entered the information into the NeverLost. "I just plug in Main Street, Napa, right?" he said. Bawart ran back to his car, waved from the open window, and roared out of sight. Rain was falling in sheets outside the little Napa cafe where they stopped. It was the wettest year in memory. The same storm system had drastically altered the shoreline of Lake Berryessa so that seasoned investigators had not recognized their own crime scene. Flooding of the Napa River which transverses downtown Napa on its way to San Pablo Bay had been a recurring problem ever since the Gold Rush town was established. The cafe windows had frosted over as it began to rain harder. Inside, they waited at a long wooden table paralleling the front window, scanned their menus, and listened to the rush of traffic on Main Street which was gleaming like gold under the street lights. Brad ordered iced tea and his regular club sandwich on sourdough bread. Jamie didn't need a menu. He was hungry for anything. Fincher, as usual, was too busy thinking about the film to eat.

Bawart finally burst in, shaking off the rain. He pulled up a chair in the cozy well-lighted room, and asked for another menu. "Hamburger with bacon and onions," he said without consulting the menu. Bawart bit into his bacon burger on a soft bun. Perfect. The bacon was cut thick with crispy edges, the onions were piled high, and the sizzling hamburger had a perfect fat to lean ratio. After Bawart had taken a few bites, he suggested they should wait until Captain Dave Jackson was back in town before they made any requests of the Vallejo police. This reminded Fincher.

"We need Jim Husted—" he said. "Where is Lieutenant Husted by the way?"

They knew that Jim Husted, an early investigator in the Zodiac case, had left the VPD, but not the reason why. Bawart knew.

"I had a murder case," he said, "where he hypnotized some of the witnesses to the homicide. This was before hypnosis in court testimony was banned [in 1982]. Hypnosis, as you probably know, is suggesting what you want them to say and try to enhance what they do. When I knew him in the seventies he was going to raise horses in the mountains. He got a divorce and married some girl who had some property up at Berryessa. The last time I saw Husted was when one of the officers from the VPD, Bob Rogers, died. I attended the funeral and a guy came up and said, 'Hey, George, how are you doing?' Turned out it was Jim Husted. He didn't look bad. He just didn't look like the guy I remembered. We had a conversation and he seemed to be doing O.K. He had ended up in Oregon selling real estate, not horses, as far as I know."

Just then Bawart remembered a package he had in his car.

"Do you want the rest of the videotapes today," he asked. Brad shook his head.

"We flew up here," Brad said. "Next time we drive, we can get them."

Fincher pushed aside his still full plate and began to prepare for tomorrow's meeting in San Francisco at the Stine crime scene in Presidio Heights. A frown crossed Fincher's face.

"Show me the letter they got the partial DNA off and find out who did the DNA test," he said. "More importantly, who can we confer with to let us know what is the selective criteria for DNA?" He was building up steam like a tea kettle. "And somebody show me the fucking fingerprint on the cab!" he shouted, tilting his head back and shaking his hands in the air, palms outward, like a thirties evangelist before his flock.

Bawart and Fincher began discussing the psychology of sociopaths, specifically pedophiles. It was a subject that interested Fincher, but made strange listening to the other patrons in the cafe.

"It's the kind of thing I never could fathom," Bawart said, "but pedophiles have got some kind of network so that they hook up with each other."

"It's true that pedophiles have networks," Fincher nodded solemnly. "Through pornography and other things they find other like-minded individuals."

"That was one of the objections to the Megan's Law," Bawart explained, "because pedophiles would go in there and say, 'I want to know how many pedophiles are living in my city.' They can look it up—the name and the address and get enough information . . ."

"To start a club," Fincher said.

"Exactly!" Bawart said. "He calls him up, 'Hey, what kind of pictures you got?' Once they get their bona fides together, he calls the guy up and says, 'I've got some neat pictures,' and they trade back and forth." Bawart sipped his Diet Coke, then said. "Leigh Allen had some unusual relationships where the curtain was pulled back a little and he revealed things that he didn't normally disclose in conversation." Bawart had been checking out everybody associated with Allen and knew most of them. "'Nasty Norm' and he were tight buddies," he continued.

"Nasty Norm?"

"When I talked to him he was working as a marine biologist and pretty straightforward. All of sudden Norm came out and said, 'Aw, I'll tell you, I've got his stuff here in my basement.' Now I'm just wondering if Allen talked to Cheney like he talked to Norm."

"Zodiac is not 'Wile E. Coyote Super Genius,' as we grew fond of calling him," Brad said. "He's a sad, pathetic, and incredibly sick person who came within inches of being caught. The rest was all in the public's head, ready and waiting for each eager imagination to mold into a powerful demon."

"Leigh Allen had a friend named George who worked with him at Ace Hardware and the corporation yard," Bawart continued. "George used to fill our police cars with gas. Not a smart stack of wood—every time he'd come in he'd always have some dirty jokes. He'd always have the raunchy type. 'Why am I listening to this shit?' I would ask myself." Bawart alluded to George in his official affidavit for a search warrant on

Allen's home on Fresno Street because his information allowed them to poke "into all the little crooks and crannies."

"He was the guy who tipped you to the fact that Allen had guns in his basement," Fincher surmised.

"Yeah, but he didn't do it by volunteering. I approached him. 'Hey, George, what's with your buddy, Arthur Leigh Allen?' No bullshit, I got him just going and so he told me, 'He's got quite a few guns.' I'm not sure he was candid with me about all the stuff. I said, 'Ever discuss the Zodiac killings? Did he ever discuss little kids?' Another tipster claimed that Leigh Allen had confessed to his psychiatrist on tape that he was Zodiac. "Here's how this business with the audio tapes went down. I was standing there talking to Pete Noyes, who worked for NBC News in Culver City, when in walked Alex Trebek and this cameraman who had the tapes. The camera man says, 'If you don't think I'm legitimate call 'Jigsaw' Jones.'"

"If you don't think I'm legitimate, call Jigsaw Jones!" Fincher laughed loudly. "He'll vouch for me. If you can't get him, call Nasty Norm."

"Actually, Jigsaw Jones is famous," Bawart explained. "He had badge No. 1, LAPD Homicide—an absolute star homicide investigator. He'd been there fifty years in 1990, and they called him Jigsaw because somewhere in his career, he found a body, the arms were over here, the legs were over there and he put it all together and made one murder case out of it. Conway called Jigsaw up and he said, 'Oh, yeah, Pete Noyes is great. If he said it, you can take it to the bank.' Noyes told me, 'We've got tapes of Arthur Leigh Allen confessing to his psychiatrist that he did the killings.' The guy the doc had working with him was supposed to be this great private detective who turned out to be a bus driver, off on disability. I finally caught up with the 'PI' and he was scared to death, thought I was going to put him in jail for misrepresenting himself. This guy was gonna have the doc build a trench around his house cause he was afraid that Arthur Leigh Allen was going to come after him—and the doc was going for this. You fall into the trench, stick yourself on bamboo sticks, get an infection, and die. As nutty as that sounds, if you can sit down with the doc, a well respected analyst, a reasonable guy who goes, 'I was really terrified for my life and literally asking what can I do, and as a joke I said that.' I met the doc in a place that was a bitch from mine. You talk about windy roads, this was a small town way up there and it's a retreat dry-out place for drunks and people with emotional problems—barracks and bunks. Rattlesnakes all over the damn place. 'Don't go over there,' the doc said, 'there's a rattlesnake. Uh, oh, there's another one on this deck.'"

"You don't have to corral all the rattlesnakes—you just have to know where they are," Fincher interjected.

"So, now Conway beat the shit out of my American Express card. 'Buy that. Buy That. George is good for it.' So, then we bomb on down there and hook up with Pete Noyes at some 'fancy-dancy' restaurant. We have drinks and lunch and this guy gives me those tapes. I thought, Oh, boy, we got all this stuff! I listened to some. Noyes kept bugging me, cause I hadn't listened to all the tapes. 'Oh, yeah,' I said, 'we'll get them back to you.' But I never did." There were two sets of tapes—taped telephone conversations recorded by the ersatz PI who called the doc's house. There was a section where he was looking for Toschi and saying, 'It's urgent, it's an absolute emergency.' The others were telephone conversations between the doc and Allen, but not the actual therapy sessions."

"Doctor-patient privilege," Fincher said. "Come on, it's thirty-five fucking years later. If you've got anything here's a chance to sort a wrinkle out that's still there. I buy the conclusion that's drawn. I buy it. It makes sense to me, but the evil genius idea, I don't see that yet in Leigh Allen. Where are the interview tapes? We got to get them from the doc. Promise him a bunch of stuff . . ."

"He doesn't have the tapes," Bawart said. "I've got 'em."

Brad grinned knowingly. "Now, we have them," he said.

"Did I give you those tapes?" Bawart asked in surprise.

"Yes, and I listened to them and it's just talking—seventy-eight sessions of just talking. 'Well, hi, Arthur. You been good this week?' 'Yeah I have.'"

"At the refinery interview Allen stated to Toschi and Armstrong that if he was the Zodiac he certainly would not tell us," Fincher said.

"Yeah, exactly," Bawart said.

"We asked Cheney," Brad said, "if Leigh was the guy at Washington and Cherry and he sees a cop car approaching as he's walking away, would he be scared? What would he feel like emotionally? And Cheney's answer was that 'Leigh was probably trying to control his laughter. He would probably think it was funny. Puttin' something over on the cops, Leigh was big into that.'"

"One of the things I need to see is the original of Mel Nicolai's DOJ report," Fincher said.

"Nicolai was a real street guy," Bawart said. "Nicolai was already a Vallejo cop when I first came on the department in 1961. So I knew him well—a good guy, helluva guy. We weren't making much money and Vallejo was kind of used as a training ground. Nicolai went from Vallejo to the DOJ and began to work as an agent. Yeah, Nicolai was a helluva guy," Bawart said as he got up to leave.

He had had a red letter day and would have been proud to work side by side with Brad, Jamie, and Fincher. Good guys, helluva guys. The door closed behind him. Through the big window, Brad, Jamie, and Fincher watched George leap into his car and roar away. He still had plenty of time to get home, kick up his feet in his barber chair, and watch *Jeopardy*.

"We have to sit down and take a hard, fast look at the Zodiac letters," Fincher said. "We have to get them down to a solid twenty-two letters they could probe, and then have SFPD tell us which they had actually tested and how much DNA they'd gotten off each. They've got to test all of these letters and do it soon. Ninhydrin is extremely destructive of DNA over a passage of time." It was already a losing proposition. Some of the letters had gone missing early in the case or taken as souvenirs in later years. They may have been lost in the labyrinth of the FBI or in the files of other jurisdictions including state level. Fincher recalled what Conway had said, "They made such a big deal about the so-called DNA off three envelopes. My frustration is that with a credible spokesman for the SFPD saying, 'We checked the known DNA of the Zodiac against Arthur Leigh Allen and we conclude that it wasn't him,' it gives people false closure."

"If they didn't get the DNA off the Paul Stine letter," Fincher said, "we don't know where the DNA came from. If it came from the 'Red Phantom letter,' which is a fake. Again, I'm not an expert but I can throw out at least three of the letters that [state handwriting expert] Sherwood Morrill corroborated."

When they got back to their hotel, Fincher called Conway to get his input about another subject. "I feel it is extremely important," Fincher told him, "that there be a scene in the movie where somebody goes, 'We would go with you right now and slap cuffs on that fat bastard and drag his ass in here if we could.' How would you do such a scene in a movie?"

"A credible district attorney told me just that in those very words," Conway replied.

"Another question—how many pictures comprise a legal lineup in California?"

"According to police procedure, if you show somebody six pictures—five. That's all you need. There's no legal standard such as there is with fingerprint analysis where twelve points is considered identification. I've had fingerprint experts get on the stand and say, 'We don't have any points at all.'"

"It's all perceived reality," Fincher said. "Just like the movies."

Conway recalled how Bawart had taken a photo lineup to LA to show surviving victim, Mike Mageau, a trip that Conway had figured as "another wild goose chase." He considered Bawart an expert at getting road trips. "Do you know how many times he's gone to Vegas on our dime?" Conway said. "I've never been to one-fifth of the road trips he's been on. Then, I remember George calling from an airport telling me, 'Mageau just picked Leigh Allen out of the lineup, for God's sakes!'"

Brad opened his briefcase, and withdrew a two-page list of possible actors—Jake Gyllenhaal, Benicio Del Toro, Philip Seymour Hoffman, Greg Kinnear, and Christian Bale. He made small notations by each name: "Av" for available and "T" for technically available if they're negotiating for something. But there was no deal yet for Zodiac, no green light, and another director might want an entirely different list of actors. Until then, this was just a wish list.

IN SACRAMENTO, OVER THE last three days, their reliable researcher, Max Daly, dark-haired, slender, and determined, had been hitting pay dirt. Yesterday, he had located stellar pictures of Mel Nicolai's office and obtained rare photos of the charming Art Deco Postal Inspectors office before its demolition. Between 1966-1982, the DOJ had been based in a cannery which still existed. Max contacted the building's owner who provided pictures and a floor plan of the old offices.

"I'm so happy!" Max reported, beaming. "I've nailed the DOJ set. I like to do enough visual research that I can freak the people out so that as they sit there in the theatre they say, 'How did they know what my office looked like thirty years ago!' Another of the things I scanned yesterday was the original of Mel Nicolai's DOJ report." He acquired photos of the slightly remodeled Mr. Ed's in Vallejo, and a building to double for the Science Dynamics building in Southern California where Cheney and Panzarella had worked.

"We can pretty much set the office up like a Univac office, with key punches etc . . ." Max said. "That set is this guy's office with a map and messenger service schedules on the wall, a hint of all the computers happening across the hall."

After an informative session in Napa with Ken Narlow, the big detective allowed Max to borrow his captain's uniform—gold braided coat and gold hat—a glorious, resplendent treasure which the researcher lovingly stowed in the trunk of his car and intended to guard with his life. As Max accelerated toward San Francisco, he thought about an interesting story Narlow had told him. On the evening of the double stabbing at Lake Berryessa, Narlow's sister-in-law had been across the street from the phone booth Zodiac had used to call the Napa Police Department after he roared down the mountain from the lake.

"She and her friends had gone to eat dinner in a restaurant on the southeastern corner of Main Street," Max concluded. "She went in to see if it was crowded. When she came out she observed a man watching the booth slumped down in the front-seat of a '58 white Chevy. 'Take a look at the angry-looking guy in that car,' she told her friends, who noted him, then went inside and ate. When they came out the glowering man was still there. Now, he was watching the cops fingerprinting the hanging receiver. "We need to know more about the man she saw," Max concluded. "She may have seen Zodiac." But all she could recall was that the man resembled a former neighbor. But, when he later searched for a photo of the neighbor, he discovered the trail had grown cold. He had also learned more about Hal Snook, the fingerprint expert who had been unable to travel to Lake Berryessa with Brad, Jamie, and Fincher. He had done a remarkable job.

At 8:50 PM, on the day of the murder, Hal Snook reached the Napa Car Wash at Main and Clinton Streets to photograph the phone booth Zodiac had used. He wrote down the phone number in his notebook, then marked the location of the receiver. "On a small shelf," he wrote, "with the mouthpiece directly under the phone unit attached to the northern corner of the eastern wall, earpiece pointing south, openings on the receiver facing the booth's east wall." Snook then processed everything for latent prints. He removed impression lifts #1 through #28, and #33 through #35 without any trouble, but heavy beads of moisture remained on latent impressions #29 through #32. These four latents could not be lifted until approximately three hours after his arrival, and then they would have to be artificially dried. Snook had waited patiently in the dark, but it wasn't until 11:49 PM, that he completed processing the booth and was able to leave the Car Wash to drive up to Lake Berryessa where they had been waiting on him.

All through his trips, Max had the feeling that he was attracting unwanted attention. He scanned the highway behind for any cars. There were none. That in itself was unusual on the heavily driven freeway. In San Francisco, he reached a one-room office on Lincoln Way directly across from Golden Gate Park. Parking in the garage, Max hefted a huge industrial-sized scanner up two-stories and knocked on a battered wooden door. Inside, he went to a small desk against the west wall crowded with an Apple computer, and art supplies. Hanging from the wall were a T-square and diagrams of the crime scenes. He plugged in his scanner and spent the day copying the author's floor-to-ceiling, three-box deep wall of documents and photos collected through blood and sweat. In 1969-1983, as information and tips arrived at the *Chronicle*, no one outside of law enforcement had seen their contents. The copies were for Brad to create an index for each document and photo so they could see what items they were missing. In turn, Brad would provide duplicates to Ron Frankel who did 3D models, motion graphics, and pre-vis. He would be in charge of the film's document section.

Before Max packed up, he perused the "VPD Return of Items" taken during the 1991 search of Leigh Allen's basement. Among the listed items were guns, pipe bombs, and a knife or bayonet with a sheath, and rivets similar to the one Zodiac used at Lake Berryessa. There was no silencer. Police had also itemized anarchist and survivalist books such as *The Poor Man's James Bond* and *Explosives and Bomb*

Disposal Guide by US Naval school instructor Robert R. Lenz who had developed bomb disposal techniques used by the military and civil units. As Max leafed through a copy of the *Bomb Disposal Guide* he stopped abruptly. His mouth was open. His eyes were riveted on an illustration on page 265 showing profiles of two bomb disposal men in square-hooded costumes. The caption to Figure 177 read: "Officer fully clothed in protective clothing."

A full page drawing depicted what could be the Zodiac costume from Lake Berryessa—the square headpiece of the hood, slits for eyes, bib coming down over the chest cinched by a military belt, and leggings. Max sat motionless, certain he was looking at the inspiration for Zodiac's "neatly sewn" executioner's costume. Was it possible that he had ordered his costume readymade and from a mail order catalogue? If that were so, there could be a paper trail, just as there could be a paper trail for the exclusive Wing Walker shoes the killer had purchased at an Air Force or Navy Base Exchange. There was that Armed Forces connection again, he thought. Only one suspect in the case had a Navy commander father, was a dependent, was a former Navy man, and had worked at Travis Air Force Base as an occasional teacher where he could have bought the rare, limited edition Wing Walker shoes.

Outside on Lincoln Way, Max could hear dogs barking, the steady tread of traffic, and wind howling through the tall trees of Golden Gate Park. There was a small kitchenette along the north wall and he made himself a cup of coffee. He had to keep awake. He still had a six-hour drive back to LA. Alone, he hoped and wondered if any strange cars might be tailing him.

CHAPTER NINETEEN
WALKING NORTH ON CHERRY

AS DAVE TOSCHI TURNED onto Jackson Street, the wind buffeted his green VW compact. It was bitter cold at 9:50 AM, frigid enough to chill the hardened investigator through his light trench coat. He still had a slight fever from his recent illness. His face was pale and lined with stress. Through clouds of steam raised by heavy machinery, he spied the vague outlines of Fincher, Brad, and Jamie huddled on the corner. Mike Billington, and Stephanie Coyote, the new San Francisco Film Commissioner, joined them in the cloud of mist. After a bumpy start, Coyote had *If Only It Were True* with Mark Rufallo revved up for production. At last, the cash-strapped city's location fortunes were improving. Other features might shoot on the Treasure Island sound stages despite the constant Bay Bridge re-construction noise. As Toschi circled looking for a space, he passed Washington and Cherry, the murder site he visited every October 11 to pay his respects. Lieutenant Nicole Greely and her longtime friend, Inspector Kelly Carroll, parked and walked over to the director. Over dinner last night, Carroll had invited a key Washington Street witness to this morning's walkthrough. Now, he had to tell Fincher that the man had to attend a funeral and was unable to come this morning. It was obvious to the gathering group of investigators and filmmakers that Fincher was irritated. He had been counting on the witness's input to make his film as accurate as possible. Well, he sighed, he would have to do with the next best thing.

"Could I look at those?" he asked, gesturing impatiently toward a sheaf of black and white police photos taken over thirty years earlier among the mansions and high marble steps. Perhaps, they might give him the information the absent witness would have provided. Fincher shuffled the glossy 8 X 10s, tucking one under another so fast they were hard to follow. "That's the actual cab door . . . that's the shirt . . ." *Zip!* "I see there was a tree here in 1969 . . ." *Zip! Zip!* "A couple of mailboxes . . . those are gone now, that's an apartment . . . gone . . . no, no, wait," *tap! tap! tap!* ". . . That's still there." He studied the building and compared it to the photo. "This is ostensibly the same dormer windows. What they've done is they have extended the dormer windows out. This is ivy here." He handed the pictures back. It was just not the same. He needed the witness.

"It's a pretty ballsy thing to shoot somebody in this neighborhood," he said. Sound remained a key component of Fincher's films. He needed to make the neighborhood speak. "Did anyone else in the canvassing of the neighborhood hear a shot?" he asked. "No one heard a *boom* and came out and said, 'What was that—a firecracker going off?' 'A vehicle accident?' 'My God, what happened?' Once, when I was shopping for a handgun, a salesman gave me some good advice about noise. 'If this is for home security you don't want to get this [gun] because the blast is so loud that when you fire it indoors you'll be deaf.'" Fincher turned to Toschi who knew his guns and was there to offer his expertise. "So, if you're in a cab—windows up, firing a 9-mm can deafen you— an extremely loud percussion. Literally, your ears will be ringing for a minute. If you haven't ever shot anybody in the back of the head at close range before, you don't realize this. So, if Zodiac's coming thinking it's going to be loud, inside a vehicle is the last place you'd want to do it unless he knows it's not going to be loud."

"Nobody heard a shot from inside the cab," Toschi said. "It was very likely muffled. Even the children across the street did not hear."

"You know because of your experience," Fincher said, "if it's a contact . . . "

"It's going to be further muffled," Toschi continued. He explained that a muzzle pressed firmly against the skin, a contact wound, produces an effective seal that expends the blast noise into the body and muffles the shot. The degree of noise depends on the barrel length, powder load, and bullet velocity. "There is probably more noise with a gun with a

slide and ejector than with the German Luger. Because everything kind
of breaks back here, the Luger's probably the quietest of all the guns.
He just put the muzzle of the gun behind the right ear and blasted. We
know that he's awfully handy with weapons—.22s and other 9-mms
and has a pretty good working knowledge of weapons. It would mean
he hunted."

"Is this the kind of neighborhood where everybody knows
everybody else?" Jamie asked. He was always interested in the human
aspect, the heart of his script.

"I don't think people here really knew each other that well," Toschi
replied.

"I mean block parties and stuff like that."

"They may have a party now and then. We handed out business
cards and found no one who heard anything. I expected more people to
come out because we had red lights everywhere and the fire department
and military police working the area. Maybe twelve or fourteen came
out." There are photos of the crowd—somewhere. "We told our guys,
'Don't let anybody near the vehicle.' We put two of our guys around it
and told them 'Don't let anyone touch anything.'"

"Their attention was drawn down here . . ." Inspector Carroll
began.

"For unexplained reasons," Fincher said, completing his sentence.

Toschi tensed, listening, obviously uncomfortable. On the frigid
street, the man who had begun the investigation eyeballed the man who
had been ordered to put the Zodiac case into mothballs.

"As soon as I saw Kelly Carroll walking up," Toschi said, as he
dropped behind, "he disturbed me by being there. Why is he interjecting
himself into the scene out here at Washington and Cherry? Who invited
him? And Carroll is more or less ignoring me. He comes across as going
over all the evidence. All he's going through is the files brought back
from Sacramento, files Armstrong and I wrote, files handled by a couple
dozen people before like an old, old story nobody cared about. David
has to pick up on the fact that Carroll doesn't have any real working
knowledge of Zodiac. How could he? He wasn't around in 1969."

Toschi was not himself today. He attributed that to his continuing
illness and increased workload because of the loss of manpower at his
job. He squared his shoulders and thought better of the situation. As

a coworker remarked of him in '71, "I know you're going to get him. You're Dave Toschi." Yes, he was. He was Dave Toschi. Get in there and fight for the facts of your case, he thought. Both combatants for the truth squared off. Toschi caught up with Fincher and Carroll. After all, Carroll was still with the department and he wasn't. Ultimately, it was the case that mattered, the justice of it all. Everyone on that windy corner was pulling for that.

"Hey! What are you doing these days?" Toschi asked Carroll.

"I'm in Juvenile," Inspector Carroll said. "I got tired of Homicide."

Both Carroll, and his partner, Michael Maloney, had transferred out of Homicide. Turning back to Fincher, Carroll continued. "I'm not clear on whether it was noise that drew their attention or somebody glanced out the window," he said. "They might think that somebody is drunk. I don't know why they came to that window, but ultimately their focus of attention was drawn down here. It doesn't seem right, so the young man says to his sister, 'Call the cops.' He comes downstairs to the ground floor which is directly across from us and he looks out and he's eyeball to eyeball." In effect, he was saying that the driver's side door was left open.

"O.K., so has anyone else ever heard before about the driver's side door being open?" Fincher asked. He looked from face to face. No one had. The implication was that Zodiac had climbed over the front seat, then exited the driver's side and left a bloody print. "So Zodiac gets out of the backseat somehow. He probably goes out the driver's side, goes into the front seat, opens the driver's side door. Now, cradling the head wouldn't make any sense. If you're going to cradle a head after a contact wound you're going to be covered in blood." Did Zodiac lean over to get the blood off the contact wound, possibly propping himself up on the dashboard? "The fact that the driver's side door is open would explain the latent print. Zodiac rubbed down the left sidebar of the cab [between the driver's door and rear seat]." Fincher paused. "The shirt is cut from the left flank or the right flank?"

"Right flank," Toschi said. "I saw it the night of the murder."

"His ass is still behind the wheel and he falls over," Fincher said. "So now Zodiac can get in, pull the shirt off, tear or cut the shirt, and he doesn't have to worry about blood getting on him because the head is away. Most of the body is between the head and the wheel well. So he takes his turn. The door's open. He looks directly across, then does this thing where he gets blood on the shirt."

"Was there any blood on the dash or was all the blood concentrated in the wheel well?" Brad asked.

"We never found any blood on the dash at all," Toschi said forcefully.

"Now, when the car is found—the photographs show the passenger side open and the guy's hand is coming out. The police didn't open that door and leave it open?"

"What you have to factor in," Carroll interjected, "and Dave knows this—I'm just riffing here—the police are called and obviously there's somebody who's been shot—then they're going to seek access. Who opened that door? It could have been the officer who first arrived at the scene. I think it was Armand."

"I remember specifically that Armand Pelissetti *did not touch* the body whatsoever!" Toschi said. "I was very concerned Armand might have pulled the body out or he might have opened the door or his partner had. 'Armand, did you touch the body at all?' I asked him. 'Did you touch the door on the passenger side?' He said, 'Dave, we found this man just the way he is right now. At first, we thought he may have had his throat slit because of all the blood and had the ambulance expedite because they felt he was probably dead, but weren't sure. We then realized he had been shot.' At no time did they touch the door or the body. 'Which way did the children tell you the killer left the vehicle?' I asked Armand. 'Just out of the passenger side,' he said, 'then swung around and went around to his right and rubbed down the left sidebar of the cab.' If you read the report, you know the children said Zodiac exited from the *passenger* side and went around the vehicle. At no time did he climb over the steering wheel. It would be absurd! Zodiac weighed over 220-230 and was not particularly agile. There's a steering wheel there, a hump in the middle for the drive shaft, a running meter your knee's liable to hit, and your arms are liable to hit the gears. It's going to block your exit unless you come out of the passenger side just like Armand said. Zodiac would have soiled every part of himself."

"That the witness saw Zodiac sitting on the driver's side behind the wheel," Fincher said, "I've only ever heard the opposite, that he was on the other side. My question has been from the beginning. 'Why would he cradle the head?' And the cradling of the head is what makes sense if he's sitting on the passenger side. What we're now being told is that he came up and sat on the other side of the car. I just want to get the facts, people, just like *Dragnet*."

"After that moment the suspect gets out of the car," Carroll continued, "walks in this direction as casually as somebody walking his dog." Toschi relaxed. That was more like it. They were moving now as a team. After all, they were all there to get the truth and sharing what they each knew was the way to get there.

"O.K., let's go down and see the escape route . . ." Fincher said.

He raised his arm in a sweeping motion like a general and led his troops north down a slight hill along a tree-shrouded walk. Fincher was aware that the sidewalk would have been heavily shadowed that night in 1969, but not dark enough to hide huge bloodstains. The detectives reached a circular drive fronting a brick wall and paused to peer down into the Presidio—a short drop over the wall, an easy escape route. If that was so, then why did Zodiac turn right off Cherry onto Jackson Street and continue walking east? This morning, Jackson Street was under heavy construction at mid-block. Clouds of dust were rising. Fincher set the stage, his hands framing scenes.

"Officers Fouke and Zelms are in their patrol car," he said. "Zelms is driving. *Take one!*" He clapped his hands—*Bang*! "The two officers see Zodiac cross into the Presidio. They're coming down after circling the whole area, waiting for communications to give them everything they've got and see this guy. They stop, not more than ten-seconds, and they ask him if he's seen anybody that looks suspicious, maybe a black man [as Police Dispatch had mistakenly and tragically radioed]. The guy pointed east, the direction he was walking, and said, 'Yeah, a few minutes ago in that direction,' and they sped off. They've got a radio car. Other vehicles are listening to communications, waiting for a description. The children are screaming into the phone—everything is confused. My question is this—the time that it takes us to walk this is about three minutes—is that about right?" Toschi nodded. "We're not talking about being stopped three minutes after the shooting, we're talking about somebody being stopped *ten minutes* after the shooting because it takes ten minutes for the first car."

Fouke and his partner, assigned to another unit, had driven over from Arguello Boulevard southwest of Cherry and Washington and were circling the area awaiting a better description. Fincher thought this could be up to fifteen minutes after the shooting, but Toschi disagreed. He estimated it was ten minutes or less when the officers saw this person who might have slipped into a doorway or hidden in some bushes.

"Their description was what the kids saw," he said. "It was perfect. Except they described him as larger and older."

"What I read," Fincher said, opening his black binder and holding the pages down against the wind, "is you have the execution shooting, the wiping down of the cab, the suspect walking casually away. He comes down this street. He is stopped approximately within a hundred feet, give or take, of this area. That [patrol] car is going this way, so the driver has the worst view, the passenger has the best view. Procedurally, would they have pulled up? Moved closer in order to ask him? Dave, was it ever described to you by the two officers who stopped him what the proximity was to them." Fincher moved to the center of the street. He planted his feet wide, straddling the road like the Colossus of Rhodes. "He's on one side of the street and they're on the other."

"He's on Jackson Street very close to the scene," Toschi said, explaining that Zelms' patrol car came up from behind the man and they asked if he had seen anyone."

"Was there any conversation?" Fincher said.

"Yes, but the officers deny that now, trying to detach themselves from it."

"They've got a pretty good view of this guy."

"Fouke, the lead guy, got the best look at the killer," Toschi said. "Zelms wasn't paying that much attention. It was Fouke who made the report a month later to us. He pulled his car over to the north side of Jackson Street when he saw this man on the south side and engaged in this ten or fifteen-seconds conversation with him. That's our killer."

"We gotta get Fouke," Fincher said as they moved back to the south side of Jackson Street. "We gotta get Pelissetti."

"When they stopped him, had he already crossed over to the north side?" Jamie asked.

"Right here," Toschi said, "right where I'm standing." He pointed down at his feet. "Just as they are approaching the intersection and see this fellow."

"So he's right here," Fincher said, "and he says, 'I saw a guy,' and points east."

"And the radio car continues on east," Toschi said, "and by the time they get a short distance away, there's a correction over the radio communications that it is a white male suspect. And they say, 'Ah, shit! We had him. That's the guy.' Then, they zoom off. By the time they circled back, the suspect was gone on Maple."

"So he comes down here," Jamie said, "crosses Jackson up there. He was walking down on this side of the street and they see him about to turn the corner."

"Both sides are equally lit up," Fincher said. He stroked his goatee, "But the thing that's always bothered me about Allen, is that he's always been this moonfaced [silent movie comedian] Fatty Arbuckle. How is it that Kathleen Johns, how is it that the two cops in the Presidio, how is it that Mike Mageau doesn't comment on that round face? In the police composite sketch you see cheekbones and you see the horn-rimmed glasses that extend beyond the cheekbones. I'm telling you, put two fucking dinner plates over Leigh Allen's eyes and you're still going to see a huge face."

The binder was opened. Mageau had described precisely such a huge face, "a heavyset, beefy-type face," as did Darlene's babysitter's description of a man parked outside the Ferrin's home. "Moonfaced . . . round-faced as an owl," she said. The three women at Lake Berryessa said the man watching them "had a round face."

"Allen with his round face in no way, shape or form resembles that composite sketch that was done here," Brad said.

Toschi agreed. "That composite is the worst thing that happened in the case," he admitted. "At first we were looking for a sloppy cabdriver killer because the robbery detail said, 'this white guy, he's been pulling a few robberies doing the same thing. Takes them out to a quiet area, sticks a gun to their head and robs them.' So we think we've got a robbery that went bad and the robber has to shoot the guy and kill him. What he gets is less than $15. Our Chief of Inspectors says, 'I want a composite put out to every cab fleet in town.' We didn't want to do it, but he was the boss." The traumatized young witness "expressed a little doubt about the sketch, but had more confidence in the revised sketch because the cops down the street had a much better, longer look at him." He said that when they found whoever was responsible, he "would really be disappointed if that sketch did not resemble the person."

"There's a report," Fincher said, "that says the two cops stop a man who is large, lumbering—they describe him as six feet, two hundred-plus pounds. They describe his outfit, potbelly etc . . . They talk about stopping him and asking if he's seen anything suspicious. And he says there was a man waving a gun—waving a gun! They have since recanted that?"

"Yes," Toschi said. "On October 17, 1969, Armstrong and I got a call from Officer Fouke and went out to Richmond Station where he worked. Fouke was teary-eyed in the Captain's office and a little shaky, and I said, 'How you doing?' When Fouke asked, 'Do you think it was him?' I said, 'Yeah.' 'Am I going to get in shit?' Which means 'Am I going to get fired?' I said, 'No, you're not going to get in trouble. It's been tearing you apart for weeks and you had to come out with something.'"

"So nobody knows that Fouke and Zelms have seen the suspect until he calls you and says, 'We got a problem with the description,'" Fincher said.

"He tells me, 'We saw a guy that was dressed like that. We passed him and it looked like him,' and he played it down and just says, 'The guy that Eric [Zelms] and I saw was heavier, was paunchy, had baggy pants, dark trousers, a crewcut, wearing glasses. We were looking for a black guy, but I'm pretty sure that this is the guy now that we know.'"

"So that's when he goes, 'O.K., look, I may have fucked up in a big way,'" Fincher said. "So then the shit hits the fan and it starts to go round and you guys start to go, 'Come on, guys, this is not police work.' He doesn't tell us that they got a very good look at him."

"When Fouke was talking to the suspect, he was staring directly at him," Toschi said. "That's how he was able to tell us the composite was a bit different from his recall. He made his face a little bit bigger, older, made him a little wider, heavier. He says, 'We just slowed down, drove past him and went on.' His memo never left headquarters and we tried to keep it confidential as possible."

"I respect that," Fincher said. "Is it your belief that they never actually stopped Zodiac."

"Oh, no, I believe they did," Toschi said.

"O.K. So now I want to ask my question again. I want to make sure I get an answer. It's your considered opinion that the patrol car did indeed stop. They did indeed make verbal contact with the suspect. They did indeed ask him a question. He responded to them. They then drove on leaving him behind them."

"Absolutely!"

"And that a month later, this story is recanted to protect these guys."

"Like a mother protecting a baby, yet we had to live with this."

Earth moving machines were clanking and wheezing up the precipitous hill making their investigation all that much tougher. A plane passed above. They heard the roar of dump trucks carting away shattered concrete, the remnants of the old street. At the intersection of Jackson and Maple Streets, the pounding and bite of picks became deafening and they had to stop. Trucks rattled by where Fouke had seen Zodiac "turn north on Maple Street." They came to a low stone wall. Beyond, lay shadowed groves of trees and a vast garrison stretching north. To escape the pandemonium, they clung to that bit of peace.

"This road is in the Presidio, but this is not," Fincher said, "because we've shut this road down before [for his movie, *The Game*]. This road takes you right out . . ." He pointed with his right arm. "Presidio Road runs straight down that way, so there's no stop signs. If your car was parked over there, you get in it and you're going to drive at least four or five blocks before you're going to have to worry about being able to be cut off."

"Can you jump the wall one block up?" Jamie asked.

"Sure," Fincher said, shrugging, "same thing."

"Why are you going down Jackson?" Jamie asked. "Why don't you just go down Cherry and jump there?"

"It was probably that Zodiac was still within sight of the crime scene," Brad said. "There is a circling car. We know that it is many minutes after the shooting."

"The question is," Jamie wondered, "why is he still this close to the scene? Even if his original plan was to watch, hop the fence, peek over for a little while before he takes off in his car, he's already changed his plan."

The route the first responding patrol car took was up Washington Street going west and they would have come up to Cherry just as Zodiac was turning the corner. A half-dozen units at Richmond Station were waiting for Dispatch to give them a full description.

"So the cars came up this way," Fincher said. "And the other ones are coming on Arguello and they turn and they come back this way. Procedurally, when Dispatch says we have a shooting they then have to wait for the nearest patrol car." Dispatch had put out a Code 217, a shooting, so they rolled quickly. "Back up," Fincher said, holding up the flat of his hand like a traffic cop. *Take Two: Bang!* "They don't have GPS, so what they will say is, 'There's a shooting at Washington and Cherry.' A car in the area will go, 'I'm at blah, blah, blah . . .' Another car may chime in with 'I'm at X, Y, and Z,' and they'll say, 'Car No. 1 . . .' What I'm getting at is, in this three and a half to four minutes, after a minute of circling—roughly five minutes [after the shooting] I'm betting arrival of the first car and the passing of Fouke and Zelms are nearly simultaneous. O.K., so it doesn't require the first car to arrive on the scene and say, 'I am here on the scene,' for the second car to be doing the circle. So Dispatch will say, 'We have a shooting at Washington and Cherry,' and then Car No. 1 chimes in and says, 'We're two blocks up. We'll take this.' And another car comes in and says, 'We're four blocks. We'll circle. Give us a description.' Those two things have already happened and the description had absolutely nothing to do with the scene, it has to do with the phone call."

"Glasses were mentioned in the wanted poster description," Brad said. "What if Zodiac had taken Paul Stine's glasses and was wearing them as a disguise when he met the patrol car?"

The sound of pile drivers drowned him out as they turned the corner onto Maple Street, a trek reminiscent of Jamie and Fincher's breathless climb to Knoxville Road at Lake Berryessa. At the summit they gazed west to the intersection of Washington and Cherry Streets a block away where Zodiac had directed the cab to stop. According to Toschi, the cab's dome light attracted the kids' attention to look down and see "some kind of struggle."

"They can see the cab driver is not moving," Jamie said. "And so they don't necessarily know if it's a shooting or not."

"I gotta stop you," said Carroll who was standing a few yards away with Greeley. "They can see the cab driver is not moving. I don't have a clear, collective understanding of their collective perspective, but they see something ain't right."

"I would say the street level straight on view is the least explanatory of the situation," Fincher said, "with the dome light on sitting in the front-seat behind the wheel. We know the wound is on the right side. So he either slumped to the left. You've got an inert person and you've maybe got a guy getting out of the back of the cab, opening the driver's side door, pushing the guy over and rummaging through, looking like trying to get a guy's wallet and a piece of the shirt. Once you're on the street you have far less perspective . . ."

That he stopped the cab on the slight decline of a hill, gravity would have worked to Zodiac's favor as he used the weight of the body to help tear the shirt. Bit by bit, they were revising their ideas and trying new ones on for size and listening to each other as Fincher took it all in. Each answer brought another question. You could feel Jamie's script growing with each question and answer.

"You might have a better perspective to identify the person, but not what is going on inside the cab," Brad said.

"Absolutely. Absolutely," Fincher said. He rubbed his hands together. "So it's the bird's-eye view is more telling that something's amiss." That was the angle he wanted to use in his movie if he shot *Zodiac*.

"Procedurally," Jamie said, "if you don't know it's a shooting, do you dispatch more than one unit?"

"Probably not," Carroll said. "The call would go out and, uh . . . I'll let Dave answer that."

"They don't know what they got," Toschi said tersely, yet warming to the various theories.

"They have hysterical children," Fincher said, "but wait a minute— because of something they don't know is going on?" He sat down on a nearby step to think. The concrete was cold. He put his chin in his hand. "If you have a robbery, do you have hysterical children? If you have hysterical children on the phone, chances are there is a slumped body."

"All they know is that something is going on in this taxi," Toschi said.

"And you're the expert here on this one," Carroll said to Toschi, who brightened at the compliment and exchange of good feelings, this joining of two generations of Zodiac investigators. "In that time there were sector car responsibilities," he said. "The sector car has responsibilities to the area, but they could have been out of service for whatever reason . . . Actually, I never got clear from Armand whether it was his car sector or not."

"Well, let me ask you about that," Fincher interrupted. "So there's three cars in this area, let's say. Dispatch is going to say, 'We have children, hysterical, semi-hysterical. There's a problem at Washington and Cherry.' Somebody's gonna respond to that and say, 'I'm close. I'll take that,' right. Somebody else is going to say, 'I'm not near, but I'll sweep.' We know the guy takes about a minute after the gunshot to walk to the car and do whatever. He takes about three and a half minutes to walk casually to Jackson. It's five or six minutes for the first car to arrive at Washington and Cherry . . . We need to find out where that car came from."

"It's literally on Zodiac's tail and he disappears around the corner as it arrives," Brad said, "then makes his way down here where Fouke and Zelms stop him."

"You know because of the address he asked for that he's coming back here. He knows he's a block further because he asks for this block. When he gets to that corner, we know that he's going to leave down Cherry and come back to Maple. Regardless of what direction a police car comes, he has to come back."

"The only decision Zodiac would have to make," Jamie said, "is whether to come down Jackson or to come down Washington. It makes sense that he goes around Cherry because he turns a corner from the cab quickly as possible. His initial destination on the trip sheet leads one to speculate that it's a perfect escape. You shoot it out up there, then you come right down this steep hill to your concealed car."

"The first car doesn't arrive until five, six or seven minutes later," Fincher said. "That means the first car's not on the scene talking to the second car that's doing a sweep because that means he's loitering for five or six more minutes than is necessary to get here."

Why would he loiter? Toschi thought. Zodiac already bought another block of walking. He knew the streetlights were working that night because he had photographs of them. So did Fincher. Ostensibly, the lighting is the same one block up. It was not the lights.

"You're not buying anything by not stopping here," Fincher said as he assumed the role of Zodiac again. "*Take Three!* The only reason not to stop here might be pedestrians. So you're driving along here and somebody is walking their dog. You go, 'Now I have to shoot this guy and walk down the street. Somebody with a dog forces me to go another block.' So that makes sense. It's not the proximity to the buildings, because that is ostensibly the same a block away. The windows were dark. Does Zodiac know that he was seen? He does not know." No one had come out, so Zodiac was obviously taking his time casually walking north on Cherry. Fincher figured the shooter was slightly adrenalized because the killing was his sick fantasy. "He's within spitting distance of any number of possible witnesses and acting causally enough not to draw attention to himself."

Then, Fincher drew upon his movie experience as Brad and Jamie had ceased doing. "As Michael Corleone does in *The Godfather*, if you know the best chance of you to become noticed, singular, and interesting is to run. He's made that decision up front and made that decision about this block because this is the address he's given. Something here [at Washington and Maple] has made him change his mind and go another block."

What was it? Fincher stood in the intersection and looked all four ways. What did Zodiac see?

Jamie theorized somebody walking this way or that way made it one block more. Zodiac had waited the interloper out, but by then the patrol car containing Zelms and Fouke was coming up behind him. Maple was an important street, because Zodiac didn't want to get too much further away and was willing to buy another block, but didn't go two or three more.

"It's not like he said, 'Maple,' then went four blocks." Jamie said. "Why didn't Zodiac have Stine take him to Jackson Street because it was closer to his possible escape route, just one block down and in, as opposed to one block over, one block down. "Was he nervous? Was he worried if he didn't say, 'one block down' instead of 'one block down and take a right' it might spook Stine? As long as you get away, I don't think it matters that people know your escape route."

"It matters if your car has been parked there for hours and might be remembered or even ticketed," Fincher said, reminding them that Sam had been caught that way. "If it's not the setting, it has to be people on the street."

Or had the reason been the street itself? What was there? Southward, Maple slides steeply downward toward a brilliantly lit intersection three blocks away—heavily traveled California Street.

"The night of the Paul Lee Stine shooting, a bunch of solos [motorcycles] came out to see the scene," Toschi added. "We didn't have a good description so they just revved up their wheels and took off."

"'Revved up their wheels and took off,' is that an accurate description?" Fincher said. "Is Zodiac's description in his letter about cops holding road races accurate?"

"Sure. Sure. Sure it is," Toschi said. "He puts on a hat, puts on a coat and doesn't look at all like the guy they stopped ten minutes before and he's getting off watching our guys spinning their wheels, going in circles and not going anywhere. Its like an arsonist. He wants to watch the fire."

"So, it's not so much about a quick getaway, but access to a quick getaway while he watches," Jamie said.

Watching and feeling superior might be what Zodiac was all about. The SFPD had had vehicles out in front, so did the MPs. Fincher looked north toward the military Presidio and the heavy foliage there, a green and solitary refuge from all this dust and clatter.

"There's a line here, that's your turf, here's ours," he said. "The Fire Department comes out, 'Glad to help,' and when the cops and five or six MPs and a captain leave at around two o'clock, they have a dead body, a bloody cab, and some children who were witnesses to what they think they saw. So let's just walk and see how many minutes it takes to get there." They walked west along Washington toward Cherry studying the buildings as they went. "Has this always been a school?" Fincher asked Toschi. He nodded. "Now were you aware that the driver's side door had been opened? Do you recall the witness saying he had had eye contact with him?"

"No!" Toschi said. "The vantage of the third floor was where the children saw Stine's head in his lap. It's in my police report."

"To enter the driver's side makes more sense," Brad said. "You're going to avoid the bloody side. You go around to the driver's side. It also explains wiping down the driver's side which doesn't make sense if you get into a cab you get into it from the passenger side."

"Not if you're picked up at the Pinecrest Restaurant," Fincher said, "because that's a One-Way Street and if he's at that corner that means he is getting into the backseat on the driver's side . . . Pulling up you're going to be getting out the right side of the cab, 'Just let me out up here,' he starts sliding out . . . You don't get out, go sit on the passenger side and go through their stuff. You go immediately to the front door, push the guy over. He bleeds into this wheel well. You take his wallet [the first time Zodiac had ever taken something from the crime scene], untuck his shirt. You get some blood on the shirt."

"You can also grab him, move him if he's on the seat, put him so the blood's going into the wheel well," Jamie said.

Perhaps, Fincher had his answer at last. "So it's consistent with the photo of the crime scene because he was slumped this way."

"But who opened the passenger side door?"

"Our officer said the door was open and the body was where the picture shows," Toschi said.

"There's no reason to lie about that," Jamie said. "Zodiac had to have gotten out the rear passenger side." Now, the screenwriter also crossed the line to switch places with Zodiac, to become the killer. "He goes to the front passenger side door, opens that. He's trying to get the blood that's present in the wheel well. 'How am I going to do this from here? Am I going to have to put a knee in the blood to get this shirt? No. Screw it! I'm going to go around to the other side.' So he walks around to the front of the cab, opens the driver's side door, gets in, blood over here, 'Oh, I can take the keys. I can get the wallet. Maybe I've already started ripping on the right side because I was reaching in . . . If your plan is to go through the driver's side door, you're going to go out the back driver's side door. You're going to get out of the cab this way, immediately go to the door. You're not going to take the longest possible route around the cab to go sit behind the wheel."

Silently, Fincher went over Officers Peda and Pelissetti's official report. He read until he came to an abbreviation he didn't recognize.

"What's a PEH," he asked.

"Park Emergency Hospital," Toschi replied.

Fincher returned to the report:

> "Witnesses saw the suspect in the front-seat of the Yellow Cab, mid-to-passenger side, with the victim slumped partially over his lap. The suspect appeared to be searching the victim's pockets.The suspect then appeared to be wiping (fingerprints) on the interior of the cab, leaning over the victim to the driver's compartment. The suspect then exited the cab by the passenger side front door, also wiping with a white rag, possibly a handkerchief. The suspect then walked around to the driver's side and proceeded to wipe the exterior of the left door area. The suspect then fled (walking) north on Cherry Street toward the Presidio of San Francisco. Witness's "observation point was directly across the street (50 feet) and unobstructed."

"As Zodiac entered Stine's cab," Toschi ventured, "he may have touched the exterior of the left door as he slid into the rear seat. In the darkness he put on the gloves, committed the crime and discarded them, explaining why he didn't wipe down the rear seat."

"The meter read $6.25 at exactly 10:46 PM," Fincher said. "10:46! An hour later?"

Toschi explained that the meter was still running from Geary and Mason. Stine never got to turn it off, but only stopped to put the cab in park. "Let's go sit down. I want to go through all this stuff more carefully."

When Carroll edged up, Brad asked him an important question about an article which stated, "Based on the results of a DNA test, Inspector Carroll and his partner in Homicide, Inspector Michael Maloney, told the *Chronicle* that, "Arthur Leigh Allen does not match the DNA developed from bona fide Zodiac Letters."

"Do we know which Zodiac letter was tested for DNA?" Brad asked.

"Again, just to be accurate," Carroll said, "—the envelope you're talking about? Off the top of my head I honestly couldn't say." In April, Inspector Carroll had spoken with the *Chronicle*. "Our hope is that from that evidence a DNA profile will be developed," he said. "I completely understand the demand of current cases, but the Zodiac always stood to me as symbolic of SFPD's commitment not to give up on unsolved homicides. If there is any realistic hope of solving the case, it would be from the physical evidence that we have."

"Was there somebody who was assigned to shepherd that whole thing," Fincher asked.

"Yeah. Me."

"So obviously," Fincher said, "we have the list of the letters they didn't have enough cells to get DNA tests, but we're not really sure in terms of chronology which of the twenty-six letters were tested. Obviously, the Paul Stine letter would have been best, anything that's got a bloody [piece of] shirt in it would have been pretty good."

"Let me interrupt you," Carroll said, "and I'll give you the short end of it. One of the first things I did upon getting this case was try to survey the evidence: What do we have? What don't we have? Where the hell is it? So we have a number of items of correspondence, the letters themselves, some of them are bona fide, some of them are not. Then, we have some envelopes. As part of my investigation, I was able to discover three envelopes that were not in police custody. They are bona fide Zodiac correspondence and they come from the letters that he sent out at the end of July in '69 to the *Ex*, the *Vallejo Times* . . . I have it all now. When I came on, I didn't have it all. I was lucky enough to discover some things [such as the three envelopes] that had been in private hands."

Toschi's face showed pain. The envelopes had been in private hands? Then, how could the police trust the evidence?

"Anyway, so now I sit down with my expert questioned documents examiner, Susan Morton," Carroll continued. "She's actually familiar with the case. She was with postal [documents examination] before she came to us. Real good gal. Sharp. So she had a history with this. I said, 'Susan, tell me what's bona fide.' 'These [letters] are bona fide.' It's a fairly simple logistical progression. The letter that includes a piece of the Paul Stine shirt is bona fide. But we can do a logical extrapolation. If this is bona fide, well this is the same person that wrote this. 'O.K., separate the bunk.'"

"When you say separate the bunk," Fincher asked, "are you including for instance the 'Red Phantom' letter?"

'Yeah."

"You claim that as bona fide because . . ."

"When I say bona fide, let me make it more accurate. Absolutely one hundred percent bona fide. I'm going to the bank that's the Zodiac correspondence. Stuff that she tells me and some of the stuff you can see yourself. She says, 'This is bona fide.' 'This is questionable.' 'This is bullshit.' I don't care about questionable and bullshit. Now, what is the corresponding envelope that brought me this bona fide stuff? Now, I submit it to the lab and I say, 'Now you please do your magic,' which is, see if there is biological material you can recover from seals or stamps, develop a DNA profile, and go from there. Now, I'll be honest with you. I couldn't tell you which."

"O.K., that's fine," Fincher said. "We have a SFPD list that says for whatever reason there's not enough biological material on the letters to test."

"Let me stop you and say, whatever list you have predates my involvement in this case," Carroll said. "There was some preliminary effort done before we had our modern lab. I got handed this case in 2000. I was a homicide detective and I took it as an assignment to investigate. The Police Department subsequently decided it's not worth investigating as an active case."

"Why?" Fincher asked. To get an answer, this master of incessant retakes asks as many questions as it takes.

"Whatever was done before is something to be taken into consideration," Carroll said. "But what was done subsequent to my involvement is that these items which have been to our lab, the items have not been completely analyzed. This case, for whatever reason, has been suspended or closed."

In April, Carroll had reported that the SFPD still had untested DNA evidence—with no immediate plans to analyze it because of an overworked crime lab.

"Look, to be real honest with you, I'll speak plainly. I don't think the Police Department sees this as a dynamic or viable case. This has taken on mythic proportions and as such, it's messy."

"These are monetary reasons? Fincher asked. "Here's what I'm saying, if it's a monetary consideration, we are not adverse to writing that check. Because we don't want to make a movie that condemns a dead man, if he can be exonerated at this point."

"I don't have the answer," Carroll said. The tension in the air grew heavier. Everyone on that busy corner could feel it.

"Is it time involvement?" Fincher asked.

"Their concern would be the time involvement," Lieutenant Greely interjected. "Someone would have to work with you and that's what we don't have right now. That's what their concern is."

"If we could define what their concerns were." Fincher said, moving into his helpful persona. "If they could say, 'Look, this is so many extra man hours.'"

"The Number One concern," Greely said moderately, "is man hours. I don't think once they got over that huge, huge [budget] issue the city's having right now, you know . . . we would never not want to not investigate something. There would be no reason to. Having someone help, I don't know, because it would be so many man hours of so many different people."

"Supervision," Fincher said.

"It's not just that," she said, "but now you would have the questioned document person. She would have to spend some time finding and doing it."

"But everything exists in one area, at least now."

"Geographically, you mean," Carroll said.

"Yeah, so if we could make a seductive enough case," Fincher said. He smiled. "We will get Scotland Yard's lab."

"Specifically, you want certain letters tested or something?" Greely asked.

"We want to follow your gut on this. If you say that there were things that could have been done . . ." As Fincher spoke his voice grew milder and milder. He was downright charming.

"Things that weren't done," Carroll said, his voice rising. "The evidence hasn't been exhausted in terms of its analysis."

Everyone had now gathered in a shaft of bright light on the street corner where Stine had been killed. They were waiting to see how the discussion was resolved.

"And if we could get a list of what that is and if we could bear the burden of going to an independent, so we don't have to tax your lab—"

"Uh, huh."

"But somebody that you would vet and say—" He was smiling more broadly. His eyes were friendly.

"It's never leaving our lab!" Carroll said suddenly. Fincher's relentless questioning had gotten to him. "I keep my mouth very quiet about this for any number of reasons!"

Fincher was taken aback. Very strong feelings and egos were involved here and likely an internal department policy of which he knew nothing—swift currents within swift currents, wheels within wheels, orders within orders. After all, the police department is a military organization which issues orders that must be obeyed. And those orders had been issued.

"Plus, we don't want to do what we do and put it out for hire," Greely explained calmly, defusing the situation. "The next guy says, 'I want to solve my son's murder. I live on Washington and Cherry so I will pay for it.'"

"Is there a way to financially remunerate the city?" Brad asked.

"You know what, we'll find out," Carroll said tersely. "I'm very clear on what you're after and I'll get an answer."

"We would need someone who already has a lot of knowledge about it," Lieutenant Greely said. "You can't take someone and start new. So how much time he's invested . . . I would deal with the department."

"I know exactly the guy," Fincher said. He was thinking of expert document examiner Lloyd Cunningham.

"But it's a huge amount of work," she said.

"When we talk about shooting on the street corner, we're talking about ninety people and taking fifty families and putting them in hotels," Fincher said brightly. "We love taking the long way around. We live for it!"

"Kelly can put some thought in it, specifically what you're thinking about. Possibly it's doable," she said.

"So much of the information that I have comes from fucking *Hard Copy* and *20/20*," these people who always look for the short cut and always look for the hearsay. I'm looking at this and thinking, 'We've got people who care and people who are looking at this.' From my standpoint, if we're making this movie we have to be fairly sure of what it is that we're saying. I'm not interested in entertaining people so much that I want to be that irresponsible. So if you can stop me now, I've got as many articles about how inconclusive the last DNA testing is as I have saying this case is now closed and we've exonerated the following suspects. And that's why being able to speak to you today is obviously a huge benefit. If there's something we could provide to give you closure that would be great for us because that would allow us to go, 'As far as SFPD is concerned these are the things that have been done.'"

"I'll get an answer," Carroll said tersely.

He was ready to leave. The mystery was as frustrating to him as it was to Toschi. Two strong men and a case that, so many years afterward, was still obsessing lives and affecting policy from a police department that seemed to just want it to go away. Obviously, there were things going on behind the scenes at SFPD. Nationally, there had been political and personal fallout from ABC's *Zodiac Primetime Special* on October 17, 2002.

"We might be interested in writing that check," Fincher said, hurling another question after them. "I will speak to Mike Billington on following that up. It's very politically charged as you can imagine because what I was told is that there are a lot of open murder cases where DNA tests have not been done and if we go in and they get money from Hollywood to do these DNA tests it would make the city look very bad. If they did do it, it would have to be under the headline essentially that because the movie was being made it reinvigorated interest in certain questions that were being raised and that they went ahead and did it."

Carroll and Greeley shook hands with Fincher, Toschi, Brad, and Jamie, then drove away.

"The other way to go," Jamie said, "and I'm just going to throw it out there, is if they completely stonewall us and this goes forward until we're near shooting, there is something to be said for giving the *Chronicle* a call and saying, 'We really want to pay for this test that won't cost the taxpayers of San Francisco anything to hopefully resolve the Zodiac thing. And the Police Department says, 'No.'"

"What I do not understand," Brad said, "is how the guy who was in charge of DNA testing of the letters doesn't know which letter they tested. It's 'I have to check on that.'"

In the strong light, Toschi's shadow had intersected Fincher's shadow so that the two had become one. Toschi's dark-brown trench coat swept back to reveal his plaid shirt. Fincher hooked his hands behind his back and leaned forward to hear what the inspector was saying. Toschi was holding his hands apart as if measuring a two-foot long fish that had gotten away. The wind caught in his white hair and swept his words away. Badly chilled, Toschi climbed back into his car and drove away. What an ordeal this has been, he thought, as he turned the heater on. His shoulders ached and his cough was worse. As he drove, he thought of Inspector Carroll's reluctance to answer Fincher's questions at Washington and Cherry with any exactitude. He smiled. He didn't doubt that Carroll wanted to solve the case as much as he did but all could be explained by an SFPD internal memo the *Chronicle* had printed in its front page section: "Under Department Directive, Inspector Kelly Carroll is prohibited from speaking with the commercial media." Presumably, this included speaking about the Zodiac.

MAX DALY FOLLOWED UP with Susan Morton, but she didn't recall which letters had been tested, and said she knew little about the Zodiac case.

The DNA test on three recovered envelopes that Zodiac had mailed to the *Chronicle*, *Examiner*, and *Vallejo Times* which exonerated Allen and two others had been conducted nationally on live TV less than two years before SFPD rendered the Zodiac case inactive. As Toschi neared his home, he was still wondering what weight that TV program had carried in making the decision to shut the case down. Wheels within wheels. His head was pounding more than ever. As far as he was concerned it had been a terrible day.

On the lonely corner of Washington and Cherry, Zodiac's secondary choice of destination, the mystery remained. It grew darker as the day passed. At night, a brilliant glow lit up the base of the steep hill down Cherry to busy California Street three blocks below.

They had no idea this spot had been carefully chosen by Zodiac. At the corner of Cherry and California Streets was a bus stop. Saturday nights in 1969, a bus stopped there every eight minutes. You could set your watch by it. If Zodiac had walked downhill to California and taken that bus west to 22nd Avenue and California, another block south would have brought him to the door of 320 22nd Avenue where the 1968-1969 San Francisco City Directory listed the name of a tenant— "ALLEN, ARTHUR— STUDENT."

Brad Fischer, Lt. Nicole Greeley, Jamie Vanderbilt,
Inspector David Toschi, and David Fincher

Inspector David Toschi, Brad Fischer, Jamie Vanderbilt,
Lt. Nicole Greeley, and David Fincher

CHAPTER TWENTY

PRESS AND PRESSURE

THE FLAG ATOP THE *Chronicle* tower cracked in the wind rushing down Mission Street. Across the way, that hardy '06 Quake survivor, the Old Mint, gold dust in every cranny, shrugged off its age and squared its marble shoulders against the gale. Similarly, the *Chronicle's* nearly one hundred year old exterior remained unaltered, except for a hasty renovation in the 1980s when careless sandblasting had worn away the sandstone facing and erased the delicate sculptured lines of the friezes. Fincher, Brad, and Jamie entered, holding down their hats. The strong wind slammed the heavy glass door behind them. A second large American flag hung inside the lobby next to a bronze wall plaque explaining the *Chronicle's* mission. Only one word was misspelled— "Journalism." Brad stopped at the guard's desk, sat down on a bench against the south wall, and consulted his want list. So far, the young producer had 'shot put the moon' and gotten an interview with the brother and sister-in-law. With a pen, he put a checkmark by their names. He added "Speak with Pelissetti" to the list. That Fincher's most recent request. They still had to find Mike Mageau (the unstoppable Arneson was at this moment tearing up the desert looking for the traumatized survivor). He closed his notebook and looked for Jamie and Fincher.

Fincher had his back to Brad. He was focusing on a pair of cramped, wood-paneled elevators which would play a part in the opening scene of *Zodiac*. He reminded himself to give the mailroom close scrutiny before they left since the film would begin there with the arrival of an anonymous letter. The elevator clanked, complained, and struggled to the third floor where a red-haired reporter greeted the filmmakers. At high speed, she guided them in a circuitous, long-legged route that ended at the editorial boardroom. All that was missing were the two oil-painted portraits of Theriot and DeYoung who no longer owned the paper. Their former rival, Hearst's *Examiner*, had won a century-long circulation war by simply buying the *Chronicle* and continuing it under their control, but retaining the *Chronicle* name.

Presently, the newspaper was hemorrhaging two million dollars a month, so management was buying out older reporters to reduce the staff. In the early eighties, it was not uncommon for passerby to glimpse veteran journalists in white shirts, cuffs rolled up, holding their desk drawers, waiting at the bus stop. It was the end of a glorious age. Yet, there was still power here. The great and near-great still came to curry favor with "The Voice of the West." Governor Arnold Schwarzenegger had visited just that morning. A sliding wall bisecting the conference room was still rolled back. Inside, metal chairs for the press were still lined up in rows. As the filmmakers left, Actor Sharon Stone's ex-husband, Executive Editor Phil Bronstein, mustached and wide-shouldered, strode out of his office into the sparsely populated City Room and boomed, "Of course you can film here!"

Nearby, was the coffee area. Jamie had been intrigued by stories of an eccentric man who sold coffee and three-day-old doughnuts to reporters. Oil stained the pink boxes the pastry came in. Clyde "Shorty" Wyatt, a tiny guy with an old man's face and shoulder-length white hair, had served "Coffee Good as Hell!" throughout the Zodiac period. His most notable characteristic was a high, cackling laugh. Cops busted Shorty one night and for ages a photo of his arrest hung above his coffee urn depicting a startled Shorty, little hands pressed against a brick wall and huge cops surrounding him.

"Shorty is going to be in the movie," Brad said. "There's a moment in the script where we see Shorty, and a reporter is getting coffee and says, 'Can I ask you a question? 'Does it bother you that people call you Shorty?' And Shorty goes, 'What do you mean?' And the reporter goes, 'Forget it.' People will see Shorty as a much beloved, though foulmouthed, character." Shorty, who lived on Knob Hill, vanished from home one day wearing only one shoe. After a citywide search they found him at Hanno's Bar where anyone with printer's ink in their veins congregated.

Their minds filled with facts, startling images, snappy dialogue, and a cackling laugh, Brad, Jamie, and Fincher, strode down a steep concrete hall, out the Fifth Street doors, and into the dank alley between the *Chronicle* and *Examiner*. It took them a moment to find Hanno's Bar which was now called the Chieftain. Ace Reporter Paul Avery had spent long evenings at the classic watering hole (and at the M&M Bar on the corner). A half-block further down the alley, he had almost had to use his gun against a man with a knife. The pub advertised Boddington's in the window. Fincher shadowed the glass and peered into the narrow wood-paneled room which contained only a few loafers, and several pool tables and video games. Fincher entered, and slumped on the first stool, rested his elbow on the bar, and considered the Herculean task before him. For the first time during their scouting trip, he seemed utterly exhausted. It was as if he had left all his energy on that windy Washington Street corner. He had felt the tension in the air. Brad and Jamie followed and sat down at a table.

Brad, was still fresh and telling jokes:

"How many development executives does it take to change a light bulb?" he asked.

"How many?" Jamie asked.

"Does it *have* to be a light bulb?"

The daylight faded. It was time to leave. At 8:45 PM, the filmmakers departed from SFX on United Flight 846 to Los Angeles. In his seat, Jamie white-knuckled the short hop for a second time. At 9:44 PM, the guys arrived back at LAX where a long, black limo picked them up. Jamie returned home not only "totally engulfed in detecting" and rewriting the script, but preoccupied with his upcoming wedding to Amber.

Brad rested on Sunday, but it was an uneasy rest. Early Monday morning, he was down all 107 steps, into his car and soon back at his desk at Phoenix Pictures. Now that they had visited the crime scenes with the original detectives and discovered important new clues, they had to repeat the ordeal with the two surviving victims—Bryan Hartnell and Mike Mageau. Because Mike had become a street person traveling from city to city, finding him seemed improbable, even impossible—yet with Arneson on the case, very possible. As for the Hartnell interview, that was still up in the air. They still had to interview Inspector William Armstrong. One problem loomed larger than all the rest. Since the meeting with Toschi at the Clift Hotel last year, the detective had remained cooperative yet steadfastly opposed to allowing them to use his real name in *Zodiac*. Brad feared that Toschi may have been offended by Inspector Carroll's presence at the Stine crime scene. As always, the case brought out strong territorial feelings between the old guard and the new guard who all had the same objective—the truth.

At 2:40 PM, Brad reached Toschi by phone to smooth out any ruffled feathers he might have. "I can't thank you enough," Brad said, "and I'm speaking for Jamie and David, for going around the corner with us and answering all those questions about Jackson and Maple." It had not escaped the young producer how sick Toschi had been and yet he had ventured into the cold to help them and dredge up old memories he would be happy to forget.

"Well," Toschi said, obviously touched that Brad had been concerned about him, "I don't know what to say." They talked awhile. He hung up and drove to his usual hangout, the Copper Penny on Masonic. "Brad wanted to apologize that Inspector Kelly Carroll showed up," Toschi told his luncheon companion. "I guess he felt the tension between us." He took a bite of "Dirty Harry" lemon meringue pie and smiled. "Carroll is liaison with the film commission and the filmmakers have to get along with them. I understand that." He only wished the department could be more forthcoming on the DNA and which letters and envelopes were tested. He suspected that higher ups in the SFPD only wanted to put the case behind them.

When Fincher spoke with Captain Conway, the veteran policeman detailed his past problems dealing with the SFPD. "They passed that case along to four, five, six different guys," he complained. "Because the Zodiac generated so much interest, officers who were about to retire, they'd give the case to somebody else. Every time, we had to reeducate whoever we were talking to on what the case was all about."

"Apparently," Fincher told Conway, "no one at the SFPD wants to be forthcoming until they find out what light they are going to be painted in. But, the truth of San Francisco is that there's nothing there but a fucking fingerprint that they can put at the scene. I also think that there were no fingerprints taken at Washington and Cherry before the cab was impounded. The sole fingerprint that showed up was a bloody fingertip. How big can it be?" Absently, he looked at the tip of his little finger. "It's ridiculous. And the fact that it doesn't exist until forty-eight hours after the car is impounded."

The next day, Tuesday, January 18, Brad climbed out of his car at Kate Mantilini to lunch with a talent manager about suitable actors. He left, more relaxed, and confident that Jamie was "going to nail the rewrite." He expected new pages from him by the weekend and he wanted to move the process along. The next day, Phoenix Pictures began finalizing the chain of title and all the legal documents they had with Warner Brothers. At 3:00 PM, their legal department dropped a bombshell. They reminded Brad that they have only a life rights deal with Toschi not to use his real name. For *Zodiac* to be accurate Fincher insisted they use all real names.

"Every day is another challenge," Brad said, "but it definitely is important to get Toschi to allow us to use his real name today." Toschi had left work for the day, but the issue was urgent enough for Brad to call him at home which he rarely did.

"My bride is just afraid I won't be treated right," Toschi explained when he came to the phone. He had been treated poorly by the press in the past.

"They'll send you the parts of Jamie's script about your character."

"I just don't know," he said. "I just don't know." Toschi couldn't be budged. This was deadly serious. Fincher wasn't going to make *Zodiac* if he couldn't use real names and Toschi's name was the most important of them all. Later that night, Brad got a head's up on another disquieting development. The trades were to run with a story tomorrow about Fincher directing *Zodiac*.

"They kind of caught us by surprise," Brad admitted. "It's always best when we can control the press as opposed to the press controlling us. We've put them off for a year, but say they have the story confirmed by Paramount and they're going with it. I haven't told Jamie yet, but left a message for him and David, too." The next morning, Inauguration Day, *The Hollywood Reporter* published an article about *Zodiac*. So did *Daily Variety*. "That front page story in *Variety* got picked up all over the world," Brad said.

At 12:25 PM, Toschi grabbed up his phone at the first ring. Brad was on the other end with a familiar question.

"I'm getting the feeling you want me to say, 'Yes,' about using my true name in the film," Toschi replied.

"I'd love you to say, 'Yes,' Dave," Brad said.

There was a long pause.

"Well, then, 'Yes.'" Toschi said.

At 2:40 PM, Toschi was again in a side booth at the Copper Penny explaining the new development to a friend. "So I said, 'Yes.'" he stated. "It wasn't a question of Brad twisting my arm. I said O.K., because I don't want to ruin this picture in any way at all. He seemed very happy about it. So don't say anything to my bride. I just wanted to let you know I will go ahead and do it."

Inspector David Toschi, SFPD

On January 27, Jamie worked all day on *Zodiac*. "By now, he and Fincher are like an old married couple," Brad said. "They get mad at each other, then make up. I have not informed anyone about the little side trip Jamie took to Washington DC. Everyone is under an impression that he has been tucked away into a cave doing nothing but *Zodiac*."

"Which I have been," Jamie added defensively, "but I was tucked away in a cave talking to people with serious national security clearance." Jamie's first draft was over two hundred pages. He had paid close attention to how Fincher conducted an interview because, when he interviewed Clarke, Brad and Fincher wouldn't be there to help him. "All it means is I have to work twice as hard and twice as fast on twice as many things." And he was doing that. "Anyway, I got the Clarke job because of the *Zodiac* script, so they knew I was in on this as well." His lunch meeting with Brad and Fincher was scheduled for 3:00 PM. Jamie got there a few minutes early with an armload of pages. "Guess who I got a call from?" Brad told him, "Bryan Hartnell's son, Benjamin. "Bryan is just getting over food poisoning he contracted on Sunday. His son is calling me and giving me updates. He said, 'My dad's going to call you, my dad's going to call you.'"

Jamie thought about this. He would not be surprised if the son sat in during any interviews because he seemed very protective of his father. By February 1, Hartnell had still not called. Brad spent the next day "working like crazy" and trying not to think about a meeting which probably was not going to happen. As he headed home in his leased BMW 330, he pulled into Hamburger Hamlet on Hollywood Boulevard for a solitary dinner, just one of a string of lonely working meals he endured after a long day. He sat down feeling a little glum. As he picked at his food, he opened the latest package of documents and spread them out on the table. "I was reading through all these Lake Herman Road reports I hadn't seen before," he recalled. "when my cell phone rang." It was Benjamin Hartnell.

"If my dad calls you right now, are you available?" he asked.

"Of course," Brad said. He hung up immediately. Too nervous to eat, he studied the burger on his plate for thirty-seconds, forty-five—. At the one minute mark, his phone rang. It was Bryan. Brad leapt to his feet, and ran outside to take the call. As he listened, cupping his ear, he began pacing up and down on Hollywood Boulevard across from the TCL Chinese Theatre on the "Walk of Fame." After initial pleasantries, Hartnell's first question was, "How can I help you?"

It was a warm, friendly voice issuing from a man as big as the Matterhorn, an immensely likable and successful man. As he paced, Brad was thinking: I'm just amazed and grateful that he's willing to talk to us. Hartnell asked what their story is. Brad took him through it. "And he just got right into it," Brad said later, "and he was going through the whole story of what happened and I learned some interesting things I didn't really know before." Brad got no sense of whether Hartnell would go back to Lake Berryessa with them. The place held horrible memories for him. By the end of the call, Hartnell had agreed to meet with them in Redlands on Friday, February 11. While engaged in a conversation he had been trying to have for over a year, Brad was kept busy fighting off panhandlers. "Of course while I was talking," Brad said, "the Hamlet where I was having dinner closed. I rapped on the glass and they let me back in to finish eating. They had even put a napkin over my burger."

It was late when Brad called Jamie who always made fun of him because he called all the time and often late at night.

"This better be good!" Jamie snapped. He had been busy on the script in his second floor office.

"I just had a two-hour conversation with Bryan Hartnell!"

There was a long pause.

"You just took that 'better be good' thing and ran with it, didn't you?" Jamie said.

"I'm really happy that he's agreed to talk with us. It is really important to the story."

"It's really important to Fincher."

There were still more people to speak with, but Hartnell had topped their wish list. The clouds parted. The end was in sight. It looked like they might pull this off against all odds.

On Tuesday, February 9, Jamie emailed Brad 130 pages of his script and promised the rest by the end of the week. Brad got some takeout and went over the new pages alone. The ratty, stain-encrusted cap which usually sat in a place of honor on his TV set, now rested on his head. Two days later, after going through the script all day with Fincher, Brad learned their Friday meeting with Hartnell had been delayed until February 25.

"I'm so exhausted," he said. "This whole week's kicked my ass. It's been so busy, but in a good way. I tell you I'm getting too old for this [Brad was not yet thirty]. I went to the William Morris Grammy Party on Sunday and I've just been paying for it all week. Oh, I got a call from a Stine witness. It sounds like he's going to talk to us. Before then, we're getting together with David on Tuesday. We were told to clear our schedules for the whole day." Last time Brad and Jamie visited Fincher's office, they did not get into the War Room to see the big board. There was restructuring to do which meant moving bunches of three by five cards around, so low tech it was just one step removed from cave painting.

On Tuesday, February 22, three days before the meeting with Hartnell, Brad, and Jamie spent the day in the Amazing Office pawing over the script, focusing on the different sequences, and the flow of the entire film. *Zodiac* not only had to encompass Fincher's truth, but do it in two and a half hours. Two and a half hours! The biggest frustration for them was that the movie could only be two and a half hours long.

"Nobody actually does the writing," Jamie said, who at this point felt the equivalent to an editor. "Fincher doesn't say a character should say this or that. I go away and write a scene dramatizing it and I bring it to him. He says, 'OK, I like this,' or maybe, 'You're going down the wrong path.' He might say, 'Maybe there's a better way to do it.'"

"By the way, Jamie, Mike Medavoy wants to know when we were going to get the damned script in," Brad said.

"Soon as we can. When I'm not with the lovely Fischer and Fincher team, I'm working."

"You seem to always be in pretty good spirits."

"That's the liquor," he joked. So far today he had only had ice water and was not only exhausted but famished. Only his enthusiasm and passion for the project kept him going. "We're getting this movie made if you have to direct it. We wouldn't be in this good position if the studios didn't want to make the movie—with David Fincher. Phoenix Pictures really doesn't have a say in whether this movie gets made or not. It's Warner Brothers and Paramount who can yea or nay it at the price and the running time that Fincher gives them. If they nay it at that price and that running time and David says, 'O.K., well fine, I'm not going to make the movie,' then we go and get another director and bring it back to that studio at the right price and the right running time. We were always going to do this much work. You know how thorough David is. The nice thing about the way we're doing the movie is that it isn't Arthur Leigh Allen telling Don Cheney about Lake Herman Road. It's Cheney telling Armstrong as it was in real life. There is not a situation where Brad and I one day say, 'You know what, we can't get this done. We give up.' That's not going to happen. By hook or by crook we're doing this film!"

In Beverly Hills, Mike Medavoy was seated behind an ornate

desk deep in thought. A line of concern creased the legendary film producer's brow. He was thinking of his men. Thoughtfully, he ran his finger along a magnificent paperweight, a Saudi gold ingot resting on a sheaf of movie contracts and assorted papers on his desk. In 1967, King Vidor, the great movie director, had attempted to solve a murder to make a movie of it just as Fincher was doing now. "I realized it was vintage stuff," Vidor had warned, his voice quavering for he was quite elderly by then and despairing of ever solving the ancient mystery. "It was the rarest vintage of all: a murder that has never been solved. One opens such a bottle at his own peril . . ." Now, nearly forty years later, Medavoy feared his director, producer, and screenwriter had uncorked just such a lethal bottle and were in terrible danger of losing themselves. Gazing about his light-filled home crowded with beautiful paintings and gorgeous prints, he carefully considered the three men. They were smart guys, yet each had lost himself in the process of chasing a murder story and crossed an invisible line. "It is what happens when you get so obsessed with something and you lose sight of what the objective is," Medavoy said. "You're bound to get lost and you're bound to destroy everything along the way . . . and it happened to every single one of them. Look at all the things that happened to the principal characters."

To Medavoy, that aspect was what was so fascinating (and perilous) about the film they were attempting to have greenlit. "David and Brad and Jamie [are] maniacal about making *Zodiac* accurate," he said, "and doing their own gumshoe work. We thought that Brad Fischer was going to become a policeman and quit show business!" It was not difficult for Medavoy to envisage the trio at work each day. They were either trying to crack Zodiac codes over at Fincher's retro office, or out beating the bushes with a covey of retired cops, or down on their hands and knees in lonely lovers lanes looking for clues, and in other ways trying to make sense of a decades-old tragedy that might mean something or might mean nothing at all. Of course, Medavoy was worried about his movie (too long and with no ending), but his most pressing thoughts were of his three filmmakers. If only they could find the missing Mike Mageau and wrap this all up. Fincher, Brad, and Jamie were hot on Mike's trail. So was the indefatigable Arneson who was drawing closer to his quarry each day.

Thursday night was Jamie's time with his friend, Jonathan

Liebesman, the director of his first produced film, *Darkness Falls*. Tonight, Brad joined them. "We were having dinner at Dan Tana's and standing by the door," he said. "Who comes out but Meg Ryan. She locks eyes with me and starts striding toward me with intent, holding her valet ticket. She is trying to retrieve her car. 'I don't work here,' I said. 'Oh, my God, I'm so sorry,' Meg Ryan says. 'I can't believe it,' Brad said to Jamie, 'that's the second time that's happened this month!'"

In Los Angeles, it was the wettest season in 150 years, a worldwide season of wild weather and dashed hopes, but more so in LA. Multimillion dollar homes precariously balanced on cliff sides pitched down muddy slopes dragging complete swimming pools with them. Highland Park was hit particularly hard. Jamie worried about Brad's imperfect roof, but not too much since Brad had ultimate confidence in the Karloff house.

"It's been standing on that hill for so long it's sunk its roots," Brad said. Rain was coursing outside the French doors and kitchen windows of the home that Brad slyly called Castle Dracula. The elegant Vanderbilt home, with a sweeping staircase and long, well-lit kitchen was anything but gloomy. Amber had designed the exquisite home so that it was a warm, friendly place to be. The kitchen was pungent with the smell of meat loaf and spice. Jamie's father, the impeccable Alfred, used to make a great meat loaf which Jamie had made before. Tonight, Amber was cooking the dish because she's a better cook than he is. Her version: bread crumbs, different kinds of sauces (including Worcestershire and barbecue sauce) and a secret ingredient.

Jamie unfolded Toschi's statement which had just arrived and flattened it out on the kitchen table. Brad sat down next to him. Together, they began to read: "Zodiac absolutely exited Stine's cab by the front passenger side," Toschi had written. Fincher had been accepting of what former homicide detective Carroll had said at Washington and Cherry, but Jamie thought a bit of that was Fincher saying that for Carroll's benefit.

CHAPTER TWENTY ONE

ABC DNA

IN OCTOBER 2002, ABC producer Harry Phillips was given permission to conduct a new DNA analysis of Zodiac evidence on a hour-long episode of *Primetime Live Thursday*. "Inspector Carroll had recovered not only the letters," Phillips explained, "but the envelopes which had contained the letters and ciphers, and a threatening greeting card. It was a mixture of fragmentary DNA taken from three separate envelopes. The three envelopes had been outside of the police chain of custody for years." How many chemical and cursory secretions had contaminated them in all that time? If the documents were police evidence, what had they been doing in private hands, and if so, who had taken them? "I was given considerable access to the SFPD's Zodiac files," Phillips told *San Francisco Magazine*. "The evidence and files were in an atrocious state, evidence had been stolen, rifled, and taken home by retired cops."

"Back in the day, when these Zodiac crimes occurred, nobody had even heard of DNA," Napa County Sheriff's Sgt. Pat McMahon, who had worked the Zodiac investigation, explained. "Things weren't preserved with that in mind." On camera, Dr. Cydne Holt, a respected forensic scientist, was to attempt to discover any DNA evidence on two letters sent to the *Chronicle*, and the *Vallejo Times-Herald* on July 31, 1969, and on a greeting card sent to the *Chronicle* on November 8, 1969. The card had earlier been processed for DNA and discovered to have only a "Few Cells," and the DNA indicators on the letters were too small to be considered useful. Next, Dr. Holt turned to the envelopes that had contained the letters and card that Zodiac had mailed to the *Chronicle* and *Times-Herald*. She removed the stamps and flaps. "I will then try to recover DNA from the cells that may have been deposited on the letter," she said into the camera.

"She uses a centrifuge to lift the cells from the sticky adhesive," moderator John Quinones said in voiceover. "She uses the newest DNA detection called polymerase chain reaction, PCR, to produce a genetic profile. It needs just fifty human cells. We start with a very small amount of material like you would have on a letter and actually make more copies of the DNA like a little Xerox machine that amplifies the areas of the DNA that are different between different individuals. She is looking for a pattern of spikes that indicate the presence of DNA."

The test on the first two envelopes produced only flat lines where she should have seen spikes. The DNA indicators were too small to be useful. Toschi had always suspected that Zodiac, who had demonstrated a knowledge of chemistry in his bomb diagrams and letters, used plain water to seal his letters and affix his stamps. Now that Dr. Holt failed to find enough material from the sealed portions of the two envelopes, the flap, and back of the stamps. She resorted to swabbing the outside of the two envelopes.

"I can't detect any DNA," Dr. Holt said. "Disappointing, Certainly not the end."

She took the envelope of November 8, 1969, which had contained the greeting card, and tested under the flap and stamps. Again, she found no genetic material from the sealed portions of the envelope. Now she resorted to swabbing the outside of the stamp, the last hope for a DNA sample on the *Primetime* Live special. She looked into the camera and said, "I found a partial DNA fingerprint from a male individual who at sometime has had contact with the stamp."

"What Dr. Holt finds," Quinones said excitedly in the closing moments of the television show, "is four out of a possible nine DNA markers, plus an indicator of gender XY. Not enough to positively identify anyone as Zodiac. But it's enough to narrow suspicions or perhaps even eliminate suspects."

This small trace of DNA from the surface of the stamp, was so thin, with so few markers able to be extracted, that it was considered inclusive, but was tested against the DNA samples from three suspects, including Allen, without a match.

"Well, based on the information that I developed," Dr. Holt said, "Arthur Leigh Allen could not have contributed to the DNA that I detected on the stamp." But DNA samples are valid for inclusion of a possible suspect, not exclusion. In its travels, the envelope and the outside of the stamp had been touched by the postman who collected it from the mailbox, US Post Office mail sorters, *Chronicle* mailroom employees, the copyboy who distributed the letter, Carol Fisher the Letters Editor, the editorial staff of the Editorial Page, reporters, the copyboy who rushed the envelope to engraving, the photoengraver who took a high resolution photo of the letter and etched it onto a copper plate, and possibly the SFPD technician who fumed it with Ninhydrin the following day.

What Dr. Holt was saying was that Arthur Leigh Allen did not match an *unknown* male individual who might or might not be Zodiac, who had at sometime touched the *outside* of the stamp on an envelope in the US Mail and not in police custody since 1969. At no time did Dr. Holt say that the DNA sample belonged to Zodiac. She didn't know. No one did. The genetic sample could belong to anybody. Nevertheless, the police department announced that Arthur Leigh Allen was cleared. After his retirement, Homicide Inspector Maloney, Inspector Carroll's former partner, disagreed. "It's premature to drop Allen out," he said. "We've got to be careful not to make assumptions on this evidence. Who knows who the print was from?" Until Zodiac's full genetic profile was developed the sample could not be tested against anyone.

VPD Lieutenant Dave Jackson agreed, "All it indicates is that the DNA on the stamp and envelope are not his. It doesn't eliminate him as a suspect." VPD Captain Tony Pearsall also disputed that the partial DNA sample cleared Allen. "It's quick to draw such a conclusion on one minuscule piece of evidence," he said. "They're assuming a lot from just the fact that the DNA is not Allen's."

Associated Press reporters Kathleen Ronaye, Don Thompson, and Michael Balsamo later confirmed in published reports that, "The partial DNA profile obtained in 2002 by Dr. Cydne Holt for 'Primetime Thursday' was collected from the *outside* of the stamp."

OVER DINNER, JAMIE REMAINED exhilarated at the progress they had made so far. The next morning, he was rocked back on his heels—the meeting with Hartnell had been postponed again. The downpour outside increased, kicking up in Jamie and Amber's swimming pool and running down the windows where he was working or trying to work. Customarily, he religiously rises at 9:30 AM, to write, but his latest series of meetings with Fincher required that he be up and out the door by 8:00 AM. That's why "very early" Friday morning, February 25, he was driving bumper to bumper in a cloudburst to the Amazing Office. He arrived just as Brad and Fincher were finishing their interview with actor Mark Ruffalo who was interested in playing the role of Toschi. Fincher had sought him out because actor Jennifer Aniston, who had played opposite him in *Rumor Has It*, had raved about Ruffalo's "ability to breathe life into a nondescript character." She thought Fincher would love him because, "He'll do so much heavy lifting." He would have to. Fincher was known for doing sixty to seventy takes of a scene. Ruffalo, who had tended bar for a decade and endured eight hundred auditions before making it in show business, was up to the task.

"Acting is a quarter of a full director's directing—it's a part of their frame," Jamie said. "It's all daunting super-wide 20 millimeter lenses. That's why these films take forever: a director wants a perfect image from A to Z." Jamie sat down across from Ruffalo and recalled how good he was as "Fanning" in *Collateral*. The Kenosha, Wisconsin native had just wrapped *All the King's Men* for Phoenix and Columbia. "I'd like to do something original," Ruffalo said, studying the script. "I was asked to reprise Steve Martin in *All of Me*—for *Just Like Heaven* [an upcoming release which had been filmed in San Francisco], not hard, but comfortable." Neither Ruffalo nor Fincher were in love with comfort. "Discomfort produces great results. It stops you from getting lazy and sloppy and relying on yesterday's tricks. So it's fine. You just go kicking and screaming."

"Some people go to the movies to be reminded that everything's okay," Fincher explained. "I don't make those kind of movies." He studied Ruffalo. He knew the guy who played Toschi had to be realistic and representative of what the investigator was really like—snappily dressed, erudite, intelligent, all of the things that Dirty Harry is not.

"You can't make this stuff up. None of us are creative enough to dream up a Dave Toschi."

"What's Toschi's hair like?" Ruffalo asked. "Is it curly?"

"It is," Jamie said. A pause. "Oh, yeah, Ruffalo's got naturally curly hair. Perfect. Mark's got Dave Toschi hair in real life!"

"Toschi's a very deflecting, into-the-side-door kind of detective," Ruffalo said. "There is a disarming simplicity to him that is deceiving, not unlike Columbo. After all, he is the model for actors who attempt to play detectives, and I am playing the one that some actors have modeled their career-making roles on." Ruffalo recalled that Toschi and Armstrong were known as the "Zodiac Twins." "I'm going to call you guys the 'Zodiac Triplets,'" he said as he left the Amazing office.

Ruffalo was represented by the William Morris Agency and manager Robert Stine. Brad was aware Mark's reps weren't thrilled that he was meeting with Fincher, something akin to: "You're going to meet with my client and you're going to convince him that this is a great movie to do and you'll offer him peanuts and—he'll take it!" Brad thought that's just the kind of person Ruffalo is. He really just wants to work on good movies. The reps will rightly say, "But Goddamit, I've got to get him a paycheck." Jamie felt Fincher had a predisposition against paying actors. "The way he looks at it is, 'If I have a seventy-five million dollar budget, I'm not going to waste ten of it on an actor.' When actors say, 'I need ten million dollars to do this movie,' Fincher says, 'O.K., well we're not going to use you,' and they say, 'Well, it's David Fincher. I mean, I can work with David Fincher. O.K., yeah! I don't need ten million dollars!'" Benicio Del Toro, who had studied with Ruffalo at Stella Adler in LA, wanted the Toschi role too, but when Brad had a conversation with his agent she started talking about how much money he's making. "Listen, you know what," Brad said, "this ain't going to work." When she started "kind of backing off a bit." Brad shook his head. "You don't understand the way this thing is happening. We have a certain amount of money to make this movie. This is not a situation where any actor's agent is going to start negotiating with the studio and try to get more money. I know exactly what we have in the budget for Dave Toschi and the place where you are starting out right now tells me this is not going to work, so let's just move on."

"Christian Bale, who we love, is really ready to do anything,"

Jamie said. "He's ready to be the best boy on this movie, he's so into this. He just wants to be in this picture." Christian Bale was the new Batman and this thrilled Jamie. When he was a kid he only read two comics, *GI Joe* and *Batman*. "And so," he said, "my biggest, great geek moment of the last year was when Christian Bale wanted to meet me." He told himself, "I'm not going to ask about Batman, I'm not going to ask about Batman." But Bale brought it up and they ended up talking about Batman for half an hour.

"They made me pull [my performance] back because it was too dark," Bale said.

"No, no, noooo," Jamie said, "the role's not too dark. Batman can't be too dark."

Early the next morning, he lobbied Fincher about getting Bale the role of Paul Avery, but Fincher had another idea. He asked, "Who else could play Avery?" The director liked Aaron Eckhart a lot. He considered Avery a great tragic figure, but also blamed him for much of what went wrong. "I think Paul is a very interesting character," he said, "but I think that he and the *Chronicle* may have done a disservice to the investigation and in a lot of ways got in the way and not in a malicious way. Getting the information from Riverside [about Zodiac] from [Captain] Irv Cross and instead of going to the SFPD, then going right to Sherwood Morrill. How does Dave Toschi look when that shows up in the papers?"

"Like a fool," Brad and Jamie said together.

Their collective feeling about Avery was that while he was fascinating in a flamboyant way, and tragic in other ways, ultimately he screwed over Toschi. By 11:50 AM, rather than writing, the Hollywood Detectives were discussing Zodiac theories in the director's Strangelovian office. Unaccountably, the letters and codes had become more interesting to them than shooting schedules and movie-making drudgery like casting. They were gripped by a passion to know. The answers were there, just out of reach, tantalizing. Yet, they could not decipher them. The National Cryptologic Society had put Brad in touch with an older codebreaker for the NSA who was involved with KGB codes.

"He could take another crack at some of the unbroken codes," Brad suggested.

"Great!" Fincher boomed from his great slab of a desk. He slammed down his palm. The Amazing Office rocked.

"Yes, we're all hooked on the case," shrugged Jamie, "but we've got to get this script done." He lifted the massive stack of paper which was his script and dropped it back on the desk with a *bang*! almost as loud as one of Fincher's handclaps. An hour passed. Jamie looked up from his work. Fincher was on the computer looking at something Zodiac-related and Brad was comparing one Zodiac letter to another and thinking back to August 4, 1971, when Leigh Allen's boss at the Greater Vallejo Recreation Department, Phil Tucker, had informed police of a visit he and his wife had made to see Leigh Allen one and a half years earlier. Allen had shown them two unusual letters. Parts of the neatly printed letters rambled; other parts were "well written with legal type vocabulary." Several pages had "symbols or codes of some type," code symbols based on plus (+) signs. Allen told the Tuckers that Joe Mitten of Atascadero Ward 18, an inmate he knew while working at Atascadero Prison in 1963, had written the letters and when he died Allen had obtained these letters. "This is where Zodiac got his code," Allen told them. That was amazing enough, but it was the plus (+) sign in the letters that intrigued Brad.

"Check this out!" he said, sitting straight up and waving a photostatic copy in the air. "I just found a plus (+) sign in the Arthur Leigh Allen handwriting exemplar. Get a load of this, Jamie." He showed him the first Zodiac letter to the *Chronicle*. "Plus (+) signs instead of *ands*."

"What are you doing?" Fincher asked.

"I think Zodiac's using pluses all the time!" Brad said.

"What?" His face lit up. He got up, came over, reached down and leafed through all the letters.

"In the three debut letters," Brad said, "Zodiac used the plus (+) sign on two of them. It's '+ the girl' on the letter to the *Chronicle* and the one to the *Examiner*, but to the *Vallejo Times-Herald* he actually writes out 'plus.' It's so common it has to be part of his natural writing."

"To me, the plus (+) sign strengthens the case against Arthur Leigh Allen," Jamie said. "It's not unheard of that people write colloquially when they are sort of writing shorthand. In making the plus (+) sign, the pen stroke goes this way. For the plus he does the slash downward, then comes up on the bottom left, and then crosses it from left to right, rather from right to left. That shows whoever wrote the letter wrote with their right hand which would be consistent to the idea that Arthur Leigh Allen was somebody who was predominately left-handed and is trying to disguise his handwriting by using his right hand. It's not that common a writing trait. Certain people do it, but it does narrow it down."

"If you get ten thousand different pieces of paper written by ten thousand different people," Fincher said. "I would be curious to see how often somebody does this." He looked at the plus (+) sign and thought back to Riverside, wondering if Zodiac had written the 'Bates Had to Die' letter after all. He studied all the different letters "with the squigglies" next to each other, then looked at some of Allen's. "I'm no handwriting expert," he said finally, "but this is actually looking a little better than I thought."

"As we go farther, certain things become more suspect in terms of some of [state handwriting expert] Sherwood Morrill's analysis," Jamie said. "From everything we know about him for years he was fantastic, and may have lost it in his twilight years. Anyway, all this is great, but we got to get back to the script. O.K., Brad we need to talk about the script."

"Yeah, but check this out about the handwriting."

"That's great, Brad, we can talk about the handwriting in a second. We are still trying to make a movie. Let's get the movie greenlit before we solve the case."

"Sure," he said. But Brad was counting plus (+) signs, a little feverishly now. He calculated there were twenty-nine plus (+) signs in the whole of the Zodiac letters, an affectation surprising in that the experts had never noticed it. This meant the *Badlands* and *Exorcist* letters were probably done by Zodiac since plus (+) signs were in both.

"The *Exorcist* letter in particular looks fantastic for that," Jamie said as he got up. "The other great thing is that when they go through all the exemplars of Leigh Allen's handwriting *and* is only spelled out once and then to start a sentence." On the other hand, Brad found plus (+) signs all through Allen's everyday writing.

"If you look at the Robert Emmett the Hippie [cipher]," Fincher said. "Zodiac promises to give you something he's not really going to

give you. But he always gives you something at the end of the line."
Fincher suspected there was a payoff of sorts in the solution.

At the end of a long, productive day, though sidetracked by three
hours on the letters, Brad had to get home. His parents were flying in
that evening and he had to meet their cab from the airport. "Brad's very
happy his parents are not staying with him," Jamie confided. "His mind
is too full of the case and the movie." "From what I understand from
the lovely and talented Mr. Arneson who's headed to Las Vegas," Brad
said, "he can find Mike Mageau, but we better be ready to find Mike
when we say, 'Find Mike' cause he's going to have him in the trunk of
his car and asking, 'Just tell me where do I take him.' We'll say, 'Find
Mike,' and then we're going to get a call saying, 'You need to be in Las
Vegas in twelve hours. We'll bring him to your hotel room.'"

In the meantime, Brad's friend, an FBI agent in LA, was unable
to help them acquire a non-redacted FBI report concerning the call to
lawyer Mel Belli by Zodiac. "Getting that is one of the most difficult
things procedurally that you do," the friend explained. Brad feared
that even an unedited report would still not provide the exact date of
Zodiac's phone call to Belli's home. They had the exact words of Belli's
housekeeper from the FBI report, but not the time. If only Zodiac had
called Belli's downtown office where Belli's secretaries were required to
read every crazy letter, take every call, and document the exact dates and
times in a red logbook. Not to do so was a fireable offense.

"If you have Belli's passport," it was suggested, "you can nail down
the day he left for Europe and authenticate the date of Zodiac's phone
call to him."

"That's an excellent idea," Brad said. He was in a good mood to
prepare for the actors' read-through, but didn't let his optimism show
through. They were almost there. But the only time you were going to
hear him say, "We've done it. *Zodiac* is greenlit," is when film is running
through the camera.

"Until Zodiac is signed, sealed, and delivered," Jamie explained,
"they don't want to say official green light because as soon as it is
officially greenlit, all the actors and David are pay or play. Warners and
Paramount wouldn't be spending this money if they weren't going to
make the film. The cold hard truth of this is that with the green light
officially they have ten days to pay the purchase price."

On Wednesday, March 2, Brad's parents accompanied him to
Phoenix Pictures. His mother was blond and effervescent; his father
tall, lean and scholarly. Both were doctors. They ate lunch with Brad
at Rita Hayworth's Dining Room, then spent the rest of the day in
his office. "They are just as emotionally involved with the project as I
am," Brad said. He cleared all his nights to be with them. Around 5:00
PM, Mike Medavoy walked in. He had just had a conversation with Jeff
Robinov and wanted to get Fincher on the phone quickly. Robinov
had a call into Fincher and Fincher didn't get the message. The topic
was, and would be for the weeks to come, the length of Jamie's script
which was rapidly growing. Fincher was not so worried about length.
He was asking different questions. On Tuesday, Jamie and Brad met at
the Amazing Office for what became "a fantastic meeting."

Fincher fanned out a sheath of location photos his scouts had sent
back from San Francisco. San Francisco had changed significantly over
the years.

"All right," he said, leaning forward, his left arm on the desktop, "we
got to paint that building out, because that wasn't there. We have to take
out this building and this building and this." His fingers darted to the
left and right, touching for a second like a magician, or blocking out a
structure with his whole hand, the artist's eye at work, the artist's hand
in motion. "We're going to have to digitally erase stuff." Fincher loved
the technical aspects of moviemaking. Using aerial cityscapes by Matte
World Digital, he could show the TransAmerica Pyramid rising as if
overnight and digitally restore the demolished Embarcadero Freeway
which many had considered an eyesore.

To establish the period look, Fincher and cinematographer Harris
Savides poured over William Eggleston and Stephen Shore's photos.
"We specifically referenced Shore's work from the early Seventies,
which was more naturally lit," Savides said. "We also worked with a lot
of photos in the actual Zodiac police files." Production Designer Don
Burt, and Warners Location Manager Rick Schuler, a lean, sharp-eyed
and polite man who knew his business, not only scouted San Francisco
locations, but sites in Los Angeles and elsewhere which could double
for the Bay Area. A building on Spring Street might stand in for the San
Francisco Hall of Justice. The lobby of the Terminal Annex building was
almost identical to the lobby of the *Chronicle*; the Los Angeles *Herald*

Examiner Building could double for its City Room, or they might build a full size set which Fincher favored. He had already reproduced the *Chronicle* City Room three-dimensionally in his computer so he could plot camera tracking and angles, even pass smoothly through walls as he had with his film, *Panic Room*. Fincher visualized the opening sequence—a front-mounted camera would follow a slow moving mail cart backwards into the *Chronicle*. Scouts posted each of the location photos on a website so that the director, Brad, and Jamie could log on, click, and see them any time.

Every time Jamie sat down and talked about the story with Fincher, it reinvigorated his excitement. "How cool is it we get to do this for a living!" he said. "Are you kidding me!" As stressed as Jamie was about page count, he and Fincher didn't make cuts so much as plot out the last forty to fifty minutes of the movie, compressing a huge amount of time in reality into forty minutes of screen time and connecting some of the investigatory dots. One problem they faced: how to get the feeling of the passage of time?

"O.K.," Fincher said, "there's three scenes where nothing happens... I feel like if you get the idea you have this clock that's kind of showing you nothing's going, nothing's going, nothing's going—you'll get an encapsulated view." He wanted to make the screen story flow in such a way that it was at the same time more truthful to what really happened and a better finish to the movie. Some of it he could do visually.

"Do we need this scene?" Jamie asked. "Or should we have a scene like this in its place?" A two-line scene in the script had Avery driving to Riverside.

"What am I going to tell the actor to do here—drive?" asked Fincher. The scene is gone.

Hollywood screenplays are very fluid and malleable. The content of scenes can change a lot on the set, usually to a film's detriment. Jamie's best case scenario was one where the picture's structure was locked down by the time they started shooting.

"David's not an improvisational guy," he explained. With a script like *Basic* or *The Rundown*, Jamie didn't have to worry about the truthfulness of it, but always had worries about page count. "The situation as it is right now is the original script is long for a regular feature film, but it would time out to about two and a half hours which is what David has to deliver with the Warner Brothers deal. Fincher told him they were not there yet and now was not the time to worry about the running time of the movie or the page count.

"I need you to write the best scene you can," he said, "and I don't want you to be counting words."

Jamie e-mailed Brad some new pages. Brad was expecting a 180 page script. "But it's much, much more than that," Jamie said. "This draft is going to be over two hundred pages. They will not be pleased with this, but one of the coolest things about it is we're actually going to cut it down. David will be in charge of cutting. That will be nice because he has a more objective perspective on that than I do. I really like David's process."

Brad forwarded Jamie's latest pages to Fincher, then called him to say, "I don't know if you got the pages Jamie sent."

"I did, Dude. I already read them," Fincher said.

Jamie called Brad and asked if he got the pages. "I did get the pages," Brad said, "and I wouldn't worry about David getting turned off, considering the fact that I emailed those pages about an hour ago and he's already read them." Brad explained that Fincher thought some of it was a little long and was tired of being inside the *Chronicle* all the time, but felt the Riverside scene had come a long way.

"I finally broke his back on the long thing," Jamie said. There was a hint of pride in his voice. "I've been working my tail off." What he had to do now was just keep the flow of the script going. There was no lack of story. The problem was: how do you show four Zodiac letters arriving at the *Chronicle* in rapid succession without boring the audience, yet still make them feel there's a passage of time and not spend twenty pages doing it?

"I just had a conversation with Mike," Brad told Jamie. "He literally said, 'Do not embarrass yourself by submitting a screenplay that's even close to 180 pages.'"

"If that's embarrassing," Jamie said, "this is gonna be downright stripped naked at your high school graduation!"

At their next meeting, Fincher discussed the secondary characters who would not appear in *Zodiac*, but contribute bits and pieces to his truth. "I think we need to come up with some kind of way to subdivide [the material]," he said. He proposed a computer almanac that would allow them to visually rocket into Northern California hour-by-hour, day-by-day, and minute-by-minute. "So the clock becomes the defining spine of the whole thing. You'd be able to kind of just click on an area, point to it, expand it and then it would run you through everything that happened in that area and see this chronologically. Calling up "Vallejo, July Fourth," and show—here's Vallejo, here's the street, here's what happens on this date." He wanted to take everything they had in a police report and build an entire visual logbook encompassing when letters are mailed. At a particular moment, they would be able to see what Jack Mulanax was doing, what Les Lundblad was doing, what Ed Rust was doing, what Leigh Allen was doing, and gage the progress of the Fourth of July water parade at that moment. He shook his head. There was no way his visual chronology could ever be complete.

"Over the years we've lost so much," he said. "We've lost so many witnesses to where the fuck Leigh was during the Riverside thing, where he misses a day of work after the Riverside murder. The supposition is that he is hiding a scratch or something but who can tell us whether or not he comes to this school with a fucking Band-Aid on his face." Brad asked if there was a record from Valley Springs of when he was fired from the school, something more definitive than March or early April, Anything that can account for Allen's whereabouts."

"I'm only concerned with Allen from the time he loses his job at Valley Springs," Fincher said. "That's all I give a shit about—1968."

"Do we want to try to capture Allen's whereabouts during Riverside, or are we discounting it?"

"I'm going to discount Riverside only because if I can connect the others I don't need it. We can include Lake Herman Road for the time being." Fincher still had grave doubts about the Lake Herman Road attack being an authentic Zodiac crime. Brad thought it was easier to include it than exclude it. Fincher said they would limit themselves to anything that they could document with a check stub, a police report, or an official record, exactly what a professional cop would do. Using Brad's flash cards, the director added firm dates, and subtracted anything without a factual basis or that fell under the category of conjecture. The Big Board was downright menacing. If it had had legs it might have stepped down and stalked across the room and pounded on Fincher's desk.

"O. K., then that's the three—we stick with Blue Rock, Berryessa, and Paul Stine," Jamie said. "I would believe Lake Herman Road less, if Zodiac said on the phone, 'I killed these kids. They're one mile east of Columbus Parkway, Goodbye.' And then the letter three and a half weeks later goes, 'I also killed these kids last Christmas.' This sounds to me more like a guy who's going, 'I'll take credit for this one too.'"

"Let's say he didn't do it, and he got the idea to do it. What's the publicity for Lake Herman Road?" Fincher asked.

"The *Vallejo Times-Herald* ran it front page, but very small. The *Chronicle* buried it [though Paul Avery had driven to the scene to cover it]."

"So there's an argument to be made for him going out to do this thing, shoot these people and get away with it for six months and the trail's getting cold. We have a police report that shows Cheney's initial story as being a hell of a lot more believable than subsequent generations. When he told his story to you, Cheney talked about the watch?"

"He did. Leigh Allen and his brother got twin Zodiac wristwatches [as gifts from their mother], very expensive even in the late sixties."

"That watch—certainly wearing that fucking Zodiac watch to the day he died is a nutty thing for someone who breaks down on KPIX and cries, 'Why don't they leave me alone?' Well, stop wearing the fucking watch! Let's start there."

Brad checked his own watch. "I have a nighttime movie date at Mike Medavoy's," he said and rose from his chair.

"This is how the other half lives," Jamie said. "Instead of going out to see the new releases, Mike calls whatever studio has new releases and they deliver a print to his house in Beverly Hills and he watches in his private screening room. It's nice work if you can get it."

After they left, Fincher pondered ways to find a Riverside witness or learn the information in another way. Jamie returned home to hack his way through the morass of pages. His upstairs office walls were covered with police reports; his desk and floor scattered with binders of transcriptions, interview tapes, and all the material provided to them by the author and the authorities of four counties. On Monday, March 7, Jamie e-mailed his 225 page script to Fincher and Brad. It took them all night to read it. Brad called Fincher "who was very pleased with it," and Fincher called Brad to say, "O.K., we're pretty much there." Except for the cutting. Everybody at Phoenix, who passed Jamie in the hall, made a scissors motion with their fingers and hissed "Cut, cut, cut, cut . . ."

"And we will cut it down," Jamie exclaimed over his shoulder. "Mike Medavoy hasn't read the draft because it is incredibly long. They are very concerned about the length, but between you and me they have no reason to be. If David is happy, I'm happy. I busted my tail to get us a good script." He knew the situation was sometimes frustrating for Brad. "Brad and I have worked out a rather interesting division of labor where I do what David asks me to do and Brad gets fired for it. The script is much more factually accurate after speaking with Toschi and the others. There's a lot more Avery. There's a lot more Toschi. I finally got his voice down. There's a lot more ensemble movie of the four characters we follow, but everybody's part is bigger."

The story was still just about the four people, but it felt very much like a Hollywood movie, a character piece and at the same time a mystery which was historically accurate and provided all the facts. If they shot the script now it would clock in at three and one half hours. Jamie knew that clocking a script was a very inexact science, especially with such a dialogue-heavy script as his with additional banter. Some pages would photograph in twenty, thirty-seconds, others in two minutes. The biggest struggle in his latest draft was to get it to the point where Fincher not only felt it was true to life (he was very invested in that), but to get the feeling of ebb and flow of the information. In the script the fingerprint on Stine's cab is a great source of debate. Jamie doesn't necessarily want to show one way or the other if Zodiac was wearing gloves. "We do see the Stine killing, but we're not going to see the face of the person." Then, there comes a time when the world's moved on and everybody has forgotten about Zodiac. Fincher said that when Zodiac stops writing for three years, they couldn't just cut to the next scene.

"We've got to feel he stops writing."

As for the structure, Jamie thought it was finally there; how the characters related to each other was there. "We balance what Toschi was doing and what Graysmith was doing. We follow both of them before they meet (a structural thing where we know the two main characters are going to be on screen together at some point, but don't know when). So when the two finally intersect, it's a really cool moment." Jamie's early *Zodiac* script had been much more like *JFK*—a final summation and a ten page monologue to convince the audience. The script had come a long way.

"I don't want this to be about convicting Arthur Leigh Allen," Fincher said. "If the characters in the movie believe Arthur Leigh Allen is the Zodiac, (though I think it's him) I'm completely fine with that, but I don't want to make a movie about convincing the audience." In the present script you see Bawart pick up the mantle and say, "You should know he's very sick. He's got diabetes. I'm just saying if we get him, he's already got, you understand." Now Jamie and Fincher were going to go back in and cut, cut, cut, cut.

By March 16, the pleasant Vanderbilt home was a madhouse. Workmen were laying bathroom tile while others were engaged in preparing for Amber and Jamie's wedding on May 7. Amber was not the type who believed the more a dress cost, the better it was. Her wedding dress was off the rack for $500. They did a little work on the dress and she said, "This is beautiful. I love it." A friend of Amber's mother arranged a string quartet and would sing at the wedding. "There will be very few Hollywood types at the ceremony," Jamie said. "We don't want to invite anybody for business purposes. I love David, but I don't think he would want to come to the wedding. I feel like a lot of times in Hollywood people sort of pretend to be friends with more important people. He's not one of those types of guys. I really respect that about him. I'm under no illusion that he and I are best of buds."

On Sunday, Amber had her bridal shower as Fincher prepared to speak with Cunningham's handwriting expert. The director had always wanted to talk to a good questioned documents inspector, one with fresh eyes. Now, he had the chance. Things were moving fast. Jamie's script had to be handed into Warner Brothers soon and they were still cutting.

The next day, Brad called Toschi three times. Each time he was interrupted by another call before he could finish a sentence: "They're having trouble getting copies of the Jim Dunbar/Mel Belli television prog—," he began. He hung up. His second call started: "The KGO people seem to think it's a radio show and—" He hung up. The third time he only got Belli's name out before he had to hang up. Brad didn't call back again that day.

Meanwhile, moviemakers had returned to San Francisco streets.

On skid row, the big-budget musical *Rent* was being filmed. It was fitting that a big production had come to this impoverished corridor of the city where Paul Avery, who had armed himself after a threat from Zodiac, had once enmeshed himself in a deadly duel—gun against knife. City officials had promised the Sixth Street block between Market and Mission Streets to the filmmakers until April 1 to recreate Manhattan's Lower East Side. Again, incentives were a problem. Treasure Island still lacked a usable sound stage. At this rate, San Francisco would not realize its dream of becoming "Hollywood *North*," though Will Smith's *Pursuit of Happyness* was slated to be filmed here, and perhaps, after that, (fingers crossed) David Fincher's *Zodiac*.

On Wednesday, Brad and Fincher conferred with the Physical Production people: Steve Pappasian, Lou Phillips, and Ceán Chaffin as Line Producer. Executive VP Lynn Harris (Production Executive for *Zodiac*) and senior VP Greg Silverman (Creative Executive for *Zodiac*) and Geoff Shaevitz would oversee the project for Warner Brothers, the lead studio on the project. Warners would take international output. Marc Evans for Paramount would handle domestic distribution. Kelly Smith-Waite, Physical Production Executive in charge of the project, would report to Pappasian. "She and Lou Phillips [Executive Producer] are together constantly," Brad said, "because they do the same job at the respective companies."

On Thursday, March 10, Jamie spoke with Sony executives to discuss his Clarke script for *Against All Enemies*. "I've kind of beat it out as a story," he told them and producer John Calley, then took them through the overall version of what he wanted it to be.

On Friday, Fincher met with Jake Gyllenhaal whom Jennifer Aniston had also recommended. After biking for three hours that morning, he arrived at the Amazing Office dressed in jeans, a gray sweater, and Converse hi-tops. Six feet tall, muscular, and roguishly good looking, Jake had huge brown eyes and a light stubble on his chin. His dark brown hair, shaven for his recent role in *Jarhead*, had grown back. There was a light stubble on his chin. "His face is accessible," director Sam Mendes said of him. "His soul is accessible." Gyllenhaal is from a liberal, civic-minded show-biz family and grew up in Hancock Park surrounded by "big personalities." Paul Newman, one of his idols, taught him to drive; Jamie Lee Curtis is his Godmother. These days,

Jake was at the top of the heap in Ang Lee's *Brokeback Mountain*, a tragic story about two cowpokes who fall in love in 1960s Wyoming. From the very beginning, Fincher thought Gyllenhaal would be "really interesting" for the Graysmith character. "I'll do it, if you'll do it," Fincher told him as he pushed the most recent version of the screenplay across the table to him. Gyllenhaal promised to read it over the weekend. The first time he read the script, he was terrified by the murders. He remembered flipping through the pages and thinking, "This is real, this actually happened. I immediately wanted to do it." Nor did the huge script, easily a three hour movie with a lengthy one hundred day shooting schedule, intimidate the athletic actor. "Hey, it *was* two hundred pages," he deadpanned.

After lunch, Brad and Fincher discussed casting with Laray Mayfield, the charming casting director with the Southern accent whom Brad had worked with on *Basic*. Laray and Fincher went back nineteen years; she had cast *Panic Room* with Jody Foster for him. Brad ran through names for the parts of Toschi and Avery. "These are actors we're going after," he told Laray. Ruffalo was still a favorite, but British actor Daniel Craig, the new James Bond, was now on their list. For authentic casting Laray needed period photos of Toschi, Avery, and Armstrong. "Later on," she said, "we should get what pictures we can of the other guys." She needed to know everyone's age so she could consider actors for the film. In 1969, the SFPD's seventeen homicide inspectors had an average age of forty-two and a half years old, had been policemen for eighteen years, inspectors for nine years and handled an average each of fourteen new homicide cases a year. Their boss, Lieutenant Charles Ellis, was a silver-haired, soft-spoken administrator whom Laray described on her casting call sheet as "50s, medium build, dark hair, intelligent, supportive, and protective of his detectives."

Her call sheet described Mel Belli, born July 29, 1907, as a cheerful, rotund character: Caucasian. Heavyset, White hair in his 50s: A world-famous attorney who basks in the spotlight. When he's summoned to a radio station for a scheduled call-in from the Zodiac Killer, he's terrified en route—but snaps into his public persona as soon as the cameras are on him. Overly dramatic, he is nonetheless dead serious when he warns the detectives on the case the killer will undoubtedly strike again. "Melvin Bellicose," as his enemies called him, "attired himself in three-piece Saville suits, spats, vermillion vests, and red silk-lined jackets. With his huge gold cufflinks, pocket watch, and snakeskin cowboy boots, he was all show business, "I'll never forget him walking into a room like the cock of the walk," Toschi recalled." Belli had four tan Italian greyhounds, Welldone Rumproasts I, II, III, and IV, and a parrot, Captain John Silver, who drank only Jim Beam. Jamie's script had two scenes with Belli—in the television studio and at his eight million dollar mansion at 2950 Broadway Street. His daughter, Gretchen, showed Fincher a box of "incredible pictures" of a penthouse patio overlooking the TransAmerica Building in mid-construction. Brad suggested that the scene where the Graysmith character is sitting with the housekeeper in Belli's parlor and hears about the phone call to Belli by Zodiac be moved to the patio "because of that unbelievable view." Jamie, intrigued that Belli had starred in an episode of *Star Trek* exactly one year before Zodiac shot Stine, referenced the attorney's role as "Gorgan," an evil super being disguised as an angel in the script.

Fincher was considering an unusual choice for the part of reporter Paul Avery, but wanted to mull his idea over before telling Jamie who was busy that weekend. After his quick trip to New York, the screenwriter's friends threw him a bachelor party onboard a cruise to Mexico. Brad was invited, but not before Amber and Jamie's brother placed him under a gag rule: "You are not to discuss *Zodiac* at all." Twenty close friends, college friends, and a couple of industry people including director Jonathan Liebesman, made sure of that as they sailed out of San Pedro on Friday. They cruised down to Ensenada, spent the day, were at sea on Sunday, and slipped back into San Pedro at 6:00 AM, Monday, March 28. Brad flew through customs and into his car, tearing up the freeway all the way to his office. He knew what lay ahead. "The whole day was insane," he said. On March 31, they delivered "an early draft" of the new script. Warners has a very strict and unforgiving page count format with rigid margins. Putting it into that format will really add pages. It's not only the margins. Any kind of camera direction takes up a totally new line; a notation of "POV" requires a new paragraph.

"It's an epic," Brad said, slumping back into his chair as if the act of lifting the script had fatigued him.

Gyllenhaal's agent (he was represented by CAA and Management 360) called Fincher and reported that Jake wanted to do *Zodiac*, but as

Gyllenhaal studied the script, he realized that for the first three-quarters his character is deferential, quiet, and watching. "But I am the hero of this movie," he said to Brad, then came back and told them, "Oh, I get it. It's a comedy." It was amusing to him that in 1970 there were no faxes and there were rotary phones. "Everything was so slow!" he said. He also found it weird visiting one of the places where the murders happened. "My God, we're at the real place." He wondered how many people had walked by that site not knowing what happened there.

Today, Gyllenhaal parked his gray Series 320 Mercedes-Benz in the lot behind Fincher's Amazing Office, popped the trunk, moved aside a basketball, basketball shoes, a catcher's mitt, and a football, grabbed a bottle of water, and went in to see Fincher. As they talked about his character, Jake fingered his sandblasted cell phone, scarred from the rigors of filming *Jarhead* near the Mexican border. "Robert Graysmith is an interesting bird," said Gyllenhaal, who wanted to be an author "in ten years." When I first met him I had told him that I was going to put him on tape because I wanted to study his mannerisms and just physically, I wanted to see how he behaved. I was really nervous. I thought to myself, 'Oh, well, what kind of personality does this guy have in order to go out into the world?' And I thought, 'I'm going to meet this guy and it's gonna be like this weird, dark exchange. What world am I going to have to go to with him to get some truth out of him? And he walks into the room and he's like this sweet, unassuming, constantly complimentary, kind of innocent man. Everything they tell you in acting school, like, 'you should always play the opposite, that's exactly what Graysmith is. He's the opposite of everything you would assume to be a man obsessed with a case like this. But then, as you spend more time with him, there is a sense of, if he wants to get a piece of information out of you and you haven't answered the first time because it's a little too close or a little too personal, he'll then insert it in this odd, syncopated way, so that you answer it and you don't even know you're answering it. He is at the same time, kind of cunning when he wants to get information, but as a human being, he's a gentle guy. It's really interesting."

Over at Phoenix Pictures, Brad's phone rang. It was the Warner Brothers's Legal Department.

"You guys are going to have to change all the names," the legal eagles said matter-of-factly.

"Excuse us?" Brad said. He knew obstacles always come up at some point, but this was a landslide just as the script was about to be evaluated by Warner's top executives.

"Yeah, you're going to have to change all the names, living or dead."

"What are you talking about?" Brad said. "That makes absolutely no sense. The dead cannot sue for right to privacy. Using real names is exactly what David Fincher wants." Frantically, Brad hung up and called Jamie. "I don't know where this is going to end up or how big a deal it's going to be. I'm getting mixed signals. The Warner Brothers's legal people, always the most conservative you can find, are raising red flags about the depiction issues portraying real people and using real names."

"They always err on the side of stupidity," Jamie said. "Lawyers want to protect the studio, obviously, but we're going to take every precaution we can. As many life rights that we can secure, the more comfortable the lawyers are going to be, but it seems they're being sort of asinine about it. Lawyers are paid to be alarmists, but their bottom line is to make millions for the studio. The only thing they are really going to be nervous about is Paul Avery." Avery comes off well in the movie, though the script shows his drinking and substance abuse and downward decline.

"What I'm going to have to do," Brad said, "is go through every single person who's still alive and try and get their life rights. But to go as far as to say they want to change real names including people who are dead! That's just crazy! David's going to walk. He won't do the movie if that's the case!"

CHAPTER TWENTY TWO

DEAD AGAIN

THE REST OF THE day passed in agony for Brad and Jamie. For six and a half hours that Tuesday, they sat gloomily in the cozy kitchen at Castle Dracula. They didn't know where to look. They didn't know what to think. They didn't know what to say. Absently, they pawed through the script word-by-word, looking for ways to shorten it. The pages seemed to have grown heavy in their fingers. They made some headway, though their hearts were not in it. For a while, they watched Sophie the dog scamper under the table and out again. Then they shooed her away, and went back to the problem which was overwhelming their every thought. "Change all the names, living or dead," they thought. "Impossible!" they said. They waited for the phone to ring. It refused to do so. They waited harder. After all their work, the movie couldn't end here.

An hour later, the phone rang.

Jamie took the call, listened silently, then hung up. His expression was unreadable.

"Well," Brad said. "What did they say?"

"Now, they've kind of backed off," Jamie said. A huge smile creased his face. "Warners Legal says we can use real names!"

Before the call, they were worried they could not work. Now, they were so excited they couldn't stop.

The next morning in the Amazing Office, Brad and Jamie were rejuvenated. The energy level was through the roof as they and Fincher made more and more cuts. Today, they were knights with crested helmets, and broadswords slashing. Each stroke was judicious, well-reasoned, and when the dust settled they were down to 189 pages. Now they were rolling. All three were running back and forth like shuttlecocks on a loom, saying, "What about this?" "What about that?" "We can cut that!" "We can consolidate that." Things were hectic, yet good in a painful way.

Jamie found it fascinating that Fincher was very protective of the material that was already in the script. "Usually, it's the reverse," he said. "You can cut this and this and the writer goes, 'No, no, no, that's incredibly important.' It's the reverse with us. We say, 'Maybe we can do this,' or Brad says, 'Maybe we can do that,' and David says, 'No, we need to keep that.' It's unusual, but great. Stuff that I originated and stuff discovered during the last year talking to everybody, visiting the sites and rewriting the script, we all sort developed together."

While they were paring the script to hit the budget mark, a couple of executives read the latest draft of the script. Their response was extremely positive, though they were still terrified of the length. One said, "This is really good. So good, I don't know where to cut." In the turmoil, Jamie had assumed a very Zen-like quality. "It's going to be what it's going to be," he said, but had a good feeling that it was going to work out. If for some reason it didn't (Jamie knocked wood), then they will keep going and get another director or get another studio or do what they needed to do. The script was not owned by any studio. That's how Brad, Jamie, and Mike Medavoy had structured the deal.

"I actually still own the script which is very rare in Hollywood to get this far," Jamie said. "Between the first draft and the draft we have now it's changed in many ways. But the overall goal of what we set out to do, I don't think it's really changed and that's sort of shocking." Jamie felt he was in "a very good position."

"I just tell Brad, I've got to go do this work and he has got to deal with these problems. Mike's his boss and not mine. I have a certain escape route. I love Mike to death, I really respect him. He's got one of those map-of-the-world faces. He is an interesting contradiction. In many ways, Mike really likes artists, but because he's been in Hollywood so long, he has control issues. Listen, I would be the same way. David believes, 'I know who is important to me in making this movie and I will deal with the people I need to deal with and that's the one guy at the studio who can say yes.' The Warner Brothers executives can't say yes or no whether this film gets made. Two guys at the studio can, a guy named Alan Horn and a guy named Jeff Robinov, second in command at Warner Brothers. Robinov's green light abilities are comparable to the powers of Superman or more aptly Green Lantern or Thor, but he has to run it by Alan Horn too. These are the Green Light Guys, who can say, 'Here's $75 million.' Pretty much every studio only has one who can say, 'Here, go make the movie.' He's also the guy who is on the hook if the movie fails."

Robinov was going to read the *Zodiac* script over the weekend. Waiting for the green light to flash, Jamie had one foot on solid ground and one foot on water, balancing and treading as fast as he could. "I suspect we are going to get greenlit at the wrap party," he said, rolling his eyes.

Laray and Fincher were in the Amazing Office casting an important role. Laray's Call sheet described the role of Arthur Leigh Allen:

> "40—must play at 38 and 56, Caucasian. Heavy Build, 6,' about 200-lbs. A large   man, he's a former military who was fired from teaching for molesting elementary school students. Drinks a quart of beer a morning, and comes off as an extremely powerful and strong man in his movements. Jack of all trades who has worked as a teacher, janitor, chemist, and hardware salesman. Lives in his mother's basement. Very creepy. He is the lead suspect in the Zodiac case. He eventually contracts diabetes."

On Saturday night, Brad, Fincher, and Ceán attended a surprise birthday party for singer Frank Black, who was in the running to play the prime suspect. "It's a very Fincherian piece of casting," Jamie explained, "like putting Meat Loaf in *Fight Club*." Later, John Carroll Lynch, a comic actor from the *Drew Carey Show*, rocked Laray with his audition and snared the Allen role. During dinner before the party, Brad saw O. J. Simpson across the restaurant. It was a surreal moment in a surreal evening. But his mind was elsewhere. "We're going to hear Jeff's response on Monday and that will be the next big thing," Brad said.

"We're going to hear from Jeff!" Jamie whooped. "We're going to hear his thoughts. We're going to hear if he loved it. If he hated it. If it's too long. If it's too short—oh, wait! He's not going to think it's too short."

Monday morning, April 4, everyone was up early awaiting Robinov's response. Brad had not slept. Jamie had not slept. Fincher had been up for hours.

Under time constraints, they turned in an allowance budget. "If we begin September 1, where are we? What's the location? How much of the script pages can we shoot in this one day?" Brad said: "When you board and budget a movie, you're not only breaking out the costs of the movie itself, you're also creating a schedule which is called in the industry "a board." Its called a board because before computers when they used to schedule a film there was actually a board with strips that corresponded to each scene that needed to be filmed and those strips could be moved around on the board depending on how the schedule needed to be laid out—before and after availability or location availability and so on. They have to figure out where in the shooting schedule they can go and shoot that day-by-day, how many nights they will need to complete that scene, how much it will cost to shoot each night, and what major actors will be required. Literally, it is a full schedule for shooting the movie—a Herculean task.

"It's like trying to figure out how to move an army around the West Coast," Jamie added. "But what we need to do right now is get the movie cash-flowed."

At 11:30 AM, Brad drove to Warner Brothers to learn what Robinov thought of the script. No matter how many times Brad visited the studio, it was always "a bit like running a gauntlet" to him. Since all the hallways looked alike, he became lost in the maze. He should know where Robinov's office was located. He had been there when it belonged to Lorenzo de Bonaventura, Jeff's predecessor. At last, he found a room decorated with beautiful Troy miniatures—Robinov's modest office.

"Robinov read the whole script over the weekend and was very happy with it," Brad reported with relief. "The midpoint of the movie is now when *Dirty Harry* premieres in San Francisco. It comes right after all the frustration about Allen and the whole thing kind of fizzles out. After *Dirty Harry* there's a time cut and life has moved on several years later, then Armstrong quits. We are really now starting to gear up.

We got the budget in—hit the number—seventy-five million dollars."
The negotiations on everything always get very complicated at this
point because they have to close the deals: Gyllenhaal as Graysmith,
Mark Ruffalo for Toschi.

In the Amazing Office, Brad and Jamie heard a new casting
possibility. "For Paul Avery what about [Fincher paused dramatically .
. . a drumroll]—Robert Downey, Jr. Well, what do you think of that?"

"I gotta be honest," Brad said. "I think it's a brilliant idea because
he's just a phenomenal actor. We're in a position to bring him back in
a big way." Brad had earlier suggested Downey in an email to Fincher
which read, "Avery equals Downey?" and gotten the director to
thinking.

"Downey is someone who can really grasp Paul's inner demons,"
Fincher said, as well as the director's own demons. Zodiac had haunted
him ever since he was a child in the North Bay. Immediately, they put
money offers out to Gyllenhaal and Ruffalo. "If everything goes right,
and I don't want to get your hopes up," Brad said, "we could potentially
be greenlit next week. We need to actively start preproduction then."
Brad then dialed CAA which represents Downey and began to get
things moving to nail down the deal for him to play Paul Avery.

Avery's widow, Margot St. James, a candidate for San Francisco
supervisor and founder of a proposed union of Prostitutes—C. O. Y.
O. T. E. (Call Off Your Old Tired Ethics), was in San Francisco when
she heard the news. Reached at Pier 23 where she was celebrating
her birthday, she watched white gulls wheeling in the blue sky as she
absorbed the information. "Paul would have loved it," she said finally.
"He and Robert Downey, Jr., had much in common." Once back home
in Bellingham, Washington, she added a footnote. "Paul was generally
paranoid and began to change his route each day. He carried a gun and
felt insecure living on a houseboat in Sausalito. I said, 'Paul, aren't you
afraid? Zodiac could be outside the *Chronicle* waiting for you.'" After
that Avery began chain smoking, drinking heavily, taking cocaine, and
gambling. He had always been living on the edge, courting danger
from the battlefield to the dark alleys of San Francisco, but this was
worse. The unsolved case had a similar effect on everyone touched by it.
Meanwhile, the search for Mike Mageau, who had been touched in the
most terrible way, went on.

"We're making our actors 'Pay or Play,'" Jamie said as the contracts were finalized. "The three leads are all going to be paid equally under what is called a favored nations payment. None of them could make more than the others. They also can't make less. With a feature film you either hire actors for run of picture where during the entire shooting schedule you are paying this amount of money and during their schedule they will be available. Or you hire somebody on a weekly basis and say we're going to pay you first week of October and first week of December and if your schedule works out with other pictures, we'll hire you."

Brad now had the whole schedule for the production, not a full board, but an early version of it. The board breaks down the screenplay into pages, then schedules the film page by page. He likes this part, but now it is more Lou Phillips and Ceán Chaffin's bailiwick in the terms of the physical aspects of making the movie. Brad loves that part too because these are the signs that the movie is becoming real; the process is no longer theoretical, but starting to become practical. Brad, a very practical man, is still officially in charge of worrying. Best of all, if the meeting doesn't get rescheduled again, he could stop worrying a little since they would finally see Bryan Hartnell next Friday. For the twentieth time, Brad told Jamie, "Keep your fingers crossed. I think it's all headed in the right direction. For a filmmaker like David, who has so many choices and does so few movies, this is an opportunity to do something that's truly great."

"I have to be honest," Jamie said, "part of me just as a film fan is excited that I could see another David Fincher movie and the fact that it is ours! When a movie does get greenlit, its like you pushed the boulder up to the peak, it goes over, and starts going down the hill on its own." That special moment required them to start official preproduction— crewing up the movie and hiring the production designer and director of photography. They'd already hired Ceán to put together the budget, a tremendous and complicated endeavor. As the film's highly experienced line producer, Ceán was responsible for hiring the crew, managing the day-to-day operation of the company, and making sure everything was running efficiently. Once the budget was done and approved, then they had to hire everybody who was going to work on the movie.

"That should be April 18, at the latest," Jamie estimated. "Ceán's already hired five or six people just to do the budget. It's such a huge undertaking. There's an accountant, assistants—we're affecting people's lives already." For the crucial budget breakdown, they needed specifics—what car Toschi drove in 1969 and how much to buy it now. Toschi had bought his 1962 Borgward red, two-door German taxicab at Earle C. Anthony's on Van Ness Avenue in San Francisco. Graysmith's $3,000, bright orange '72 VW Rabbit, also bought on Van Ness, was much easier to find.

FOR HIS DECEMBER 2004 film, *Collateral*, director Michael Mann had used the FilmStream/S.two systems for short portions and recorded its video images to Sony HDCAM SR tapes, a medium that couldn't support HD high data files. Mann had addressed this drawback by compressing the data and reducing the data rate. But when data is compressed, crucial decisions about color balance, contrast, and brightness have to be made on the spot because once the results were compressed, any subsequent modifications degraded image quality.

Legendary cinematographer Harris Savides had used the FilmStream/S.two systems for the first time to shoot Fincher's Motorola TV commercial. He had especially been impressed with Fincher's modifications to the Viper.

"David took it," Savides stated, "shook it, and said, 'Don't do it this way. We're making a movie. This isn't a football game. We're capturing the image onto a drive and sending it off to start editing,'" Fincher's first modifications to the Viper were to add an automatic electronic slate and make alterations in playback so captured images could be immediately viewed on set via a 57-inch plasma monitor. In this way, the director could delete unsatisfactory takes and feed the rest to a rotating group of 20 D.MAG removable hard drives loaded in S.two digital film recorders. They were shaping the future.

Software engineer Andreas Wacker and Film editor Angus Wall worked with Fincher to perfect a tapeless workflow system for *Zodiac*. Wacker's job was to write the software and design the data workflow. Wall had long favored Final Cut Pro which uses "off the shelf technology" which allowed him to cut with 30 and 23 inch displays and have several timelines up to move pieces around. He would design the post production system. He could begin with Apple Power Mac G5s so

Fincher could see the cut on a 65-inch plasma screen in HD resolution, along with dailies, location, notes, costumes, and casting.

If necessary, Wall could enlist several Mac Minis to help render the workload. Any discrepancies could be fixed by nine LUTs using Final Touch software for on set and dailies. At night, the dailies could be generated on Compressed QuickTime clips on a secure online viewing system linked to a time code where Jamie and Brad could check in and make comments. Collaborating with Technicolor Digital Intermediates (TDI), Savides equipped the Viper with Zeiss DigiPrime lenses and started tests to 'break' the camera." He needed to see how far he could push an image before it broke apart.

There were drawbacks. With no video signal processing in the Viper, Savides had to compensate for a pronounced green bias inherent in the FilmStream output by using a CC Magenta 30 filter. A digital camera does not handle a backlit situation as well as film. To handle this, he would use muted colors, a consistent level of grain throughout, and work as wide open as possible.

There were advantages. The Viper's Dynamic Pixel Management allowed the camera to change its aspect ratio by vertically ganging pixels. This permitted Savides to shoot at different aspect ratios without cropping the image or using anamorphic lenses. Not only that, but he could use inexpensive software in postproduction, and never lose a negative. With a digital camera, Fincher could work at very low light levels and shoot night exteriors with one-third the light he would normally need. He was creating the look of new films to come.

BRAD WAS VERY BRIEFLY away in Vancouver, but constantly in touch. If there were any difficulties with actors or other creative issues that might come up where he might be helpful, then he would be helpful. Right now, he was thinking about *Zodiac*. The tentative start date for the first day of shooting *Zodiac* was August 15, in the electrically charged atmosphere of Lake Berryessa, a setting that still gave Brad and Jamie the willies.

Fincher, juggling a thousand things, had not ceased his detective work. The Zodiac case had gripped him as no other. He sifted the clues on his long desk so many face cards, mostly the Ace of Spades. What could he learn from them? The Zodiac letters might hold the answer.

He reached for his binder. The plus sign (+) had been an exciting breakthrough and possibly linked the main suspect to the Riverside slaying. With that in mind, he consulted Conway and Bawart about handwriting analysis. He needed to know more.

"A great source of frustration," Conway replied when they touched base. "George and I spent quite a bit of time with the best handwriting analyst in the state—[forensic documents examiner] Lloyd Cunningham. I was totally satisfied with him being the best of the best. What! You guys haven't tracked down Lloyd Cunningham yet?"

"No."

"Like the DA," Conway said, "Cunningham was sensitive about the implications of him saying, 'This is a match.' There was little doubt in my mind that Arthur Leigh Allen did the writing [in the Zodiac letters]. The problem with handwriting, because we got a whole education about that and George and I have a critical eye for handwriting now, is that unless they saw the guy write it himself they won't do the top-of-the-line finding. The writings we knew were Arthur Leigh Allen's taken from his house in the search warrant we took to Lloyd Cunningham. We sat there with him. He had spent days with it before we even met with him."

"And what did he say?" Fincher asked expectantly.

"Well," Conway said, "and this is why I'm telling you that Arthur Leigh Allen was an evil genius, its possible for him to have been an ambidextrous writer because we had evidence of him doing all kinds of things with either his left hand or his right hand." Ralph Spinelli had confirmed that. So had Spinelli's manager, Preston, who had watched him play pool at the Crazy Horse and even played him.

"Sure, I buy that," Fincher said. "Years ago if you were born left-handed the school would pressure you to switch to your right hand." This was usually a sharp slap from a ruler anytime you used your left hand. "That was to force bi-lateralization of function—the right side of your brain controls the left side of your body, the left side of your brain controls the right side of your body. Often, people who are prone to violence and sociopathic behavior have what is called non-bilateralization. The left side controls the left side; the right side controls the right side. It is very common in multiple personalities disorders that you don't have a cross."

"The left hand/right hand thing was the closest we got Cunningham to acknowledge that's the explanation of these little, teenie, minor anomalies he found 'cause he did it with his left hand. I oversimplify what I know about handwriting analysis, but basically their mentality is, 'If I can find one little teeny wriggle that's different, then I discount any possibility of a match.' What's fascinating to me, is a guy inside the DA's office would have a full mouthful of shit and won't say, 'I've got shit in my mouth,' because their whole reputation, their whole being is on the line. They won't do it."

"Handwriting examination ranks just above holography as far as I am concerned," Bawart said. He always spoke his mind and could be as direct as Fincher. In 1991-1992, Bawart had found the DOJ very difficult to deal with on handwriting because this was such an old case. "They were still looking at cases two or three years old they had not been able to find time for. It went all the way down the line. Unless you had something really on the front burner, the DOJ was not the place to go. It could sit there for years. So that's why we took all their stuff to Cunningham who was working for major companies and getting paid big dollars. He just didn't want to come out and say, 'This could be or maybe could be.'"

"But now this guy's future is not on the line," Fincher said. "We are trying to put together a roster of four of five handwriting analysts who had never seen Zodiac stuff before, and we want to put all of it in front of them at the same time. Personally, I look at Riverside [ballpoint pen desktop writing] and I go, 'Take it off.' I look at the 'Red Phantom' letter and I say, 'Take it off.' One of the most ludicrous notions is that that handwriting matches in any way, shape, or form. Anyway it's included in the twenty-six known Zodiac letters. There's a couple of other letters that I go, 'I don't know.'"

"I've got one for you," Bawart said. "There was a suspect about twenty-two or twenty-three years old when the killings were going on. He was a bodybuilder," he said, "steroids and all that kind of stuff can make you go wacky. I went out and interviewed him well after [state handwriting expert] Sherwood Morrill was dead, but he wasn't a weird guy. He didn't try to disguise his hand printing—sort of a chicken scratch. His hand printing is dead on to Zodiac's. It was so good we took it to Cunningham. He said, 'No, it's very close, but it's not him.'

Because it looked so close to us, we took it to somebody else and they also said it wasn't him. But, boy, it sure looked good."

Returning to his desk, Fincher was still thinking about ambidextrous writing. He opened SFPD's report for Wednesday, September 6, 1972, the date Inspector Armstrong had hand-delivered Allen's file to Dr. David Cook at Sonoma State Hospital. "Would Allen revert to the use of his right hand under emotional stress?" Armstrong asked. He listened carefully and as carefully jotted down Cook's answer:

> 1. Suspect in his psychotic state or when upset, reverts to childlike ego state. This is confirmed by all family and close friends. 2. Zodiac writes his letters to *Chronicle* when he is in similar state (other self) according to evaluation by MDs and psychologists. 3. Suspect is left-handed. Writes normally with left hand, but is ambidextrous. When he was a child he was made to write with his right hand." Armstrong asked himself, "If this subject is in child ego state which hand would he write with ??—Right hand. But would the writing be different than left hand normal state of writing—???

Two days later, Armstrong rang questioned documents examiner Terry Pascoe at CI&I in Sacramento. Surprisingly, the expert disagreed with the findings of his boss, Sherwood Morrill. "Writing can be a product of mental state," Pascoe explained. "The known writing of this suspect can be different when in a different mental state [especially] with the talents of our suspect Allen who writes with both hands, has a high IQ, and has made a study of handwriting." "When I was in elementary school," the suspect once explained to Toschi and Armstrong, "the policy was to make left-handed children write with their right hands. I conformed, but later reverted to my left hand. When I boxed I could not use my right hand with any success. In high school there were no right-handed baseball gloves. I had to use a left-handed glove on my left hand to catch the ball, then take the glove off so I could throw the ball with my left hand."

Next, Fincher asked Toschi about ambidexterity. "Inspector," he said. "My understanding is that people can be equally adept as an archer or shoot a basketball with both hands, but that writing has a specific character that has something to do with actual motor coordination. There is a different slant to handwriting even if you are ambidextrous." Fincher knew it has something to do with how the brain is connected to different sides of the body and even though someone may not be as adept in terms of prime motor coordination there is still a personality for each. "Is it your understanding of Leigh Allen that he's equally proficient at firing a gun?"

Toschi said, "Yes."

"So, Inspector, tell me about the feeling you had at the Refinery questioning. Could you at that moment have asked him for a handwriting sample? You didn't do that. Because he could say, 'No, fuck you.' Once you have a warrant you can say, 'You need to provide us with a sample.'"

"'You *will* give us a sample,'" Toschi said. "We were trying to build a case slowly. As frustrating as it may be, you can't be overzealous." That was a sore point to Fincher who stated that, "You never see in a film the excruciatingly long time it takes to lay the groundwork for a case. You only see them kicking down the door."

A week or two earlier, Toschi had bumped into Lloyd Cunningham at a dinner at Original Joe's for thirty-two retired SFPD homicide detectives. He considered Cunningham a first class guy and good friend. "He has a private practice and has been dealing very, very closely with the federal government on Questioned Documents," Toschi said. "He was in vice for many years, got tired of it and wanted to get into fraud. He told me, 'I would like to have some kind of experience to start a career when I retire and what better than questioned documents.'" Cunningham had gotten into the field through perseverance. The SFPD had no one who could help him so Cunningham contacted John Shimoda, a US Postal Inspector in San Bruno, and said, "Teach me." For the longest time, Shimoda brushed him off, saying, "I don't want to deal with San Francisco." Finally, Cunningham told him, "I'm really serious. You're the best and I can come over there any time you want." So Shimoda took him under his wing and spent hours teaching him. That is how Cunningham got very good at it. It impressed Toschi that Cunningham was looking at one particular Zodiac letter and except for one little comma thought he might have a match. At the dinner, Cunningham took Toschi aside and said, "Hey, Dave, of all the guys I want to tell this to, it's you with all the years you worked on the Zodiac case. We are close to getting the Zodiac,' he whispered. "We think we are going to be able to find out who he is and where he is. The Feds are working on it very, very quietly and I just wanted you to know."

"Are you talking about a sure thing, Lloyd?" Toschi asked.

"No.

"I'll be very surprised if they get a hit."

Fincher thanked Toschi for the background information and went back to work. As he studied Allen's handprinted home recipe cards, he thought he saw a similarity to the Zodiac letters. "It's kind of astounding," he said. The director had a keen eye for spatial differences and similarities, the relationship of one object to one another, traits inherent in a great film director as well as in a first class handwriting expert like Lloyd Cunningham.

At the Vanderbilt home, Jamie was thinking about Zodiac hand printing too. "Conway is saying at the 1993 Zodiac conference, the one thing about Zodiac handwriting in the letters is that it doesn't change from beginning to end at all," Jamie said. "And I thought, 'Whoa! That's not true.' So we really want to get someone who's never looked at the stuff before just to get his take on it." On Friday afternoon, Jamie and Lou Phillips met with a handwriting expert. "You should talk to Lloyd Cunningham," the expert told them. "He knows all about the case." It was a familiar refrain.

"That's the opposite of who we want," Phillips explained. "We are looking for fresh eyes."

"Well, I can't help you. You should call Lloyd Cunningham." Then the expert completely changed his tune, and went from very enthusiastic to passing on them. Jamie did not understand what had gotten into him. "Maybe he's afraid to go on the record," he said. The SFPD was now equally cold to them. Everyone told Brad to call Cunningham. Finally, he did. Cunningham referred them to a top man in the field, Gerald McMenamin, an internationally known Forensics-Linguistic expert, professor of linguistics at California State University, and author of *Forensic Linguistics.*

The night before their trip up to see McMenamin, Brad rang Jamie at 8:00 PM. "I just want to be sure you're coming with us," he said.

"I'm really sorry, but I can't go," Jamie said. Among his other projects, he was preparing for his wedding.

"I can't believe this. It's really important. We're going to have all this time on the trip with David to go through the script. I can't believe you can't come."

"Well, I can't because I have to do this and that and I'm really sorry."

"I can't believe you wouldn't do this for the project!"

"How dare you accuse me of not giving everything to the project!"

They began yelling at each other. Brad stopped abruptly and got up.

"Hold on a second," he said. "I'm going to go close the door to my office."

His assistant, John, huddled in the other room, and covered his ears as the boys enjoyed a fine twenty minutes of shouting at each other. By the end, they were laughing at each other. "I was yelling at the top of my lungs," Jamie recalled afterward. "Brad was too. It was a real fight. Like an old married couple we just had to yell at each other for a while."

Now, they had blown off steam, gotten it out of their system, and cleared the air.

The next morning, Brad and David made the trip to their hired expert alone. "David Fincher wanted me to do the work I would do for court," McMenamin wrote of the meeting. "I didn't pay much attention to the codes because that is an artificial language. It is in the natural language that the unconscious mind is at work [that I am interested in]." McMenamin scanned the handwriting samples, beginning with a copy of the right-handed printing that Toschi had Allen write in his trailer in September 1972. It was the only known right-handed writing from the prime suspect who, while naturally left-handed, was known to have some ability with his right hand. McMenamin began by saying, "Guys, I just don't see it." They talked a bit more and he said, "Is there any other writing that you have?"

"Well, I have these videotapes that the police seized from his house," Brad said, "There's writing on those. And I have these folded pieces of paper Allen tucked inside the cardboard sleeves as video indexes in pencil and ink." Brad got them out and handed them to McMenamin who unfolded them and spread them out on his examination desk. He pondered one sample, then a few more.

"I gotta be honest," he said, looking up at them. "You could make a credible case for it being him."

The expert had not only studied the patterns of the printing, but focused on the content and grammatical patterns of the writer, how he formed his sentences, word structure, and spelling. "As a forensic linguist," McMenamin said, 'the two things you look for are disguise and how the writer would break down the words. The exhibits I made an examination on related to the issue of disguise. Did the Zodiac attempt to disguise his writing? Yes, Allen was ambidextrous and his weak hand was his right hand. His strong hand was his left hand, which he normally used for writing and other tasks. What I noticed in the Zodiac's writing was the division of his words into syllables and morphemes [the smallest meaningful unit in the grammar of language] which carry a semantic interpretation." That's where you see the pattern and that's what I look at—how he divides his words.

The expert bent to his work again. It was silent in the room as minutes passed. "This is interesting," he said, raising his head from the samples. He had found some commonalities between Allen's writing and the Zodiac's, but in a way that nobody had seen before. It was as amazing a discovery as the Berryessa map Jamie had found and the North Beach parking ticket Brad had made significant.

"It has to do with the way that people split words on individual lines where you hyphenate," McMenamin said. He took up his pencil and showed them what he meant on a piece of paper. "As a rule, you split the word on the vowel that ends the first part or by syllable. Zodiac letters are broken oddly [killing as kill-ing]. There are two aspects to his breaking the word, in some he ran out of room and he would split the word inappropriately . . . There is one example of Allen's right hand. I found five lines and three divisions in that writing that were comparable to the Zodiac. My personal conclusion? *It is the same word separations or word segmentation in those five lines.*"

The room was absolutely still.

Now that they could see it, it was completely obvious. When Zodiac printed out individual words, he separated parts of the words. The first part of the word was set apart a little bit from the second part in a certain place. So if you're writing out a word such as "television" it's not split from one line to the next, but on a single line. But Zodiac separated the last three letters of the word off a little bit, something also common in Allen's natural hand printing.

McMenamin believed that Brad's theory of the plus (+) sign for the word *and* was significant. "There are two aspects to it," he said. "One is in terms of its significance whether there is a certain rule that is followed depending on when he uses the word *and,* and when he uses a plus (+) sign."

"He almost always uses a plus (+) sign," Brad said, "and hardly ever uses *and*."

"The other thing you can do is just statistically take five thousand to ten thousand examples of an individual's handwriting and see what their ampersands are and how often a plus (+) sign comes up as opposed to the word *and*." Zodiac's use of "shall" and "will" were very significant aspects of his letters too. The "shall/will" structure is used to give information about predictions of future events and to express conditional ideas such as threats, promises, and requests. It is common in military-style orders: "The regiment *will* attack at dawn." Zodiac used predictions as a way of giving orders. The use of *will* is a matter of intent. *Shall* is as if ordained. With *will* you are absolutely going to do it. '*Will you,*' is used with firm instructions or orders, but not requests. To be certain, McMenamin consulted a professor of history of language who said Zodiac uses shall/will correctly, which was even more remarkable. In the US, its common usage had all but disappeared by the 1930s.

"Even in the sixties [when the letters were written] it wasn't common at all." Brad said. "It would have been common as something that was taught in Catholic school." Fincher told the expert about Allen's interrogation tape. McMenamin said his colleague would be interested in listening to Allen's recorded voice. "The professor can listen to anyone speak and tell within miles exactly where they were from or where they had grown up."

"And Brad will do a report for us," Jamie added later. "Once again, Brad Fischer, beloved by all, has charmed his way into this man's heart." When Brad returned to Jamie's house, he studied Allen's 'To Whom' final letter found in the suspect's computer after his death:

> This will disappoint the thugs and bullies in the higher echelons of the police Department (who must have spent an astronomical amount of taxpayers money in their efforts to fabricate a case against me). Their efforts were doomed from the start. If that sounds presumptuous it is based on hard facts. I have never killed anyone and

I don't intend to, though there are some policemen who I wouldn't be too sad about if I saw their names in the obituary column and even those thugs would probably be missed by someone, however unpleasant they may be.

"Sounds like have a little list, 'Those who would never be missed.'" Brad said, referencing Zodiac's July 26, 1970, letter to the *Chronicle.* He read on:

Let me say I have known a few good police officers. They were officers and gentlemen. Sadly, they are a minority at least in Vallejo. I guess it helps to be a jerk in this city if you wear blue. The police are wrong and all their lies can not change that. There are two groups of people in the world who are consummate liars, fishermen and police and not necessarily in that order. At least the fishermen's lies are harmless. I certainly can't say that for the Vallejo police. I wish the world all the best, all the world except, of course, the Vallejo police. I wish them all the worst. They richly deserve it. Arthur L. Allen.

What to make of the prime suspect's final words? So much anger and bitterness. He had not used contractions, just as Zodiac did not: "all their lies *can not* change that." Brad dispatched the full letter and Rolodex cards to McMenamin to see what he thought of the similarities, word separations, and cadence. Over the next few days, Brad pressed the expert for an answer. "Hi, Jerry," he wrote, "just confirming that you received the photocopies of Allen's Rolodex cards. Anything substantive or significant in that?"

"What appears frequently is the same kind of word divisions I noticed frequently in the Zodiac writings," McMenamin replied, "separations at morpheme boundaries and separations at seeming-syllable boundaries, a common aspect of the Zodiac writings. Maybe I should make a list of the clear cases in Zodiac and the clear cases in known-Allen."

"What about showing some of this material to forensics expert Terry Pascoe?" Brad suggested.

"Sure," McMenamin said, "I can write a short summary of comments, findings with evidence and you or I can send it to him." McMenamin's all-over feeling was that Allen cannot be ruled out—and he was applying the same stringent rules he would apply if he were taking a case to court. He could not rule the suspect out or in based on what he had seen. McMenamin believed that whoever is the writer of the Zodiac letters he was using intentional deception to mask his true handwriting and intentionally misspelling words. *"I do think Allen wrote the Zodiac letters, but it is one thing to think that and another to prove it in court,"* he stated.

"The answer has to be very clear. I have to satisfy my peers to make the evidence scientific and to do that I have to establish a pattern." To accomplish this he needed more samples of Allen's handwriting. Brad went about gathering them. The Hollywood detectives were back on the hunt and doing everything a pack of bloodhounds would do except bay at the moon. At home, Jamie discovered this eye of the hurricane to be an interesting interval. For the first time in nine months, he had a few hours of downtime to swim and kick back. *Zodiac* was now in the hands of the angels. "We're going to go through another round of cutting the script down," he said. "We're going to need some judicious visuals since the story spans thirty years. I've got to be honest, I'm feeling very optimistic."

At noon on Friday, April 8, Brad saw the exact budget which had had to be compiled under impossible time constraints and by many hands. "Ceán had to deliver a budget of $75 million," he said, "The budget came in at $74,999,888. We're looking in pretty good shape here. Warners is going to start cash flowing to us on Monday which means that we are effectively in preproduction then."

Friday evening, Brad got a "fairly astonishing fax" from Bawart in Vallejo in response to a request for more of Allen's writing. The cover page said, "This is a list of what I'm sending you—a copy of an invoice, letter from Arthur Leigh Allen . . ." Then, Brad came to something unexpected.

"I've never, ever seen this before," Brad exclaimed and got Jamie on the line. "Jamie!" I got this fax from Bawart. It's unbelievable what's in here."

"What? What is it?"

Just then, Fincher called on his other line. "Jamie," Brad said. "I'll call you back." When he called back, Brad said. "Did you know Bawart interviewed Officer Fouke in 1991? Did you know that Bawart put a picture of Arthur Leigh Allen in front of him?" Brad intended to slowly draw out the suspense without telling him where he was going.

"What's coming, Brad?" Jamie asked impatiently. He drummed his fingers.

"No, no, no," Brad said. "Don't ruin the ending."

"Vallejo Police Department 9-18-91 1330 Hrs.," he read aloud. "Donald Fouke arrived at the Vallejo Police Department. Fouke had already been informed that we were investigating the old Zodiac case. I asked Fouke to describe what had occurred on October 11, 1969, that later turned out to be relevant to this case: Fouke told Bawart that when he got the radio call about a shooting at Cherry and Washington Streets he was already about eight to ten blocks north of the location and began driving south towards Washington looking for a black male [a mistake in communications] heading his direction. Fouke told Bawart it was dark, but illuminated by street lights. He observed a rather large individual wearing a dark blue windbreaker-type jacket, baggy pleated pants, and engineer boots walking towards him on Jackson Street.

"Fouke described the white male as over six feet, approximately 230 to 240 pounds, about thirty-five to forty-five years old with a crewcut with a receding hairline. He wore horn-rimmed glasses and his face was oval or round. Fouke continued on past and two blocks later the police radio put up an updated description. Fouke immediately realized that he had observed the responsible. He didn't make a U-turn, but went around the block to intercept him, but when he got there no one was on the street. Bawart advised Fouke that this was in conflict with what he initially felt happened, that possibly he and Zelms had spoken to this individual. Fouke told him no. Fouke indicated at his residence in North Bend, Oregon, he is able to get KTVU-Channel 2 out of Oakland and that he did view an interview with a suspect located in Vallejo wherein the suspect indicated [to Rita Williams] that he was being harassed by the police. Fouke indicated that the person's face was blacked and he could not tell what the individual looked like.

"Bawart told Fouke he had some photographs to show him and advised him that the responsible from October 11, 1969, that he observed may or may not be amongst these photographs and merely because he was showing him photographs he did not have to identify anyone. Fouke knew this because he had given similar lineup admonishments himself. Bawart then showed Fouke a previously prepared, stapled together photographic lineup of six photos, primarily Soundex driver's license pictures. Fouke viewed this lineup for approximately fifteen-seconds. He then pointed to the photograph of Arthur Leigh Allen indicating that this was the same type of face as the individual he had seen on October 11, 1969 walking from the direction of the crime scene. He indicated that it was difficult to tell if this person had a crewcut from the person he was looking at today, that his hair went back in a similar manner which he described like a widow's peak. He then pointed to the photograph [a filler picture] just to the right of Arthur Leigh Allen's photograph and indicated that this individual had the same type of round face, however the jowls were too large . . .

"Fouke was asked if he was identifying this photo also. He indicated he was not. He was merely pointing out that the same round features existed in their faces. Fouke was asked how positive his identification of the photograph of Arthur Leigh Allen was. He indicated that he could not positively say that this was the same person he had observed on October 11, 1969, but the facial features were very similar.

"Fouke was then shown an 8 x 10 photograph [recovered during a VPD search] which depicted Allen sitting on a sailboat. In this photograph Allen is wearing a wet suit. Fouke . . . indicated build of the individual on the sailboat was the same as the build of the person he had observed on October 11, 1969. This picture showed more of a profile of Arthur Leigh Allen and Fouke indicated that the hair was the same type as the individual as the person he had observed on October 11, 1969. He could not positively make an identification, but indicated that this person strongly resembled the person he had seen on October 11, 1969. Fouke told Bawart that after observing the individual on October 11, 1969, he later wrote a scratch [a memo] to Toschi and Armstrong and that he did not participate in any composite of the suspect. Fouke told Bawart the composite drawing made by the SFPD, although similar to the person he observed, "looked younger and the face was not round enough."

"That big round face of Allen's is the first thing everyone comments on," Brad told Jamie who was listening to every word. "This document resolves to a great degree this problem of the misleading composite at Washington and Cherry. Fouke pointed to Arthur Leigh Allen."

"I think this a huge piece of evidence!" Jamie said.

"So do I," Brad said.

The past was reliving itself. Bawart had shown Mike Mageau an identical photo lineup which he looked at for 20 to 30 seconds before pointing to Leigh Allen's picture. "That's the man!" Mageau had said. "That's the man who shot me at Blue Rock Springs."

Preproduction started on Saturday, April 9, but the absolute final, final word, the official green light, might not come for two weeks. Brad thought they were "pretty much there . . . looking very good." By April 18, they had to have hired everybody. They would hire a bunch on Monday, though there would be actors with one line that hadn't yet been cast.

"We have a nice race against time at the end," Jamie said. "I'm very superstitious. I don't want to shave my *Zodiac* goatee until we are greenlit, but I have to shave it for the wedding. By then, I have to be clean-shaven and somewhat short-haired—or else." Right now it was going to take five months to shoot the movie. A movie is so like a mobile army that people talk about it in military terms—the director's the general with different lieutenants in charge of different departments.

"We're finally winning some battles," Jamie said on Monday as money began to flow. "When a movie studio decides to commit a couple hundred thousand dollars to something, it usually is an indication that they intend on committing more." Cash flow for two weeks of preproduction was about $400,000. Right now, they were spending over a quarter of a million dollars to cash-flow them for four weeks. "Warner Brothers and Paramount collectively okaying a 198 page script may go on record as the longest script ever greenlit in Hollywood." During rewrites Brad had been all over Jamie. "Now the worm has turned," Jamie gloated. Brad missed having the upper hand. "Now I'm calling Jamie," Brad said, "and saying, 'What's going on? What's going on?'" Hollywood had been trying to make *Zodiac* into a movie since it was published. "It's taken them almost twenty years," Jamie said, "but there was lots of big, good news today." At this moment, actors' agents were negotiating every detail which Jamie found "an interesting, ridiculous exercise" to go through, but little things like billing matter greatly, not as much to the actors as to their people. Working out billing on a teaser poster was tricky: Gyllenhaal's name on the left, a little lower than Ruffalo's, and Downey's name below both of them.

At 3:00 PM, the next day, Fincher and Gyllenhaal met at the Chateau Marmont. They were almost through with the deal. Jake's agent had called that morning saying they had gone over the entire agreement with Jake and that he was in. As for money, it was roughly the same amount Brad had offered. Now, the news was coming fast. "We just closed the three leads," Brad said. "We're going to do a reading of the script. We'll get a conference room and we'll have the actors there, Jake, Mark, Robert Downey, Jr., and other actors playing multiple parts, and see what we'll learn from the script reading. When a script is read you notice things you don't when you're reading it yourself quietly. The read-through is just for us, not Warner's."

At noon on Tuesday, April 19, Brad was on his way to have lunch with Ceán, who was producing along with Fincher, Jamie, and Phoenix principals, Medavoy, Messer, and Brad. "We continue to be headed in the right direction," Brad said. And on the legal front? "I'm waiting to hear officially. I got walked through with Lynn Harris. The Warner Legal Department's standpoint is to have as many release forms as they get from anyone and everyone. They'd be happy if they could get release forms from people who came to see the movie." The only outstanding issue, as far as he could see barring any sudden surprises, that remained was the two hour and forty-five minute running time.

"It's not a question of can the movie be 2/45, it's what happens if they watch the movie and it seems like it's running slow and whether Warner Brothers will have a right to release a shorter version or whether David will have the final say. Of course, David has final cut at 2/45 [2 hours and 45 minutes long] or at 2/25 [2 hours and 25 minutes long]. The question is, which version?" Fincher would take into consideration the way the film plays and insist on having the ultimate decision of which version gets released. A meeting to discuss the running time was set between Fincher, Robinov, and Harris. Once they were over that hurdle, the conditions of the green light, from a legal standpoint, were only that they deliver a budget vetted at seventy-five million dollars or less. "So they have to look at that," Brad explained, "and vet it. They have to say, 'Yes, in our opinion this is a good budget. It can be done for that price.' That shouldn't be a problem. We're still working on the Hartnell meeting. It got canceled again. This week has been crazy, crazy, crazy!"

There was still no sign of Mike Mageau. The movie might have to be done without finding him and getting his input, but Fincher would not like it. Mageau was part of his search for his truth. Arneson continued hunting for him, but time was running out. Fincher's big meeting with Robinov and Harris was set for 1:00 PM. Brad got to Warner Brothers at 1:30 PM, and he and Jamie waited outside Warner Brothers executive Greg Silverman's office while Fincher spoke inside.

"We are biting our fingernails," Brad said, "and hoping we still have a movie when the meeting is over."

"I am just a deer in headlights, hoping that nothing horrible is going to come down," Jamie said.

Inside Silverman's office, Fincher was stressing the importance of having *Zodiac* run 2/45. "There are confidences among people who have given us their life rights whom we have told, 'We are telling the real story, we're not going to water it down, we're not going to be reductive—we want people to appreciate the frustrations of every blind alley, the emotional consequences of not having closure.' It's important to them and important to us and it's not a responsibility that we're taking lightly." We tried to make the movie as short as we could, but assured people that they would not be turned into plot devices. Whenever possible, we tried to make good on these promises."

"The closer it gets to being real," Jamie said nervously as he waited, "the more careful we are about assuming it's going to be real. If I start getting used to the idea that this will work out, it won't work out."

Fincher smiled as he came out and said the studio told him, "Make it as long as you want!"

Brad and Jamie let out a whoop. The 2 hour and 45 minute length had been approved! Everybody filed into the conference room, sat down, went through their notes on the film, and saw that what was left to be settled was fairly minor stuff. Brad and Jamie ordered chopped salads for lunch, Rubinov had a Subway sandwich, and Fincher had a sandwich he found unpalatable. They ate and did not eat and discussed the script and did not discuss the script until 3:30 PM. Brad felt great when he left. "It is such a pleasurable experience when you know this is the right director for the movie and a studio that understands what you're trying to achieve." The meeting had gone so well, so speedily, that as they were leaving, Fincher turned, grinned and said to the execs,

"That's it? We had to come all the way down here for this?" He was pleased they had agreed to spend another four weeks of money—a total of $800,000 so far, all working toward beginning to shoot on August 8 or a couple of days earlier. As the schedule stood, there were five or six weeks in San Francisco and the remainder in Los Angeles. But under that timetable they would have to give the crew the long Labor Day weekend, then go back up to San Francisco. Ceán had a great idea. She suggested they start earlier so they could wrap in San Francisco by Labor Day, give everybody the Labor Day weekend off, then start again in Los Angeles.

"Ceán is fantastic at her job," Brad said, as he recalled how she had been compelled to put the budget together "like lightning" under extreme pressure. At 4:30 PM, he attended a meeting with Fincher and the production designer who had ID pictures of everyone they needed, all except Carol Fischer, the secretary who had opened many of the Zodiac letters. Her part was not yet cast. Immediately after the conference, Brad returned to Phoenix Pictures and looked in on Mike Medavoy.

"The two hour and forty-five minute length is approved," Brad said.

"Really?"

"You're shocked, aren't you?"

"Yeah."

On Friday, Jamie was so confident that the movie would be greenlit that he prepared to shave off the *Zodiac* rally. It was a giddy moment. He clipped it with scissors until it was very sparse, reached for his Mach 3 razor, and lathered up with the best bargain shaving foam they made. He deleted the goatee with a few quick, confident strokes, wiped his face with a towel and realized that he would not be able to attend the cast read-through. That would be impossible. It was the same day as his wedding. Fincher, who allegedly didn't have a sentimental bone in his body, couldn't understand this.

"Why can't he come anyway?" he asked.

Meanwhile, they had buttoned Ruffalo up for the Toschi part, but there was a scheduling clash with Downey who was set to top-line in Warner's *Kiss Kiss Bang Bang*, *The Shaggy Dog*, and *Fur* with Nicole Kidman. Downey had no conflict for production, only rehearsal.

Fincher, who wanted three weeks of rehearsal, was "very big" on having the actors rehearse, spend a week or three going through the script, do the scenes repeatedly, and talk about the characters. Jamie and Brad were confident they could work out Downey's scheduling problem. "We're going to go balls to the walls on this one." Downey said of *Zodiac*. There was a wedding in his life too. On August 27, he was to wed producer Susan Levin, "a tough cookie" who helped him "toe the line" and make a tremendous change in his life for the better.

At noon, Jamie was preparing for his own wedding when Laray called and said, "We had this guy do the cast breakdown [of all the characters in the movie to be mailed out to agents]." There are companies that break down a script into the different parts, describe each part, how it fits into the movie and how many scenes and lines for every single speaking part, then mail the breakdown to agencies and agents. "It's all flowery," Laray told Jamie, "and there are no specifics in there. Is there any way you can put in some more specific information?" Busy as he was, Jamie spent a couple of hours punching up the breakdown. He outlined Sherwood Morrill who had been described in the book as "a scholarly man in a three-piece pinstripe suit in thick glasses." Jamie's version:

> "Sherwood Morrill: 50s, Caucasian. Heavyset. Balding with an intense face. A meticulous, temperamental man; he is the unquestioned expert in his field. Sherwood works closely with the police throughout the Zodiac investigation, and later helps Graysmith with his search."

That afternoon, Brad conferred with David, Ceán, Production Designer Don Burt, and Warners Location Manager Rick Schuler. Candace (Ceán's assistant), and Fincher's daughter, and her friends arrived. Before dinner everyone played a little football in the parking lot at the rear of Fincher's office.

"David's kind of had a bad back which he treats with acupuncture," Brad said, "so we're tossing the football around and I threw it to him a little short and as it landed he tried to stop it with his foot and twisted his ankle."

"The last time this happened," Fincher said, rising painfully, "I was in physical therapy for a month."

"That's exactly what I need to hear, David, that's I've injured my director." They went to dinner, but David hobbled into the restaurant. Brad suspected he was pulling his leg.

"Are you O.K.?" he asked again.

"I dunno," Fincher said. "It's a little swollen. If nothing else it's quite an insurance claim."

On April 21, Brad and Graysmith had their legal grilling via conference call. "I don't think it is the more public aspect of the case the lawyers are nervous about," he said, "it's more some of the private stuff. We're not looking to make anybody feel horrible. I wish making this movie wasn't going to make the brother and sister-in-law's lives harder. It is. And it will make Bryan Hartnell's life harder." The meeting dealt with only ten topics, none earthshaking. A week later, Don Burt and Rick Schuler flew up to San Francisco to check out suitable locations. First, they visited Graysmith's old apartment on 3rd Avenue to recreate it as a sound stage set, but were unable to see the Toschi residence. Mrs. Toschi preferred they didn't. Respectful of her wishes, Burt and Schuler refused to even drive by the Toschi house. Brad phoned about the problem and caught her washing dishes. After a good conversation, their first in depth, she was still opposed to strangers in her home and he too was respectful of that. Toschi solved the problem. His mother's album contained rare family photos of birthday and Christmas parties that showed the cozy home as it had been in 1969. He sent that to Burt. To double for the opening scene at Blue Rock Springs, they chose Bouquet Canyon Road in Angeles National Forest in Saugus. The revised Time of Day Breakdown would read:

> Int. Corvair—night, 9:00 PM July 4, 1969. Ext. Mr. Ed's—night, 9:15 PM Ext. Blue Rock Springs--Parking Lot—Night, 9:45 PM INT. Darlene's car—night, 9:45 PM. Omitted scene 5 is replaced by 5A, Ext. Blue Rock Springs—night 10:00 PM [The new Continuity Breakdown now read:] Int. Corvair—Darlene Ferrin picks up Mike Mageau. (Mike wore more than 1 shirt). Ext. Mr. Ed's—Darlene and Mike pull in, decide to go to Blue Rock. Ext. Blue Rock Springs--Corvair pulls into lot of local golf course. Int. Darlene's Car—A cop approaches passenger door, fires at M. then D., walks away. He returns & fires twice more. 5A/ Ext/ Blue Rock Springs. POV of cop's headlight finds a bloody Mike and Darlene. VO reports murders into phone.

On Friday, April 29, Brad was at Marcus Nispel's house discussing his film *Pathfinder* when the Warner Brothers and Paramount production departments reached him about *Zodiac*. Their reply: a seven page memo that should have had a black border around it. Their notes were "extremely productive, extremely enlightening," but of deep concern. Earth shattering was more like it. One of the conditions that had to be met to be greenlit was the vetting of the budget. The Warners and Paramount production departments had three weeks to review and vet it. Brad turned to the entry and felt the room revolve under his feet. He steadied himself. In essence it was devastating news.

"The budget was extremely well prepared," Warner's physical production person Kelly Smith-Wait, noted, "however we believe it could be off by as much as *two and one half million dollars.*"

The memo said a lot about how Ceán had done a fantastic job, but claimed there was some stuff that was missed. Brad doubted this. "Preparing budgets is what Ceán does," he said, "and she's extremely good at it.

"But at first, we got really worried that we had submitted a budget under what they said we need. Listen," Brad said, "this is the head of physical production. This is all these people do. Both Warners and Paramount had to get together and vet it. And they all met in the same room. Ceán and Lou Phillips were there. They said, 'You guys are off. You guys are wrong. You guys are off about two and a half-million.'"

Brad wasn't having any of this. He got on the phone.

"You guys are off about two and half million," Warner's repeated.

"Oh, really, Brad said. "Where?"

"People shouted," Jamie reported. "We got really upset. We were understandably freaked out at this late stage when they are already spending money on the movie. I don't think they will pull the plug, but two and one half million dollars!" Fincher's deal called for him to pay one hundred percent of any money over budget. Jamie was really scared Fincher was going to say, "Screw 'em! I told them the movie I want to make. I'm not going to give them two and one half million dollars." As Fincher had warned, he was not in the habit of financing movies. Of all the problems they had faced, this was the most insurmountable. Surely, this meant the end of their movie.

CHAPTER TWENTY THREE

THE SPLENDIFEROUS WEDDING

THEN, BRAD HAD A second thought. "But what if we're right," he said. "What if they're just being dicks?" Brad looked at the budget again. It did *not* look like it was off. "Ceán," he explained, "did a phenomenal job under tremendous pressure and it came in at under seventy-five million. Both David and Ceán looked over the budget and said, 'No, we feel that this is solid and we can do the movie at this price.' We all felt that the budget prepared was rock solid and basically told Warner Brothers that we stand behind it." Warners still insisted it was off. "I think Warners felt it was low in locations and in some areas," Brad explained. We said, 'Well, we disagree.' It was them saying, 'You're over,' and us saying, 'No, we're not,' them saying, 'Yes, you are.'"

On Monday, May 2, Ceán, Phillips, and the accountant got together to decide whether or not to just green light the movie at seventy-five million and deal with the other issues as they progressed and got more information. Brad called Jamie that afternoon, and purposely left a very dour message: "I have an update. Call me."

An update, Jamie thought. More bad news. What else could go wrong? He called back.

"What's going on?" he said slowly, measuring his words. He was in no mood to hear additional bad news.

"Well, what do you think Warners and Paramount said about the budget?" Brad said.

"They probably said, 'Well, it's your problem and it's gotta come out of the script and we got to scramble and take two and one half-million out or we don't have a movie."

A beat.

"They gave it to us!" Brad shouted. "Warner Brothers said, 'Well, we still disagree, however we're going to give this the extra two and a half.'"

"Holy shit!"

"Ultimately, I think everyone was concerned enough about it that both Paramount and Warners came back to us very quickly and said, 'You know what? We're going to give you the other two and one-half million dollars.'"

"That never happens!" Jamie said, walking in circles about the sunny kitchen and grinning broadly.

"It really is to Warner's and Paramount's credit that they did this because they didn't have to do it. They could have been dicks. They could have said, 'We had an agreement at seventy-five million. You guys are on the hook for overages, so whatever else it is it's your problem not ours.' They acted like true partners! It is extremely rare. I gotta give props to Dan Fury [the Warners business affairs executive in charge of negotiating the deal for the movie]. Dan Fury has been fantastic."

The best part was this. In the end, the movie came in *under* budget at two and a half million dollars." Ceán had been right on the money! Brad and Jamie had expected nothing less. She wasn't just one the best, she was the best.

"A piece of paper still needs to be drafted and sent to Warner Brothers business affairs," Jamie said. "But they said the word. They said it! The other thing that strikes me is that they really want to make this movie. They really want to do this."

"Once that piece of paper gets sent," Brad said breathlessly, "we have all our actors in place, and an agreed upon length of the movie. David Fincher now needs to sign a piece of paper that says he is available to make this his next movie, which he will—then we are formally greenlit ten days from receipt of that rights agreement at Warner Brothers. As soon as *Zodiac* is officially greenlit they are making the movie and everyone is pay or play."

"And that, as they say, is that," Jamie said.

"A sorta-kinda congratulations," Brad said. He always stopped short of saying something was going to happen until it was definitely happening. But, gosh, he thought, it's certainly more likely happening than not happening. When it started off at seventy-five million and two hours and twenty-five minutes we now have seventy-seven and one-half-million and two hours and forty-five minutes. They had come remarkably close to the eighty-million dollars Fincher had insisted on a year earlier. As Jamie and Brad had said at the beginning, "Fincher knows what shit costs."

Right after his staff meeting, Brad called one of the Stine witnesses again and left a message. He had just gotten off the phone with Pam Kersh, one of the vetting lawyers, when the witness called back and agreed to meet with them that night in San Francisco at 8:30. "We got him on our own," Brad told Fincher. At 3:30 PM, Brad, Fincher, Burt, and Schuler hopped on a plane and checked into the Hotel Adagio across from the Clift and just around the corner from the meeting place. Brad did not bring any police documents or a recorder to the meeting. He wanted to keep it casual. Fincher was only interested in sitting down with the witness, telling him what they were doing, and what they wanted from him. They went down to the hotel lobby to meet the witness who was a half hour late because he thought they were going to meet at a bar instead.

"Nobody in that neighborhood," he explained, "as far as I know, still lives there from that period." This was disheartening. Fincher needed to recreate the scene as accurately as possible, and for that, needed the help of people who had lived there. "You and your brother and sister are the only people that can help me do that," he said. "I want to get a computer simulation, an accurate rendering of what happened and show it to you and have you tell us where it's off, what's right, and what's wrong. I need something I can show the actors to say this is what you're going to do. This is where you're going to go. This is everything that happened as realistically as possible. What different things drew you to the window? A flash? A struggle? Or did you just randomly go up there? I need to clarify all of these things. I want to put you on tape because I want the DVD to have interviews with everyone. I want to get into that house, put a camera in there, and shoot it from the perspective that you saw."

Fincher explained the scene: three kids making noise. Their names will not be referenced.

"My sister is a really nice girl and if you called her she might talk to you," the witness said, "and she might not. If you call my brother, he's gonna be a heck of a lot less polite than I will and you'll be lucky if all you hear is the click of the phone hanging up. As far as my mother is concerned, she's a grown woman over twenty-one, she can decide for herself. But if you ask me, the odds of you guys getting into that house are about zero."

Another setback, but they took it in stride. They understood. It had been a horrible, and lingering experience for the Cherry and Washington Streets neighborhood.

Meanwhile, Jamie's parents, Alison and Alfred, "Al and Al," were flying from New York to LA. As they sat in First Class, Jamie's mom looked around. "That guy looks really familiar," she said. "Yeah, he does," Alfred agreed. "He's an actor. He's the guy who looks like Toby Maguire, but isn't Toby Maguire."

"I think that's Jake Gyllenhaal," Alison said.

"I think you're right," Alfred said.

Mrs. Vanderbilt got up, went over and said, "I'm sorry to bother you, are you Mr. Jake G.?" She used an initial because she was worried she'd mess up his last name. Jake started laughing and said, "Yeah, but I never heard 'Jake G.' before."

"Very sorry to bother you," she said, "but I heard you're doing *Zodiac* and I just wanted to say hello because my son wrote the screenplay."

"Oh, that's amazing. That's such a great script! Do you know how good a writer your son is?"

"Yes, of course I do."

By 11:00 PM, Brad had returned to LA and was headed to a meeting with director Greg Hoblet on a television series. The next day entailed more *Zodiac* work, including fine-tuning two key pieces of casting. On Thursday, May 5, Fincher and Laray decided that Anthony Edwards, tall, slender, blond, and pale would be superb as Inspector William Armstrong, the intelligent, responsible investigator. Personable and well briefed, Edwards was also tall, dignified, serious, slender and pale. Edwards and Fincher lived in the same neighborhood (Edwards is a Santa Barbara boy) and their kids played together. "I've always loved him as an actor, a wonderful actor," Fincher said, "but I've always thought of him as the guy who lives up the street. When it was time to cast the part of Armstrong, I knew I needed the most decent person I could find, because he would be the balance of the movie." Edwards, who consistently turned in "astonishingly underplayed performances—minimalist and empathetic," saw Armstrong as a man of integrity who would never let the department down. Edwards saw the killer as "someone who has disassociated himself from the actual killing; he is not there."

Fincher was thinking about Inspector Armstrong. "This guy's notes—unbelievable," he said. "I have to speak with him." Armstrong was located and immediately refuted the notion that he didn't want anyone to find him. He added, "I got kinda cold on Arthur Leigh Allen. I felt the evidence just didn't work. He just wasn't the guy and that DNA test just proved it." He had heard a policeman say: "We can now discount Arthur Leigh Allen as a suspect because the DNA didn't match."

"That DNA test was pretty controversial," Brad said. "We spoke to the person who helmed that test and he couldn't even tell us which letter was tested." It had not been revealed that the DNA was on the outside of the stamp where some unknown person had touched it.

"Jillions of actors are showing up," Laray said. "It's a huge project. Of course, we have the extra added attraction of David and people love to work with him. Yesterday afternoon, I auditioned kids for the roles of Bryan and Cecelia." Laray's casting call description of Cecelia described her as "22, Caucasian. 5'2" and 100 pounds, blonde, slender build. "I took them out into the parking lot here at the office and put them on tape. We got the police called on us because the girls were so authentic sounding in their screaming. People thought we had something horrible going on. The girl we finally got for Cecilia, Pell James, is just so good, you'll freak out. When you start seeing these scenes come together piece by piece you realize it's coming to life." She had cast forty of the seventy-six speaking parts, but had not made official offers because she did not have their new schedule yet. Candy Clark, an Academy Award nominee for *American Graffiti*, snared the Carol Fisher part. During the hunt for Zodiac the SFPD homicide squad had practically lived at Original Joes' Restaurant. If Fincher filmed at that San Francisco restaurant, Laray knew she could use the same busboy, Manuel Loaisa, and the same waiter, Angelo Viducic, who had waited on Toschi and Armstrong in 1969. She would have to be quick. Original Joes would soon undergo a complete renovation.

"If I were to cast a twenty-five year old actress who looks a little haggard," she said, "what do you think of Bijou Phillips for Linda, Darlene Ferrin's sister? We tried her for Cecilia Shepherd, but she's just not quite right." Next, they filled the role of Jack Mulanax. The Call sheet read: "40's, Caucasian, medium build, receding hairline, mutton chops. He's a blue collar homicide detective with a prominent nose." Laray wrote. She knew who had a nose exactly like Mulanax's—the handsome, Canadian actor of Greek parentage who had acted in *The Thin Red Line*, Elias Koteas. She cast him. Elias was balding so they would fit him with a wig which he would eventually discard. Laray and Fincher's choice for the role of Ken Narlow ("30's, Slim. 6'1, should come off as pragmatic and unexcitable") was comic actor Donal Logue who played Mark Ruffalo's best friend in *Just Like Heaven*. Chloe Sevigny, a lissome blond actor, got the part of Melanie Graysmith. The role of Kathleen Johns went to Ione Skye, the raven-haired daughter of folk singer, Donovan [Leitch] who composed 1966's "Hurdy Gurdy Man," which Fincher would feature on the soundtrack of *Zodiac*.

"Give our 'Toschi' and our 'Armstrong' a copy of our Murder Book [a collection of all the reports that the author had collected, Max Daly had scanned, and that Brad had collated]," Fincher said. He had taken "a little bit of liberty" with a scene with Toschi and Armstrong. "We put that [conversation] in the car to make it seem more surreptitious," he explained. "We just wanted to put it out into the world so that you could see the neighborhood and the sheepishness of Fouke and Zelms, so you could look out the window and see how far away a person would be. So you kind of understand the predicament that they're in where they're reacting to something and trying to do it as quickly as possible. Here's this guy walking down the street." Brad agreed it was good to get them out of the office and have a patrol car at night passing Jackson and Maple.

"Do you know George Bawart?" Brad asked Armstrong.

"That name sounds kind of familiar."

"He's the guy who served the warrant at the Fresno Street house [in Vallejo] and didn't find the smoking gun, but did find a hell of a lot of other stuff—guns, bombs, clippings. Did you know that Bawart found Mike Mageau and showed him a photo lineup and that Mageau identified Arthur Leigh Allen?"

"Are you kidding?" Armstrong said. "Wow."

Then, Brad told him about the Fouke report to Bawart in 1991 and his identification of Allen. "He was blown away," Brad reported. "He didn't know any of that. David and I are going to go up and speak to him next weekend. I gotta tell you the letters keep working." But inexplicably Armstrong canceled their meeting after an article appeared inaccurately portraying his character in the film. "Fix it," Fincher said. Brad said he would and placed a call to Armstrong to straighten the misconception out.

When Armstrong called Brad back, it developed that the problem had been exactly what they had suspected—an erroneous article. Armstrong told Brad his letter made him feel a lot better. "He's agreed to meet with us," Jamie reported. "We just feel really bad we got off on the wrong foot because of a publication, rather than us. I wish we could figure out how that got in *Variety*. Maybe somebody's agent who hadn't read the script heard one line and misinterpreted it." He just wanted to sit down with Armstrong and let him know they were going to portray him in the best possible light as somebody who worked really hard. "I understand it's a scary thing. Our lawyers said we don't think we need him to sign anything because the portrayal is so good, levelheaded, and balanced." Jamie was just sorry that they had caused Armstrong some consternation. They met with him and explained their aims, their point of view, and how they would handle Allen in the film. "Are we wrong about this?" Jamie asked him. "Are we wrong about that? We want to be sure we portray you accurately in this movie. We put out a lot of facts, but haven't really scratched the surface of how many facts there are."

In the process of moving *Zodiac* toward being officially green lighted, Medavoy and Brad held a big DVD meeting. Brad never saw so many people from two major studios in a single room than for this meeting—all the people who were on the creative side of the movie at Warner Brothers and Paramount, all the DVD executives at Warner Brothers and Paramount, including the international marketing people.

"It's incredible when David Fincher starts doing a DVD, how many people suddenly show up at his door," Brad said. "This DVD is going to be huge." It should be with a budget of over $1 million. Warner's, by precedent, doesn't pay anybody for interviews on any DVD—ever. If they paid one person they would have to pay everybody. There might be five to ten hours of extras."

At last, David, Brad, and Jamie were about to meet with Hartnell. The Hollywood Detectives arrived at the Hilton at 5:30 PM, and met him in the restaurant a few minutes later. He was impossibly tall, handsome, and glowing with health and success.

"I was just really struck how together he was as a person," Jamie said. "There's a lot of stuff he didn't remember because it was a long time ago." Hartnell went back and forth about what he remembered of that terrible day at Lake Berryessa—"Did I say that?" He put on headphones and they played him the audio of Arthur Leigh Allen's interrogation tape for comparison. Bryan couldn't rule him in or out. "Obviously, this is an old man," he said. They left him a couple of other tapes to listen to because the audio was poor on the first tape.

The next day, Brad spoke again to the Stine murder witnesses they had met in San Francisco and got a decisive, "No." If they couldn't get into the house on Washington Street, Fincher could film from a crane just outside the second story window where the children saw the murder and achieve the same effect. An hour later, Bawart sent Brad another report. He had just found his official police interview with the female Stine witness from Washington Street after he showed her a lineup containing a driver's license Soundex of Leigh Allen. "After viewing this lineup for a period of time," Brad told Fincher, "she was unable to make any type of identification other than pointing to Allen's face indicating that was the approximate shape of the person's face she had observed on 10-11-69."

"O.K., let me get this straight," Fincher said. "We've got Mageau, Fouke, and this girl all pointing to Arthur Leigh Allen."

Jamie and Brad went, "Yep."

Fincher looked at them and said, "Well, our work is done here." Then he extended his arms as if he was Superman flying away.

Two days after that meeting, Max Daly sensed the SFPD was not only growing chilly, but icy toward Fincher's project.

"I don't know," he said. "It seems like they just clammed up. I was supposed to go by and visit them last month. Brad put me in touch with places like Benicia and Solano who were all helpful. But there were no pictures of Blue Rock Springs at the Solano County Coroner's Office, though it says in the report they were taken. As for the SFPD, they just want it to go away." Daly had spoken with Sergeant Carrington, who works with the film commission, to make sure they had the permits set up and told him he wanted to come see an evidence lockup and the Zodiac files. When he showed up a few weeks later "he seemed to kind of forget I was there to see the evidence." They had a card on Paul Stine and the case number, but when they went down to evidence, they could not find it and said it was down at Hunter's Point. Daly said he was going there tomorrow and Carrington said he would let him know if that had been cleared. Daly suspected there was some disconnect between the upper tier and the mid-tier of the department. "From that point forward it's just been up in the air from a number of different directions."

"Max got the runaround," Jamie said, "but it's understandable. They're a major police department. We're simple movie folk. We could use their help at this point in terms of double and triple-checking of facts. The cops only kept repeating, 'It's an open case.'"

Brad was more direct: "I got told in the most polite way—fuck off!"

Strong pressure was being applied on Mayor Newsom's office by the Washington and Cherry neighbors. "It's not looking like we're going to get to shoot at night at Washington and Cherry," Brad said. "There was a meeting and the mother showed up. She's been rallying all the neighbors against the production." Suddenly, the city permit to shoot on that corner was in jeopardy. Jamie did not understand it. "San Francisco will still make money," he said. "We are shooting other things in the city—the HOJ, the car ride with Mel Belli, the *Chronicle*. I don't know if it's politics, but we already have everything we need." Ceán got on the phone and resolved the matter. "We can shoot until 10:00 PM," she said, "but not after."

"If we can't shoot at Washington and Cherry," Fincher snapped, "then we will shoot somewhere else and use computers. It's not slowing us down. Fuck 'em! They won't let us shoot at the actual location due to the exclusivity of the high-rent neighborhood, then we'll use computers and fake Washington Street." He would use photogrammetry, a process where they establish certain points within three dimensional space.

"Remember in *Panic Room*," Brad said, "we were able to move through impossible spaces. We can do that. It's going to be expensive because we have to do it on stage and we have to build."

Don Burt provided the visual effects team all they needed to build computer-based geographic models of the homes and texture them with period facades. He made a detailed drawing of the intersection as it was in 1969 and took photos from every possible angle with a high-resolution digital camera. Digital Domain would handle most of the movie's two hundred-plus effects shots and piece together matte paintings based on Burt's photos. For the six minute Washington and Cherry sequence, Fincher resolved to film the actors in a minimalist setting at the Downey Stages to allow for the later insertion of background plates. He planned to place twenty by twenty-five foot blue screens on dollies and roll them behind the actors as they walked the cab scene. The background plates would then be inserted along with 3D versions of vintage police motorcycles, squad cars, a fire truck and street lights. Ultimately, after all that work, the only scene filmed at the site would be a closeup of Zodiac's expended casing.

In spite of these expensive, extensive setbacks, Brad was still able to see everything coming together. So could Jamie. "David is going through the script again and again and again," he said, "refining little things until it all seems so real." Every dollar was now under the microscope since the producers were on the hook for every over-budget dollar, but even this cheered Brad as just another of the physical, tangible signs that the movie was starting to happen. Forgetting his hesitancy, he considered asking about a new BMW M 3 convertible. "It's basically a rocket," said Jamie, who already had a new car, the same kind of SUV he and Amber had driven to Bawart's house.

Fincher, still under the spell of the investigation, thirsted for the last two items on his list to make *Zodiac* a truthful document. He had to find Mike Mageau; he had to speak to Officer Armand Pelissetti to find out if Stine's cab door was open or closed when the police arrived and where Zodiac had entered the front-seat. Was it from the driver's side or the passenger side? Was the window up or down? Brad located

Pelissetti. Fincher would soon have his answers. "There's one mystery that's just been plaguing us," Brad told Pelissetti, "and you're the only person we've talked to so far who can answer it. When you and your partner arrived at the scene, was the front passenger-side door of Stine's cab open or closed?" Brad knew how important this was to Fincher's search for truth. He didn't have long to wait for an answer.

"Closed," Pelissetti said firmly.

And that was the final word from the man who was there and should know. "All four doors were closed when we first got there," he amplified, "and the bloody print was also there when we got there before the crowd, before any other police officer had arrived." The driver's side window was down where he observed the body. The kids were there," Pelisseti said, "and the first thing I wanted to do was get them inside. They gave me the description." Pelissetti passed that on to his partner, then started north on Cherry, the direction the kids had told them the shooter had gone. He checked the bushes along the way and when he got to the corner saw Fouke and Zelms coming around in their cruiser.

"Fouke told me," Brad related, "that when he saw Pelissetti at the corner, Pelissetti said to him, 'I'm looking for a white guy,' and that's when Fouke realized they'd just screwed up. So Pelissetti then made a decision to go left or right and went right, walking along Zodiac's escape route down Jackson. He saw a guy who did not match the description walking his dog." Ah, thought Fincher, there was a dog walker just as they had surmised and that might have made Zodiac ask Stine to go an extra block. "Pelissetti kept going and headed back to the crime scene on Maple. When he got back to the cab some of the other police officers were there and Stine's arm was now hanging out."

"So the print was left either by Zodiac," Brad said, "or—and here's my conspiracy theory—one of the kids. When you think about it, the bloody print never matched anyone in a criminal database. How crazy that would be."

Brad was shivering before a thousand foot waterfall, encircled by twenty-five huge Vikings, three big draft horses, and a tribe of Indians when the call came. He was in Vancouver checking out Marcus Nispels's *Pathfinder*. Ten hours earlier, he and Sean Penn had been watching Mike Medavoy's star being placed on the Hollywood Walk of Fame. Two hours after the call, Brad was in Las Vegas listening to Mark

Arneson.

"You've been looking for Mike Mageau for ages," Arneson said, "and I found him! He's here in jail, but we have to hurry. He's about to be released."

They ran all the way to the Vegas Correctional Facility, a huge, colorless monolith within walking distance of the Golden Nugget. Inside, Brad hurried to the videophone bank and got the chance to speak to Mike for thirty minutes. As backup he took notes, voraciously trying to write down every word that the surviving victim said, and checking his watch as he did. The stress was incredible. "Mageau was lucid," Brad recalled, "talking a mile a minute and eager to tell his side of the story. He said he was followed on the way to Blue Rock Springs that Fourth of July night." That confirmed something Brad had always believed. "The guy was someone who had been following Darlene Ferrin. She was always being followed from the moment she became a part of his life. She was used to it. This guy in particular was extremely dangerous and sounded like a jilted lover or someone trying to keep tabs on her. My brother once had a gun pointed at him by this guy and warned me away. 'He'll kill you. He'll shoot you,' he told me. When Darlene arrived that night she knew she was being followed."

Mike told Brad he had run out of the house because he knew someone was right behind her. They argued over who was going to drive, but she insisted on driving. "Darlene hadn't eaten in twenty-four hours," he said. "Both of us were starving so we went to Mr. Ed's. We were followed to Mr. Ed's by this guy." Mageau hadn't wanted to get out of the car because he and Darlene both thought he was going to shoot then and there. Darleen said, "Oh, he's not going to do anything to you. He's not going to kill you. He's got a secret to keep. He might not kill you, but he sure as hell will kill me." At Mike's suggestion they sped to Blue Rock Springs. "The guy chased us, actually hit our bumper . . ." At that, the video phone suddenly shut down. Time was up. Visiting hours were over. Mageau was being cut loose, so Brad stationed Arneson at the door.

"Unfortunately," Brad told Fincher later, "Mike went out a different exit before Mark had a chance to corral him and vanished again." The hunt for Mike Mageau began all over again. There were more questions to answer, but now it was more important to find

Mageau and offer him help because he was so troubled.

"I went to Vegas right after Brad," Jamie said. "So while he was trying to track down Mageau again, Amber and I had a very nice night at the tables—and we lost horribly—about a thousand dollars."

Finally, a new private investigator they had just hired, Tom Elfmont, along with Bryan Hartnell, his son and spouse, and a small crew headed by David Prior found Mageau again. Moonlight was streaming down as they walked the Beaumont, California, roads, calling out his name, and looking behind bushes and in doorways at every likely spot. Finally, they headed toward the freeway and it was there they found him. He was sick, starving, and sleeping in a culvert under a freeway offramp. Brad rushed to the scene. "And Mike and Bryan saw each other for the first time in twenty years," he said. "How amazing is that! We got Mike bedded down at a motel and fed and later interviewed him with Hartnell. Mike remembered Bawart's photo lineup well."

A few hours later, Bawart phoned to find out how Mike was. Mageau was okay considering how he had suffered. They would do all they could for him.

"Our rescue went fine," Prior said, "but Mageau is worried about Darlene's sister, Pam. 'She didn't do as well as me after the murder,' he said. 'I did just fine.'" Prior studied the ragged, malnourished man. "You did?" the astonished Prior asked. "Oh, yeah," Mageau replied. "I did just fine." The next time Brad and Prior spoke with Mageau was at Phoenix Pictures for the record and on camera for Fincher.

Saturday, May 7, was a lovely day in the low-sixties in LA. The actors arrived at Fincher's Amazing Office and took their seats around the long table. Some actors do a read-through completely flat because they don't want to commit themselves to any character choices so early on. Other actors go wild. There were so many speaking parts in the script that today some actors would read five parts. Fincher wanted to hear the revised White Shooting Script for *Zodiac* (codenamed *Chronicles* for security purposes) read aloud just for Brad and Laray. On the front of each copy, Warner Brothers had requested that all involved be "incredibly sensitive regarding the disclosure of any information relating to the *Chronicles* script. All drafts that have previously been issued are being destroyed and it is everyone's best interest to maintain confidentiality regarding all material aspects of this script." Gyllenhaal,

Ruffalo, Downey, and Chloe Savigny began at noon as Fincher's assistant videotaped the reading and fed it straight into the director's computer. If Brad was going to drive to Jamie and Amber's wedding and be there on time, he would have to leave the instant the read-through was done. It was running late because the energy in the room was so high and the actors were so inspired.

Jake Gyllenhaal and Mark Ruffalo

Several hours later, thrilled by the energy of the collaborative performances and the realization of his own expectations, Brad leapt up. He thanked everybody, grabbed a copy of the taped run-through he had promised Jamie, and sprinted to his new BMW 330. He slid behind the wheel, intending to race to Jamie and Amber's wedding in Santa Barbara "like a bat out of hell." It was over an hour's drive and he needed to be there by 6:00 PM. "Get me to the church on time," he hummed as he sped north along 101. In his tux, he felt very "James Bond-ish." On the seat beside him lay the all important actor's tape and the enormous script which was so thick it kept flying apart. *Zodiac* might be an epic movie, but the studio had used the same puny copper fasteners that hold together a normal sized script. Brad studied Jamie and Amber's gold engraved invitation:

> Mr. Allan L. Freeman; Mr. and Mrs. James T. McDonough request the pleasure of your company at the marriage of their daughter Amber Lydia-Ann Freeman to James Platten Vanderbilt son of Mr. and Mrs. Alfred G. Vanderbilt, Jr.

Tracing the coastline, he swept by Camarillo, then Ventura. The Channel Islands were to his left. Santa Rosa Island was ahead. The ultramarine Pacific was no match for the rainbow of colors which had been unleashed upon Santa Barbara this special day. Before the crowds of summer, the artists of the I Madonnari Street Painting Fair had put their hearts into the 150 portraits and landscapes in colored chalk pastel. Their brilliant work covered the courtyard of the Old Mission. From downtown Santa Barbara a pleasant breeze carried the scent of orchids from a festival. White doves were turning in the sky as the brilliant colors became the white of a glorious and unforgettable wedding.

At 6:00 PM, a solemn faced little flower girl, Portia Freeman, Amber's niece, began scattering rose petals to the altar. In an opera box above, a string quartet played. Strawberry Saroyan was covering the wedding for the *New York Times* and interviewing guests in beautiful designer gowns and tuxes. Even former James Bond girl Maud Adams was there, looking fit enough to take on 007 himself. The bride and groom, caught in a flood of light streaming through the huge archway window and lower side windows on either side, moved in an arc of unearthly radiance. Outside, above a strip of verdant golf course lit by the setting sun magically floated above the Pacific.

Brad wheeled off Hot Springs Road. His heart was beating fast. Because the run-through had run long and he had encountered fierce traffic, he was going to be a little late. Wheeling onto Summit Road, he reached the Montecito Country Club, one of the most prestigious and well-designed venues in Santa Barbara. Brad hurried through the double-doored entrance as the Reverend Dr. Linda Logan was completing the ceremony. Even the serious little flower girl was coaxed into a smile as Brad rushed over crushed rose petals, and past dapper groomsmen in morning coats holding silver-headed canes. He slid silently into his seat as the Reverend Dr. Linda Logan was completing the ceremony. The vows had been spoken. The only interruption to Dr. Logan was Amber's joyous and premature, "I do!" answered before the all-important question had been asked.

Brad wanted to be among the first to wish newlyweds good luck and deliver Jamie's own copy of the all-star run-through. They had crossed the finish line. The year-and-a-half-long race was won, though a road of revised pages—white, blue, pink, yellow, green, goldenrod, buff, cherry, tan and the rainbow all over again, were in their future.

The wedding was glorious—cocktails, dinner and dancing and Brad finally got to eat, something he had neglected to do all day. The young producer and one hundred and seventy other guests ate candied walnut and goat cheese salad and sweet sake-seared duckling on Portobello mushrooms. Brad dug into grilled petite filet and prawns in a scampi style garlic *beurre blanc* sauce. No matter how fast he ate, he was not able to get enough. The wedding cake was a zesty lemon sponge filled with raspberries and vanilla bean custard, but Brad opted for a bittersweet chocolate cake layered with milk chocolate mousse. The chase had been long, exhausting, and the wedding glorious— cocktails, dinner and dancing with Mrs. Vanderbilt as newsreel cameras rolled. Brad slipped Jamie his own copy of the all-star run-through of his *Zodiac* script. He looked his friend in the eye. Both men smiled. The streets were dry again. All was right in their little portion of the world.

"It's a good day," Jamie Vanderbilt said.

"We are officially greenlit," Brad Fischer said.

In the Amazing Office, David Fincher looked over a 207-page document that would translate into two hours and forty-five minutes of screen time. Along the way he, Brad, and Jamie had combed forests, traveled the state, found witnesses and uncovered new clues, taken on powerful men and befriended great detectives as they created art. Fincher had never doubted that they would achieve the impossible. The sun was going down and golden rays cut into the high-ceilinged room. It glittered on the copper brads holding the bound script on his desk. He had found his truth. He knew where all the rattlesnakes were.

David Fincher was shooting *Zodiac*.

ACKNOWLEDGMENTS

SPECIAL THANKS to the legendary Mike Medavoy whose kindness and sensitivity I will never forget. He came up to me during the premiere of David Fincher's classic movie to see that I was okay. It was at Mike's home that I also spent time with Bryan Hartnell, a man whose bravery and accomplishments are as tall as he is. To Jake Gyllenhaal, an actor whose talent grows by the day and who is everything I am not though he played me to a *T*. Thanks to Mark Ruffalo who made me realize what a great heart full of compassion he has. And extra special thanks to Ceán Chaffin, Arnold Messer, Louis Phillips, David Shire, Harris Savides, Laray Mayfield, Donald Graham Burt, William Armstrong, Santo Paul Panzarella, Don Cheney, and the others who made it all happen.

To Brian Cox (*privately, my all time favorite actor—don't tell the others*), Anthony Edwards, Robert Downey Jr, John Carroll Lynch, Richmond Arquette, who spent an hour with me at Lake Berryessa, John Getz who called me at home to learn more about the character he was playing, Ione Skye for her sensitive, heartbreaking scene on a country road, Charles Fleischer who bid me, "Goodnight, Mr. Graysmith," which I consider the best tombstone ever, Chloë Sevigny, Candy Clark, Elias Koteas, Dermot Mulroney, Donal Logue, Lee Norris, Patrick Scott Lewis, Pell James, Philip Baker Hall, James Carraway, Zach Grenier, Adam Goldberg, James Le Gros, Clea DuVall, Penny Wallace, Jack Samson, Mindy Bazar, Barbara Harris, Alyssa Rand, Kristan Berona, Kristine Kelly, David Collins, Don DiStefano, Jim Dunbar, Donald Fouke, Jonathan Hartnell, Richard Hoffman, Pam Huckaby, Holly Kang, Terrence Pascoe, Armond Pelissetti, John Robertson,

Capt. Roy Conway, Hal Snook, and Candice Taylor. Paul Avery who sat a few desks from me at the *San Francisco Chronicle* and who spoke with me in Sacramento at his new paper to discuss his part in the case, Margot St. James, Amy Carr, Jan Bawart, Max Daly, Mike Billington, Capt. Dave Jackson, Mayor Gavin Newsom, Chief Heather Fong, Lt. Nicole Greeley, Inspector Kelly Carroll, Scott Messer, Robert Ressler, Ralph Spinelli. Harry Phillips, Mark Arneson, Tom Elfmont, Steve Pappasian, Lynn Harris, Greg Silverman, Geoff Shaevitz, Marc Evans, Kelly Smith-Waite, Rita Williams and Kevin Fagan. And of course to the three heroes, the three amigos, you know who you are—the best.

To Jerry Lentz and Steve Kellener, who so graciously looked out for me in Los Angeles during the filming of *Zodiac*, especially for taking me to see *King Kong* (where I squirmed in my seat during the worm pit sequence). Heather Taylor for her dedicated eye and extensive knowledge. To David Smith, always an inspiration, Margot Graysmith who is always there, the ever amazing Wilailak Prakhe, Rayluk Smith, Harmony Smith, Zoe Smith, Strephon Taylor, Nik Caesar, Tiffany Hearsey, and Bill Riling.

To my editor and sounding board Aaron Smith, who was not only an inspiration and a great voice of wisdom, but a patient yet demanding taskmaster, without whom, this book would not be what it is today.

And a special tip of my newsboy cap to Brad Fischer who read this book off and suggested corrections. As Brad said no one has ever had such access as I have.

And to David Fincher who would hate being called "Brilliant," but as he says, "I can't help what people think."

SOURCES

This book is based on the author's face to face recorded interviews on audio cassette tapes and telephonic update interviews conducted between 2003 and 2007. All photographs were taken by the author on the scene with the original investigators and the three filmmakers, unless otherwise noted. Original rare police photos and copies of reports are from the author's collection or were recovered from the prime suspect during a search warrant served by George Bawart, found in the suspect's computer, and from VPD police photos and forensic examinations. Thanks to Producer Brad Fischer for reading and fact-checking this entire book.

BIBLIOGRAPHY

Selected References

Beebe, Lucius. *The Big Spenders*. Garden City, New York: Doubleday & Co., 1966.

Belli, Melvin, and Kaiser, Robert Blair. *My Life on Trial*. New York: William Morrow & Co., Inc., 1976.

Knapp, Laurence F. David Fincher Interviews. Jackson: University of Mississippi: 2014. Nev Pierce's interviews are particularly penetrating.

Medavoy, Mike, with Young, Josh. *You're Only as Good As Your Next One*. NewYork: Pocket Books, 2002.

Shaw, Mark, and Belli, Melvin. *King of the Courtroom*. Fort Lee, New Jersey: Barricade Books, 2007.

Sifakis, Carl. *America's Most Vicious Criminals*. New York: Checkmark Books, 2001.

Snyder, Lemoyne. *Homicide Investigation*. Springfield, Illinois: Charles C. Thomas, 1969.

Stewart, James B. *Disney War*. New York: Simon and Schuster, Co., 1977.

Swallow, James. *Dark Eye, The Films of David Fincher*. London: Reynolds and Hearn Ltd., 2003.

Waxman, Sharon. *Rebels on the Backlot*. New York: Harper Entertainment/an imprint of Harper Collins Publishers, 2005.

Newspapers and Periodicals

San Francisco Chronicle: "FILES SHUT ON ZODIAC'S DEADLY TRAIL; The SFPD renders 35 year case inactive."April 7, 2004, p.1.

Corkery, P.J. "Column." *San Francisco Examiner*, August 30, 2004, p. 3.

Dineen J.K. "Hollywood/San Francisco." *San Francisco Examiner*, February 23, 2005.

Dineen, J.K. "Hollywood North." *San Francisco Examiner*, July 13, 2005. p.5.

Dineen J.K. "Fading to Black." *San Francisco Examiner*, August 31, 2004, p. 5.

Donat, Hank. *San Francisco Independent*, April 27, 2004.

Gafni, Matthias. *Vallejo Times-Herald*, October 16, 2002.

Goodyear, Charlie. "Interview with Homicide Lt. John Hennessey." *San Francisco Chronicle*, April 7, 2004.

Hurwitz, Matt. "Crime Scenes and Compression Schemes." *Videography*, March 2007, p. 18.

Jouvenal, Justin. "Newsom: SF to be Digital Hollywood." *San Francisco Examiner*, July 14, 2005. p. 3.

King, Daniel, with Allen Johnson. "Margot St. James." *San Francisco Chronicle*, October 5, 2005.

Mockenhaupt, Brian. "The Curious Case of David Fincher." *Esquire*, March 2007, p.159.

Paramount Handbook of Production Information. "*Zodiac* Production Notes." February, 2007.

Peters, Oliver. "Zodiac: Solving Tapeless Mysteries." *Videography*, January 2007, p. 36.

Penthouse, March 2007, p27.

Pierce, Nev. "David Fincher on Movies and the modern world." *The Guardian*, September 27, 2004.

Premiere, February 2007.

Premiere. "Jake Gyllenhaal Q & A." February 2006.

People. "A Fresh Start. Downey Wedding." September 12, 2005.

Peterson, Dave. "Zodiac Link to Santa Barbara Murders." *Vallejo News-Chronicle*, 1969.

Raab, Scott. "The Quiet One," *Esquire*, March 2007, p.146.

Rebello, Stephen. Interview with David Fincher. September 16, 2014. Excellent informative interview.

Ronaye, Kathleen. "Partial DNA profile obtained in 2002 by Dr. Cydne Holt for the ABC television show, *Primetime Thursday*, was collected from the outside of the stamp." Associated Press, May 9, 2018.

Russo, Charles, "Zodiac: The Killer Who Would Not Die." *San Francisco Magazine*, March 2007, p. 132. Saroyan, Strawberry. "Vows, Amber Freeman and Jamie Vanderbilt." *New York Times*, May 22, 2005.

Sella, Marshall, "The Two Jakes." *GQ,* February 2007.

Spines, Christine. "Mark Ruffalo." *Entertainment Weekly*, March 9, 2007, p. 27.

Starr, Kevin. "The City's Supercop." *San Francisco Examiner*, August 13, 1977.
Weiss Mike. "Interview with Inspectors Kelly Carroll and Michael Maloney." *San Francisco Chronicle*, October 15, 2002.

Author Robert Graysmith with Fincher, Fischer, and Vanderbilt 'Untouchables'
(*Photo by Margot Graysmith*)

ABOUT THE AUTHOR

ROBERT GRAYSMITH is an author and illustrator. He was the political cartoonist for the *San Francisco Chronicle* when the letters and cryptograms from the infamous Zodiac killer began arriving to the paper. He was present when they were opened in the morning editorial meetings, and has been investigating & writing ever since. He lives in San Francisco where he continues to write and illustrate.

www.robertgraysmith.com
www.facebook.com/RobertGraysmithInk

MONKEY'S PAW PUBLISHING, INC.

www.monkeyspawpublishing.com

follow us on social media at

www.facebook.com/MonkeysPawPub
www.instagram.com/MonkeysPawPub
twitter.com/MonkeysPawPub

CPSIA information can be obtained
at www.ICGtesting.com
Printed in the USA
LVHW091106100921
697538LV00017B/619/J